Save Thousands on Your Mortgage

Save Thousands on Your Mortgage

The Best Investment You Can Make

Warren Boroson

Edited By
N. Everett Picchione, C.P.A.
Dome Financial Services

Collier Books/Macmillan Publishing Company
New York
Collier Macmillan Publishers
London

Collier Books
Macmillan Publishing Company
866 Third Avenue, New York, N.Y. 10022
Collier Macmillan Canada, Inc.

Library of Congress Cataloging-in-Publication Data
Boroson, Warren.
    Save thousands on your mortgage : the best investment you can
make / by Warren Boroson : edited by N. Everett Picchione.
        p.   cm.
    ISBN 0-02-028345-8
    1. Mortgage loans. 2. Prepayment of debts.   I. Picchione, Nicholas.
II. Title.
HG2040.15.B67   1990
332.7'22—dc20   90-31148   CIP

Macmillan books are available at special discounts for bulk purchases for sales promotions, premiums, fund-raising, or educational use. For details, contact:
        Special Sales Director
        Macmillan Publishing Company
        866 Third Avenue
        New York, N.Y. 10022

10 9 8 7 6 5 4 3 2 1

Printed in the United States of America

Contents

Save Thousands on Your Mortgage

Introduction

This Book Is Reader Friendly

If you can barely manage addition and subtraction, and division and multiplication scare the heck out of you, then this book is written with you in mind. It's written simply, with short sentences, crystal-clear ideas. And every so often, we'll remind you of what you've learned.

The message of this book is simple, too.

You can save an incredible amount of money . . . have more cash available for possible emergencies . . . and even retire earlier . . . if you shrink the amount of money you still owe on your mortgage.

To reap these wonderful rewards all you need do is use your extra cash to pay down the amount you owe on your mortgage. Just send in that extra cash with your regular monthly mortgage payments. You can send in a regular amount (like $50) every month, or vary the payments ($50, $25, $75, $100). You can start when the mortgage is brand-new . . . or when it's 5, 10, 15, or 20 years old—any time at all. Even 16 years and 4 months. And it doesn't matter whether yours is a fixed-rate mortgage or an adjustable-rate mortgage.

We suspect, though, that you may suffer not only from math anxiety. You might also have a tough time explaining exactly what a "mortgage" is . . . and tables full of little black buglike figures may make you shudder . . . and you have no idea whether the guys who own your mortgage would sock you with a penalty if you started paying off your mortgage early.

1

So we'll take you by the hand and lead you, kindly and gently. (In fact, if you want to know the precise meanings of the words we'll be bandying about—from "adjustable-rate mortgage" to "title insurance"—read Chapter 11 before reading Chapter 1.) This book is written to be user friendly. And the advice and guidance it gives should prove just the medicine you need for your financial health.

Chapter 1

The Stunning Amounts
You Can Save

The interest you pay on any long-term loan is horrendous, especially with the most common kind of mortgage, a 30-year mortgage.

Let's say that you borrow $100,000 to buy a house costing about $125,000 (You've made a 20 percent down payment.) And let's say that the interest rate you pay is 10 percent. That means a monthly mortgage payment of $877.57. After 30 years, you'll have paid back that $100,000, all right. (The loan is "self-amortizing," which means that you'll pay off both your principal and the interest during those 30 years.) But you'll also have paid almost $216,000 in interest charges! Think about it. You borrowed $100,000. You pay $877.57 a month on your mortgage. And you paid the lender $216,000 in interest over the course of the loan. That's over twice the amount of money you borrowed!

$216,000. That could go a long way toward financing your retirement—not to overlook sending your kids through Sarah Lawrence College, and allowing you and your spouse to take a luxurious round-the-world cruise.

But you don't have to shell out that $216,000.

Just pay an extra $31.13 a month every month (in addition to your $877.57) to lower your principal (the money you borrowed), and your mortgage will be paid up after 25 years, not

30. You'll reduce your interest charges by $43,000. Just pay an extra $87.45 a month, and you can tear up your mortgage-payment coupons after only 20 years . . . and you'll save $84,308 in interest charges! Obviously, the more extra money you pay toward the principal of your mortgage, the more you'll save.

The bigger your mortgage, the more you'll save by prepaying—because you'll owe less money on which you must pay interest. And the higher your interest rate, the more you'll save by prepaying.

Just to prove it, now let's say that your interest rate is 12 percent and your mortgage lasts 30 years. Your balance is $200,000. You're paying $2,057.23 a month on your mortgage payment. Pay $25 a month extra toward your principal, and you'll lower your total interest charges by $64,316—and reduce your mortgage term by 44 months, or 3.66 years. Pay $50 a month extra, and you'll lower your total interest charges by $109,887—and the term of your mortgage by 60 months, or 5 years. Pay $100 a month extra, and you'll lower your total interest charges by $172,814—and shorten the life of your mortgage by 96 months (8 years). Pay $200 a month extra, and you'll lower your interest charges by $247,884—and shorten the life of your mortgage by 141 months (11.75 years).

Okay, you're convinced. We're talking big bucks here. And, naturally, you're looking for a catch. Are there any charges for repaying your principal? No. Is there a penalty? In a few states, there may be a small penalty. (See page 37.) And you may not be able to pay down a "graduated-payment mortgage," an unusual type of mortgage.

What about interest deductions for your income taxes? Don't you lose them? You'll lose a bit, but they're not worth much anymore anyway. (See pages 30–35.)

So you see, there really *is* no catch.

That's why we say that paying down your mortgage balance is probably the best solid investment you'll ever make. In later chapters, we'll tell you why paying down your mortgage is such a terrific money- and time-saver—and the simple way you can go about doing it.

Chapter 2

Who *Shouldn't* Pay Down a Mortgage?

We'll be honest. Not every single human being in the whole country should pay off his or her mortgage early. Some people out there—they exist, we've met them—have old, old mortgages that charge interest as low as 4 percent. If that's the case with you, *don't* pay off your mortgage. In fact, you might want to give this book to a friend who is paying a higher interest rate.

But we figure that the interest rate on your mortgage is higher than 4 percent—higher than the interest you could earn from a money-market account or from a 6-month or 1-year certificate of deposit. (*Interest,* confusingly, can mean both the charge you pay for borrowing someone else's money—and the money you get for lending someone else *your* money.) And if the interest rate on your mortgage is typical for today's market, then the advice in this book may be perfect for you.

Another reason not to pay down a mortgage: Interest rates have climbed sky high. If you have a mortgage with a 10 percent interest rate, and interest rates in general climb to 12 percent and seem poised to remain there, think twice about paying down your mortgage. There's nothing wrong with paying 10 percent to borrow money when you can lend out money for 12 percent (via a money-market fund).

Still another reason not to prepay your mortgage is if it's near the end of its term. If your mortgage payments stop after 30

5

years, and 28 years have gone by, most of your monthly payments now go toward paying off the principal—the money you borrowed, not the interest. So why bother?

It's also true that if you just bought your house, you probably won't have much spare cash available to pay down your mortgage. You scrimped and scraped to come up with the down payment; now you have to buy new curtains and drapes, new furniture, a lawn mower, a dehumidifier, whatever. You have to build up a supply of cash for emergencies—six months' income is the rule of thumb. So you aren't going to have much, if any, cash left to pay down your mortgage.

But if: (a) You do have a little spare cash, (b) Your mortgage interest rate is normal, not way below current rates, and (c) Your 30-year mortgage has 10 or more years to run, you should *very* seriously consider paying down the balance of your mortgage. It's that simple. After all, some of the best ideas in life are simple.

Chapter 3

Why You Can Save
Such Colossal Amounts

The basic reason you can save a king's ransom by paying down your mortgage is that *for 30 years* you're paying for the use of that money your borrowed to buy your house. Year after year. And you're suffering the black magic of compound interest.

If you *lent* someone money for 30 years, you would expect to make a fortune yourself, wouldn't you? That's what you're doing when a bank or other lending institution lends you money for 30 years. The lender is making the fortune—off of you.

In fact, the simplest explanation of why paying down your mortgage is such a good idea is: The bank that lent you the money got a great business deal out of it. And now you're turning around and getting out of the bank's great business deal. So it's a great business deal for *you.*

Let's say that you borrow $100,000 for a $120,000 house, and the interest rate you pay is 10 percent. The loan term is 30 years, or 360 months. The amount of money you'll pay every month, to pay off your principal (the money you borrowed) and your interest over the course of 30 years, is $877.57. That doesn't include property taxes, which your lender will send to your town; and it doesn't include hazard insurance payments, which your lender may collect to send to your insurance company. Your monthly payment might actually be $1100 or so, but only that $877.57 goes toward your mortgage—to repay the money you borrowed and the interest you're being charged.

Most of your payments early on go toward paying off that interest you owe on that $100,000. In the first year of any mortgage, in fact, a typical 95 cents of every dollar you pay covers interest payments. Gradually, your mortgage payments cover less and less interest—and more and more of your principal.

You might think that after making 15 years of payments toward a 30-year mortgage you would have paid off half your principal. Think again. Usually it will be over 20 years before your mortgage payments will be evenly split between interest and principal. If you have a 10 percent mortgage, it will be 23.5 years before you'll have paid off half your principal. Only after 20 to 25 years does your mortgage money pay as much toward your principal as it does toward your interest!

Now, here's what an amortization table looks like on a $100,000 mortgage at 10 percent interest for 30 years (360 months):

MORTGAGE LOAN ANALYSIS

Principal	$100,000
Annual interest	10.00%
Term (years)	30
Periods per year	12
Start date	12/89
Monthly Payment	$877.57
No. of Payments	360

Payment Number	Payment Date	Beginning Balance	Interest	Principal	Ending Balance	Cumulative Interest
1	12/89	100,000.00	833.33	44.24	99,955.76	833.33
2	1/90	99,955.76	832.96	44.61	99,911.15	1,666.30
3	2/90	99,911.15	832.59	44.98	99,866.18	2,498.89
4	3/90	99,866.18	832.32	45.35	99,820.82	3,981.11
5	4/90	99,820.82	831.84	45.73	99,775.09	4,162.95
6	5/90	99,775.09	831.46	46.11	99,728.98	4,994.41
7	6/90	99,728.98	831.07	46.50	99,682.48	5,825.48
8	7/90	99,682.48	830.69	46.88	99,635.60	6,656.17
9	8/90	99,635.60	830.30	47.27	99,588.32	7,486.47

MORTGAGE LOAN ANALYSIS *(continued)*

Payment Number	Payment Date	Beginning Balance	Interest	Principal	Ending Balance	Cumulative Interest
10	9/90	99,588.32	829.90	47.67	99,540.65	8,316.37
11	10/90	99,540.65	829.51	48.07	99,492.59	9,145.88
12	11/90	99,492.59	829.10	48.47	99,444.12	9,974.98
13	12/90	99,444.12	828.70	48.87	99,395.25	10,803.68
14	1/91	99,395.25	828.29	49.28	99,345.97	11,631.98
15	2/91	99,345.97	827.88	49.69	99,296.28	12,459.86
16	3/91	99,296.28	827.47	50.10	99,246.18	13,287.33
17	4/91	99,246.18	827.05	50.52	99,195.66	14,114.38
18	5/91	99,195.66	826.63	50.94	99,144.72	14,941.01
19	6/91	99,144.72	826.21	51.37	99,093.36	15,767.22
20	7/91	99,093.36	825.78	51.79	99,041.56	16,592.99
21	8/91	99,041.56	825.35	52.23	98,989.34	17,418.34
22	9/91	98,989.34	824.91	52.66	98,936.68	18,243.25
23	10/91	98,936.68	824.47	53.10	98,883.58	19,067.72
24	11/91	98,883.58	824.03	53.54	98,830.04	19,891.75
25	12/91	98,830.04	823.58	53.99	98,776.05	20,715.34
26	1/92	98,776.05	823.13	54.44	98,721.61	21,538.47
27	2/92	98,721.61	822.68	54.89	98,666.72	22,361.15
28	3/92	98,666.72	822.22	55.35	98,611.37	23,183.37
29	4/92	98,611.37	821.76	55.81	98,555.56	24,005.13
30	5/92	98,555.56	821.30	56.28	98,499.28	24,826.43
31	6/92	98,499.28	820.83	56.74	98,442.54	25,647.26
32	7/92	98,442.54	820.35	57.22	98,385.32	26,467.61
33	8/92	98,385.32	819.88	57.69	98,327.63	27,287.49
34	9/92	98,327.63	819.40	58.17	98,269.45	28,106.89
35	10/92	98,269.45	818.91	58.66	98,210.79	28,925.80
36	11/92	98,210.79	818.42	59.15	98,151.65	29,744.22
37	12/92	98,151.65	817.93	59.64	98,092.00	30,562.15
. . . .						
343	6/18	14,612.29	121.77	755.80	13,856.49	214,863.54
344	7/18	13,856.49	115.47	762.10	13,094.39	214,979.01
345	8/18	13,094.39	109.12	768.45	12,325.94	215,088.13
346	9/18	12,325.94	102.72	774.86	11,551.08	215,190.84
347	10/18	11,551.08	96.26	781.31	10,769.77	215,287.10
348	11/18	10,769.77	89.75	787.82	9,981.95	215,376.85
349	12/18	9,981.95	83.18	794.39	9,187.56	215,460.03
350	1/19	9,187.56	76.56	801.01	8,386.55	215,536.60
351	2/19	8,386.55	69.89	807.68	7,578.86	215,606.49
352	3/19	7,578.86	63.16	814.41	6,764.45	215,669.64

Payment Number	Payment Date	Beginning Balance	Interest	Principal	Ending Balance	Cumulative Interest
353	4/19	6,764.45	56.37	821.20	5,943.25	215,726.01
354	5/19	5,943.25	49.53	828.04	5,115.20	215,775.54
355	6/19	5,115.20	42.63	834.94	4,280.26	215,818.17
356	7/19	4,220.26	35.67	841.90	3,438.36	215,853.84
357	8/19	3,438.36	28.65	848.92	2,589.44	215,882.49
358	9/19	2,589.44	21.58	855.99	1,733.45	215,904.07
359	10/19	1,733.45	14.45	863.13	870.32	215,918.51
360	11/19	870.32	7.25	870.32	0.00	215,925.77

Remember, your monthly mortgage payment is $877.57, and for the very first month the bulk of it goes toward paying the bank the interest it charges—$833.33. The rest, $44.24, goes toward paying back your principal ($833.33 + $44.24 = $877.57). Where did that $833.33 come from? Multiply the $100,000 you borrowed by the 10 percent-a-year interest rate—$10,000. Now divide by twelve months—and you get $833.33.

With payment 2, the balance you owe on your principal is now $99,955.76 ($100,000 − $44.24 = $99,955.76). So you multiply that by 10 percent ($9,995.57), and divide by twelve—to get your next monthly interest payment, $832.96.

Now look at payment 359. Your balance from the previous month is $1,733.45. Multiply by 10 percent, divide by twelve, and you get $14.45.

But what happens when, along with payment one, you send in, say, an extra $44.61? (That's the principal you would have paid the following month.) Answer: You lop an entire month off your 30-year mortgage—and save over $830 in interest. Money you would have owed in interest if you hadn't paid that debt for 29 years and 11 months. Now you know how paying off your principal early can save you so much!

For the next month (and only that month), you can skip your mortgage payment (but not, of course, the money you owe for property taxes and possibly insurance). Or, if you send in your regular payment, $877.57, it will go toward payment 3. You'll have reduced your 30-year mortgage to a 29 year, 11 month mortgage.

10

In other words, the faster and sooner you can erase your principal on your mortgage, the more money you'll save in the long run on interest payments. For example, suppose that when you first took out your $100,000 mortgage at 10 percent for 30 years, in addition to your first monthly payment of $877.57, you also tacked on the principal amounts that are due for the second, third, and fourth months. According to the table on page 8, that would come out to a total of $134.94 ($44.61 + $44.98 + $45.35 = $134.94). If you were to pay that extra $134.94, along with your first monthly payment of $877.57, you would immediately shave three months off your 30-year mortgage and save over $2,490 in interest payments! You have to admit—it's not too shabby an investment for just an extra $134.94.

Of course, you don't have to start prepaying a mortgage when the very first payment is due. You can begin when the mortgage is any age—15 years, 10 years, 17 years and 6 months—whenever you have spare money. But the sooner you start, the better—to reduce the mountain of debt you would owe otherwise.

Table A: How Much Will You Save (see pages 45–88)

This table shows:

(a) How much you'll shrink the amount of the interest you would otherwise have to pay on your mortgage, and

(b) How many months you'll take off your loan term—just by sending in extra regular amounts of money with your monthly mortgage.

In the table, we've given $25 to $200 a month as the amounts you might regularly send in, but you could send in less—or more. The principal amounts range from $10,000 to $200,000. The interest rates range from 7 percent to 17.75 percent. To use this table, find the page with your mortgage interest rate. Check the loan amount on the left side of that page, and run your eyes across to the prepayment amount. The numbers will tell you how many dollars you'll save and how many months of payments you'll lop off the term.

Chapter 4

Other Fine Reasons
to Pay Down a Mortgage

We've given you two wonderful reasons to pay down the balance you owe on your mortgage: (1) To reduce that mountain of interest you would otherwise have to pay, and (2) To shorten the life of that mortgage, so the day when you own your house free and clear comes sooner.

Here are some other excellent reasons:

3. Tax deductions aren't as worthwhile anymore.

Interest on loans backed by your residence—home-equity loans—are still usually 100 percent deductible. And that's not true of consumer loans, such as auto loans. The interest on consumer loans is only 10 percent deductible in 1990, and after that—zilch.

Big deal.

A few years ago, before the Tax Reform Act of 1986, you might have been in the 38 percent tax bracket. That means that the last dollars of your taxable income were subject to that 38 percent slice—and you wound up with only 62 cents on every dollar. Deductions were thus worth 38 percent on the dollar. A $1,000 deduction saved you $380.

But now you may be in the 15 percent, 28 percent, or 33 percent tax bracket. A $1,000 deduction saves you only $150, $280, or $330. Deductions aren't what they used to be.

4. You may not even be able to deduct your mortgage interest payments.

In return for lowering tax rates, Congress took away or limited a lot of deductions you enjoyed in the past. Now, you cannot deduct medical expenses unless they exceed a floor of 7.5 percent of your adjusted gross income—the last line on the first page of Form 1040. You cannot deduct miscellaneous expenses—for business costs for which you're not reimbursed, for investment expenses—unless they surpass 2 percent of your adjusted gross income. With casualty and theft losses, you must deduct $100 per occurrence, and the remainder must exceed a floor of 10 percent of your adjusted gross income.

The upshot is you may not be able to itemize—to list all your deductions on Schedule A. And that includes your mortgage interest payments. To itemize, your deductions must exceed the standard deduction to which you're entitled. And with so many deductions vanishing or being curtailed, you may have to accept the standard deduction instead of itemizing.

5. The standard deduction has gone way, way up.

For a married couple filing jointly, the standard deduction was $5,200 in 1989. You would have to incur a lot of deductible expenses to surpass $5,200. And by itemizing instead of taking the standard deduction, you would have far more paperwork with which to contend—and heftier payments to your tax preparer. Besides which, by taking the standard deduction instead of itemizing your deductions, you lower your chances of ticking off the IRS with any questionable deductions.

For more about deductions and mortgage payments, see pages 30–35.

6. Prepaying your mortgage can get to be a habit—and a way of forcing yourself to save.

Over in the world of insurance, there's long been a raging argument about whether you should buy pure insurance ("term" insurance) or whole-life insurance, which is pure insurance plus a savings account and costs far more. Usually, the smarter course is to buy pure insurance—and invest the difference between the cost. In the long run, you'll do better. Trouble is, many of the people who buy term insurance don't invest the difference. They spend it.

But with a mortgage, you're in a much better situation. Every month, you must make out a check to pay your debt. If it's not a habit with you now, it will get to be one. So it shouldn't be hard just to add some extra dollars to the check you write once a month.

Unlike people who buy term insurance and don't invest the difference, people intent on paying down their mortgage do prepay their mortgages. Because they have 12 times a year reminders. Besides, the money you save by prepaying your mortgage sure beats the money you save up by buying whole-life insurance. For one thing, you're not paying anyone any commissions.

7. If you intend to invest regularly in the stock market instead, you might stop when you get frightened.

The stock market can bless you with enormous profits—if you hold on and don't sell when the market goes down. But that's what all too many individual investors do. They buy when prices are rising—because they want to climb onto the bandwagon. So they're buying expensive stocks. They stop buying stocks when the market falls—which it does, every so often, and by stomach-turning amounts. So people stop investing in stocks—just when they're getting cheap. Or, worst of all, when the market plummets they sell—fearing that the market will go down even further. In short, they buy high and sell low, which is a surefire way to lose money. To make money in the stock market, you must be a sophisticated investor. You must do something that seems to conflict with all your experience in other areas of your life—buy when prices go down, sell when prices go up. Very few investors—even professional investors—ever become that sophisticated. And we won't even go into the difficulty of picking the right stocks or the right mutual funds.

But you don't have to be all that knowledgeable to invest in paying down your mortgage. Just send in your $25, $50, $75, or $100 every month. Without worrying whether stock prices are too high or too low, and whether you should buy or sell.

8. You'll have an alternative to putting money into investments you don't understand.

Stockbrokers and other salespeople are forever peddling all sorts of weird investments these days—like "naked options" and "residuals of collateralized mortgage obligations." Many of these newfangled investments from the Dr. Frankensteins of finance are just as risky as they sound. Ask people who have invested in high-yield ("junk") bonds, or limited partnerships, if they're happy with their returns. Very, very few will be. Many stockbrokers not only guide you toward risky, wacky investments but toward investments that give them huge commissions. They might recommend a mutual fund with a sales charge as high as 8.5 percent, which means that if you give them $5,000, they get $425. You have only $4,575 of the $5,000 you forked over working for you.

With limited partnerships, the commissions can be even higher—12 percent. That's also the case with some forms of whole-life insurance, the kind that comes with a savings account. Half of your first year's premium may go toward commissions. As for annuities, all the extra charges can really kill your returns. And with most annuities, such as an IRA, you face a tax penalty for withdrawing your money before age 59½. You may also face a penalty from the insurance company for withdrawing your money in the first 3, 5, or 10 years.

Well, why not certificates of deposit? Compare the interest rate you're paying on your mortgage with the interest rate you're getting from a 6-month or 1-year CD. Which is higher? This should be no big surprise. After all, the way your bank makes a profit is to pay you less for money you deposit than it charges you for money you borrow.

Now, let's look at paying down your mortgage—purely as an investment: It's simple to understand; you have no commissions to pay; there's no salesperson to mislead you.

15

9. It's perfectly safe.

The stocks you buy may plummet—because the stock market plummets, or because the company that issued the stock gets into hot water. Even IBM stock, a so-called blue chip, as of January 1990, is selling for less than it did after the crash of October 19, 1987. The junk bonds you buy because of their high yield may sink in price—because investors doubt that many of the companies issuing these bonds can continue those payments and avoid going into bankruptcy. The high-grade bonds you buy may suddenly become junk bonds—because someone took over the company and is issuing new bonds, making your bonds subordinate and junky. Or the company may pay you off early because interest rates have fallen. And now you have lots of money—and no place to invest it for a decent yield.

As for Treasuries and CDs, if you want a high yield, you must buy them with long maturities—5 years or longer. Trouble is, inflation may return during that time, and what you considered a high interest rate may become a very meager interest rate. Okay, short-term CDs (that come due in a year or less) are safe. So are Treasury bills, which come due in no more than a year. But once again, compare your income from such safe, short-term investments with the amount you can save by paying off your mortgage early. It's no contest.

10. House prices aren't appreciating much, if at all, in most parts of the country.

In real estate, the best time to use leverage—borrowing power—is when prices are soaring. The less of your own money you have invested in your house, the more money you're making on your money. When house prices were appreciating 20 to 30 percent a year, it was a great time to have a very expensive house and an enormous mortgage. But, for a variety of reasons, the real estate market has cooled down in most parts of the country. That means that the money you've borrowed to buy your house isn't working very hard for you. So you would be better off with less of a mortgage.

Real estate prices probably won't go up very much in the

16

years to come, either. Because of the birth dearth—the smaller number of Americans born after the baby boom directly after World War II—there are fewer first-time homebuyers. That means that, for many years to come, the prices of first houses will be soft. And that will affect the prices of houses further up the scale. If the owners of "starter" houses can't make much profit on them, they can't pay much for move-up houses—and the entire chain of houses, from hovels to mansions, won't appreciate much.

Houses will still be far more enjoyable to live in than most apartments, and almost everyone will still want to live in a house. But, financially, it won't make as much sense to borrow as much as possible to put into a house.

11. You're building up your estate.

Every time you send in a monthly prepayment, you're adding to your wealth and the wealth of your family. No ifs, ands, or buts. That money goes to work for you immediately. You instantly and automatically have more equity in your house— "equity" means free-and-clear ownership.

12. You have more emergency money.

If there's an emergency and you suddenly need a lot of money—let's say that the IRS claims you underpaid your taxes and hits you with a penalty (Heaven forbid!)—you will have a ready source of money. You can refinance your mortgage or get a second mortgage (a home-equity loan). And because you've been paying down your balance, you'll have access to much more money.

Whereas, if you've been putting your extra money into the stock market or the bond market, you may have to withdraw your money just at the wrong time, when stock prices are low, or when interest rates are high (and bonds worth less).

13. Once you pay off your mortgage, you can start saving for other good reasons.

Once your mortgage is paid up, it shouldn't be hard to continue saving $25, $50, $75, or $100 a month. Go on doing it—to save more money for your retirement, to build up a hoard for a princely vacation, whatever.

14. If you move before your mortgage is paid off, you'll be able to afford a larger down payment on your next house—or a bigger, better house.

Typically, when you sell your house, you use the money the buyer gives you (from his or her mortgage) to pay off your own mortgage. The less money you owe on your mortgage, the less money you'll need to pay off that mortgage—and the more you'll have available to make a larger downpayment on your next house and to afford a higher mortgage. You can thus afford to buy a more expensive house. If you don't buy a more expensive house, you can still make a larger down payment on your next residence. Usually, the bigger the down payment, the lower the interest rate you'll pay and the better terms you'll get in general. (The bank is taking less of a risk.)

In short, paying down your mortgage is almost the perfect investment. It's conservative. It pays a gigantic return. It's simple and easy to understand.

Professional analysts rate investments on how much profit they can bless you with, as against how much risk you must assume. Usually the riskier the investment, the more profit you can make. The more conservative the investment, the less of a profit you can make. Prepaying your mortgage combines the best of both worlds. It's very conservative and it's very profitable. The best investment, very likely, that you or any other homeowner could ever make.

Chapter 5

It's a Snap to Do!

Stop reading—fetch your monthly mortgage coupon, and read it. A typical payment coupon will give:

> The payment number
> Your name
> The due date
> The amount due

Then there will be a friendly warning, AVOID LATE FEES—PAY PROMPTLY.

Below that, over on the right, may be the line: "After this date, pay this amount." The date will be the date when your mortgage is overdue, and the payment amount will include a penalty. Further below: the name and address of the lender. And over on the right, a list of payments:

> ADDITIONAL PRINCIPAL
> ADDITIONAL TAX OR INSURANCE
> OTHER
> TOTAL PAYMENT

All you have to do is write $25, $50, $75, $100, or whatever the coupon lists as ADDITIONAL PRINCIPAL. Then add that amount to the amount due; write the total payment; and send in a check for that amount—and it's all done. (To make things

19

really straightforward, write out a separate check for your prepayment and mail that with your regular payment.) Your additional payment will reduce the principal on which your next payment is based—and save you lots of interest.

If your coupon doesn't have a line for ADDITIONAL PRINCI-PAL, just add whatever amount you want to the amount due. Enclose a note to whomever is servicing your mortgage:

Dear Sirs:
> I am including an extra payment with my mortgage coupon this month, to reduce the balance of my principal.

And, while you're at it, if you don't have one, you might add:

> Please send me an amortization table.

If you don't enclose such a note, a bank clerk may think you made a mistake—and send your extra payment back. Or phone you to ask why you sent in that extra money. Or the bank may apply the payment to next month's entire mortgage payment—not just to the principal. (Some homeowners pay their mortgages in advance when they're going away for a while.) But even better than enclosing a note is to phone your lender's mortgage officer. Some lenders have their own unique policies, so it's best to be on the safe side and ask questions.

- "I want to pay down my principal balance. Can I just add an extra payment to my monthly check?"
- "Is there a prepayment penalty?"
- "What's the smallest amount I can prepay a month?"
- "Should I send you two checks—one for the regular payment and one to prepay my principal?"
- "Will you provide me with updated schedules showing the effect of my prepayments?"
- "Is it okay if I vary the size of my payments?"

What if your bank gives you a hard time? A few banks seem to go out of their way to make life difficult for their customers.

Some banks have even been known to want to charge their customers who prepay a mortgage. (Which is usually illegal.) In that case, ask the clerk for the name of the bank's president, and his or her phone number. If that doesn't do the trick, consider writing a letter of complaint to your state's banking commissioner.

But chances are 99 out of 100 that your bank will be helpful. Banks really don't care one way or another whether you pay off your mortgage early. In fact, they may appreciate it. The more cash a bank has, the more new mortgages it can write. And these days banks make a good deal of their money just by originating new mortgages. (Note: Some lenders may want you to give them a few months' notice before you begin paying down your mortgage balance. Still others may insist that you prepay only a specified amount every month—such as your monthly principal. Check with your lender, or read your mortgage contract.)

Chapter 6

How Much to Prepay

You can send in whatever you can afford ($100, $50, $30), a set amount, or the amount of the following month's principal payment (from your mortgage schedule). But it's better to send in a fixed amount, like $50 or $100. For one thing, you'll get accustomed to one number. You won't have to keep a list of varying sets of figures, to make sure the bank hasn't fouled up on your payments. You might even experiment. Send in $50 one month, $150 the next, just to see whether you're a little short of cash for the month when you pay the larger amount. So, one way to decide how much to prepay is to find out how much you can spare. Another way is to decide when you want your mortgage paid off. A good time is when you plan to retire. If your income is going to sink because you're leaving your job, you may also want to see your expenses decline. Table B on pages 91–156 will help you calculate how much you must send in every month to pay off your mortgage in any particular number of years.

Here are some other ways to decide how much to prepay:

- Pay the amount of principal that's due the next month. Your amortization schedule will provide you with the number— and you'll have a convenient schedule to follow. And it will be easy for you to figure out how much interest you'll save, and how much time you'll slice off your mortgage's term.

  The trouble with this method is that your prepayments will

22

gradually increase (because your payments of principal become higher). And it's better to pay more at the beginning than later on.

- Divide your mortgage payment by 12, and add that amount to each month. If your mortgage payment is $877.57 on a $100,000 loan at 10 percent interest, dividing by 12 gives you $73.13. So, every month, instead of paying $877.57, you would pay $950.70. After a year, you would have paid off an extra month's debt. And over the course of 30 years, you would have saved over $70,000 in interest payments—and eventually lop off close to 10 years from the term of your mortgage.
- Pay an extra 5 percent or 10 percent of your monthly mortgage. For $877.57 you would pay $43.88, at a 5 percent rate. Or $87.76, for 10 percent.

Still, the most realistic way to go about it, as mentioned, is to experiment—see what amount of prepayment you're comfortable with. If you have trouble meeting your regular bills at the end of any month, consider lowering your prepayments. If you find yourself with extra cash, consider upping your prepayments.

Table B: When Your Mortgage Will Be Paid (see pages 91–156)

Let's say that you have a 15-year or 30-year mortgage. These tables will tell you how much you would have to prepay every month to pay off your mortgage completely—in 25, 20, or 15 years (for a 30-year mortgage), or for 12½, 10, or 7½ years (for a 15-year mortgage).

First, look for the tables that apply either to a 30-year or a 15-year mortgage. Find the applicable table for you. Over on the left, find the remaining balance on your mortgage. Follow that line over to the right. There you'll see the amount you must prepay every month in order to shave off the desired number of years from your current mortgage.

Example: You have a 30-year mortgage, at 10 percent, and

the balance is $100,000. You want to pay off that mortgage in 20 years. You'll have to pay $87.45 a month. And you'll save $84,308 in interest.

What if you have an adjustable-rate mortgage? Obviously, you can only estimate how long it will take you to pay off your mortgage—because you won't know what your mortgage's interest rate will be in the future.

Chapter 7

Refinancing Your Mortgage

Refinancing your mortgage—dumping your old one and getting a new one—is almost another story entirely from paying down your balance. But you can combine the two techniques. You can start prepaying your existing mortgage and then, if it becomes worthwhile, refinance your mortgage and start paying that one down.

Why not just refinance your mortgage for a lower amount? If you have $80,000 remaining on your mortgage, why not refinance for just $60,000? Fine, if you can afford it. But paying $20,000 or more up front is a horse of a very different color from paying an extra $50 a month, to gradually shrink your mortgage.

The rule of thumb is that you should consider dumping your old mortgage and getting a new one when current mortgage rates are two percentage points below the interest rate on the mortgage you have. But this is just a rule of thumb. The fact is that many homeowners refinance their mortgages when there's no difference in rates just to get out of a volatile adjustable-rate mortgage and into a stable fixed-rate mortgage.

Whether or not you'll save money by refinancing depends on:

- The difference between your current mortgage interest rate and what you could get today.
- Your closing costs (usually between 3 percent and 6 percent of your mortgage), which may include lawyer's fees, the cost

of a new survey, new title insurance, and—above all—points. Points are special charges a bank assesses to keep the interest rate down. One point is equal to 1 percent of the mortgage amount.

- How long you think you'll remain in your house and keep that new mortgage.

This is where refinancing a mortgage and paying down a mortgage intersect. When you calculate how long your mortgage will last, you should also consider the effects of paying down that mortgage.

Here's an example of refinancing a mortgage:

Let's say that you took out a 30-year ARM in 1987 for $70,000, indexed to a one-year Treasury bill. The ARM had a 2 percentage point yearly limit on the amount it could rise and a lifetime cap of 2 percentage points.

The first year your interest rate was 7.5 percent. Normally your rate would have been 9.36 percent—the 6.61 percent T-bill rate plus the lender's 2.75 percent margin for profit. Rounded up, your monthly payment of principal and interest was $490. In July 1988 your interest rate leaped by the 2 percentage point limit, to 9.5 percent. So your monthly payment of principal and interest became $587, and your balance $69,355. In July 1989 interest rates jumped to 11.5 percent. Your monthly payment became $688, and your balance was $68,881.

But now you refinance.

Closing costs are 3 percent of your balance, or $2,066. Let's add them to your balance, just to make things simpler. Your new mortgage is around $71,000. You take out a 30-year fixed-rate mortgage at 9.5 percent—2 percentage points below your current mortgage rate. Your new monthly principal and interest payment is $597.

The difference between your current monthly principal-and-interest payment and your previous payment: $91 a month. Divide that into your closing costs of $2,066 and you get $23.

Divide that by 12 (months) to get 1.9 years—the length of time it would take to recoup your closing costs.

In sum, your new mortgage would begin saving you money in less than 2 years.

Chapter 8

The Truth About 15-Year Mortgages and Biweekly Mortgages

Instead of paying off a 30-year mortgage early, you could switch to a mortgage that's paid off in 15 years. Is it a good idea?

Not as good as paying down your 30-year mortgage, and for two reasons: You'll have to pay closing costs to turn your 30-year mortgage into a 15-year mortgage, and a 30-year mortgage gives you more flexibility.

When interest rates are normal you can pay down your principal on a 30-year mortgage with your extra money—or forget it if you *don't* have extra money. (The monthly payment on a 15-year mortgage is, of course, much higher than on a 30-year mortgage.) When interest rates are low compared to your mortgage, you can pay down your mortgage as much as you can possibly afford—or refinance. And when interest rates are high compared to your mortgage, you can stop paying down your mortgage and invest your extra money in a high-paying money-market fund.

If you already have a 15-year mortgage, of course, there's nothing to stop you from paying it down.

What about getting a biweekly mortgage, where you make half your regular monthly mortgage payments every 2 weeks? You make 26 payments a year (13 months)—and wind up with a month's worth of extra payments (because a monthly mortgage entails only 12 payments). This way you can slice off a month's payments every year.

Again, you may have to obtain a new mortgage and pay closing costs. And paying down your mortgage gives you more flexibility: You can adjust your prepayments to your pocketbook and to the state of current interest rates. Besides which, some mortgage brokers actually charge to make the arrangements for you to make biweekly payments. You can do the same thing yourself—free of charge—just by paying down your principal on your own, without any outside help.

Another reason to choose prepayments over a biweekly mortgage: Lenders report that homeowners who have locked themselves into biweekly payments wind up making a mess of things. "It's hard enough for most homeowners to remember their monthly payments," says one mortgage banker. "Those who are supposed to make biweekly payments are always late."

So forget about gimmicks like turning your 30-year mortgage into a 15-year mortgage, or getting a biweekly mortgage. Stick with the flexibility, ease, simplicity, and thrift that paying down your 30-year mortgage provides.

Chapter 9

What Homeowners Should Know About Taxes

One of the biggest objections some people have about prepaying their mortgages is: "We don't want to lose the tax deductions we get from paying the mortgage interest." So let's answer this question in some detail.

First, you will still be able to deduct all of your property taxes. And, if you're intent on itemizing rather than just taking the standard deduction, those property taxes may enable you to itemize.

Second, as mentioned earlier, deductions aren't worth that much anymore—because tax brackets have shrunk, because the standard deduction has been increased, and because you may not be able to itemize your deductions now that they've been curtailed or tossed out the window.

Third, you won't lose your interest deductions for a good number of years. They will be eliminated gradually.

Finally, remember that while deductions can be fine, not spending money you don't have to spend is plain wonderful. To get a tax deduction, you must spend money. All the deduction does is take away a little of the pain. If you don't spend your money wisely, any deduction you get for spending that money isn't much solace.

Let's say that you pay a quack $20,000 to cure your dandruff. Sure, part of that $20,000 may be deductible—so you may be out only, say, $14,400. But wouldn't it have been better not to have wasted that $20,000 in the first place? (If you're in the 28 percent marginal tax bracket and your medical expenses have exceeded 7.5 percent of your adjusted income, a $20,000 expense—if it was deductible—would cost only $14,400.)

The same logic holds for prepaying your mortgage. It's far better not to have spent your money unwisely than to rejoice because you didn't spend quite so much because of the tax savings. Another way of looking at the whole subject is to recall all the other tax benefits homeowners enjoy—and which you won't lose by paying down your mortgage.

First, we'll deal with the $125,000 exclusion. You can exclude up to $125,000 of capital gains (your profit) from your taxes on the sale or exchange of your main home if:

- You or your spouse were 55 or older on the date of the sale or exchange. (*Not* at the end of the year.)
- You owned and lived in your main home for at least 3 years of the 5-year period ending on the date of the sale or exchange. (If the spouse who otherwise qualified was in a home for the disabled during part of that time, the requirement is only 1 year.)
- Neither you nor your spouse sold a home and excluded the capital gains on the sale since July 26, 1978.

Another benefit that homeowners get is the deferral tactic. You may postpone paying some or all of the taxes on the sale or exchange of your main home if:

- You buy and live in a new main home costing at least as much as the adjusted sales price of your old home.
- You buy and live in the new home 2 years after, or 2 years before, the sale of the old home.
- You lived in the home you're selling for 2 years or more and haven't postponed paying taxes on the gains from the sale of a previous residence within the past 2 years. (Exception: if you're selling your current home for job-related reasons.)

The amount of gain you postponed paying taxes on is subtracted from the purchase price of your new home. In other words, you may some day have to pay taxes on that gain.

What these 2 tax-saving strategies add up to is this: After you reach the age of 55, if you sell your main home for a profit of $125,000, you can avoid all capital gains taxes and also make full use of the deferral technique by purchasing a new home for $250,000. You will make use of the $125,000 exclusion and defer the full $125,000 gain.

Some other tips for homeowners:

- There's a big advantage to remaining in the same house all your life. That way neither you nor your heirs will ever have to pay income taxes on the gain from the sale of your home—because you haven't sold it. If you need money, you could check into a reverse-annuity mortgage, where an investor or a banker will pay you in return for the eventual ownership of your house.
- If you want to move to a smaller house, but you want the tax-deferral advantage, buy a smaller house in a swankier community, or a smaller but newer house, or a smaller house with larger grounds. Or you could buy a smaller, cheaper house and, within 2 years of your selling your old one, spring for improvements, like additional rooms or a swimming pool. These improvements will raise your purchase price for tax purposes, and lower your taxable gains.
- If you need money from the sale of your house, but can wait, consider an installment sale in which you give the buyers a first or second mortgage. You'll receive your payments over several years, and perhaps be in a lower tax bracket and have a smaller tax bill to pay. Of course, if the tax rates go up, this strategy will not be as effective. One drawback of an installment sale: You must have confidence that the buyers will keep paying you. That's why an installment sale of your house to your children, if they want it, usually makes the most sense.
- If you are definitely going to be socked with capital-gains

taxes the year you sell your house, try to match your gains with losses. Sell any stocks you own on which you have losses. And boost any other deductions you can, such as charitable contributions. You might also time the sale of your home to coincide with a year in which your income will be less and your tax bracket will be lower. For example, the year you retire.

- Other ways to lower any taxes you might owe:

1. Reduce the profit on the sale of your home. To calculate the gain, add together the original purchase price, closing costs, and the original cost of any improvements (not repairs). Subtract them from your selling price. You won't forget improvements like central air conditioning, but you might overlook new bookshelves, a new stove that went with the house, a lawn-sprinkling system, new shrubs, and new locks and doorbells. If you don't have canceled checks or sales slips to back up your improvements, you can submit other evidence, like property-tax records or even before-and-after photographs of your house. (You cannot add in the cost of repairs, which only keep the house functioning.) Also subtract from your gain any closing costs you paid, such as a broker's commission, legal fees, appraisal fees, state and local transfer-tax fees, along with other expenses connected with selling the house.

2. Finally, if you buy a less expensive home, deduct "fix-up expenses" from your sales price—the cost of work you paid for to help you sell your old home, such as for painting and gardening. To qualify, these fix-up expenses must be performed 90 days before you sell the house and must be paid for within 30 days of the sale.

Here's an example of these calculations:

Your *selling expenses* were $5,000. You spent $900 on new blinds and on a new water heater. You also spent $800 on painting your house, and satisfied the rules regarding such fix-up expenses.

1. Selling price of old home: $61,400
2. Selling expenses: $5,000

33

3. Amount realized (1 minus 2): $56,400
4. Tax basis of old home: $45,000
5. Improvements (blinds, heater): $900
6. Adjusted basis of old home (4 plus 5): $45,900
7. Gain on old home (3 minus 6) $10,500

Now you buy and live in another home that cost $54,600 within 2 years of selling your old one. As a result, you can defer paying taxes on most of that $10,500 gain.

8. Amount realized from old home: $56,400
9. Fix-up expenses (painting): $800
10. Adjusted sales price (8 minus 9): $55,600
11. Cost of replacement home: $54,600
12. Gain not postponed (10 minus 1): $1,000 (taxable)
13. Gain postponed (7 minus 12): $9,500
14. Cost of new home: $54,600
15. Adjusted basis of new home (14 minus 13): $45,100

Here's an example of taking the $125,000 exclusion *and* deferring the tax you owe on your remaining profit:

You're 55, and sell your main residence for $400,000 after living there for 3 of the past 5 years. The basis—your investment (including the original purchase price) for tax purposes—of your house was $75,000.

1. Sales price of your old home: $400,000
2. Tax basis of old home: $75,000
3. Gain (1 minus 2): $325,000
4. Exclusion: $125,000
5. Taxable gain (3 minus 4): $200,000

Now you buy a house for $450,000—and use the deferral strategy.

6. Sales price: $400,000 (as above)
7. Gain: $325,000 (as above)

8. Exclusion: $125,000
9. Net taxable gain: $200,00
10. Price of new home: $450,000
11. Tax basis of new home (10 minus 9): $250,000

Chapter 10

Smart Questions, Easy Answers

Q. Should I consider paying down the principal on other loans? Not just mortgages?

A. Sure. The longer any loan lasts, and the higher the interest rate, the better the argument for paying it down early.

Q. What's the difference between paying down your mortgage and a home-equity loan?

A. They're sort of opposites. With the first, you lower the amount you owe on your mortgage; with the second, you boost your mortgage debt by obtaining a second mortgage. A home-equity loan can be a good idea if you need extra money for a very good reason such as buying a car, or for a tempting business opportunity. But it can be dangerous if you forget that if you can't repay the debt, you can lose your house. Don't spend the money frivolously. As the saying goes, "Don't lose your house for a blouse."

Q. Which is better, a fixed-rate mortgage or an adjustable-rate mortgage?

A. A fixed-rate mortgage is the devil you know. You will never suffer interest-rate shock when your mortgage interest rate shoots up. But if you plan to remain in your house only a few years, an ARM may make sense. ARM interest rates usually start out at bargain rates, then leap up. You also may qualify for a larger mortgage with an ARM, and, if you have trouble qualifying at all, an ARM may be the easier mortgage to get.

Q. Will my bank charge me extra if I make prepayments toward the principal on my mortgage?
A. In general, no, but check with your bank first.

Q. Will my bank charge me a "prepayment penalty"?
A. In a few states lenders may charge such penalties, but typically only during the first year of the loan. That's to compensate the lender for the paperwork in setting up the loan.

Prepayment penalties usually don't apply to loans backed by the Federal Housing Administration or the Veterans Administration. You're more likely to face a prepayment penalty with an adjustable-rate mortgage than a fixed-rate mortgage because ARMs usually start with low interest rates. But check whether the mortgage agreements assess a prepayment penalty only if you pay off the entire balance of the mortgage within a few years, not if you begin a program of paying down your mortgage. A typical prepayment penalty is 5 percent of the amount you pay back early.

Q. What if I intend to sell my house soon? Will prepaying my mortgage still make sense?
A. Sure. Because of those prepayments you'll have more equity in your house. "Equity" means free-and-clear ownership. So, when you sell, you'll receive more cash from your buyer than you would if you hadn't started prepaying your mortgage.

With that extra cash, you can afford to buy a more expensive house. The reason is that you'll have more money to put into a down payment. If you buy a house that's only as expensive as the one you sold, or a house that's less expensive, you can make an even greater down payment than the usual 20 percent. That will lower the mortgage payments you'll have to make every month—and probably persuade the lender to give you a lower interest rate than normal on your mortgage.

Q. When should I consider stopping paying down my mortgage?

A. Obviously when you cannot afford it anymore. Maybe you've experienced some financial reverses, or you've suffered a loss of income. Some other reasons:
- When you're nearing the end of the term of your mortgage, and principal payments automatically make up by far the biggest portion of your monthly payments.
- When you discover what you think is a better investment opportunity—which will be very rare indeed.
- When interest rates shoot up and they promise to remain there. If you're paying 10 percent on a mortgage when you can get 15 percent from a money-market fund, it's time to stop paying down your mortgage. Put your money into a high-paying money-market fund instead.

Q. How can I tell that my bank is crediting my prepayments properly?

A. After you make a payment wait a week or so and phone the bank to inquire about your mortgage balance. Make sure that it agrees with your own figures.

Q. If I start sending in $25 a month to pay down my balance can I stop? Or am I locked into paying that $25 a month—even if I'm strapped for money?

A. You can stop anytime you want. And resume anytime you want. And you're not stuck with $25. You can vary the amount, upward or downward.

Q. What if instead of prepaying my mortgage with $50 a month, I send $50 a month to a stock mutual fund? Will I come out better or worse with the fund?

A. Who knows? Stocks go up, down, or sideways. But if you prepay your principal you know without any doubt that you'll make a princely profit.

Q. I don't have an amortization schedule. How much am I paying every month for my mortgage?

A. The next table will guide you.

Table C: Figuring Out Your Monthly Mortgage Payment (see pages 158–245)

This table will enable you to figure out how much your mortgage payment is every month—not including payments for property taxes or for insurance (if your lender collects your insurance payments).

First, check the page that has your mortgage interest rate. Read down the left-hand column until you find your precise loan amount. Move to the right until you find the length in years of your mortgage. The appropriate number below in that column represents your monthly mortgage payment.

To illustrate, let's say you took a mortgage of $100,000 at 10 percent. Simply refer to Table C and find the pages that have 10 percent for interest rates. From there, scan down the page for a loan of $100,000. Now refer to the right for, say, a 30-year mortgage. Your monthly payment would be $877.57. If you wanted to take out a mortgage of 25 years, the mortgage payment would be $908.70, and so forth.

Chapter 11

Coming to Terms:
What the Words Mean

Adjustable-Rate Mortgage (ARM). A mortgage with an interest rate that bobs up and down in accordance with an outside index of interest rates, like 1-year Treasury bills.

Amortization Table. A table of numbers that shows the payments you must make every month over the term of the mortgage; how much of that payment goes toward interest and how much goes toward principal; and your balance after each payment.

Annual Percentage Rate. The interest you pay on a loan, plus other charges, such as points for a mortgage. When you search for a mortgage, focus on the APR, because the APR is what you will actually be paying.

Appreciation. Rise in value, as of property.

Balance. The amount of your principal that remains to be paid.

Cap. The limit on how much an adjustable-rate mortgage can climb in 1 year or over the length of the mortgage.

Closing Costs. The total amount of expenses to obtain a new mortgage (the chief one being points); that is, what you'll be expected to pay at your closing.

Deduction. An expense you can subtract from your taxable income—if you itemize (list all your deductions on Schedule A instead of taking the standard deduction).

Default. To fail to make your mortgage payments.

Down Payment. The amount of cash you must come up with to obtain a mortgage. Usually it's 20 percent of the house's value, though you may pay less if you have private mortgage insurance, or obtain a mortgage backed by the Veterans Administration or the Federal Housing Administration.

Equity. Your free-and-clear ownership of a house. If your house is worth $100,000, and you owe $75,000 on your mortgage but have no other debts secured by your house, your equity is $25,000.

Escrow. The depositing of money with a third party, to cover expenses that are scheduled to come due. A bank that collects property taxes may keep the money in escrow.

Fixed-Rate Mortgage. A mortgage with an interest rate that doesn't change, as opposed to an adjustable-rate mortgage.

Foreclosure. The legal proceeding that the holder of a mortgage sets up to repossess the property in order to cover the mortgage money he or she lent and the person who obtained the mortgage has failed to repay.

Graduated-Payment Mortgage. A mortgage in which the early principal payments are less than the later payments. Designed for young people whose incomes supposedly will grow.

Home-Equity Loan. A second mortgage. With some types, the borrower can draw whatever money he or she needs, via special checks or a credit card, and not owe interest until he or she does withdraw the money.

Interest. The money you must regularly pay for the privilege of using someone else's money. Expressed as a percentage of the money borrowed—a 10 percent interest rate, for example, means you must pay $10 for every $100 you borrow.

Leverage. Borrowing money to invest, as in obtaining a mortgage to buy property.

Money-Market Fund. An investment group that buys short-term debt instruments, so shareholders receive interest in line with current rates.

Mortgage. A loan, backed by real estate. If the borrower doesn't pay back the interest and principal in accordance with the terms, the mortgage holder can try to repossess the property and then try to sell it to get his or her money back. *See* Foreclosure.

Mortgagee. The lender of mortgage money.

Mortgagor. The borrower of mortgage money.

PITI. An abbreviation for the regular payments you must make on a house you have purchased with a mortgage—for Principal, Interest, Taxes, and Insurance.

Points. Special charges a lender may assess to provide a mortgage. Points lower the interest rate. Each point equals 1 percent of the loan; on a $100,000 mortgage, three points is $3,000.

Prepayment. Paying off all or part of a debt early.

Prepayment Penalty. A small financial charge that a lender is permitted to assess, in a few states, if a mortgage borrower pays off the mortgage early.

Principal. The money you borrowed and must repay.

Property Taxes. Taxes you must pay to your state and city government—for local schools, police, and so forth. Although it is not part of the monthly mortgage, lenders usually collect such taxes and pay them.

Refinancing. Paying off your old mortgage and getting a new one.

Starter House. A small inexpensive house (or condominium, or townhouse), typically for young people just starting out as homeowners.

Term. The length a mortgage lasts—usually 15, 20, 25, or 30 years.

Title Insurance. Insurance you may have to buy to protect the lender, and yourself, against the possibility that the person who sold you property didn't own it, or own all of it.

Table A

How Much
Will You Save

7% How Much Will You Save

TABLE A

AMOUNT OF LOAN	AMOUNT OF MONTHLY PRE-PAYMENT	15 YEAR MORTGAGE		30 YEAR MORTGAGE	
		Amount Saved	Months Reduced	Amount Saved	Months Reduced
$ 5,000.00	$25.00	1,600	87	5,020	240
	50.00	2,098	116	5,802	285
	100.00	2,490	141	6,316	317
	200.00	2,750	158	6,618	337
10,000.00	25.00	2,179	58	7,990	185
	50.00	3,201	87	10,040	240
	100.00	4,196	116	11,604	285
	200.00	4,980	141	12,632	317
25,000.00	25.00	2,791	29	12,626	113
	50.00	4,700	49	18,173	167
	100.00	7,161	77	23,560	223
	200.00	9,732	107	27,903	272
50,000.00	25.00	3,083	15	15,827	69
	50.00	5,582	29	25,253	113
	100.00	9,400	49	36,347	167
	200.00	14,322	77	47,120	223
75,000.00	25.00	3,195	11	17,334	50
	50.00	5,958	20	29,160	85
	100.00	10,505	36	44,637	134
	200.00	17,019	60	61,468	190
100,000.00	25.00	3,254	08	18,214	39
	50.00	6,166	15	31,654	69
	100.00	11,165	29	50,507	113
	200.00	18,800	49	72,695	167
125,000.00	25.00	3,290	06	18,792	32
	50.00	6,299	13	33,390	58
	100.00	11,603	24	54,899	97
	200.00	20,065	42	81,768	149
150,000.00	25.00	3,315	05	19,200	27
	50.00	6,390	11	34,668	50
	100.00	11,916	20	58,320	85
	200.00	21,010	36	89,275	134
200,000.00	25.00	3,346	04	19,740	21
	50.00	6,508	08	36,428	39
	100.00	12,333	15	63,308	69
	200.00	22,330	29	101,014	113
250,000.00	25.00	3,365	03	20,080	17
	50.00	6,581	06	37,584	32
	100.00	12,598	13	66,780	58
	200.00	23,207	24	109,799	97
300,000.00	25.00	3,379	02	20,314	14
	50.00	6,630	05	38,401	27
	100.00	12,781	11	69,337	50
	200.00	23,832	20	116,640	85

7¼% How Much Will You Save

TABLE A

AMOUNT OF LOAN	AMOUNT OF MONTHLY PRE-PAYMENT	15 YEAR MORTGAGE		30 YEAR MORTGAGE	
		Amount Saved	Months Reduced	Amount Saved	Months Reduced
$ 5,000.00	$25.00	1,672	88	5,257	242
	50.00	2,188	117	6,065	287
	100.00	2,595	142	6,596	318
	200.00	2,864	159	6,909	338
10,000.00	25.00	2,279	59	8,394	187
	50.00	3,344	88	10,515	242
	100.00	4,377	117	12,131	287
	200.00	5,190	142	13,193	318
25,000.00	25.00	2,926	29	13,341	115
	50.00	4,920	50	19,116	169
	100.00	7,483	77	24,695	225
	200.00	10,155	107	29,185	274
50,000.00	25.00	3,236	16	16,801	71
	50.00	5,852	29	26,683	115
	100.00	9,841	50	38,232	169
	200.00	14,967	77	49,391	225
75,000.00	25.00	3,355	12	18,446	52
	50.00	6,251	21	30,897	88
	100.00	11,008	37	47,073	136
	200.00	17,805	61	64,551	192
100,000.00	25.00	3,417	08	19,411	41
	50.00	6,472	16	33,603	71
	100.00	11,705	29	53,367	115
	200.00	19,682	50	76,164	169
125,000.00	25.00	3,456	07	20,046	34
	50.00	6,612	14	35,494	60
	100.00	12,170	25	58,098	99
	200.00	21,016	43	86,126	151
150,000.00	25.00	3,482	06	20,496	29
	50.00	6,710	12	36,892	52
	100.00	12,502	21	61,795	88
	200.00	22,016	37	94,146	136
200,000.00	25.00	3,516	04	21,091	22
	50.00	6,835	08	38,822	41
	100.00	12,944	16	67,207	71
	200.00	23,411	29	106,734	115
250,000.00	25.00	3,536	04	21,468	18
	50.00	6,913	07	40,092	34
	100.00	13,225	14	70,989	60
	200.00	24,340	25	116,197	99
300,000.00	25.00	3,551	03	21,728	15
	50.00	6,965	06	40,992	29
	100.00	13,420	12	73,785	52
	200.00	25,004	21	123,590	88

7½% How Much Will You Save

TABLE A

AMOUNT OF LOAN	AMOUNT OF MONTHLY PRE-PAYMENT	15 YEAR MORTGAGE		30 YEAR MORTGAGE	
		Amount Saved	Months Reduced	Amount Saved	Months Reduced
$ 5,000.00	$25.00	1,744	88	5,498	242
	50.00	2,280	118	6,332	287
	100.00	2,700	142	6,880	318
	200.00	2,979	159	7,203	338
10,000.00	25.00	2,382	59	8,805	188
	50.00	3,488	88	10,997	242
	100.00	4,560	118	12,665	287
	200.00	5,401	142	13,761	318
25,000.00	25.00	3,064	30	14,078	116
	50.00	5,144	51	20,079	170
	100.00	7,811	78	25,849	226
	200.00	10,583	108	30,482	274
50,000.00	25.00	3,392	17	17,814	72
	50.00	6,129	30	28,156	116
	100.00	10,289	51	40,158	170
	200.00	15,623	78	51,699	226
75,000.00	25.00	3,518	12	19,605	53
	50.00	6,550	21	32,695	89
	100.00	11,521	38	49,572	138
	200.00	18,604	61	67,694	193
100,000.00	25.00	3,585	09	20,662	41
	50.00	6,785	17	35,628	72
	100.00	12,258	30	56,312	116
	200.00	20,579	51	80,316	170
125,000.00	25.00	3,626	07	21,360	34
	50.00	6,934	14	37,685	61
	100.00	12,749	25	61,401	101
	200.00	21,987	43	90,590	152
150,000.00	25.00	3,654	06	21,855	29
	50.00	7,037	12	39,211	53
	100.00	13,101	21	65,390	89
	200.00	23,042	38	99,145	138
200,000.00	25.00	3,690	05	22,513	23
	50.00	7,170	09	41,325	41
	100.00	13,570	17	71,256	72
	200.00	24,516	30	112,624	116
250,000.00	25.00	3,711	04	22,930	19
	50.00	7,253	07	42,720	34
	100.00	13,868	14	75,371	61
	200.00	25,499	25	122,803	101
300,000.00	25.00	3,727	03	23,217	16
	50.00	7,309	06	43,711	29
	100.00	14,074	12	78,423	53
	200.00	26,203	21	130,781	89

7¾% How Much Will You Save

TABLE A

AMOUNT OF LOAN	AMOUNT OF MONTHLY PRE-PAYMENT	15 YEAR MORTGAGE		30 YEAR MORTGAGE	
		Amount Saved	Months Reduced	Amount Saved	Months Reduced
$ 5,000.00	$25.00	1,817	88	5,743	243
	50.00	2,372	118	6,602	287
	100.00	2,807	142	7,167	318
	200.00	3,095	159	7,500	338
10,000.00	25.00	2,487	59	9,225	189
	50.00	3,635	88	11,486	243
	100.00	4,745	118	13,205	287
	200.00	5,615	142	14,335	318
25,000.00	25.00	3,205	30	14,835	117
	50.00	5,373	51	21,062	171
	100.00	8,144	78	27,021	226
	200.00	11,017	109	31,796	274
50,000.00	25.00	3,552	17	18,864	73
	50.00	6,411	30	29,671	117
	100.00	10,747	51	42,124	171
	200.00	16,289	78	54,043	226
75,000.00	25.00	3,686	12	20,815	54
	50.00	6,857	21	34,554	90
	100.00	12,044	38	52,135	139
	200.00	19,416	62	70,895	194
100,000.00	25.00	3,757	09	21,970	42
	50.00	7,105	17	37,729	73
	100.00	12,823	30	59,343	117
	200.00	21,494	51	84,249	171
125,000.00	25.00	3,801	07	22,736	35
	50.00	7,263	14	39,965	62
	100.00	13,342	25	64,809	102
	200.00	22,977	43	95,159	153
150,000.00	25.00	3,830	06	23,282	30
	50.00	7,372	12	41,630	54
	100.00	13,715	21	69,109	90
	200.00	24,088	38	104,271	139
200,000.00	25.00	3,868	05	24,007	23
	50.00	7,514	09	43,941	42
	100.00	14,210	17	75,458	73
	200.00	25,646	30	118,686	117
250,000.00	25.00	3,891	04	24,467	19
	50.00	7,602	07	45,473	35
	100.00	14,526	14	79,931	62
	200.00	26,685	25	129,618	102
300,000.00	25.00	3,908	03	24,786	16
	50.00	7,661	06	46,564	30
	100.00	14,745	12	83,260	54
	200.00	27,430	21	138,218	90

8% How Much Will You Save

TABLE A

AMOUNT OF LOAN	AMOUNT OF MONTHLY PRE-PAYMENT	15 YEAR MORTGAGE		30 YEAR MORTGAGE	
		Amount Saved	Months Reduced	Amount Saved	Months Reduced
$ 5,000.00	$25.00	1,892	87	5,991	243
	50.00	2,466	117	6,875	286
	100.00	2,915	141	7,457	317
	200.00	3,212	158	7,800	337
10,000.00	25.00	2,593	58	9,652	189
	50.00	3,784	87	11,982	243
	100.00	4,932	117	13,751	286
	200.00	5,831	141	14,914	317
25,000.00	25.00	3,350	29	15,615	118
	50.00	5,606	50	22,066	171
	100.00	8,482	78	28,211	226
	200.00	11,456	108	33,126	274
50,000.00	25.00	3,716	16	19,954	73
	50.00	6,700	29	31,230	118
	100.00	11,212	50	44,132	171
	200.00	16,964	78	56,422	226
75,000.00	25.00	3,858	11	22,075	54
	50.00	7,171	21	36,476	90
	100.00	12,578	37	54,762	139
	200.00	20,242	61	74,154	194
100,000.00	25.00	3,933	08	23,338	42
	50.00	7,433	16	39,908	73
	100.00	13,400	29	62,460	118
	200.00	22,425	50	88,264	171
125,000.00	25.00	3,980	06	24,179	35
	50.00	7,600	13	42,337	62
	100.00	13,949	24	68,323	102
	200.00	23,986	43	99,832	153
150,000.00	25.00	4,011	05	24,779	30
	50.00	7,716	11	44,150	54
	100.00	14,342	21	72,953	90
	200.00	25,157	37	109,525	139
200,000.00	25.00	4,051	04	25,578	23
	50.00	7,866	08	46,677	42
	100.00	14,866	16	79,817	73
	200.00	26,800	29	124,920	118
250,000.00	25.00	4,075	03	26,087	18
	50.00	7,961	06	48,358	35
	100.00	15,201	13	84,674	62
	200.00	27,898	24	136,647	102
300,000.00	25.00	4,094	02	26,440	15
	50.00	8,023	05	49,559	30
	100.00	15,433	11	88,300	54
	200.00	28,685	21	145,906	90

8¼% How Much Will You Save

TABLE A

AMOUNT OF LOAN	AMOUNT OF MONTHLY PRE-PAYMENT	15 YEAR MORTGAGE		30 YEAR MORTGAGE	
		Amount Saved	Months Reduced	Amount Saved	Months Reduced
$ 5,000.00	$25.00	1,967	87	6,242	243
	50.00	2,560	117	7,151	287
	100.00	3,024	141	7,749	318
	200.00	3,331	158	8,103	337
10,000.00	25.00	2,701	59	10,087	190
	50.00	3,934	87	12,485	243
	100.00	5,121	117	14,303	287
	200.00	6,049	141	15,499	318
25,000.00	25.00	3,497	29	16,415	119
	50.00	5,843	50	23,089	172
	100.00	8,824	78	29,418	227
	200.00	11,900	108	34,471	274
50,000.00	25.00	3,884	16	21,083	75
	50.00	6,995	29	32,831	119
	100.00	11,687	50	46,179	172
	200.00	17,649	78	58,837	227
75,000.00	25.00	4,034	11	23,387	55
	50.00	7,492	21	38,462	92
	100.00	13,123	37	57,454	140
	200.00	21,083	61	77,470	195
100,000.00	25.00	4,114	08	24,767	43
	50.00	7,769	16	42,167	75
	100.00	13,990	29	65,663	119
	200.00	23,374	50	92,359	172
125,000.00	25.00	4,164	07	25,689	35
	50.00	7,946	13	44,801	63
	100.00	14,569	24	71,945	103
	200.00	25,014	43	104,611	155
150,000.00	25.00	4,197	05	26,348	30
	50.00	8,069	11	46,775	55
	100.00	14,984	21	76,924	92
	200.00	26,247	37	114,908	140
200,000.00	25.00	4,239	04	27,229	23
	50.00	8,228	08	49,535	43
	100.00	15,538	16	84,335	75
	200.00	27,980	29	131,326	119
250,000.00	25.00	4,265	03	27,790	19
	50.00	8,328	07	51,379	35
	100.00	15,892	13	89,603	63
	200.00	29,138	24	143,891	103
300,000.00	25.00	4,284	02	28,180	16
	50.00	8,395	05	52,696	30
	100.00	16,138	11	93,550	55
	200.00	29,968	21	153,848	92

8½% How Much Will You Save

TABLE A

AMOUNT OF LOAN	AMOUNT OF MONTHLY PRE-PAYMENT	15 YEAR MORTGAGE		30 YEAR MORTGAGE	
		Amount Saved	Months Reduced	Amount Saved	Months Reduced
$ 5,000.00	$25.00	2,043	88	6,497	244
	50.00	2,656	117	7,430	287
	100.00	3,134	141	8,044	318
	200.00	3,450	158	8,408	337
10,000.00	25.00	2,811	59	10,530	191
	50.00	4,087	88	12,994	244
	100.00	5,312	117	14,860	287
	200.00	6,269	141	16,089	318
25,000.00	25.00	3,648	30	17,238	120
	50.00	6,085	50	24,133	173
	100.00	9,172	78	30,642	228
	200.00	12,349	108	35,830	274
50,000.00	25.00	4,056	16	22,253	76
	50.00	7,296	30	34,476	120
	100.00	12,170	50	48,267	173
	200.00	18,345	78	61,285	228
75,000.00	25.00	4,215	11	24,753	56
	50.00	7,820	21	40,510	93
	100.00	13,680	37	60,208	142
	200.00	21,938	61	80,842	196
100,000.00	25.00	4,299	08	26,260	44
	50.00	8,113	16	44,507	76
	100.00	14,592	30	68,953	120
	200.00	24,341	50	96,534	173
125,000.00	25.00	4,352	07	27,269	36
	50.00	8,300	13	47,362	64
	100.00	15,203	24	75,675	105
	200.00	26,063	43	109,491	156
150,000.00	25.00	4,388	05	27,993	31
	50.00	8,430	11	49,507	56
	100.00	15,640	21	81,021	93
	200.00	27,360	37	120,417	142
200,000.00	25.00	4,432	04	28,963	24
	50.00	8,599	08	52,520	44
	100.00	16,226	16	89,015	76
	200.00	29,184	30	137,906	120
250,000.00	25.00	4,459	03	29,584	19
	50.00	8,705	07	54,539	36
	100.00	16,601	13	94,724	64
	200.00	30,407	24	151,350	105
300,000.00	25.00	4,480	03	30,014	16
	50.00	8,776	05	55,986	31
	100.00	16,861	11	99,015	56
	200.00	31,281	21	162,043	93

8¾% How Much Will You Save

TABLE A

AMOUNT OF LOAN	AMOUNT OF MONTHLY PRE-PAYMENT	15 YEAR MORTGAGE		30 YEAR MORTGAGE	
		Amount Saved	Months Reduced	Amount Saved	Months Reduced
$ 5,000.00	$25.00	2,121	89	6,754	245
	50.00	2,752	118	7,712	288
	100.00	3,245	142	8,342	319
	200.00	3,570	159	8,716	338
10,000.00	25.00	2,923	60	10,980	193
	50.00	4,242	89	13,509	245
	100.00	5,505	118	15,424	288
	200.00	6,490	142	16,685	319
25,000.00	25.00	3,801	31	18,082	123
	50.00	6,331	52	25,196	176
	100.00	9,525	79	31,883	229
	200.00	12,803	109	37,205	276
50,000.00	25.00	4,232	17	23,465	78
	50.00	7,603	31	36,164	123
	100.00	12,662	52	50,393	176
	200.00	19,051	79	63,767	229
75,000.00	25.00	4,400	12	26,175	58
	50.00	8,156	22	42,624	95
	100.00	14,247	38	63,026	144
	200.00	22,807	62	84,270	198
100,000.00	25.00	4,489	09	27,818	46
	50.00	8,465	17	46,931	78
	100.00	15,207	31	72,329	123
	200.00	25,324	52	100,787	176
125,000.00	25.00	4,545	08	28,923	38
	50.00	8,663	14	50,021	66
	100.00	15,851	26	79,513	107
	200.00	27,131	44	114,474	158
150,000.00	25.00	4,583	06	29,718	33
	50.00	8,800	12	52,351	58
	100.00	16,312	22	85,249	95
	200.00	28,495	38	126,052	144
200,000.00	25.00	4,630	05	30,785	25
	50.00	8,979	09	55,636	46
	100.00	16,931	17	93,862	78
	200.00	30,414	31	144,659	123
250,000.00	25.00	4,659	04	31,469	21
	50.00	9,091	08	57,846	38
	100.00	17,327	14	100,042	66
	200.00	31,702	26	159,027	107
300,000.00	25.00	4,680	04	31,946	18
	50.00	9,167	06	59,436	33
	100.00	17,601	12	104,702	58
	200.00	32,624	22	170,498	95

9% How Much Will You Save

TABLE A

AMOUNT OF LOAN	AMOUNT OF MONTHLY PRE-PAYMENT	15 YEAR MORTGAGE		30 YEAR MORTGAGE	
		Amount Saved	Months Reduced	Amount Saved	Months Reduced
$ 5,000.00	$25.00	2,199	89	7,015	246
	50.00	2,850	118	7,996	289
	100.00	3,357	142	8,643	319
	200.00	3,691	159	9,026	338
10,000.00	25.00	3,037	60	11,438	194
	50.00	4,399	89	14,031	246
	100.00	5,700	118	15,992	289
	200.00	6,714	142	17,286	319
25,000.00	25.00	3,958	31	18,948	124
	50.00	6,581	52	26,279	177
	100.00	9,883	79	33,140	230
	200.00	13,263	109	38,593	276
50,000.00	25.00	4,413	17	24,719	79
	50.00	7,917	31	37,896	124
	100.00	13,162	52	52,558	177
	200.00	19,767	79	66,281	230
75,000.00	25.00	4,590	12	27,654	59
	50.00	8,499	22	44,803	97
	100.00	14,826	39	65,907	145
	200.00	23,690	63	87,751	199
100,000.00	25.00	4,684	09	29,443	47
	50.00	8,826	17	49,438	79
	100.00	15,835	31	75,792	124
	200.00	26,325	52	105,117	177
125,000.00	25.00	4,743	08	30,652	39
	50.00	9,035	14	52,780	68
	100.00	16,513	26	83,462	109
	200.00	28,221	44	119,559	159
150,000.00	25.00	4,784	07	31,524	33
	50.00	9,180	12	55,308	59
	100.00	16,999	22	89,607	97
	200.00	29,653	39	131,814	145
200,000.00	25.00	4,833	05	32,698	26
	50.00	9,369	09	58,887	47
	100.00	17,653	17	98,877	79
	200.00	31,670	31	151,585	124
250,000.00	25.00	4,864	04	33,453	21
	50.00	9,487	08	61,304	39
	100.00	18,071	14	105,560	68
	200.00	33,026	26	166,925	109
300,000.00	25.00	4,886	04	33,979	18
	50.00	9,568	07	63,049	33
	100.00	18,361	12	110,616	59
	200.00	33,999	22	179,215	97

9¼% How Much Will You Save

TABLE A

AMOUNT OF LOAN	AMOUNT OF MONTHLY PRE-PAYMENT	15 YEAR MORTGAGE		30 YEAR MORTGAGE	
		Amount Saved	Months Reduced	Amount Saved	Months Reduced
$ 5,000.00	$25.00	2,279	89	7,279	247
	50.00	2,949	118	8,283	289
	100.00	3,470	142	8,945	319
	200.00	3,814	159	9,338	338
10,000.00	25.00	3,152	60	11,903	195
	50.00	4,558	89	14,558	247
	100.00	5,898	118	16,566	289
	200.00	6,940	142	17,891	319
25,000.00	25.00	4,119	31	19,835	126
	50.00	6,836	52	27,381	178
	100.00	10,247	80	34,414	231
	200.00	13,728	109	39,995	277
50,000.00	25.00	4,598	17	26,015	81
	50.00	8,238	31	39,671	126
	100.00	13,672	52	54,762	178
	200.00	20,494	80	68,828	231
75,000.00	25.00	4,784	12	29,190	60
	50.00	8,851	22	47,048	98
	100.00	15,416	39	68,850	147
	200.00	24,587	63	91,286	200
100,000.00	25.00	4,885	09	31,139	48
	50.00	9,196	17	52,031	81
	100.00	16,476	31	79,343	126
	200.00	27,344	52	109,524	178
125,000.00	25.00	4,946	08	32,460	40
	50.00	9,416	14	55,640	69
	100.00	17,190	26	87,519	110
	200.00	29,332	44	124,745	161
150,000.00	25.00	4,989	07	33,415	34
	50.00	9,569	12	58,381	60
	100.00	17,703	22	94,096	98
	200.00	30,833	39	137,700	147
200,000.00	25.00	5,041	05	34,707	27
	50.00	9,770	09	62,278	48
	100.00	18,392	17	104,062	81
	200.00	32,953	31	158,687	126
250,000.00	25.00	5,074	04	35,539	22
	50.00	9,893	08	64,920	40
	100.00	18,833	14	111,280	69
	200.00	34,380	26	175,039	110
300,000.00	25.00	5,098	04	36,122	19
	50.00	9,979	07	66,831	34
	100.00	19,139	12	116,763	60
	200.00	35,406	22	188,193	98

9½% How Much Will You Save

TABLE A

AMOUNT OF LOAN	AMOUNT OF MONTHLY PRE-PAYMENT	15 YEAR MORTGAGE		30 YEAR MORTGAGE	
		Amount Saved	Months Reduced	Amount Saved	Months Reduced
$ 5,000.00	$25.00	2,359	88	7,546	246
	50.00	3,048	117	8,572	288
	100.00	3,584	141	9,251	318
	200.00	3,937	158	9,653	337
10,000.00	25.00	3,270	60	12,374	195
	50.00	4,719	88	15,092	246
	100.00	6,097	117	17,145	288
	200.00	7,168	141	18,502	318
25,000.00	25.00	4,283	30	20,744	126
	50.00	7,095	51	28,501	178
	100.00	10,615	79	35,703	231
	200.00	14,198	108	41,410	276
50,000.00	25.00	4,787	16	27,355	81
	50.00	8,566	30	41,489	126
	100.00	14,190	51	57,003	178
	200.00	21,230	79	71,406	231
75,000.00	25.00	4,984	11	30,787	60
	50.00	9,211	21	49,360	98
	100.00	16,018	38	71,854	147
	200.00	25,499	62	94,873	200
100,000.00	25.00	5,090	08	32,906	48
	50.00	9,574	16	54,710	81
	100.00	17,132	30	82,978	126
	200.00	28,381	51	114,006	178
125,000.00	25.00	5,155	07	34,349	40
	50.00	9,807	13	58,604	69
	100.00	17,882	25	91,688	110
	200.00	30,463	44	130,029	161
150,000.00	25.00	5,200	06	35,396	34
	50.00	9,968	11	61,574	60
	100.00	18,423	21	98,720	98
	200.00	32,037	38	143,709	147
200,000.00	25.00	5,256	04	36,815	26
	50.00	10,180	08	65,812	48
	100.00	19,149	16	109,420	81
	200.00	34,264	30	165,957	126
250,000.00	25.00	5,290	03	37,733	21
	50.00	10,310	07	68,698	40
	100.00	19,614	13	117,209	69
	200.00	35,764	25	183,376	110
300,000.00	25.00	5,315	03	38,374	18
	50.00	10,400	06	70,792	34
	100.00	19,937	11	123,149	60
	200.00	36,846	21	197,440	98

9¾%   How Much Will You Save

TABLE A

AMOUNT OF LOAN	AMOUNT OF MONTHLY PRE-PAYMENT	15 YEAR MORTGAGE		30 YEAR MORTGAGE	
		Amount Saved	Months Reduced	Amount Saved	Months Reduced
$ 5,000.00	$25.00	2,441	89	7,815	247
	50.00	3,149	117	8,865	289
	100.00	3,699	141	9,558	318
	200.00	4,061	158	9,970	337
10,000.00	25.00	3,389	60	12,853	197
	50.00	4,882	89	15,631	247
	100.00	6,299	117	17,730	289
	200.00	7,398	141	19,117	318
25,000.00	25.00	4,450	30	21,675	127
	50.00	7,359	51	29,640	179
	100.00	10,988	79	37,007	231
	200.00	14,673	109	42,838	276
50,000.00	25.00	4,980	17	28,738	83
	50.00	8,900	30	43,350	127
	100.00	14,719	51	59,281	179
	200.00	21,976	79	74,014	231
75,000.00	25.00	5,189	11	32,444	61
	50.00	9,579	22	51,736	100
	100.00	16,632	38	74,921	149
	200.00	26,426	62	98,511	201
100,000.00	25.00	5,300	09	34,747	49
	50.00	9,961	17	57,477	83
	100.00	17,801	30	86,701	127
	200.00	29,438	51	118,562	179
125,000.00	25.00	5,368	07	36,322	41
	50.00	10,207	13	61,675	70
	100.00	18,589	25	95,965	112
	200.00	31,614	44	135,412	162
150,000.00	25.00	5,416	06	37,468	35
	50.00	10,378	11	64,889	61
	100.00	19,159	22	103,473	100
	200.00	33,265	38	149,843	149
200,000.00	25.00	5,475	04	39,026	27
	50.00	10,601	09	69,494	49
	100.00	19,923	17	114,954	83
	200.00	35,603	30	173,403	127
250,000.00	25.00	5,512	03	40,037	22
	50.00	10,737	07	72,644	41
	100.00	20,415	13	123,351	70
	200.00	37,179	25	191,930	112
300,000.00	25.00	5,538	03	40,747	19
	50.00	10,833	06	74,936	35
	100.00	20,756	11	129,779	61
	200.00	38,319	22	206,947	100

10% How Much Will You Save

TABLE A

AMOUNT OF LOAN	AMOUNT OF MONTHLY PRE-PAYMENT	15 YEAR MORTGAGE		30 YEAR MORTGAGE	
		Amount Saved	Months Reduced	Amount Saved	Months Reduced
$ 5,000.00	$25.00	2,524	89	8,088	248
	50.00	3,251	118	9,159	289
	100.00	3,815	141	9,868	318
	200.00	4,186	158	10,290	337
10,000.00	25.00	3,511	60	13,339	198
	50.00	5,048	89	16,176	248
	100.00	6,502	118	18,318	289
	200.00	7,630	141	19,736	318
25,000.00	25.00	4,621	31	22,627	129
	50.00	7,627	52	30,797	181
	100.00	11,366	79	38,325	232
	200.00	15,153	109	44,279	277
50,000.00	25.00	5,178	17	30,165	84
	50.00	9,242	31	45,254	129
	100.00	15,255	52	61,595	181
	200.00	22,733	79	76,651	232
75,000.00	25.00	5,398	11	34,163	64
	50.00	9,955	22	54,181	102
	100.00	17,259	38	78,047	151
	200.00	27,368	62	102,200	203
100,000.00	25.00	5,516	09	36,664	50
	50.00	10,357	17	60,331	84
	100.00	18,485	31	90,508	129
	200.00	30,511	52	123,191	181
125,000.00	25.00	5,588	07	38,381	42
	50.00	10,617	14	64,853	72
	100.00	19,313	25	100,353	113
	200.00	32,788	44	140,891	164
150,000.00	25.00	5,638	06	39,635	37
	50.00	10,797	11	68,327	64
	100.00	19,911	22	108,363	102
	200.00	34,518	38	156,095	151
200,000.00	25.00	5,701	04	41,346	28
	50.00	11,032	09	73,328	50
	100.00	20,715	17	120,662	84
	200.00	36,970	31	181,016	129
250,000.00	25.00	5,740	03	42,460	23
	50.00	11,176	07	76,763	42
	100.00	21,234	14	129,706	72
	200.00	38,626	25	200,706	113
300,000.00	25.00	5,767	03	43,241	20
	50.00	11,277	06	79,271	37
	100.00	21,594	11	136,655	64
	200.00	39,822	22	216,726	102

10¼% How Much Will You Save

TABLE A

AMOUNT OF LOAN	AMOUNT OF MONTHLY PRE-PAYMENT	15 YEAR MORTGAGE		30 YEAR MORTGAGE	
		Amount Saved	Months Reduced	Amount Saved	Months Reduced
$ 5,000.00	$25.00	2,607	90	8,363	248
	50.00	3,353	119	9,456	289
	100.00	3,932	142	10,180	318
	200.00	4,312	159	10,611	337
10,000.00	25.00	3,634	61	13,831	199
	50.00	5,215	90	16,726	248
	100.00	6,707	119	18,912	289
	200.00	7,864	142	20,360	318
25,000.00	25.00	4,795	32	23,600	131
	50.00	7,900	53	31,972	183
	100.00	11,750	80	39,658	234
	200.00	15,639	110	45,731	278
50,000.00	25.00	5,381	18	31,638	86
	50.00	9,591	32	47,200	131
	100.00	15,801	53	63,945	183
	200.00	23,501	80	79,317	234
75,000.00	25.00	5,613	13	35,946	65
	50.00	10,340	23	56,692	104
	100.00	17,897	40	81,234	152
	200.00	28,324	64	105,937	205
100,000.00	25.00	5,737	10	38,659	52
	50.00	10,763	18	63,276	86
	100.00	19,182	32	94,401	131
	200.00	31,603	53	127,890	183
125,000.00	25.00	5,813	08	40,530	44
	50.00	11,036	15	68,139	74
	100.00	20,052	27	104,849	116
	200.00	33,984	45	146,464	166
150,000.00	25.00	5,866	07	41,901	38
	50.00	11,227	13	71,892	65
	100.00	20,680	23	113,384	104
	200.00	35,794	40	162,469	152
200,000.00	25.00	5,933	05	43,779	30
	50.00	11,474	10	77,318	52
	100.00	21,527	18	126,552	86
	200.00	38,364	32	188,802	131
250,000.00	25.00	5,974	04	45,004	24
	50.00	11,627	08	81,061	44
	100.00	22,072	15	136,279	74
	200.00	40,105	27	209,699	116
300,000.00	25.00	6,002	04	45,867	21
	50.00	11,732	07	83,803	38
	100.00	22,454	13	143,784	65
	200.00	41,360	23	226,768	104

10½% How Much Will You Save

TABLE A

AMOUNT OF LOAN	AMOUNT OF MONTHLY PRE-PAYMENT	15 YEAR MORTGAGE		30 YEAR MORTGAGE	
		Amount Saved	Months Reduced	Amount Saved	Months Reduced
$ 5,000.00	$25.00	2,692	90	8,641	250
	50.00	3,457	119	9,755	290
	100.00	4,049	143	10,493	320
	200.00	4,439	159	10,934	338
10,000.00	25.00	3,759	61	14,329	201
	50.00	5,384	90	17,282	250
	100.00	6,915	119	19,510	290
	200.00	8,099	143	20,987	320
25,000.00	25.00	4,973	32	24,594	133
	50.00	8,178	53	33,165	184
	100.00	12,139	81	41,006	235
	200.00	16,129	110	47,196	279
50,000.00	25.00	5,589	18	33,154	88
	50.00	9,946	32	49,188	133
	100.00	16,357	53	66,330	184
	200.00	24,279	81	82,012	235
75,000.00	25.00	5,833	13	37,793	66
	50.00	10,733	23	59,270	105
	100.00	18,547	40	84,479	154
	200.00	29,295	64	109,722	206
100,000.00	25.00	5,963	10	40,733	53
	50.00	11,178	18	66,309	88
	100.00	19,893	32	98,377	133
	200.00	32,715	53	132,660	184
125,000.00	25.00	6,044	08	42,771	45
	50.00	11,465	15	71,537	76
	100.00	20,807	27	109,457	117
	200.00	35,203	46	152,132	167
150,000.00	25.00	6,100	07	44,269	39
	50.00	11,667	13	75,586	66
	100.00	21,466	23	118,540	105
	200.00	37,094	40	168,959	154
200,000.00	25.00	6,171	05	46,327	30
	50.00	11,927	10	81,467	53
	100.00	22,357	18	132,618	88
	200.00	39,787	32	196,754	133
250,000.00	25.00	6,215	04	47,674	25
	50.00	12,089	08	85,542	45
	100.00	22,931	15	143,075	76
	200.00	41,614	27	218,914	117
300,000.00	25.00	6,243	04	48,628	21
	50.00	12,200	07	88,539	39
	100.00	23,334	13	151,172	66
	200.00	42,933	23	237,081	105

10¾% How Much Will You Save

TABLE A

AMOUNT OF LOAN	AMOUNT OF MONTHLY PRE-PAYMENT	15 YEAR MORTGAGE		30 YEAR MORTGAGE	
		Amount Saved	Months Reduced	Amount Saved	Months Reduced
$ 5,000.00	$25.00	2,778	90	8,921	251
	50.00	3,562	119	10,056	291
	100.00	4,168	143	10,809	320
	200.00	4,567	159	11,260	338
10,000.00	25.00	3,887	62	14,835	202
	50.00	5,556	90	17,842	251
	100.00	7,124	119	20,112	291
	200.00	8,337	143	21,619	320
25,000.00	25.00	5,155	32	25,609	134
	50.00	8,461	53	34,374	185
	100.00	12,533	81	42,367	236
	200.00	16,625	110	48,671	279
50,000.00	25.00	5,802	18	34,716	89
	50.00	10,310	32	51,218	134
	100.00	16,923	53	68,749	185
	200.00	25,066	81	84,734	236
75,000.00	25.00	6,058	13	39,705	68
	50.00	11,135	23	61,914	107
	100.00	19,210	40	87,783	155
	200.00	30,281	64	113,553	207
100,000.00	25.00	6,196	10	42,809	55
	50.00	11,604	18	69,433	89
	100.00	20,620	32	102,437	134
	200.00	33,846	53	137,498	185
125,000.00	25.00	6,281	08	45,106	46
	50.00	11,906	15	75,045	77
	100.00	21,578	27	114,171	119
	200.00	36,442	46	157,891	169
150,000.00	25.00	6,340	07	46,742	40
	50.00	12,117	13	79,410	68
	100.00	22,271	23	123,828	107
	200.00	38,421	40	175,567	155
200,000.00	25.00	6,415	05	48,996	31
	50.00	12,392	10	85,778	55
	100.00	23,208	18	138,866	89
	200.00	41,241	32	204,875	134
250,000.00	25.00	6,461	04	50,479	26
	50.00	12,563	08	90,212	46
	100.00	23,812	15	150,090	77
	200.00	43,156	27	228,342	119
300,000.00	25.00	6,491	04	51,528	22
	50.00	12,680	07	93,485	40
	100.00	24,235	13	158,820	68
	200.00	44,542	23	247,656	107

TABLE A

AMOUNT OF LOAN	AMOUNT OF MONTHLY PRE-PAYMENT	15 YEAR MORTGAGE		30 YEAR MORTGAGE	
		Amount Saved	Months Reduced	Amount Saved	Months Reduced
$ 5,000.00	$25.00	2,864	90	9,204	250
	50.00	3,668	118	10,359	290
	100.00	4,288	142	11,127	319
	200.00	4,696	158	11,587	337
10,000.00	25.00	4,016	61	15,346	202
	50.00	5,729	90	18,408	250
	100.00	7,336	118	20,718	290
	200.00	8,576	142	22,254	319
25,000.00	25.00	5,340	31	26,644	135
	50.00	8,748	53	35,601	186
	100.00	12,932	80	43,741	235
	200.00	17,125	109	50,158	278
50,000.00	25.00	6,019	17	36,323	90
	50.00	10,681	31	53,289	135
	100.00	17,497	53	71,202	186
	200.00	25,864	80	87,482	235
75,000.00	25.00	6,289	12	41,683	68
	50.00	11,547	22	64,625	108
	100.00	19,886	39	91,144	156
	200.00	31,283	63	117,430	207
100,000.00	25.00	6,434	09	45,127	55
	50.00	12,039	17	72,647	90
	100.00	21,363	31	106,578	135
	200.00	34,995	53	142,404	186
125,000.00	25.00	6,524	07	47,537	46
	50.00	12,357	14	78,667	77
	100.00	22,366	26	118,994	120
	200.00	37,704	45	163,740	169
,150,000.00	25.00	6,586	06	49,323	40
	50.00	12,579	12	83,366	68
	100.00	23,094	22	129,251	108
	200.00	39,773	39	182,289	156
200,000.00	25.00	6,666	04	51,791	31
	50.00	12,869	09	90,255	55
	100.00	24,079	17	145,294	90
	200.00	42,726	31	213,157	135
250,000.00	25.00	6,715	03	53,423	25
	50.00	13,049	07	95,075	46
	100.00	24,714	14	157,334	77
	200.00	44,732	26	237,989	120
300,000.00	25.00	6,746	03	54,581	22
	50.00	13,173	06	98,646	40
	100.00	25,158	12	166,732	68
	200.00	46,189	22	258,502	108

11¼% How Much Will You Save

TABLE A

AMOUNT OF LOAN	AMOUNT OF MONTHLY PRE-PAYMENT	15 YEAR MORTGAGE		30 YEAR MORTGAGE	
		Amount Saved	Months Reduced	Amount Saved	Months Reduced
$ 5,000.00	$25.00	2,952	90	9,489	251
	50.00	3,774	118	10,664	290
	100.00	4,409	142	11,446	319
	200.00	4,826	158	11,915	337
10,000.00	25.00	4,147	61	15,863	203
	50.00	5,905	90	18,978	251
	100.00	7,549	118	21,329	290
	200.00	8,818	142	22,893	319
25,000.00	25.00	5,530	32	27,700	137
	50.00	9,040	53	36,843	187
	100.00	13,336	80	45,127	236
	200.00	17,631	109	51,656	279
50,000.00	25.00	6,242	17	37,976	91
	50.00	11,060	32	55,401	137
	100.00	18,081	53	73,687	187
	200.00	26,673	80	90,255	236
75,000.00	25.00	6,526	12	43,729	70
	50.00	11,968	22	67,402	110
	100.00	20,576	40	94,561	158
	200.00	32,299	64	121,352	209
100,000.00	25.00	6,679	09	47,451	56
	50.00	12,485	17	75,953	91
	100.00	22,120	32	110,802	137
	200.00	36,163	53	147,374	187
125,000.00	25.00	6,774	07	50,069	47
	50.00	12,819	14	82,400	79
	100.00	23,172	26	123,923	121
	200.00	38,990	45	169,679	170
150,000.00	25.00	6,839	06	52,015	42
	50.00	13,052	12	87,458	70
	100.00	23,936	22	134,804	110
	200.00	41,152	40	189,122	158
200,000.00	25.00	6,924	04	54,717	32
	50.00	13,358	09	94,902	56
	100.00	24,971	17	151,906	91
	200.00	44,241	32	221,605	137
250,000.00	25.00	6,976	03	56,508	26
	50.00	13,549	07	100,139	47
	100.00	25,638	14	164,800	79
	200.00	46,344	26	247,847	121
300,000.00	25.00	7,007	03	57,783	23
	50.00	13,678	06	104,031	42
	100.00	26,105	12	174,916	70
	200.00	47,873	22	269,609	110

11½% How Much Will You Save

TABLE A

AMOUNT OF LOAN	AMOUNT OF MONTHLY PRE-PAYMENT	15 YEAR MORTGAGE		30 YEAR MORTGAGE	
		Amount Saved	Months Reduced	Amount Saved	Months Reduced
$ 5,000.00	$25.00	3,041	91	9,776	251
	50.00	3,882	119	10,972	291
	100.00	4,530	143	11,768	319
	200.00	4,956	159	12,246	337
10,000.00	25.00	4,281	62	16,386	204
	50.00	6,082	91	19,553	251
	100.00	7,765	119	21,944	291
	200.00	9,061	143	23,536	319
25,000.00	25.00	5,723	32	28,776	139
	50.00	9,337	53	38,102	189
	100.00	13,746	80	46,527	238
	200.00	18,142	110	53,163	280
50,000.00	25.00	6,471	18	39,673	94
	50.00	11,446	32	57,552	139
	100.00	18,675	53	76,204	189
	200.00	27,493	80	93,054	238
75,000.00	25.00	6,769	13	45,841	71
	50.00	12,398	24	70,245	111
	100.00	21,277	41	98,033	159
	200.00	33,331	65	125,316	209
100,000.00	25.00	6,929	09	49,862	58
	50.00	12,942	18	79,347	94
	100.00	22,892	32	115,105	139
	200.00	37,351	53	152,408	189
125,000.00	25.00	7,030	07	52,703	49
	50.00	13,292	14	86,250	81
	100.00	23,995	26	128,959	124
	200.00	40,300	45	175,702	173
150,000.00	25.00	7,099	07	54,822	42
	50.00	13,538	13	91,682	71
	100.00	24,796	24	140,490	111
	200.00	42,554	41	196,067	159
200,000.00	25.00	7,189	04	57,778	34
	50.00	13,859	09	99,724	58
	100.00	25,884	18	158,695	94
	200.00	45,785	32	230,210	139
250,000.00	25.00	7,243	03	59,743	28
	50.00	14,061	07	105,406	49
	100.00	26,585	14	172,500	81
	200.00	47,991	26	257,918	124
300,000.00	25.00	7,276	04	61,147	23
	50.00	14,198	07	109,644	42
	100.00	27,076	13	183,365	71
	200.00	49,593	24	280,981	111

11¾% How Much Will You Save

TABLE A

AMOUNT OF LOAN	AMOUNT OF MONTHLY PRE-PAYMENT	15 YEAR MORTGAGE		30 YEAR MORTGAGE	
		Amount Saved	Months Reduced	Amount Saved	Months Reduced
$ 5,000.00	$25.00	3,131	91	10,066	253
	50.00	3,991	119	11,281	292
	100.00	4,653	143	12,091	320
	200.00	5,088	159	12,578	338
10,000.00	25.00	4,416	63	16,915	206
	50.00	6,262	91	20,133	253
	100.00	7,982	119	22,562	292
	200.00	9,306	143	24,182	320
25,000.00	25.00	5,920	33	29,872	141
	50.00	9,640	54	39,376	190
	100.00	14,161	82	47,939	239
	200.00	18,657	111	54,681	281
50,000.00	25.00	6,704	19	41,417	96
	50.00	11,840	33	59,744	141
	100.00	19,280	54	78,752	190
	200.00	28,322	82	95,878	239
75,000.00	25.00	7,017	13	48,023	73
	50.00	12,837	24	73,154	113
	100.00	21,992	41	101,559	161
	200.00	34,378	65	129,323	211
100,000.00	25.00	7,187	10	52,359	60
	50.00	13,408	19	82,834	96
	100.00	23,680	33	119,488	141
	200.00	38,560	54	157,505	190
125,000.00	25.00	7,293	08	55,441	51
	50.00	13,777	15	90,211	83
	100.00	24,836	28	134,100	125
	200.00	41,630	47	181,810	174
150,000.00	25.00	7,365	07	57,746	44
	50.00	14,035	13	96,046	73
	100.00	25,674	24	146,308	113
	200.00	43,984	41	203,118	161
200,000.00	25.00	7,460	05	60,977	35
	50.00	14,374	10	104,718	60
	100.00	26,816	19	165,669	96
	200.00	47,361	33	238,976	141
250,000.00	25.00	7,517	05	63,135	29
	50.00	14,587	08	110,882	51
	100.00	27,555	15	180,423	83
	200.00	49,672	28	268,200	125
300,000.00	25.00	7,552	04	64,681	25
	50.00	14,730	07	115,493	44
	100.00	28,071	13	192,093	73
	200.00	51,349	24	292,617	113

12%   How Much Will You Save

TABLE A

AMOUNT OF LOAN	AMOUNT OF MONTHLY PRE-PAYMENT	15 YEAR MORTGAGE		30 YEAR MORTGAGE	
		Amount Saved	Months Reduced	Amount Saved	Months Reduced
$ 5,000.00	$25.00	3,222	91	10,358	254
	50.00	4,100	120	11,591	292
	100.00	4,776	143	12,415	320
	200.00	5,220	159	12,912	338
10,000.00	25.00	4,553	63	17,450	207
	50.00	6,444	91	20,717	254
	100.00	8,201	120	23,183	292
	200.00	9,552	143	24,831	320
25,000.00	25.00	6,121	33	30,986	142
	50.00	9,947	55	40,666	191
	100.00	14,580	82	49,362	240
	200.00	19,177	111	56,207	281
50,000.00	25.00	6,942	19	43,205	97
	50.00	12,242	33	61,973	142
	100.00	19,894	55	81,332	191
	200.00	29,161	82	98,725	240
75,000.00	25.00	7,272	13	50,273	75
	50.00	13,286	24	76,126	115
	100.00	22,720	41	105,139	162
	200.00	35,441	65	133,371	212
100,000.00	25.00	7,451	10	54,946	61
	50.00	13,885	19	86,411	97
	100.00	24,485	33	123,947	142
	200.00	39,788	55	162,664	191
125,000.00	25.00	7,563	08	58,283	52
	50.00	14,275	16	94,291	85
	100.00	25,693	28	139,342	127
	200.00	42,985	47	188,003	175
150,000.00	25.00	7,638	07	60,792	45
	50.00	14,545	13	100,546	75
	100.00	26,573	24	152,253	115
	200.00	45,441	41	210,278	162
200,000.00	25.00	7,738	06	64,321	36
	50.00	14,902	10	109,893	61
	100.00	27,770	19	172,823	97
	200.00	48,970	33	247,895	142
250,000.00	25.00	7,798	05	66,688	30
	50.00	15,127	08	116,567	52
	100.00	28,550	16	188,582	85
	200.00	51,386	28	278,685	127
300,000.00	25.00	7,836	04	68,388	25
	50.00	15,277	07	121,584	45
	100.00	29,091	13	201,092	75
	200.00	53,146	24	304,506	115

12¼% How Much Will You Save

TABLE A

AMOUNT OF LOAN	AMOUNT OF MONTHLY PRE-PAYMENT	15 YEAR MORTGAGE		30 YEAR MORTGAGE	
		Amount Saved	Months Reduced	Amount Saved	Months Reduced
$ 5,000.00	$25.00	3,314	92	10,652	254
	50.00	4,211	120	11,904	293
	100.00	4,900	143	12,742	320
	200.00	5,353	159	13,247	338
10,000.00	25.00	4,693	63	17,990	208
	50.00	6,628	92	21,305	254
	100.00	8,422	120	23,809	293
	200.00	9,801	143	25,484	320
25,000.00	25.00	6,326	33	32,121	144
	50.00	10,258	55	41,969	193
	100.00	15,006	82	50,797	240
	200.00	19,703	111	57,743	281
50,000.00	25.00	7,186	19	45,039	99
	50.00	12,653	33	64,242	144
	100.00	20,517	55	83,939	193
	200.00	30,012	82	101,594	240
75,000.00	25.00	7,534	13	52,593	76
	50.00	13,746	24	79,164	117
	100.00	23,463	41	108,769	164
	200.00	36,519	66	137,458	213
100,000.00	25.00	7,722	10	57,624	63
	50.00	14,373	19	90,078	99
	100.00	25,306	33	128,484	144
	200.00	41,034	55	167,879	193
125,000.00	25.00	7,840	08	61,235	53
	50.00	14,782	16	98,483	86
	100.00	26,569	28	144,689	129
	200.00	44,364	47	194,273	177
150,000.00	25.00	7,919	07	63,961	46
	50.00	15,068	13	105,187	76
	100.00	27,492	24	158,328	117
	200.00	46,926	41	217,538	164
200,000.00	25.00	8,024	06	67,812	37
	50.00	15,444	10	115,249	63
	100.00	28,747	19	180,157	99
	200.00	50,612	33	256,968	144
250,000.00	25.00	8,087	05	70,408	31
	50.00	15,681	08	122,471	53
	100.00	29,565	16	196,966	86
	200.00	53,139	28	289,378	129
300,000.00	25.00	8,127	04	72,274	26
	50.00	15,839	07	127,923	46
	100.00	30,137	13	210,374	76
	200.00	54,984	24	316,656	117

12½% How Much Will You Save

TABLE A

AMOUNT OF LOAN	AMOUNT OF MONTHLY PRE-PAYMENT	15 YEAR MORTGAGE		30 YEAR MORTGAGE	
		Amount Saved	Months Reduced	Amount Saved	Months Reduced
$ 5,000.00	$25.00	3,407	91	10,948	254
	50.00	4,322	119	12,218	292
	100.00	5,025	142	13,070	319
	200.00	5,487	158	13,583	337
10,000.00	25.00	4,835	62	18,535	209
	50.00	6,814	91	21,897	254
	100.00	8,645	119	24,437	292
	200.00	10,051	142	26,140	319
25,000.00	25.00	6,535	33	33,274	144
	50.00	10,575	54	43,288	193
	100.00	15,436	81	52,242	240
	200.00	20,233	110	59,288	281
50,000.00	25.00	7,436	18	46,918	100
	50.00	13,071	33	66,548	144
	100.00	21,151	54	86,576	193
	200.00	30,873	81	104,485	240
75,000.00	25.00	7,802	12	54,981	77
	50.00	14,215	23	82,265	117
	100.00	24,218	41	112,451	164
	200.00	37,612	65	141,584	213
100,000.00	25.00	8,000	09	60,392	63
	50.00	14,873	18	93,836	100
	100.00	26,143	33	133,096	144
	200.00	42,302	54	173,153	193
125,000.00	25.00	8,124	08	64,299	53
	50.00	15,302	15	102,792	87
	100.00	27,465	27	150,135	129
	200.00	45,768	46	200,624	177
150,000.00	25.00	8,208	06	67,258	46
	50.00	15,605	12	109,963	77
	100.00	28,431	23	164,530	117
	200.00	48,436	41	224,902	164
200,000.00	25.00	8,317	05	71,456	37
	50.00	16,000	09	120,785	63
	100.00	29,747	18	187,672	100
	200.00	52,286	33	266,192	144
250,000.00	25.00	8,384	04	74,299	30
	50.00	16,248	08	128,598	53
	100.00	30,605	15	205,584	87
	200.00	54,930	27	300,271	129
300,000.00	25.00	8,426	03	76,349	26
	50.00	16,416	06	134,517	46
	100.00	31,210	12	219,927	77
	200.00	56,863	23	329,060	117

12¾% How Much Will You Save

TABLE A

AMOUNT OF LOAN	AMOUNT OF MONTHLY PRE-PAYMENT	15 YEAR MORTGAGE		30 YEAR MORTGAGE	
		Amount Saved	Months Reduced	Amount Saved	Months Reduced
$ 5,000.00	$25.00	3,500	91	11,246	255
	50.00	4,435	119	12,534	292
	100.00	5,151	142	13,399	320
	200.00	5,622	158	13,921	337
10,000.00	25.00	4,978	63	19,085	210
	50.00	7,001	91	22,493	255
	100.00	8,870	119	25,069	292
	200.00	10,303	142	26,798	320
25,000.00	25.00	6,748	33	34,444	146
	50.00	10,897	54	44,621	194
	100.00	15,872	82	53,698	241
	200.00	20,768	110	60,841	281
50,000.00	25.00	7,693	18	48,840	101
	50.00	13,497	33	68,889	146
	100.00	21,795	54	89,242	194
	200.00	31,744	82	107,397	241
75,000.00	25.00	8,076	13	57,441	79
	50.00	14,696	24	85,427	119
	100.00	24,987	41	116,181	166
	200.00	38,721	65	145,747	214
100,000.00	25.00	8,284	10	63,255	64
	50.00	15,386	18	97,681	101
	100.00	26,995	33	137,779	146
	200.00	43,591	54	178,484	194
125,000.00	25.00	8,414	08	67,472	55
	50.00	15,835	15	107,216	88
	100.00	28,380	27	155,679	131
	200.00	47,194	47	207,052	179
150,000.00	25.00	8,504	06	70,682	48
	50.00	16,153	13	114,883	79
	100.00	29,392	24	170,854	119
	200.00	49,974	41	232,363	166
200,000.00	25.00	8,618	05	75,256	38
	50.00	16,569	10	126,510	64
	100.00	30,772	18	195,363	101
	200.00	53,991	33	275,559	146
250,000.00	25.00	8,688	04	78,367	31
	50.00	16,829	08	134,944	55
	100.00	31,670	15	214,432	88
	200.00	56,760	27	311,359	131
300,000.00	25.00	8,734	03	80,620	27
	50.00	17,008	06	141,365	48
	100.00	32,306	13	229,767	79
	200.00	58,785	24	341,709	119

How Much Will You Save

TABLE A

AMOUNT OF LOAN	AMOUNT OF MONTHLY PRE-PAYMENT	15 YEAR MORTGAGE		30 YEAR MORTGAGE	
		Amount Saved	Months Reduced	Amount Saved	Months Reduced
$ 5,000.00	$25.00	3,595	91	11,546	255
	50.00	4,548	119	12,852	292
	100.00	5,278	142	13,729	320
	200.00	5,758	158	14,261	337
10,000.00	25.00	5,124	63	19,641	211
	50.00	7,191	91	23,093	255
	100.00	9,097	119	25,704	292
	200.00	10,557	142	27,459	320
25,000.00	25.00	6,966	33	35,634	149
	50.00	11,224	55	45,967	196
	100.00	16,312	82	55,165	243
	200.00	21,309	110	62,403	283
50,000.00	25.00	7,955	18	50,807	104
	50.00	13,933	33	71,268	149
	100.00	22,449	55	91,934	196
	200.00	32,625	82	110,331	243
75,000.00	25.00	8,357	14	59,970	81
	50.00	15,185	25	88,652	122
	100.00	25,770	42	119,960	168
	200.00	39,847	67	149,946	216
100,000.00	25.00	8,575	10	66,208	67
	50.00	15,910	18	101,615	104
	100.00	27,866	33	142,537	149
	200.00	44,898	55	183,869	196
125,000.00	25.00	8,712	09	70,760	56
	50.00	16,381	16	111,752	90
	100.00	29,313	29	161,323	133
	200.00	48,645	48	213,552	180
150,000.00	25.00	8,807	07	74,238	50
	50.00	16,714	14	119,940	81
	100.00	30,371	25	177,304	122
	200.00	51,541	42	239,921	168
200,000.00	25.00	8,927	05	79,217	40
	50.00	17,151	10	132,416	67
	100.00	31,820	18	203,230	104
	200.00	55,732	33	285,075	149
250,000.00	25.00	9,001	05	82,620	32
	50.00	17,425	09	141,520	56
	100.00	32,762	16	223,505	90
	200.00	58,626	29	322,647	133
300,000.00	25.00	9,049	04	85,095	29
	50.00	17,615	07	148,476	50
	100.00	33,428	14	239,880	81
	200.00	60,742	25	354,609	122

13¼% How Much Will You Save

TABLE A

AMOUNT OF LOAN	AMOUNT OF MONTHLY PRE-PAYMENT	15 YEAR MORTGAGE		30 YEAR MORTGAGE	
		Amount Saved	Months Reduced	Amount Saved	Months Reduced
$ 5,000.00	$25.00	3,691	92	11,848	257
	50.00	4,663	120	13,171	294
	100.00	5,406	143	14,061	321
	200.00	5,895	159	14,601	338
10,000.00	25.00	5,271	64	20,201	213
	50.00	7,383	92	23,696	257
	100.00	9,326	120	26,342	294
	200.00	10,813	143	28,122	321
25,000.00	25.00	7,188	34	36,840	150
	50.00	11,556	56	47,326	198
	100.00	16,758	83	56,642	243
	200.00	21,853	112	63,972	283
50,000.00	25.00	8,222	20	52,818	106
	50.00	14,377	34	73,681	150
	100.00	23,113	56	94,653	198
	200.00	33,516	83	113,284	243
75,000.00	25.00	8,644	14	62,569	83
	50.00	15,686	25	91,938	123
	100.00	26,569	42	123,787	170
	200.00	40,986	67	154,180	217
100,000.00	25.00	8,874	11	69,258	69
	50.00	16,445	20	105,637	106
	100.00	28,754	34	147,362	150
	200.00	46,226	56	189,307	198
125,000.00	25.00	9,018	09	74,164	59
	50.00	16,940	16	116,405	93
	100.00	30,264	29	167,060	135
	200.00	50,121	48	220,127	182
150,000.00	25.00	9,119	07	77,928	51
	50.00	17,289	14	125,138	83
	100.00	31,372	25	183,876	123
	200.00	53,138	42	247,574	170
200,000.00	25.00	9,244	06	83,344	41
	50.00	17,749	11	138,516	69
	100.00	32,891	20	211,275	106
	200.00	57,509	34	294,725	150
250,000.00	25.00	9,322	05	87,062	34
	50.00	18,037	09	148,328	59
	100.00	33,880	16	232,810	93
	200.00	60,529	29	334,120	135
300,000.00	25.00	9,374	04	89,779	30
	50.00	18,239	07	155,857	51
	100.00	34,578	14	250,276	83
	200.00	62,744	25	367,753	123

13½% How Much Will You Save

TABLE A

AMOUNT OF LOAN	AMOUNT OF MONTHLY PRE-PAYMENT	15 YEAR MORTGAGE		30 YEAR MORTGAGE	
		Amount Saved	Months Reduced	Amount Saved	Months Reduced
$ 5,000.00	$25.00	3,788	93	12,152	258
	50.00	4,778	120	13,491	294
	100.00	5,535	143	14,394	321
	200.00	6,032	159	14,943	338
10,000.00	25.00	5,421	65	20,766	214
	50.00	7,577	93	24,304	258
	100.00	9,556	120	26,983	294
	200.00	11,070	143	28,788	321
25,000.00	25.00	7,414	35	38,064	152
	50.00	11,893	56	48,698	199
	100.00	17,209	83	58,128	244
	200.00	22,402	112	65,550	283
50,000.00	25.00	8,496	20	54,872	107
	50.00	14,829	35	76,129	152
	100.00	23,787	56	97,397	199
	200.00	34,419	83	116,256	244
75,000.00	25.00	8,939	14	65,238	84
	50.00	16,197	25	95,282	125
	100.00	27,380	43	127,658	171
	200.00	42,141	67	158,449	218
100,000.00	25.00	9,180	11	72,399	70
	50.00	16,992	20	109,745	107
	100.00	29,659	35	152,259	152
	200.00	47,575	56	194,795	199
125,000.00	25.00	9,332	09	77,682	60
	50.00	17,513	16	121,171	94
	100.00	31,236	29	172,890	137
	200.00	51,623	49	226,773	184
150,000.00	25.00	9,438	08	81,756	53
	50.00	17,878	14	130,477	84
	100.00	32,395	25	190,565	125
	200.00	54,760	43	255,317	171
200,000.00	25.00	9,570	06	87,640	42
	50.00	18,361	11	144,798	70
	100.00	33,985	20	219,491	107
	200.00	59,319	35	304,518	152
250,000.00	25.00	9,652	05	91,700	35
	50.00	18,665	09	155,364	60
	100.00	35,026	16	242,342	94
	200.00	62,473	29	345,781	137
300,000.00	25.00	9,707	04	94,676	30
	50.00	18,877	08	163,512	53
	100.00	35,757	14	260,954	84
	200.00	64,791	25	381,130	125

13¾% How Much Will You Save

TABLE A

AMOUNT OF LOAN	AMOUNT OF MONTHLY PRE-PAYMENT	15 YEAR MORTGAGE		30 YEAR MORTGAGE	
		Amount Saved	Months Reduced	Amount Saved	Months Reduced
$ 5,000.00	$25.00	3,886	92	12,457	257
	50.00	4,894	120	13,813	293
	100.00	5,664	142	14,728	320
	200.00	6,170	158	15,286	337
10,000.00	25.00	5,573	64	21,335	214
	50.00	7,773	92	24,914	257
	100.00	9,789	120	27,627	293
	200.00	11,329	142	29,457	320
25,000.00	25.00	7,645	34	39,305	152
	50.00	12,236	56	50,083	199
	100.00	17,665	83	59,623	244
	200.00	22,956	111	67,134	283
50,000.00	25.00	8,776	19	56,969	108
	50.00	15,290	34	78,610	152
	100.00	24,472	56	100,166	199
	200.00	35,331	83	119,247	244
75,000.00	25.00	9,241	13	67,975	85
	50.00	16,721	24	98,686	126
	100.00	28,205	42	131,575	172
	200.00	43,314	66	162,750	218
100,000.00	25.00	9,495	10	75,637	71
	50.00	17,553	19	113,938	108
	100.00	30,581	34	157,220	152
	200.00	48,945	56	200,333	199
125,000.00	25.00	9,654	08	81,320	60
	50.00	18,100	16	126,047	95
	100.00	32,230	28	178,814	138
	200.00	53,147	48	233,484	184
150,000.00	25.00	9,765	07	85,718	53
	50.00	18,483	13	135,951	85
	100.00	33,442	24	197,372	126
	200.00	56,411	42	263,151	172
200,000.00	25.00	9,905	05	92,109	42
	50.00	18,990	10	151,274	71
	100.00	35,106	19	227,876	108
	200.00	61,162	34	314,441	152
250,000.00	25.00	9,992	04	96,539	35
	50.00	19,309	08	162,641	60
	100.00	36,201	16	252,094	95
	200.00	64,460	28	357,629	138
300,000.00	25.00	10,050	03	99,797	30
	50.00	19,531	07	171,436	53
	100.00	36,966	13	271,902	85
	200.00	66,885	24	394,745	126

14%   How Much Will You Save

TABLE A

AMOUNT OF LOAN	AMOUNT OF MONTHLY PRE-PAYMENT	15 YEAR MORTGAGE		30 YEAR MORTGAGE	
		Amount Saved	Months Reduced	Amount Saved	Months Reduced
$ 5,000.00	$25.00	3,985	92	12,764	258
	50.00	5,011	120	14,136	294
	100.00	5,794	142	15,064	320
	200.00	6,309	158	15,630	338
10,000.00	25.00	5,727	64	21,908	215
	50.00	7,971	92	25,528	258
	100.00	10,023	120	28,273	294
	200.00	11,589	142	30,128	320
25,000.00	25.00	7,880	34	40,562	154
	50.00	12,583	56	51,479	200
	100.00	18,126	83	61,128	245
	200.00	23,515	111	68,725	283
50,000.00	25.00	9,063	19	59,107	110
	50.00	15,760	34	81,124	154
	100.00	25,167	56	102,959	200
	200.00	36,253	83	122,256	245
75,000.00	25.00	9,551	13	70,782	87
	50.00	17,255	25	102,148	128
	100.00	29,047	42	135,534	173
	200.00	44,501	67	167,083	219
100,000.00	25.00	9,817	10	78,968	72
	50.00	18,126	19	118,215	110
	100.00	31,521	34	162,248	154
	200.00	50,334	56	205,919	200
125,000.00	25.00	9,985	08	85,074	62
	50.00	18,699	16	131,035	97
	100.00	33,244	29	184,824	139
	200.00	54,698	48	240,265	185
150,000.00	25.00	10,101	07	89,823	54
	50.00	19,102	13	141,565	87
	100.00	34,511	25	204,297	128
	200.00	58,094	42	271,068	173
200,000.00	25.00	10,249	05	96,753	44
	50.00	19,634	10	157,937	72
	100.00	36,252	19	236,431	110
	200.00	63,042	34	324,497	154
250,000.00	25.00	10,340	04	101,584	37
	50.00	19,970	08	170,148	62
	100.00	37,398	16	262,071	97
	200.00	66,488	29	369,649	139
300,000.00	25.00	10,402	03	105,148	31
	50.00	20,203	07	179,646	54
	100.00	38,204	13	283,130	87
	200.00	69,023	25	408,594	128

14¼% How Much Will You Save

TABLE A

AMOUNT OF LOAN	AMOUNT OF MONTHLY PRE-PAYMENT	15 YEAR MORTGAGE		30 YEAR MORTGAGE	
		Amount Saved	Months Reduced	Amount Saved	Months Reduced
$ 5,000.00	$25.00	4,085	92	13,072	258
	50.00	5,129	120	14,460	294
	100.00	5,926	142	15,400	320
	200.00	6,449	158	15,975	338
10,000.00	25.00	5,883	64	22,486	216
	50.00	8,171	92	26,145	258
	100.00	10,259	120	28,921	294
	200.00	11,852	142	30,801	320
25,000.00	25.00	8,120	34	41,835	156
	50.00	12,936	56	52,888	202
	100.00	18,593	83	62,641	246
	200.00	24,079	111	70,324	284
50,000.00	25.00	9,356	19	61,288	113
	50.00	16,240	34	83,670	156
	100.00	25,872	56	105,776	202
	200.00	37,186	83	125,282	246
75,000.00	25.00	9,868	13	73,659	89
	50.00	17,800	25	105,664	129
	100.00	29,902	43	139,537	174
	200.00	45,703	67	171,447	220
100,000.00	25.00	10,148	10	82,395	75
	50.00	18,713	19	122,576	113
	100.00	32,480	34	167,340	156
	200.00	51,745	56	211,553	202
125,000.00	25.00	10,324	08	88,950	63
	50.00	19,312	16	136,135	99
	100.00	34,276	29	190,923	141
	200.00	56,276	48	247,110	187
150,000.00	25.00	10,446	07	94,067	56
	50.00	19,737	13	147,318	89
	100.00	35,600	25	211,329	129
	200.00	59,805	43	279,074	174
200,000.00	25.00	10,602	05	101,575	46
	50.00	20,296	10	164,790	75
	100.00	37,426	19	245,153	113
	200.00	64,961	34	334,680	156
250,000.00	25.00	10,698	04	106,836	38
	50.00	20,649	08	177,901	63
	100.00	38,624	16	272,271	99
	200.00	68,552	29	381,847	141
300,000.00	25.00	10,764	03	110,735	32
	50.00	20,893	07	188,135	56
	100.00	39,474	13	294,637	89
	200.00	71,201	25	422,659	129

14½% How Much Will You Save

TABLE A

AMOUNT OF LOAN	AMOUNT OF MONTHLY PRE-PAYMENT	15 YEAR MORTGAGE		30 YEAR MORTGAGE	
		Amount Saved	Months Reduced	Amount Saved	Months Reduced
$ 5,000.00	$25.00	4,186	94	13,382	260
	50.00	5,248	121	14,786	295
	100.00	6,058	143	15,738	321
	200.00	6,590	159	16,321	339
10,000.00	25.00	6,041	66	23,068	218
	50.00	8,373	94	26,765	260
	100.00	10,496	121	29,573	295
	200.00	12,116	143	31,477	321
25,000.00	25.00	8,364	36	43,123	157
	50.00	13,294	57	54,308	203
	100.00	19,065	84	64,162	246
	200.00	24,648	113	71,928	284
50,000.00	25.00	9,657	21	63,508	113
	50.00	16,728	36	86,246	157
	100.00	26,589	57	108,616	203
	200.00	38,130	84	128,324	246
75,000.00	25.00	10,194	15	76,602	91
	50.00	18,357	26	109,236	132
	100.00	30,771	44	143,578	177
	200.00	46,923	68	175,840	222
100,000.00	25.00	10,487	11	85,918	75
	50.00	19,314	21	127,017	113
	100.00	33,457	36	172,492	157
	200.00	53,179	57	217,232	203
125,000.00	25.00	10,673	09	92,942	65
	50.00	19,940	17	141,341	100
	100.00	35,329	30	197,109	142
	200.00	57,876	50	254,015	188
150,000.00	25.00	10,800	08	98,455	58
	50.00	20,388	15	153,204	91
	100.00	36,714	26	218,473	132
	200.00	61,543	44	287,156	177
200,000.00	25.00	10,965	06	106,581	46
	50.00	20,974	11	171,836	75
	100.00	38,628	21	254,034	113
	200.00	66,914	36	344,985	157
250,000.00	25.00	11,066	05	112,305	39
	50.00	21,346	09	185,885	65
	100.00	39,880	17	282,683	100
	200.00	70,659	30	394,218	142
300,000.00	25.00	11,136	04	116,567	34
	50.00	21,601	08	196,910	58
	100.00	40,776	15	306,408	91
	200.00	73,428	26	436,947	132

14¾% How Much Will You Save

TABLE A

AMOUNT OF LOAN	AMOUNT OF MONTHLY PRE-PAYMENT	15 YEAR MORTGAGE		30 YEAR MORTGAGE	
		Amount Saved	Months Reduced	Amount Saved	Months Reduced
$ 5,000.00	$25.00	4,288	94	13,694	261
	50.00	5,368	121	15,113	296
	100.00	6,190	144	16,077	322
	200.00	6,731	159	16,668	339
10,000.00	25.00	6,202	66	23,654	219
	50.00	8,577	94	27,388	261
	100.00	10,736	121	30,226	296
	200.00	12,381	144	32,154	322
25,000.00	25.00	8,612	36	44,426	158
	50.00	13,657	58	55,738	204
	100.00	19,541	85	65,691	247
	200.00	25,220	113	73,539	284
50,000.00	25.00	9,962	21	65,768	115
	50.00	17,225	36	88,853	158
	100.00	27,315	58	111,476	204
	200.00	39,083	85	131,383	247
75,000.00	25.00	10,525	15	79,612	93
	50.00	18,926	26	112,863	134
	100.00	31,656	44	147,660	178
	200.00	48,159	69	180,263	223
100,000.00	25.00	10,835	11	89,532	77
	50.00	19,925	21	131,537	115
	100.00	34,451	36	177,707	158
	200.00	54,630	58	222,953	204
125,000.00	25.00	11,030	09	97,058	68
	50.00	20,583	17	146,655	103
	100.00	36,406	30	203,374	145
	200.00	59,502	50	260,982	190
150,000.00	25.00	11,164	08	102,987	60
	50.00	21,051	15	159,225	93
	100.00	37,852	26	225,727	134
	200.00	63,313	44	295,320	178
200,000.00	25.00	11,337	06	111,775	48
	50.00	21,671	11	179,065	77
	100.00	39,851	21	263,075	115
	200.00	68,902	36	355,415	158
250,000.00	25.00	11,443	05	117,994	41
	50.00	22,061	09	194,116	68
	100.00	41,167	17	293,310	103
	200.00	72,812	30	406,749	145
300,000.00	25.00	11,518	04	122,648	36
	50.00	22,328	08	205,974	60
	100.00	42,103	15	318,451	93
	200.00	75,704	26	451,455	134

15% How Much Will You Save
TABLE A

AMOUNT OF LOAN	AMOUNT OF MONTHLY PRE-PAYMENT	15 YEAR MORTGAGE		30 YEAR MORTGAGE	
		Amount Saved	Months Reduced	Amount Saved	Months Reduced
$ 5,000.00	$25.00	4,391	94	14,006	261
	50.00	5,488	121	15,441	296
	100.00	6,324	144	16,416	322
	200.00	6,873	159	17,015	339
10,000.00	25.00	6,364	66	24,244	220
	50.00	8,783	94	28,013	261
	100.00	10,977	121	30,882	296
	200.00	12,648	144	32,833	322
25,000.00	25.00	8,866	36	45,744	161
	50.00	14,025	58	57,179	206
	100.00	20,023	85	67,229	249
	200.00	25,797	113	75,156	286
50,000.00	25.00	10,276	21	68,068	118
	50.00	17,732	36	91,488	161
	100.00	28,051	58	114,358	206
	200.00	40,046	85	134,458	249
75,000.00	25.00	10,866	15	82,690	95
	50.00	19,507	26	116,541	135
	100.00	32,558	44	151,781	180
	200.00	49,408	69	184,712	224
100,000.00	25.00	11,192	12	93,242	80
	50.00	20,552	21	136,137	118
	100.00	35,464	36	182,977	161
	200.00	56,103	58	228,716	206
125,000.00	25.00	11,397	09	101,291	68
	50.00	21,242	17	152,075	104
	100.00	37,505	31	209,723	146
	200.00	61,157	50	268,010	190
150,000.00	25.00	11,537	08	107,662	61
	50.00	21,732	15	165,381	95
	100.00	39,015	26	233,083	135
	200.00	65,116	44	303,562	180
200,000.00	25.00	11,720	06	117,152	50
	50.00	22,384	12	186,485	80
	100.00	41,104	21	272,275	118
	200.00	70,929	36	365,955	161
250,000.00	25.00	11,832	05	123,910	41
	50.00	22,795	09	202,582	68
	100.00	42,485	17	304,150	104
	200.00	75,011	31	419,446	146
300,000.00	25.00	11,911	04	128,981	37
	50.00	23,074	08	215,325	61
	100.00	43,464	15	330,763	95
	200.00	78,031	26	466,167	135

15¼% How Much Will You Save

TABLE A

AMOUNT OF LOAN	AMOUNT OF MONTHLY PRE-PAYMENT	15 YEAR MORTGAGE		30 YEAR MORTGAGE	
		Amount Saved	Months Reduced	Amount Saved	Months Reduced
$ 5,000.00	$25.00	4,495	93	14,321	261
	50.00	5,610	120	15,770	295
	100.00	6,458	143	16,757	321
	200.00	7,016	158	17,364	338
10,000.00	25.00	6,529	66	24,837	220
	50.00	8,991	93	28,642	261
	100.00	11,220	120	31,540	295
	200.00	12,916	143	33,514	321
25,000.00	25.00	9,124	35	47,077	162
	50.00	14,400	57	58,630	206
	100.00	20,510	84	68,773	248
	200.00	26,378	112	76,779	285
50,000.00	25.00	10,596	20	70,407	119
	50.00	18,249	35	94,154	162
	100.00	28,800	57	117,260	206
	200.00	41,020	84	137,547	248
75,000.00	25.00	11,214	14	85,834	95
	50.00	20,100	26	120,270	136
	100.00	33,472	44	155,937	180
	200.00	50,674	68	189,189	224
100,000.00	25.00	11,556	11	97,047	80
	50.00	21,192	20	140,815	119
	100.00	36,498	35	188,308	162
	200.00	57,600	57	234,521	206
125,000.00	25.00	11,773	09	105,644	70
	50.00	21,918	16	157,599	106
	100.00	38,622	30	216,150	147
	200.00	62,836	50	275,090	192
150,000.00	25.00	11,920	07	112,483	62
	50.00	22,429	14	171,669	95
	100.00	40,200	26	240,541	136
	200.00	66,944	44	311,875	180
200,000.00	25.00	12,113	05	122,723	50
	50.00	23,113	11	194,094	80
	100.00	42,385	20	281,630	119
	200.00	72,997	35	376,616	162
250,000.00	25.00	12,231	04	130,057	42
	50.00	23,546	09	211,289	70
	100.00	43,836	16	315,199	106
	200.00	77,245	30	432,300	147
300,000.00	25.00	12,315	03	135,576	37
	50.00	23,840	07	224,967	62
	100.00	44,858	14	343,338	95
	200.00	80,401	26	481,083	136

15½% How Much Will You Save

TABLE A

AMOUNT OF LOAN	AMOUNT OF MONTHLY PRE-PAYMENT	15 YEAR MORTGAGE		30 YEAR MORTGAGE	
		Amount Saved	Months Reduced	Amount Saved	Months Reduced
$ 5,000.00	$25.00	4,600	94	14,636	262
	50.00	5,732	121	16,100	296
	100.00	6,593	143	17,098	322
	200.00	7,159	158	17,714	339
10,000.00	25.00	6,695	66	25,434	222
	50.00	9,201	94	29,273	262
	100.00	11,465	121	32,200	296
	200.00	13,186	143	34,197	322
25,000.00	25.00	9,387	36	48,422	163
	50.00	14,778	58	60,091	207
	100.00	21,002	85	70,325	249
	200.00	26,965	112	78,407	285
50,000.00	25.00	10,924	20	72,782	120
	50.00	18,774	36	96,844	163
	100.00	29,557	58	120,182	207
	200.00	42,004	85	140,650	249
75,000.00	25.00	11,571	14	89,041	97
	50.00	20,704	26	124,051	138
	100.00	34,402	44	160,131	181
	200.00	51,958	68	193,692	225
100,000.00	25.00	11,930	11	100,941	82
	50.00	21,848	20	145,564	120
	100.00	37,549	36	193,689	163
	200.00	59,115	58	240,365	207
125,000.00	25.00	12,157	09	110,120	71
	50.00	22,606	17	163,224	107
	100.00	39,763	30	222,651	149
	200.00	64,539	50	282,226	193
150,000.00	25.00	12,313	07	117,450	63
	50.00	23,143	14	178,083	97
	100.00	41,409	26	248,102	138
	200.00	68,804	44	320,263	181
200,000.00	25.00	12,517	05	128,484	52
	50.00	23,860	11	201,882	82
	100.00	43,697	20	291,129	120
	200.00	75,098	36	387,378	163
250,000.00	25.00	12,641	04	136,429	44
	50.00	24,315	09	220,240	71
	100.00	45,212	17	326,448	107
	200.00	79,526	30	445,303	149
300,000.00	25.00	12,730	03	142,440	38
	50.00	24,627	07	234,901	63
	100.00	46,287	14	356,166	97
	200.00	82,819	26	496,205	138

15¾% How Much Will You Save

TABLE A

AMOUNT OF LOAN	AMOUNT OF MONTHLY PRE-PAYMENT	15 YEAR MORTGAGE		30 YEAR MORTGAGE	
		Amount Saved	Months Reduced	Amount Saved	Months Reduced
$ 5,000.00	$25.00	4,706	94	14,953	262
	50.00	5,855	121	16,431	296
	100.00	6,729	143	17,441	321
	200.00	7,303	158	18,064	338
10,000.00	25.00	6,864	66	26,034	222
	50.00	9,413	94	29,906	262
	100.00	11,711	121	32,862	296
	200.00	13,458	143	34,882	321
25,000.00	25.00	9,654	36	49,782	165
	50.00	15,163	58	61,562	208
	100.00	21,498	85	71,884	250
	200.00	27,555	112	80,041	286
50,000.00	25.00	11,260	20	75,194	122
	50.00	19,309	36	99,564	165
	100.00	30,326	58	123,124	208
	200.00	42,996	85	143,768	250
75,000.00	25.00	11,938	14	92,312	99
	50.00	21,322	26	127,878	139
	100.00	35,349	44	164,359	183
	200.00	53,254	69	198,219	226
100,000.00	25.00	12,313	11	104,928	84
	50.00	22,520	20	150,388	122
	100.00	38,618	36	199,128	165
	200.00	60,652	58	246,248	208
125,000.00	25.00	12,552	09	114,711	73
	50.00	23,310	17	168,947	109
	100.00	40,927	30	229,231	151
	200.00	66,272	50	289,417	194
150,000.00	25.00	12,717	07	122,561	65
	50.00	23,876	14	184,625	99
	100.00	42,645	26	255,757	139
	200.00	70,698	44	328,718	183
200,000.00	25.00	12,932	05	134,439	53
	50.00	24,626	11	209,856	84
	100.00	45,040	20	300,776	122
	200.00	77,237	36	398,256	165
250,000.00	25.00	13,062	04	143,040	45
	50.00	25,104	09	229,422	73
	100.00	46,621	17	337,895	109
	200.00	81,855	30	458,462	151
300,000.00	25.00	13,155	04	149,577	39
	50.00	25,435	07	245,122	65
	100.00	47,752	14	369,250	99
	200.00	85,290	26	511,515	139

How Much Will You Save

TABLE A

AMOUNT OF LOAN	AMOUNT OF MONTHLY PRE-PAYMENT	15 YEAR MORTGAGE		30 YEAR MORTGAGE	
		Amount Saved	Months Reduced	Amount Saved	Months Reduced
$ 5,000.00	$25.00	4,813	95	15,271	263
	50.00	5,979	122	16,763	296
	100.00	6,865	144	17,784	321
	200.00	7,448	159	18,415	338
10,000.00	25.00	7,035	68	26,638	223
	50.00	9,626	95	30,543	263
	100.00	11,959	122	33,526	296
	200.00	13,731	144	35,568	321
25,000.00	25.00	9,927	37	51,153	166
	50.00	15,553	59	63,041	209
	100.00	22,000	86	73,449	250
	200.00	28,150	114	81,679	286
50,000.00	25.00	11,601	22	77,642	124
	50.00	19,855	37	102,307	166
	100.00	31,106	59	126,083	209
	200.00	44,000	86	146,899	250
75,000.00	25.00	12,313	15	95,647	101
	50.00	21,953	27	131,753	141
	100.00	36,309	46	168,619	184
	200.00	54,567	70	202,770	227
100,000.00	25.00	12,706	12	109,007	86
	50.00	23,203	22	155,284	124
	100.00	39,710	37	204,614	166
	200.00	62,212	59	252,167	209
125,000.00	25.00	12,956	10	119,422	75
	50.00	24,032	18	174,770	111
	100.00	42,115	32	235,878	152
	200.00	68,030	52	296,660	195
150,000.00	25.00	13,132	08	127,821	66
	50.00	24,626	15	191,294	101
	100.00	43,907	27	263,506	141
	200.00	72,619	46	337,239	184
200,000.00	25.00	13,358	07	140,591	55
	50.00	25,412	12	218,014	86
	100.00	46,406	22	310,568	124
	200.00	79,420	37	409,229	166
250,000.00	25.00	13,495	05	149,894	46
	50.00	25,913	10	238,845	75
	100.00	48,064	18	349,540	111
	200.00	84,231	32	471,756	152
300,000.00	25.00	13,590	05	156,995	40
	50.00	26,265	08	255,643	66
	100.00	49,253	15	382,588	101
	200.00	87,815	27	527,012	141

16¼% How Much Will You Save

TABLE A

AMOUNT OF LOAN	AMOUNT OF MONTHLY PRE-PAYMENT	15 YEAR MORTGAGE		30 YEAR MORTGAGE	
		Amount Saved	Months Reduced	Amount Saved	Months Reduced
$ 5,000.00	$25.00	4,921	95	15,590	264
	50.00	6,104	122	17,095	297
	100.00	7,002	144	18,128	322
	200.00	7,594	159	18,767	339
10,000.00	25.00	7,208	68	27,244	225
	50.00	9,842	95	31,181	264
	100.00	12,208	122	34,191	297
	200.00	14,005	144	36,256	322
25,000.00	25.00	10,205	38	52,538	169
	50.00	15,948	60	64,530	211
	100.00	22,507	86	75,021	252
	200.00	28,749	114	83,323	287
50,000.00	25.00	11,950	22	80,125	126
	50.00	20,410	38	105,077	169
	100.00	31,896	60	129,061	211
	200.00	45,014	86	150,042	252
75,000.00	25.00	12,696	16	99,043	103
	50.00	22,597	28	135,674	143
	100.00	37,286	46	172,915	185
	200.00	55,898	70	207,345	228
100,000.00	25.00	13,109	12	113,174	88
	50.00	23,901	22	160,251	126
	100.00	40,820	38	210,154	169
	200.00	63,792	60	258,122	211
125,000.00	25.00	13,372	10	124,253	77
	50.00	24,771	18	180,689	114
	100.00	43,322	32	242,597	155
	200.00	69,812	52	303,949	198
150,000.00	25.00	13,558	09	133,220	68
	50.00	25,393	16	198,087	103
	100.00	45,194	28	271,349	143
	200.00	74,572	46	345,830	185
200,000.00	25.00	13,793	07	146,935	57
	50.00	26,218	12	226,349	88
	100.00	47,803	22	320,502	126
	200.00	81,641	38	420,309	169
250,000.00	25.00	13,940	05	156,983	49
	50.00	26,744	10	248,506	77
	100.00	49,542	18	361,378	114
	200.00	86,645	32	485,195	155
300,000.00	25.00	14,038	05	164,689	42
	50.00	27,116	09	266,440	68
	100.00	50,787	16	396,174	103
	200.00	90,389	28	542,699	143

16½% How Much Will You Save

TABLE A

AMOUNT OF LOAN	AMOUNT OF MONTHLY PRE-PAYMENT	15 YEAR MORTGAGE		30 YEAR MORTGAGE	
		Amount Saved	Months Reduced	Amount Saved	Months Reduced
$ 5,000.00	$25.00	5,030	96	15,911	265
	50.00	6,229	122	17,429	298
	100.00	7,140	144	18,472	322
	200.00	7,740	159	19,119	339
10,000.00	25.00	7,383	68	27,854	226
	50.00	10,060	96	31,822	265
	100.00	12,459	122	34,859	298
	200.00	14,281	144	36,945	322
25,000.00	25.00	10,487	38	53,934	169
	50.00	16,348	60	66,027	212
	100.00	23,018	87	76,599	252
	200.00	29,352	114	84,971	287
50,000.00	25.00	12,308	22	82,641	127
	50.00	20,974	38	107,869	169
	100.00	32,696	60	132,055	212
	200.00	46,037	87	153,198	252
75,000.00	25.00	13,088	16	102,498	104
	50.00	23,252	28	139,639	144
	100.00	38,279	46	177,239	187
	200.00	57,243	71	211,942	229
100,000.00	25.00	13,522	12	117,428	89
	50.00	24,616	22	165,282	127
	100.00	41,948	38	215,739	169
	200.00	65,392	60	264,110	212
125,000.00	25.00	13,798	10	129,196	79
	50.00	25,528	18	186,700	115
	100.00	44,555	32	249,384	156
	200.00	71,624	52	311,286	199
150,000.00	25.00	13,992	09	138,767	70
	50.00	26,177	16	204,996	104
	100.00	46,505	28	279,278	144
	200.00	76,559	46	354,478	187
200,000.00	25.00	14,240	07	153,481	58
	50.00	27,045	12	234,857	89
	100.00	49,233	22	330,564	127
	200.00	83,897	38	431,478	169
250,000.00	25.00	14,397	05	164,319	50
	50.00	27,597	10	258,392	79
	100.00	51,056	18	373,401	115
	200.00	89,110	32	498,769	156
300,000.00	25.00	14,498	05	172,668	43
	50.00	27,985	09	277,534	70
	100.00	52,354	16	409,992	104
	200.00	93,010	28	558,557	144

16¾% How Much Will You Save

TABLE A

AMOUNT OF LOAN	AMOUNT OF MONTHLY PRE-PAYMENT	15 YEAR MORTGAGE		30 YEAR MORTGAGE	
		Amount Saved	Months Reduced	Amount Saved	Months Reduced
$ 5,000.00	$25.00	5,139	95	16,232	264
	50.00	6,356	121	17,764	297
	100.00	7,279	143	18,818	321
	200.00	7,887	158	19,472	338
10,000.00	25.00	7,561	68	28,467	226
	50.00	10,279	95	32,465	264
	100.00	12,712	121	35,528	297
	200.00	14,558	143	37,636	321
25,000.00	25.00	10,774	37	55,343	171
	50.00	16,754	59	67,532	214
	100.00	23,535	86	78,183	253
	200.00	29,960	113	86,623	288
50,000.00	25.00	12,674	21	85,190	130
	50.00	21,549	37	110,687	171
	100.00	33,508	59	135,065	214
	200.00	47,070	86	156,367	253
75,000.00	25.00	13,489	15	106,011	106
	50.00	23,922	27	143,646	146
	100.00	39,287	46	181,594	188
	200.00	58,603	70	216,561	230
100,000.00	25.00	13,947	11	121,770	92
	50.00	25,348	21	170,380	130
	100.00	43,098	37	221,375	171
	200.00	67,016	59	270,131	214
125,000.00	25.00	14,236	09	134,256	81
	50.00	26,300	18	192,801	117
	100.00	45,813	31	256,235	158
	200.00	73,463	52	318,670	200
150,000.00	25.00	14,438	08	144,458	71
	50.00	26,979	15	212,023	106
	100.00	47,844	27	287,293	146
	200.00	78,575	46	363,188	188
200,000.00	25.00	14,699	06	160,218	60
	50.00	27,894	11	243,541	92
	100.00	50,696	21	340,761	130
	200.00	86,197	37	442,750	171
250,000.00	25.00	14,864	05	171,903	52
	50.00	28,472	09	268,512	81
	100.00	52,601	18	385,602	117
	200.00	91,626	31	512,470	158
300,000.00	25.00	14,970	04	180,942	44
	50.00	28,876	08	288,917	71
	100.00	53,959	15	424,047	106
	200.00	95,689	27	574,587	146

17%   How Much Will You Save

TABLE A

AMOUNT OF LOAN	AMOUNT OF MONTHLY PRE-PAYMENT	15 YEAR MORTGAGE		30 YEAR MORTGAGE	
		Amount Saved	Months Reduced	Amount Saved	Months Reduced
$ 5,000.00	$25.00	5,250	95	16,554	265
	50.00	6,483	121	18,099	297
	100.00	7,418	143	19,164	322
	200.00	8,035	159	19,826	338
10,000.00	25.00	7,740	68	29,083	227
	50.00	10,500	95	33,109	265
	100.00	12,967	121	36,199	297
	200.00	14,837	143	38,328	322
25,000.00	25.00	11,067	37	56,762	173
	50.00	17,165	60	69,045	215
	100.00	24,056	86	79,772	254
	200.00	30,572	113	88,281	289
50,000.00	25.00	13,047	22	87,772	132
	50.00	22,135	37	113,525	173
	100.00	34,330	60	138,091	215
	200.00	48,113	86	159,545	254
75,000.00	25.00	13,901	15	109,583	108
	50.00	24,606	27	147,698	148
	100.00	40,310	46	185,979	189
	200.00	59,980	70	221,201	231
100,000.00	25.00	14,380	12	126,198	94
	50.00	26,094	22	175,544	132
	100.00	44,270	37	227,051	173
	200.00	68,660	60	276,183	215
125,000.00	25.00	14,685	09	139,432	83
	50.00	27,089	18	198,991	119
	100.00	47,092	32	263,152	159
	200.00	75,324	52	326,100	201
150,000.00	25.00	14,896	08	150,287	73
	50.00	27,802	15	219,167	108
	100.00	49,213	27	295,396	148
	200.00	80,621	46	371,959	189
200,000.00	25.00	15,170	06	167,156	62
	50.00	28,761	12	252,397	94
	100.00	52,189	22	351,088	132
	200.00	88,541	37	454,102	173
250,000.00	25.00	15,343	05	179,728	53
	50.00	29,371	09	278,864	83
	100.00	54,178	18	397,983	119
	200.00	94,185	32	526,305	159
300,000.00	25.00	15,456	04	189,507	46
	50.00	29,792	08	300,575	73
	100.00	55,605	15	438,334	108
	200.00	98,426	27	590,792	148

17¼% How Much Will You Save

TABLE A

AMOUNT OF LOAN	AMOUNT OF MONTHLY PRE-PAYMENT	15 YEAR MORTGAGE		30 YEAR MORTGAGE	
		Amount Saved	Months Reduced	Amount Saved	Months Reduced
$ 5,000.00	$25.00	5,361	95	16,878	266
	50.00	6,611	122	18,435	298
	100.00	7,558	143	19,510	323
	200.00	8,183	159	20,180	339
10,000.00	25.00	7,921	68	29,701	229
	50.00	10,723	95	33,756	266
	100.00	13,223	122	36,871	298
	200.00	15,117	143	39,021	323
25,000.00	25.00	11,364	38	58,193	174
	50.00	17,581	60	70,566	216
	100.00	24,583	87	81,367	255
	200.00	31,188	114	89,941	289
50,000.00	25.00	13,427	22	90,384	133
	50.00	22,729	38	116,387	174
	100.00	35,162	60	141,133	216
	200.00	49,167	87	162,735	255
75,000.00	25.00	14,322	15	113,212	110
	50.00	25,302	28	151,786	149
	100.00	41,351	46	190,392	191
	200.00	61,372	71	225,859	231
100,000.00	25.00	14,824	12	130,711	95
	50.00	26,855	22	180,769	133
	100.00	45,458	38	232,774	174
	200.00	70,324	60	282,266	216
125,000.00	25.00	15,146	09	144,718	84
	50.00	27,896	18	205,269	121
	100.00	48,395	32	270,126	161
	200.00	77,216	52	333,572	203
150,000.00	25.00	15,366	08	156,260	75
	50.00	28,645	15	226,424	110
	100.00	50,605	28	303,573	149
	200.00	82,703	46	380,785	191
200,000.00	25.00	15,654	06	174,290	63
	50.00	29,648	12	261,422	95
	100.00	53,711	22	361,539	133
	200.00	90,917	38	465,548	174
250,000.00	25.00	15,836	05	187,810	55
	50.00	30,293	09	289,437	84
	100.00	55,793	18	410,539	121
	200.00	96,790	32	540,252	161
300,000.00	25.00	15,955	04	198,363	47
	50.00	30,732	08	312,521	75
	100.00	57,291	15	452,849	110
	200.00	101,211	28	607,146	149

17½% How Much Will You Save

TABLE A

AMOUNT OF LOAN	AMOUNT OF MONTHLY PRE-PAYMENT	15 YEAR MORTGAGE		30 YEAR MORTGAGE	
		Amount Saved	Months Reduced	Amount Saved	Months Reduced
$ 5,000.00	$25.00	5,474	96	17,202	266
	50.00	6,740	122	18,772	298
	100.00	7,699	143	19,857	322
	200.00	8,332	159	20,535	338
10,000.00	25.00	8,105	69	30,322	229
	50.00	10,948	96	34,405	266
	100.00	13,480	122	37,545	298
	200.00	15,399	143	39,715	322
25,000.00	25.00	11,667	39	59,634	176
	50.00	18,003	61	72,094	217
	100.00	25,114	88	82,968	255
	200.00	31,808	115	91,607	289
50,000.00	25.00	13,816	23	93,026	135
	50.00	23,334	39	119,268	176
	100.00	36,006	61	144,189	217
	200.00	50,228	88	165,937	255
75,000.00	25.00	14,754	16	116,895	112
	50.00	26,012	29	155,915	152
	100.00	42,408	48	194,831	193
	200.00	62,779	72	230,536	233
100,000.00	25.00	15,278	13	135,302	97
	50.00	27,633	23	186,053	135
	100.00	46,669	39	238,537	176
	200.00	72,012	61	288,379	217
125,000.00	25.00	15,617	11	150,113	86
	50.00	28,723	19	211,632	122
	100.00	49,724	33	277,164	163
	200.00	79,135	54	341,082	204
150,000.00	25.00	15,848	09	162,375	78
	50.00	29,509	16	233,790	112
	100.00	52,024	29	311,831	152
	200.00	84,816	48	389,662	193
200,000.00	25.00	16,152	07	181,616	65
	50.00	30,557	13	270,604	97
	100.00	55,267	23	372,106	135
	200.00	93,338	39	477,075	176
250,000.00	25.00	16,342	06	196,131	56
	50.00	31,234	11	300,226	86
	100.00	57,447	19	423,264	122
	200.00	99,448	33	554,329	163
300,000.00	25.00	16,469	05	207,526	49
	50.00	31,697	09	324,750	78
	100.00	59,019	16	467,581	112
	200.00	104,049	29	623,663	152

17¾% How Much Will You Save

TABLE A

AMOUNT OF LOAN	AMOUNT OF MONTHLY PRE-PAYMENT	15 YEAR MORTGAGE		30 YEAR MORTGAGE	
		Amount Saved	Months Reduced	Amount Saved	Months Reduced
$ 5,000.00	$25.00	5,587	97	17,528	267
	50.00	6,869	123	19,110	298
	100.00	7,841	144	20,205	322
	200.00	8,481	160	20,890	338
10,000.00	25.00	8,290	70	30,946	230
	50.00	11,175	97	35,056	267
	100.00	13,739	123	38,220	298
	200.00	15,682	144	40,411	322
25,000.00	25.00	11,975	39	61,085	177
	50.00	18,430	62	73,630	218
	100.00	25,650	88	84,573	256
	200.00	32,432	115	93,276	290
50,000.00	25.00	14,215	23	95,698	137
	50.00	23,951	39	122,170	177
	100.00	36,860	62	147,260	218
	200.00	51,300	88	169,147	256
75,000.00	25.00	15,195	17	120,629	113
	50.00	26,737	29	160,083	152
	100.00	43,479	48	199,297	193
	200.00	64,203	72	235,232	233
100,000.00	25.00	15,744	13	139,974	99
	50.00	28,430	23	191,397	137
	100.00	47,902	39	244,341	177
	200.00	73,720	62	294,520	218
125,000.00	25.00	16,099	11	155,618	88
	50.00	29,570	19	218,072	124
	100.00	51,079	34	284,253	164
	200.00	81,077	54	348,633	205
150,000.00	25.00	16,344	09	168,621	78
	50.00	30,390	17	241,259	113
	100.00	53,474	29	320,166	152
	200.00	86,958	48	398,595	193
200,000.00	25.00	16,663	07	189,142	67
	50.00	31,489	13	279,949	99
	100.00	56,860	23	382,794	137
	200.00	95,805	39	488,683	177
250,000.00	25.00	16,862	06	204,708	58
	50.00	32,198	11	311,236	88
	100.00	59,141	19	436,145	124
	200.00	102,159	34	568,507	164
300,000.00	25.00	16,996	05	216,977	50
	50.00	32,688	09	337,243	78
	100.00	60,780	17	482,519	113
	200.00	106,948	29	640,332	152

Table B

When Your Mortgage
Will Be Paid

When Your Mortgage Will Be Paid
TABLE B

A 30 Year Mortgage Will Be Paid In 25 Years If You Pre-Pay The Following:

		INTEREST RATES			
		7%	7¼%	7½%	7¾%
Loan Amount Pre-Pay Per Month	$ 1,000.00	.41	.41	.40	.39
Loan Amount Pre-Pay Per Month	2,000.00	.83	.81	.80	.78
Loan Amount Pre-Pay Per Month	3,000.00	1.24	1.22	1.19	1.17
Loan Amount Pre-Pay Per Month	4,000.00	1.66	1.63	1.59	1.56
Loan Amount Pre-Pay Per Month	5,000.00	2.07	2.03	1.99	1.95
Loan Amount Pre-Pay Per Month	10,000.00	4.15	4.06	3.98	3.89
Loan Amount Pre-Pay Per Month	15,000.00	6.22	6.09	5.97	5.84
Loan Amount Pre-Pay Per Month	20,000.00	8.30	8.13	7.96	7.78
Loan Amount Pre-Pay Per Month	25,000.00	10.37	10.16	9.94	9.73
Loan Amount Pre-Pay Per Month	50,000.00	20.74	20.32	19.89	19.46
Loan Amount Pre-Pay Per Month	75,000.00	31.11	30.47	29.83	29.19
Loan Amount Pre-Pay Per Month	100,000.00	41.48	40.63	39.78	38.92
Loan Amount Pre-Pay Per Month	125,000.00	51.85	50.79	49.72	48.65
Loan Amount Pre-Pay Per Month	150,000.00	62.22	60.95	59.67	58.37
Loan Amount Pre-Pay Per Month	175,000.00	72.58	71.10	69.61	68.10
Loan Amount Pre-Pay Per Month	200,000.00	82.95	81.26	79.55	77.83
Loan Amount Pre-Pay Per Month	225,000.00	93.32	91.42	89.50	87.56
Loan Amount Pre-Pay Per Month	250,000.00	103.69	101.58	99.44	97.29
Loan Amount Pre-Pay Per Month	275,000.00	114.06	111.73	109.39	107.02
Loan Amount Pre-Pay Per Month	300,000.00	124.43	121.89	119.33	116.75
Loan Amount Pre-Pay Per Month	325,000.00	134.80	132.05	129.27	126.48
Loan Amount Pre-Pay Per Month	350,000.00	145.17	142.21	139.22	136.21
Loan Amount Pre-Pay Per Month	375,000.00	155.54	152.36	149.16	145.94
Loan Amount Pre-Pay Per Month	400,000.00	165.91	162.52	159.11	155.67
Loan Amount Pre-Pay Per Month	450,000.00	186.65	182.84	179.00	175.12

When Your Mortgage Will Be Paid
TABLE B

A 30 Year Mortgage Will Be Paid In 20 Years If You Pre-Pay The Following:

		INTEREST RATES			
		7%	7¼%	7½%	7¾%
Loan Amount Pre-Pay Per Month	$ 1,000.00	1.10	1.08	1.06	1.05
Loan Amount Pre-Pay Per Month	2,000.00	2.20	2.16	2.13	2.09
Loan Amount Pre-Pay Per Month	3,000.00	3.30	3.25	3.19	3.14
Loan Amount Pre-Pay Per Month	4,000.00	4.40	4.33	4.26	4.18
Loan Amount Pre-Pay Per Month	5,000.00	5.50	5.41	5.32	5.23
Loan Amount Pre-Pay Per Month	10,000.00	11.00	10.82	10.64	10.45
Loan Amount Pre-Pay Per Month	15,000.00	16.50	16.23	15.96	15.68
Loan Amount Pre-Pay Per Month	20,000.00	22.00	21.64	21.28	20.91
Loan Amount Pre-Pay Per Month	25,000.00	27.50	27.05	26.59	26.13
Loan Amount Pre-Pay Per Month	50,000.00	55.00	54.10	53.19	52.27
Loan Amount Pre-Pay Per Month	75,000.00	82.50	81.15	79.78	78.40
Loan Amount Pre-Pay Per Month	100,000.00	110.00	108.20	106.38	104.54
Loan Amount Pre-Pay Per Month	125,000.00	137.50	135.25	132.97	130.67
Loan Amount Pre-Pay Per Month	150,000.00	164.99	162.30	159.57	156.80
Loan Amount Pre-Pay Per Month	175,000.00	192.49	189.35	186.16	182.94
Loan Amount Pre-Pay Per Month	200,000.00	219.99	216.40	212.76	209.07
Loan Amount Pre-Pay Per Month	225,000.00	247.49	243.45	239.35	235.21
Loan Amount Pre-Pay Per Month	250,000.00	274.99	270.50	265.95	261.34
Loan Amount Pre-Pay Per Month	275,000.00	302.49	297.55	292.54	287.47
Loan Amount Pre-Pay Per Month	300,000.00	329.99	324.60	319.14	313.61
Loan Amount Pre-Pay Per Month	325,000.00	357.49	351.65	345.73	339.74
Loan Amount Pre-Pay Per Month	350,000.00	384.99	378.70	372.33	365.88
Loan Amount Pre-Pay Per Month	375,000.00	412.49	405.75	398.92	392.01
Loan Amount Pre-Pay Per Month	400,000.00	439.99	432.80	425.51	418.15
Loan Amount Pre-Pay Per Month	450,000.00	494.98	486.90	478.70	470.41

When Your Mortgage Will Be Paid
TABLE B

A 30 Year Mortgage Will Be Paid In 15 Years If You Pre-Pay The Following:

		INTEREST RATES			
		7%	**7¼%**	**7½%**	**7¾%**
Loan Amount $ 1,000.00 **Pre-Pay Per Month**		2.34	2.31	2.28	2.25
Loan Amount 2,000.00 **Pre-Pay Per Month**		4.67	4.61	4.56	4.50
Loan Amount 3,000.00 **Pre-Pay Per Month**		7.01	6.92	6.83	6.75
Loan Amount 4,000.00 **Pre-Pay Per Month**		9.34	9.23	9.11	8.99
Loan Amount 5,000.00 **Pre-Pay Per Month**		11.68	11.53	11.39	11.24
Loan Amount 10,000.00 **Pre-Pay Per Month**		23.35	23.07	22.78	22.49
Loan Amount 15,000.00 **Pre-Pay Per Month**		35.03	34.60	34.17	33.73
Loan Amount 20,000.00 **Pre-Pay Per Month**		46.71	46.14	45.56	44.97
Loan Amount 25,000.00 **Pre-Pay Per Month**		58.38	57.67	56.95	56.22
Loan Amount 50,000.00 **Pre-Pay Per Month**		116.76	115.34	113.90	112.43
Loan Amount 75,000.00 **Pre-Pay Per Month**		175.14	173.01	170.85	168.65
Loan Amount 100,000.00 **Pre-Pay Per Month**		233.53	230.69	227.80	224.86
Loan Amount 125,000.00 **Pre-Pay Per Month**		291.91	288.36	284.75	281.08
Loan Amount 150,000.00 **Pre-Pay Per Month**		350.29	346.03	341.70	337.30
Loan Amount 175,000.00 **Pre-Pay Per Month**		408.67	403.70	398.65	393.51
Loan Amount 200,000.00 **Pre-Pay Per Month**		467.05	461.37	455.60	449.73
Loan Amount 225,000.00 **Pre-Pay Per Month**		525.43	519.04	512.55	505.94
Loan Amount 250,000.00 **Pre-Pay Per Month**		583.81	576.72	569.49	562.16
Loan Amount 275,000.00 **Pre-Pay Per Month**		642.20	634.39	626.44	618.37
Loan Amount 300,000.00 **Pre-Pay Per Month**		700.58	692.06	683.39	674.59
Loan Amount 325,000.00 **Pre-Pay Per Month**		758.96	749.73	740.34	730.81
Loan Amount 350,000.00 **Pre-Pay Per Month**		817.34	807.40	797.29	787.02
Loan Amount 375,000.00 **Pre-Pay Per Month**		875.72	865.07	854.24	843.24
Loan Amount 400,000.00 **Pre-Pay Per Month**		934.10	922.75	911.19	899.45
Loan Amount 450,000.00 **Pre-Pay Per Month**		1,050.87	1,038.09	1,025.09	1,011.89

When Your Mortgage Will Be Paid
TABLE B

A 15 Year Mortgage Will Be Paid In 12½ Years If You Pre-Pay The Following:

		INTEREST RATES			
		7%	7¼%	7½%	7¾%
Loan Amount Pre-Pay Per Month	$ 1,000.00	1.03	1.03	1.02	1.02
Loan Amount Pre-Pay Per Month	2,000.00	2.07	2.06	2.04	2.03
Loan Amount Pre-Pay Per Month	3,000.00	3.10	3.08	3.07	3.05
Loan Amount Pre-Pay Per Month	4,000.00	4.13	4.11	4.09	4.07
Loan Amount Pre-Pay Per Month	5,000.00	5.17	5.14	5.11	5.08
Loan Amount Pre-Pay Per Month	10,000.00	10.33	10.28	10.22	10.16
Loan Amount Pre-Pay Per Month	15,000.00	15.50	15.42	15.33	15.25
Loan Amount Pre-Pay Per Month	20,000.00	20.67	20.56	20.44	20.33
Loan Amount Pre-Pay Per Month	25,000.00	25.83	25.70	25.55	25.41
Loan Amount Pre-Pay Per Month	50,000.00	51.67	51.39	51.11	50.82
Loan Amount Pre-Pay Per Month	75,000.00	77.50	77.09	76.66	76.23
Loan Amount Pre-Pay Per Month	100,000.00	103.33	102.78	102.22	101.64
Loan Amount Pre-Pay Per Month	125,000.00	129.16	128.48	127.77	127.05
Loan Amount Pre-Pay Per Month	150,000.00	155.00	154.17	153.33	152.46
Loan Amount Pre-Pay Per Month	175,000.00	180.83	179.87	178.88	177.87
Loan Amount Pre-Pay Per Month	200,000.00	206.66	205.56	204.43	203.28
Loan Amount Pre-Pay Per Month	225,000.00	232.49	231.26	229.99	228.69
Loan Amount Pre-Pay Per Month	250,000.00	258.33	256.95	255.54	254.09
Loan Amount Pre-Pay Per Month	275,000.00	284.16	282.65	281.10	279.50
Loan Amount Pre-Pay Per Month	300,000.00	309.99	308.35	306.65	304.91
Loan Amount Pre-Pay Per Month	325,000.00	335.82	334.04	332.21	330.32
Loan Amount Pre-Pay Per Month	350,000.00	361.66	359.74	357.76	355.73
Loan Amount Pre-Pay Per Month	375,000.00	387.49	385.43	383.32	381.14
Loan Amount Pre-Pay Per Month	400,000.00	413.32	411.13	408.87	406.55
Loan Amount Pre-Pay Per Month	450,000.00	464.99	462.52	459.98	457.37

When Your Mortgage Will Be Paid
TABLE B

A 15 Year Mortgage Will Be Paid In 10 Years If You Pre-Pay The Following:

		INTEREST RATES			
		7%	7¼%	7½%	7¾%
Loan Amount Pre-Pay Per Month	$ 1,000.00	2.62	2.61	2.60	2.59
Loan Amount Pre-Pay Per Month	2,000.00	5.25	5.22	5.20	5.18
Loan Amount Pre-Pay Per Month	3,000.00	7.87	7.83	7.80	7.76
Loan Amount Pre-Pay Per Month	4,000.00	10.49	10.45	10.40	10.35
Loan Amount Pre-Pay Per Month	5,000.00	13.11	13.06	13.00	12.94
Loan Amount Pre-Pay Per Month	10,000.00	26.23	26.11	26.00	25.88
Loan Amount Pre-Pay Per Month	15,000.00	39.34	39.17	39.00	38.82
Loan Amount Pre-Pay Per Month	20,000.00	52.45	52.23	52.00	51.77
Loan Amount Pre-Pay Per Month	25,000.00	65.56	65.29	65.00	64.71
Loan Amount Pre-Pay Per Month	50,000.00	131.13	130.57	130.00	129.42
Loan Amount Pre-Pay Per Month	75,000.00	196.69	195.86	195.00	194.12
Loan Amount Pre-Pay Per Month	100,000.00	262.26	261.15	260.01	258.83
Loan Amount Pre-Pay Per Month	125,000.00	327.82	326.43	325.01	323.54
Loan Amount Pre-Pay Per Month	150,000.00	393.38	391.72	390.01	388.25
Loan Amount Pre-Pay Per Month	175,000.00	458.95	457.01	455.01	452.95
Loan Amount Pre-Pay Per Month	200,000.00	524.51	522.30	520.01	517.66
Loan Amount Pre-Pay Per Month	225,000.00	590.08	587.58	585.01	582.37
Loan Amount Pre-Pay Per Month	250,000.00	655.64	652.87	650.01	647.08
Loan Amount Pre-Pay Per Month	275,000.00	721.21	718.16	715.01	711.78
Loan Amount Pre-Pay Per Month	300,000.00	786.77	783.44	780.02	776.49
Loan Amount Pre-Pay Per Month	325,000.00	852.33	848.73	845.02	841.20
Loan Amount Pre-Pay Per Month	350,000.00	917.90	914.02	910.02	905.91
Loan Amount Pre-Pay Per Month	375,000.00	983.46	979.30	975.02	970.61
Loan Amount Pre-Pay Per Month	400,000.00	1,049.03	1,044.59	1,040.02	1,035.32
Loan Amount Pre-Pay Per Month	450,000.00	1,180.15	1,175.16	1,170.02	1,164.74

7%

When Your Mortgage Will Be Paid
TABLE B

A 15 Year Mortgage Will Be Paid In 7½ Years If You Pre-Pay The Following:

		INTEREST RATES			
		7%	7¼%	7½%	7¾%
Loan Amount Pre-Pay Per Month	$ 1,000.00	5.33	5.31	5.29	5.27
Loan Amount Pre-Pay Per Month	2,000.00	10.65	10.62	10.58	10.55
Loan Amount Pre-Pay Per Month	3,000.00	15.98	15.93	15.87	15.82
Loan Amount Pre-Pay Per Month	4,000.00	21.30	21.23	21.16	21.09
Loan Amount Pre-Pay Per Month	5,000.00	26.63	26.54	26.46	26.37
Loan Amount Pre-Pay Per Month	10,000.00	53.25	53.08	52.91	52.73
Loan Amount Pre-Pay Per Month	15,000.00	79.88	79.63	79.37	79.10
Loan Amount Pre-Pay Per Month	20,000.00	106.50	106.17	105.82	105.47
Loan Amount Pre-Pay Per Month	25,000.00	133.13	132.71	132.28	131.84
Loan Amount Pre-Pay Per Month	50,000.00	266.26	265.42	264.56	263.67
Loan Amount Pre-Pay Per Month	75,000.00	399.39	398.13	396.84	395.51
Loan Amount Pre-Pay Per Month	100,000.00	532.52	530.85	529.12	527.35
Loan Amount Pre-Pay Per Month	125,000.00	665.65	663.56	661.40	659.18
Loan Amount Pre-Pay Per Month	150,000.00	798.78	790.27	793.60	791.02
Loan Amount Pre-Pay Per Month	175,000.00	931.91	928.98	925.96	922.85
Loan Amount Pre-Pay Per Month	200,000.00	1,065.04	1,061.69	1,058.24	1,054.69
Loan Amount Pre-Pay Per Month	225,000.00	1,198.17	1,194.40	1,190.52	1,186.53
Loan Amount Pre-Pay Per Month	250,000.00	1,331.30	1,327.11	1,322.80	1,318.36
Loan Amount Pre-Pay Per Month	275,000.00	1,464.43	1,459.83	1,455.08	1,450.20
Loan Amount Pre-Pay Per Month	300,000.00	1,597.55	1,592.54	1,587.36	1,582.04
Loan Amount Pre-Pay Per Month	325,000.00	1,730.68	1,725.25	1,719.64	1,713.87
Loan Amount Pre-Pay Per Month	350,000.00	1,863.81	1,857.96	1,851.92	1,845.71
Loan Amount Pre-Pay Per Month	375,000.00	1,996.94	1,990.67	1,984.20	1,977.54
Loan Amount Pre-Pay Per Month	400,000.00	2,130.07	2,123.38	2,116.48	2,109.38
Loan Amount Pre-Pay Per Month	450,000.00	2,396.33	2,388.81	2,381.05	2,373.05

8%

When Your Mortgage Will Be Paid
TABLE B

A 30 Year Mortgage Will Be Paid In 25 Years If You Pre-Pay The Following:

		INTEREST RATES			
		8%	8¼%	8½%	8¾%
Loan Amount $ 1,000.00 **Pre-Pay Per Month**		.38	.37	.36	.35
Loan Amount 2,000.00 **Pre-Pay Per Month**		.76	.74	.73	.71
Loan Amount 3,000.00 **Pre-Pay Per Month**		1.14	1.12	1.09	1.06
Loan Amount 4,000.00 **Pre-Pay Per Month**		1.52	1.49	1.45	1.42
Loan Amount 5,000.00 **Pre-Pay Per Month**		1.90	1.86	1.82	1.77
Loan Amount 10,000.00 **Pre-Pay Per Month**		3.81	3.72	3.63	3.54
Loan Amount 15,000.00 **Pre-Pay Per Month**		5.71	5.58	5.45	5.32
Loan Amount 20,000.00 **Pre-Pay Per Month**		7.61	7.44	7.26	7.09
Loan Amount 25,000.00 **Pre-Pay Per Month**		9.51	9.30	9.08	8.86
Loan Amount 50,000.00 **Pre-Pay Per Month**		19.03	18.59	18.16	17.72
Loan Amount 75,000.00 **Pre-Pay Per Month**		28.54	27.89	27.24	26.58
Loan Amount 100,000.00 **Pre-Pay Per Month**		38.05	37.18	36.31	35.44
Loan Amount 125,000.00 **Pre-Pay Per Month**		47.56	46.48	45.39	44.30
Loan Amount 150,000.00 **Pre-Pay Per Month**		57.08	55.78	54.47	53.16
Loan Amount 175,000.00 **Pre-Pay Per Month**		66.59	65.07	63.55	62.03
Loan Amount 200,000.00 **Pre-Pay Per Month**		76.10	74.37	72.63	70.89
Loan Amount 225,000.00 **Pre-Pay Per Month**		85.62	83.66	81.71	79.75
Loan Amount 250,000.00 **Pre-Pay Per Month**		95.13	92.96	90.78	88.61
Loan Amount 275,000.00 **Pre-Pay Per Month**		104.64	102.25	99.86	97.47
Loan Amount 300,000.00 **Pre-Pay Per Month**		114.15	111.55	108.94	106.33
Loan Amount 325,000.00 **Pre-Pay Per Month**		123.67	120.85	118.02	115.19
Loan Amount 350,000.00 **Pre-Pay Per Month**		133.18	130.14	127.10	124.05
Loan Amount 375,000.00 **Pre-Pay Per Month**		142.69	139.44	136.18	132.91
Loan Amount 400,000.00 **Pre-Pay Per Month**		152.21	148.73	145.25	141.77
Loan Amount 450,000.00 **Pre-Pay Per Month**		171.23	167.33	163.41	159.49

8% When Your Mortgage Will Be Paid
TABLE B

A 30 Year Mortgage Will Be Paid In 20 Years If You Pre-Pay The Following:

		INTEREST RATES			
		8%	8¼%	8½%	8¾%
Loan Amount Pre-Pay Per Month	$ 1,000.00	1.03	1.01	.99	.97
Loan Amount Pre-Pay Per Month	2,000.00	2.05	2.02	1.98	1.94
Loan Amount Pre-Pay Per Month	3,000.00	3.08	3.02	2.97	2.91
Loan Amount Pre-Pay Per Month	4,000.00	4.11	4.03	3.96	3.88
Loan Amount Pre-Pay Per Month	5,000.00	5.13	5.04	4.95	4.85
Loan Amount Pre-Pay Per Month	10,000.00	10.27	10.08	9.89	9.70
Loan Amount Pre-Pay Per Month	15,000.00	15.40	15.12	14.84	14.55
Loan Amount Pre-Pay Per Month	20,000.00	20.54	20.16	19.78	19.40
Loan Amount Pre-Pay Per Month	25,000.00	25.67	25.20	24.73	24.25
Loan Amount Pre-Pay Per Month	50,000.00	51.34	50.40	49.45	48.51
Loan Amount Pre-Pay Per Month	75,000.00	77.01	75.60	74.18	72.76
Loan Amount Pre-Pay Per Month	100,000.00	102.68	100.80	98.91	97.01
Loan Amount Pre-Pay Per Month	125,000.00	128.34	126.00	123.64	121.26
Loan Amount Pre-Pay Per Month	150,000.00	154.01	151.20	148.36	145.52
Loan Amount Pre-Pay Per Month	175,000.00	179.68	176.40	173.09	169.77
Loan Amount Pre-Pay Per Month	200,000.00	205.35	201.60	197.82	194.02
Loan Amount Pre-Pay Per Month	225,000.00	231.02	226.80	222.55	218.27
Loan Amount Pre-Pay Per Month	250,000.00	256.69	252.00	247.27	242.53
Loan Amount Pre-Pay Per Month	275,000.00	282.36	277.20	272.00	266.78
Loan Amount Pre-Pay Per Month	300,000.00	308.03	302.40	296.73	291.03
Loan Amount Pre-Pay Per Month	325,000.00	333.70	327.60	321.46	315.28
Loan Amount Pre-Pay Per Month	350,000.00	359.36	352.80	346.18	339.54
Loan Amount Pre-Pay Per Month	375,000.00	385.03	378.00	370.91	363.79
Loan Amount Pre-Pay Per Month	400,000.00	410.70	403.20	395.64	388.04
Loan Amount Pre-Pay Per Month	450,000.00	462.04	453.60	445.09	436.55

8%

When Your Mortgage Will Be Paid
TABLE B

A 30 Year Mortgage Will Be Paid In 15 Years If You Pre-Pay The Following:

		INTEREST RATES		
		8%	8¼%	8½%	8¾%
Loan Amount $ 1,000.00 Pre-Pay Per Month		2.22	2.19	2.16	2.13
Loan Amount 2,000.00 Pre-Pay Per Month		4.44	4.38	4.32	4.25
Loan Amount 3,000.00 Pre-Pay Per Month		6.66	6.57	6.47	6.38
Loan Amount 4,000.00 Pre-Pay Per Month		8.88	8.75	8.63	8.51
Loan Amount 5,000.00 Pre-Pay Per Month		11.09	10.94	10.79	10.64
Loan Amount 10,000.00 Pre-Pay Per Month		22.19	21.89	21.58	21.27
Loan Amount 15,000.00 Pre-Pay Per Month		33.28	32.83	32.37	31.91
Loan Amount 20,000.00 Pre-Pay Per Month		44.38	43.77	43.17	42.55
Loan Amount 25,000.00 Pre-Pay Per Month		55.47	54.72	53.96	53.19
Loan Amount 50,000.00 Pre-Pay Per Month		110.94	109.44	107.91	106.37
Loan Amount 75,000.00 Pre-Pay Per Month		166.42	164.16	161.87	159.56
Loan Amount 100,000.00 Pre-Pay Per Month		221.89	218.87	215.83	212.75
Loan Amount 125,000.00 Pre-Pay Per Month		277.36	273.59	269.78	265.94
Loan Amount 150,000.00 Pre-Pay Per Month		332.83	328.31	323.74	319.12
Loan Amount 175,000.00 Pre-Pay Per Month		388.30	383.03	377.70	372.31
Loan Amount 200,000.00 Pre-Pay Per Month		443.78	437.75	431.65	425.50
Loan Amount 225,000.00 Pre-Pay Per Month		499.25	492.47	485.61	478.68
Loan Amount 250,000.00 Pre-Pay Per Month		554.72	547.18	539.57	531.87
Loan Amount 275,000.00 Pre-Pay Per Month		610.19	601.90	593.52	585.06
Loan Amount 300,000.00 Pre-Pay Per Month		665.66	656.62	647.48	638.24
Loan Amount 325,000.00 Pre-Pay Per Month		721.13	711.34	701.43	691.43
Loan Amount 350,000.00 Pre-Pay Per Month		776.61	766.06	755.39	744.62
Loan Amount 375,000.00 Pre-Pay Per Month		832.08	820.78	809.35	797.81
Loan Amount 400,000.00 Pre-Pay Per Month		887.55	875.50	863.30	850.99
Loan Amount 450,000.00 Pre-Pay Per Month		998.49	984.93	971.22	957.37

8% When Your Mortgage Will Be Paid
TABLE B

A 15 Year Mortgage Will Be Paid In 12½ Years If You Pre-Pay The Following:

		INTEREST RATES			
		8%	8¼%	8½%	8¾%
Loan Amount Pre-Pay Per Month	$ 1,000.00	1.01	1.00	1.00	.99
Loan Amount Pre-Pay Per Month	2,000.00	2.02	2.01	2.00	1.98
Loan Amount Pre-Pay Per Month	3,000.00	3.03	3.01	2.99	2.98
Loan Amount Pre-Pay Per Month	4,000.00	4.04	4.02	3.99	3.97
Loan Amount Pre-Pay Per Month	5,000.00	5.05	5.02	4.99	4.96
Loan Amount Pre-Pay Per Month	10,000.00	10.10	10.04	9.98	9.92
Loan Amount Pre-Pay Per Month	15,000.00	15.16	15.07	14.97	14.88
Loan Amount Pre-Pay Per Month	20,000.00	20.21	20.09	19.96	19.83
Loan Amount Pre-Pay Per Month	25,000.00	25.26	25.11	24.95	24.79
Loan Amount Pre-Pay Per Month	50,000.00	50.52	50.22	49.91	49.59
Loan Amount Pre-Pay Per Month	75,000.00	75.78	75.33	74.86	74.38
Loan Amount Pre-Pay Per Month	100,000.00	101.04	100.43	99.81	99.17
Loan Amount Pre-Pay Per Month	125,000.00	126.30	125.54	124.76	123.97
Loan Amount Pre-Pay Per Month	150,000.00	151.56	150.65	149.72	148.76
Loan Amount Pre-Pay Per Month	175,000.00	176.83	175.76	174.67	173.55
Loan Amount Pre-Pay Per Month	200,000.00	202.09	200.87	199.62	198.35
Loan Amount Pre-Pay Per Month	225,000.00	227.35	225.98	224.57	223.14
Loan Amount Pre-Pay Per Month	250,000.00	252.61	251.09	249.53	247.93
Loan Amount Pre-Pay Per Month	275,000.00	277.87	276.19	274.48	272.73
Loan Amount Pre-Pay Per Month	300,000.00	303.13	301.30	299.43	297.52
Loan Amount Pre-Pay Per Month	325,000.00	328.39	326.41	324.38	322.31
Loan Amount Pre-Pay Per Month	350,000.00	353.65	351.52	349.34	347.11
Loan Amount Pre-Pay Per Month	375,000.00	378.91	376.63	374.29	371.90
Loan Amount Pre-Pay Per Month	400,000.00	404.17	401.74	399.24	396.69
Loan Amount Pre-Pay Per Month	450,000.00	454.69	451.95	449.15	446.28

8% When Your Mortgage Will Be Paid
TABLE B

A 15 Year Mortgage Will Be Paid In 10 Years If You Pre-Pay The Following:

	INTEREST RATES			
	8%	8¼%	8½%	8¾%
Loan Amount $ 1,000.00 **Pre-Pay Per Month**	2.58	2.56	2.55	2.54
Loan Amount 2,000.00 **Pre-Pay Per Month**	5.15	5.13	5.10	5.08
Loan Amount 3,000.00 **Pre-Pay Per Month**	7.73	7.69	7.65	7.61
Loan Amount 4,000.00 **Pre-Pay Per Month**	10.30	10.26	10.20	10.15
Loan Amount 5,000.00 **Pre-Pay Per Month**	12.88	12.82	12.76	12.69
Loan Amount 10,000.00 **Pre-Pay Per Month**	25.76	25.64	25.51	25.38
Loan Amount 15,000.00 **Pre-Pay Per Month**	38.64	38.46	38.27	38.07
Loan Amount 20,000.00 **Pre-Pay Per Month**	51.52	51.28	51.02	50.76
Loan Amount 25,000.00 **Pre-Pay Per Month**	64.41	64.10	63.78	63.45
Loan Amount 50,000.00 **Pre-Pay Per Month**	128.81	128.19	127.56	126.91
Loan Amount 75,000.00 **Pre-Pay Per Month**	193.22	192.29	191.34	190.36
Loan Amount 100,000.00 **Pre-Pay Per Month**	257.62	256.39	255.12	253.82
Loan Amount 125,000.00 **Pre-Pay Per Month**	322.03	320.48	318.90	317.27
Loan Amount 150,000.00 **Pre-Pay Per Month**	386.44	384.58	382.68	380.73
Loan Amount 175,000.00 **Pre-Pay Per Month**	450.84	448.68	446.46	444.18
Loan Amount 200,000.00 **Pre-Pay Per Month**	515.25	512.77	510.23	507.64
Loan Amount 225,000.00 **Pre-Pay Per Month**	579.65	576.87	574.01	571.09
Loan Amount 250,000.00 **Pre-Pay Per Month**	644.06	640.96	637.79	634.55
Loan Amount 275,000.00 **Pre-Pay Per Month**	708.47	705.06	701.57	698.00
Loan Amount 300,000.00 **Pre-Pay Per Month**	772.87	769.16	765.35	761.46
Loan Amount 325,000.00 **Pre-Pay Per Month**	837.28	833.25	829.13	824.91
Loan Amount 350,000.00 **Pre-Pay Per Month**	901.68	897.35	892.91	888.37
Loan Amount 375,000.00 **Pre-Pay Per Month**	966.09	961.45	956.69	951.82
Loan Amount 400,000.00 **Pre-Pay Per Month**	1,030.50	1,025.54	1,020.47	1,015.28
Loan Amount 450,000.00 **Pre-Pay Per Month**	1,159.31	1,153.74	1,148.03	1,142.18

When Your Mortgage Will Be Paid
TABLE B

A 15 Year Mortgage Will Be Paid In 7½ Years If You Pre-Pay The Following:

		INTEREST RATES			
		8%	8¼%	8½%	8¾%
Loan Amount $ 1,000.00 Pre-Pay Per Month		5.26	5.24	5.22	5.20
Loan Amount 2,000.00 Pre-Pay Per Month		10.51	10.47	10.43	10.39
Loan Amount 3,000.00 Pre-Pay Per Month		15.77	15.71	15.65	15.59
Loan Amount 4,000.00 Pre-Pay Per Month		21.02	20.95	20.87	20.79
Loan Amount 5,000.00 Pre-Pay Per Month		26.28	26.18	26.09	25.99
Loan Amount 10,000.00 Pre-Pay Per Month		52.55	52.36	52.17	51.97
Loan Amount 15,000.00 Pre-Pay Per Month		78.83	78.55	78.26	77.96
Loan Amount 20,000.00 Pre-Pay Per Month		105.10	104.73	104.34	103.95
Loan Amount 25,000.00 Pre-Pay Per Month		131.38	130.91	130.43	129.94
Loan Amount 50,000.00 Pre-Pay Per Month		262.76	261.82	260.86	259.87
Loan Amount 75,000.00 Pre-Pay Per Month		394.14	392.73	391.29	389.81
Loan Amount 100,000.00 Pre-Pay Per Month		525.52	523.64	521.72	519.74
Loan Amount 125,000.00 Pre-Pay Per Month		656.90	654.55	652.15	649.68
Loan Amount 150,000.00 Pre-Pay Per Month		788.28	785.46	782.57	779.61
Loan Amount 175,000.00 Pre-Pay Per Month		919.66	916.37	913.00	909.55
Loan Amount 200,000.00 Pre-Pay Per Month		1,051.04	1,047.28	1,043.43	1,039.49
Loan Amount 225,000.00 Pre-Pay Per Month		1,182.42	1,178.19	1,173.86	1,169.42
Loan Amount 250,000.00 Pre-Pay Per Month		1,313.80	1,309.10	1,304.29	1,299.36
Loan Amount 275,000.00 Pre-Pay Per Month		1,445.18	1,440.02	1,434.72	1,429.29
Loan Amount 300,000.00 Pre-Pay Per Month		1,576.55	1,570.93	1,565.15	1,559.23
Loan Amount 325,000.00 Pre-Pay Per Month		1,707.93	1,701.84	1,695.58	1,689.17
Loan Amount 350,000.00 Pre-Pay Per Month		1,839.31	1,832.75	1,826.01	1,819.10
Loan Amount 375,000.00 Pre-Pay Per Month		1,970.69	1,963.66	1,956.44	1,949.04
Loan Amount 400,000.00 Pre-Pay Per Month		2,102.07	2,094.57	2,086.87	2,078.97
Loan Amount 450,000.00 Pre-Pay Per Month		2,364.83	2,356.39	2,347.72	2,338.84

9%

When Your Mortgage Will Be Paid
TABLE B

A 30 Year Mortgage Will Be Paid In 25 Years If You Pre-Pay The Following:

	INTEREST RATES			
	9%	9¼%	9½%	9¾%
Loan Amount $ 1,000.00 **Pre-Pay Per Month**	.35	.34	.33	.32
Loan Amount 2,000.00 **Pre-Pay Per Month**	.69	.67	.66	.64
Loan Amount 3,000.00 **Pre-Pay Per Month**	1.04	1.01	.99	.96
Loan Amount 4,000.00 **Pre-Pay Per Month**	1.38	1.35	1.31	1.28
Loan Amount 5,000.00 **Pre-Pay Per Month**	1.73	1.69	1.64	1.60
Loan Amount 10,000.00 **Pre-Pay Per Month**	3.46	3.37	3.28	3.20
Loan Amount 15,000.00 **Pre-Pay Per Month**	5.19	5.06	4.93	4.80
Loan Amount 20,000.00 **Pre-Pay Per Month**	6.91	6.74	6.57	6.40
Loan Amount 25,000.00 **Pre-Pay Per Month**	8.64	8.43	8.21	8.00
Loan Amount 50,000.00 **Pre-Pay Per Month**	17.29	16.85	16.42	15.99
Loan Amount 75,000.00 **Pre-Pay Per Month**	25.93	25.28	24.63	23.99
Loan Amount 100,000.00 **Pre-Pay Per Month**	34.57	33.71	32.84	31.98
Loan Amount 125,000.00 **Pre-Pay Per Month**	43.22	42.13	41.05	39.98
Loan Amount 150,000.00 **Pre-Pay Per Month**	51.86	50.56	49.26	47.97
Loan Amount 175,000.00 **Pre-Pay Per Month**	60.50	58.99	57.47	55.97
Loan Amount 200,000.00 **Pre-Pay Per Month**	69.15	67.41	65.68	63.97
Loan Amount 225,000.00 **Pre-Pay Per Month**	77.79	75.84	73.90	71.96
Loan Amount 250,000.00 **Pre-Pay Per Month**	86.43	84.27	82.11	79.96
Loan Amount 275,000.00 **Pre-Pay Per Month**	95.08	92.69	90.32	87.95
Loan Amount 300,000.00 **Pre-Pay Per Month**	103.72	101.12	98.53	95.95
Loan Amount 325,000.00 **Pre-Pay Per Month**	112.36	109.55	106.74	103.94
Loan Amount 350,000.00 **Pre-Pay Per Month**	121.01	117.97	114.95	111.94
Loan Amount 375,000.00 **Pre-Pay Per Month**	129.65	126.40	123.16	119.94
Loan Amount 400,000.00 **Pre-Pay Per Month**	138.29	134.83	131.37	127.93
Loan Amount 450,000.00 **Pre-Pay Per Month**	155.58	151.68	147.79	143.92

9%

When Your Mortgage Will Be Paid
TABLE B

A 30 Year Mortgage Will Be Paid In 20 Years If You Pre-Pay The Following:

		INTEREST RATES			
		9%	9¼%	9½%	9¾%
Loan Amount Pre-Pay Per Month	$ 1,000.00	.95	.93	.91	.89
Loan Amount Pre-Pay Per Month	2,000.00	1.90	1.86	1.83	1.79
Loan Amount Pre-Pay Per Month	3,000.00	2.85	2.80	2.74	2.68
Loan Amount Pre-Pay Per Month	4,000.00	3.80	3.73	3.65	3.57
Loan Amount Pre-Pay Per Month	5,000.00	4.76	4.66	4.56	4.47
Loan Amount Pre-Pay Per Month	10,000.00	9.51	9.32	9.13	8.94
Loan Amount Pre-Pay Per Month	15,000.00	14.27	13.98	13.69	13.40
Loan Amount Pre-Pay Per Month	20,000.00	19.02	18.64	18.26	17.87
Loan Amount Pre-Pay Per Month	25,000.00	23.78	23.30	22.82	22.34
Loan Amount Pre-Pay Per Month	50,000.00	47.55	46.60	45.64	44.68
Loan Amount Pre-Pay Per Month	75,000.00	71.33	69.89	68.46	67.02
Loan Amount Pre-Pay Per Month	100,000.00	95.10	93.19	91.28	89.36
Loan Amount Pre-Pay Per Month	125,000.00	118.88	116.49	114.10	111.70
Loan Amount Pre-Pay Per Month	150,000.00	142.66	139.79	136.92	134.04
Loan Amount Pre-Pay Per Month	175,000.00	166.43	163.08	159.73	156.38
Loan Amount Pre-Pay Per Month	200,000.00	190.21	186.38	182.55	178.72
Loan Amount Pre-Pay Per Month	225,000.00	213.98	209.68	205.37	201.07
Loan Amount Pre-Pay Per Month	250,000.00	237.76	232.98	228.19	223.41
Loan Amount Pre-Pay Per Month	275,000.00	261.53	256.28	251.01	245.75
Loan Amount Pre-Pay Per Month	300,000.00	285.31	279.57	273.83	268.09
Loan Amount Pre-Pay Per Month	325,000.00	309.09	302.87	296.65	290.43
Loan Amount Pre-Pay Per Month	350,000.00	332.86	326.17	319.47	312.77
Loan Amount Pre-Pay Per Month	375,000.00	356.64	349.47	342.29	335.11
Loan Amount Pre-Pay Per Month	400,000.00	380.41	372.77	365.11	357.45
Loan Amount Pre-Pay Per Month	450,000.00	427.97	419.36	410.75	402.13

9% When Your Mortgage Will Be Paid
TABLE B

A 30 Year Mortgage Will Be Paid In 15 Years If You Pre-Pay The Following:

	INTEREST RATES			
	9%	9¼%	9½%	9¾%
Loan Amount $ 1,000.00 **Pre-Pay Per Month**	2.10	2.07	2.03	2.00
Loan Amount 2,000.00 **Pre-Pay Per Month**	4.19	4.13	4.07	4.00
Loan Amount 3,000.00 **Pre-Pay Per Month**	6.29	6.20	6.10	6.01
Loan Amount 4,000.00 **Pre-Pay Per Month**	8.39	8.26	8.13	8.01
Loan Amount 5,000.00 **Pre-Pay Per Month**	10.48	10.33	10.17	10.01
Loan Amount 10,000.00 **Pre-Pay Per Month**	20.96	20.65	20.34	20.02
Loan Amount 15,000.00 **Pre-Pay Per Month**	31.45	30.98	30.51	30.03
Loan Amount 20,000.00 **Pre-Pay Per Month**	41.93	41.30	40.67	40.04
Loan Amount 25,000.00 **Pre-Pay Per Month**	52.41	51.63	50.84	50.05
Loan Amount 50,000.00 **Pre-Pay Per Month**	104.82	103.26	101.69	100.10
Loan Amount 75,000.00 **Pre-Pay Per Month**	157.23	154.89	152.53	150.16
Loan Amount 100,000.00 **Pre-Pay Per Month**	209.64	206.52	203.37	200.21
Loan Amount 125,000.00 **Pre-Pay Per Month**	262.05	258.15	254.21	250.26
Loan Amount 150,000.00 **Pre-Pay Per Month**	314.47	309.78	305.06	300.31
Loan Amount 175,000.00 **Pre-Pay Per Month**	366.88	361.40	355.90	350.36
Loan Amount 200,000.00 **Pre-Pay Per Month**	419.29	413.03	406.74	400.42
Loan Amount 225,000.00 **Pre-Pay Per Month**	471.70	464.66	457.58	450.47
Loan Amount 250,000.00 **Pre-Pay Per Month**	524.11	516.29	508.43	500.52
Loan Amount 275,000.00 **Pre-Pay Per Month**	576.52	567.92	559.27	550.57
Loan Amount 300,000.00 **Pre-Pay Per Month**	628.93	619.55	610.11	600.62
Loan Amount 325,000.00 **Pre-Pay Per Month**	681.34	671.18	660.95	650.68
Loan Amount 350,000.00 **Pre-Pay Per Month**	733.75	722.81	711.80	700.73
Loan Amount 375,000.00 **Pre-Pay Per Month**	786.16	774.44	762.64	750.78
Loan Amount 400,000.00 **Pre-Pay Per Month**	838.58	826.07	813.48	800.83
Loan Amount 450,000.00 **Pre-Pay Per Month**	943.40	929.33	915.17	900.94

9% When Your Mortgage Will Be Paid
TABLE B

A 15 Year Mortgage Will Be Paid In 12½ Years If You Pre-Pay The Following:

		INTEREST RATES			
		9%	9¼%	9½%	9¾%
Loan Amount Pre-Pay Per Month	$ 1,000.00	y .99	.98	.97	.96
Loan Amount Pre-Pay Per Month	2,000.00	1.97	1.96	1.94	1.93
Loan Amount Pre-Pay Per Month	3,000.00	2.96	2.94	2.92	2.89
Loan Amount Pre-Pay Per Month	4,000.00	3.94	3.91	3.89	3.86
Loan Amount Pre-Pay Per Month	5,000.00	4.93	4.89	4.86	4.82
Loan Amount Pre-Pay Per Month	10,000.00	9.85	9.79	9.72	9.65
Loan Amount Pre-Pay Per Month	15,000.00	14.78	14.68	14.58	14.47
Loan Amount Pre-Pay Per Month	20,000.00	19.70	19.57	19.44	19.30
Loan Amount Pre-Pay Per Month	25,000.00	24.63	24.46	24.30	24.12
Loan Amount Pre-Pay Per Month	50,000.00	49.26	48.93	48.59	48.25
Loan Amount Pre-Pay Per Month	75,000.00	73.89	73.39	72.89	72.37
Loan Amount Pre-Pay Per Month	100,000.00	98.52	97.86	97.18	96.49
Loan Amount Pre-Pay Per Month	125,000.00	123.15	122.32	121.48	120.62
Loan Amount Pre-Pay Per Month	150,000.00	147.78	146.79	145.77	144.74
Loan Amount Pre-Pay Per Month	175,000.00	172.42	171.25	170.07	168.87
Loan Amount Pre-Pay Per Month	200,000.00	197.05	195.72	194.37	192.99
Loan Amount Pre-Pay Per Month	225,000.00	221.68	220.18	218.66	217.11
Loan Amount Pre-Pay Per Month	250,000.00	246.31	244.65	242.96	241.24
Loan Amount Pre-Pay Per Month	275,000.00	270.94	269.11	267.25	265.36
Loan Amount Pre-Pay Per Month	300,000.00	295.57	293.58	291.55	289.48
Loan Amount Pre-Pay Per Month	325,000.00	320.20	318.04	315.85	313.61
Loan Amount Pre-Pay Per Month	350,000.00	344.83	342.51	340.14	337.73
Loan Amount Pre-Pay Per Month	375,000.00	369.46	366.97	364.44	361.86
Loan Amount Pre-Pay Per Month	400,000.00	394.09	391.44	388.73	385.98
Loan Amount Pre-Pay Per Month	450,000.00	443.35	440.37	437.32	434.23

When Your Mortgage Will Be Paid
TABLE B

A 15 Year Mortgage Will Be Paid In 10 Years If You Pre-Pay The Following:

		INTEREST RATES			
		9%	9¼%	9½%	9¾%
Loan Amount Pre-Pay Per Month	$ 1,000.00	2.52	2.51	2.50	2.48
Loan Amount Pre-Pay Per Month	2,000.00	5.05	5.02	5.00	4.97
Loan Amount Pre-Pay Per Month	3,000.00	7.57	7.53	7.49	7.45
Loan Amount Pre-Pay Per Month	4,000.00	10.10	10.05	9.99	9.93
Loan Amount Pre-Pay Per Month	5,000.00	12.62	12.56	12.49	12.42
Loan Amount Pre-Pay Per Month	10,000.00	25.25	25.11	24.98	24.83
Loan Amount Pre-Pay Per Month	15,000.00	37.87	37.67	37.46	37.25
Loan Amount Pre-Pay Per Month	20,000.00	50.50	50.23	49.95	49.67
Loan Amount Pre-Pay Per Month	25,000.00	63.12	62.78	62.44	62.08
Loan Amount Pre-Pay Per Month	50,000.00	126.25	125.57	124.88	124.17
Loan Amount Pre-Pay Per Month	75,000.00	189.37	188.35	187.31	186.25
Loan Amount Pre-Pay Per Month	100,000.00	252.49	251.13	249.75	248.34
Loan Amount Pre-Pay Per Month	125,000.00	315.61	313.92	312.19	310.42
Loan Amount Pre-Pay Per Month	150,000.00	378.74	376.70	374.63	372.51
Loan Amount Pre-Pay Per Month	175,000.00	441.86	439.49	437.06	434.59
Loan Amount Pre-Pay Per Month	200,000.00	504.98	502.27	499.50	496.68
Loan Amount Pre-Pay Per Month	225,000.00	568.11	565.05	561.94	558.76
Loan Amount Pre-Pay Per Month	250,000.00	631.23	627.84	624.38	620.85
Loan Amount Pre-Pay Per Month	275,000.00	694.35	690.62	686.81	682.93
Loan Amount Pre-Pay Per Month	300,000.00	757.47	753.40	749.25	745.02
Loan Amount Pre-Pay Per Month	325,000.00	820.60	816.19	811.69	807.10
Loan Amount Pre-Pay Per Month	350,000.00	883.72	878.97	874.13	869.19
Loan Amount Pre-Pay Per Month	375,000.00	946.84	941.76	936.57	931.27
Loan Amount Pre-Pay Per Month	400,000.00	1,009.96	1,004.54	999.00	993.36
Loan Amount Pre-Pay Per Month	450,000.00	1,136.21	1,130.11	1,123.88	1,117.53

When Your Mortgage Will Be Paid
TABLE B

A 15 Year Mortgage Will Be Paid In 7½ Years If You Pre-Pay The Following:

		INTEREST RATES			
		9%	9¼%	9½%	9¾%
Loan Amount Pre-Pay Per Month	$ 1,000.00	5.18	5.16	5.14	5.11
Loan Amount Pre-Pay Per Month	2,000.00	10.35	10.31	10.27	10.23
Loan Amount Pre-Pay Per Month	3,000.00	15.53	15.47	15.41	15.34
Loan Amount Pre-Pay Per Month	4,000.00	20.71	20.63	20.54	20.46
Loan Amount Pre-Pay Per Month	5,000.00	25.89	25.78	25.68	25.57
Loan Amount Pre-Pay Per Month	10,000.00	51.77	51.57	51.35	51.14
Loan Amount Pre-Pay Per Month	15,000.00	77.66	77.35	77.03	76.71
Loan Amount Pre-Pay Per Month	20,000.00	103.54	103.13	102.71	102.28
Loan Amount Pre-Pay Per Month	25,000.00	129.43	128.91	128.39	127.85
Loan Amount Pre-Pay Per Month	50,000.00	258.86	257.83	256.77	255.69
Loan Amount Pre-Pay Per Month	75,000.00	388.29	386.74	385.16	383.54
Loan Amount Pre-Pay Per Month	100,000.00	517.72	515.66	513.54	511.39
Loan Amount Pre-Pay Per Month	125,000.00	647.15	644.57	641.93	639.23
Loan Amount Pre-Pay Per Month	150,000.00	776.58	773.48	770.32	767.08
Loan Amount Pre-Pay Per Month	175,000.00	906.01	902.40	898.70	894.93
Loan Amount Pre-Pay Per Month	200,000.00	1,035.45	1,031.31	1,027.09	1,022.77
Loan Amount Pre-Pay Per Month	225,000.00	1,164.88	1,160.23	1,155.47	1,150.62
Loan Amount Pre-Pay Per Month	250,000.00	1,294.31	1,289.14	1,283.86	1,278.47
Loan Amount Pre-Pay Per Month	275,000.00	1,423.74	1,418.05	1,412.25	1,406.32
Loan Amount Pre-Pay Per Month	300,000.00	1,553.17	1,546.97	1,540.63	1,534.16
Loan Amount Pre-Pay Per Month	325,000.00	1,682.60	1,675.88	1,669.02	1,662.01
Loan Amount Pre-Pay Per Month	350,000.00	1,812.03	1,804.80	1,797.40	1,789.86
Loan Amount Pre-Pay Per Month	375,000.00	1,941.46	1,933.71	1,925.79	1,917.70
Loan Amount Pre-Pay Per Month	400,000.00	2,070.89	2,062.62	2,054.18	2,045.55
Loan Amount Pre-Pay Per Month	450,000.00	2,329.75	2,320.45	2,310.95	2,301.24

10% When Your Mortgage Will Be Paid
TABLE B

A 30 Year Mortgage Will Be Paid In 25 Years If You Pre-Pay The Following:

		INTEREST RATES			
		10%	10¼%	10½%	10¾%
Loan Amount Pre-Pay Per Month	$ 1,000.00	.31	.30	.29	.29
Loan Amount Pre-Pay Per Month	2,000.00	.62	.61	.59	.57
Loan Amount Pre-Pay Per Month	3,000.00	.93	.91	.88	.86
Loan Amount Pre-Pay Per Month	4,000.00	1.25	1.21	1.18	1.14
Loan Amount Pre-Pay Per Month	5,000.00	1.56	1.51	1.47	1.43
Loan Amount Pre-Pay Per Month	10,000.00	3.11	3.03	2.94	2.86
Loan Amount Pre-Pay Per Month	15,000.00	4.67	4.54	4.42	4.29
Loan Amount Pre-Pay Per Month	20,000.00	6.23	6.06	5.89	5.72
Loan Amount Pre-Pay Per Month	25,000.00	7.78	7.57	7.36	7.15
Loan Amount Pre-Pay Per Month	50,000.00	15.56	15.14	14.72	14.31
Loan Amount Pre-Pay Per Month	75,000.00	23.35	22.71	22.08	21.46
Loan Amount Pre-Pay Per Month	100,000.00	31.13	30.28	29.44	28.61
Loan Amount Pre-Pay Per Month	125,000.00	38.91	37.85	36.80	35.76
Loan Amount Pre-Pay Per Month	150,000.00	46.69	45.42	44.16	42.92
Loan Amount Pre-Pay Per Month	175,000.00	54.48	52.99	51.52	50.07
Loan Amount Pre-Pay Per Month	200,000.00	62.26	60.56	58.88	57.22
Loan Amount Pre-Pay Per Month	225,000.00	70.04	68.13	66.25	64.38
Loan Amount Pre-Pay Per Month	250,000.00	77.82	75.70	73.61	71.53
Loan Amount Pre-Pay Per Month	275,000.00	85.61	83.28	80.97	78.68
Loan Amount Pre-Pay Per Month	300,000.00	93.39	90.85	88.33	85.83
Loan Amount Pre-Pay Per Month	325,000.00	101.17	98.42	95.69	92.99
Loan Amount Pre-Pay Per Month	350,000.00	108.95	105.99	103.05	100.14
Loan Amount Pre-Pay Per Month	375,000.00	116.73	113.56	110.41	107.29
Loan Amount Pre-Pay Per Month	400,000.00	124.52	121.13	117.77	114.45
Loan Amount Pre-Pay Per Month	450,000.00	140.08	136.27	132.49	128.75

10% When Your Mortgage Will Be Paid
TABLE B

A 30 Year Mortgage Will Be Paid In 20 Years If You Pre-Pay The Following:

		INTEREST RATES			
		10%	10¼%	10½%	10¾%
Loan Amount **Pre-Pay Per Month**	$ 1,000.00	.87	.86	.84	.82
Loan Amount **Pre-Pay Per Month**	2,000.00	1.75	1.71	1.67	1.63
Loan Amount **Pre-Pay Per Month**	3,000.00	2.62	2.57	2.51	2.45
Loan Amount **Pre-Pay Per Month**	4,000.00	3.50	3.42	3.35	3.27
Loan Amount **Pre-Pay Per Month**	5,000.00	4.37	4.28	4.18	4.09
Loan Amount **Pre-Pay Per Month**	10,000.00	8.75	8.55	8.36	8.17
Loan Amount **Pre-Pay Per Month**	15,000.00	13.12	12.83	12.55	12.26
Loan Amount **Pre-Pay Per Month**	20,000.00	17.49	17.11	16.73	16.35
Loan Amount **Pre-Pay Per Month**	25,000.00	21.86	21.39	20.91	20.44
Loan Amount **Pre-Pay Per Month**	50,000.00	43.73	42.77	41.82	40.87
Loan Amount **Pre-Pay Per Month**	75,000.00	65.59	64.16	62.73	61.31
Loan Amount **Pre-Pay Per Month**	100,000.00	87.45	85.54	83.64	81.75
Loan Amount **Pre-Pay Per Month**	125,000.00	109.31	106.93	104.55	102.18
Loan Amount **Pre-Pay Per Month**	150,000.00	131.18	128.31	125.46	122.62
Loan Amount **Pre-Pay Per Month**	175,000.00	153.04	149.70	146.37	143.06
Loan Amount **Pre-Pay Per Month**	200,000.00	174.90	171.08	167.28	163.50
Loan Amount **Pre-Pay Per Month**	225,000.00	196.76	192.47	188.19	183.93
Loan Amount **Pre-Pay Per Month**	250,000.00	218.63	213.86	209.10	204.37
Loan Amount **Pre-Pay Per Month**	275,000.00	240.49	235.24	230.01	224.81
Loan Amount **Pre-Pay Per Month**	300,000.00	262.35	256.63	250.92	245.24
Loan Amount **Pre-Pay Per Month**	325,000.00	284.21	278.01	271.83	265.68
Loan Amount **Pre-Pay Per Month**	350,000.00	306.08	299.40	292.74	286.12
Loan Amount **Pre-Pay Per Month**	375,000.00	327.94	320.78	313.65	306.55
Loan Amount **Pre-Pay Per Month**	400,000.00	349.80	342.17	334.56	326.99
Loan Amount **Pre-Pay Per Month**	450,000.00	393.53	384.94	376.38	367.86

10%

When Your Mortgage Will Be Paid
TABLE B

A 30 Year Mortgage Will Be Paid In 15 Years If You Pre-Pay The Following:

		INTEREST RATES		
		10%	10¼%	10½%	10¾%
Loan Amount $ 1,000.00 Pre-Pay Per Month		1.97	1.94	1.91	1.87
Loan Amount 2,000.00 Pre-Pay Per Month		3.94	3.88	3.81	3.75
Loan Amount 3,000.00 Pre-Pay Per Month		5.91	5.82	5.72	5.62
Loan Amount 4,000.00 Pre-Pay Per Month		7.88	7.75	7.63	7.50
Loan Amount 5,000.00 Pre-Pay Per Month		9.85	9.69	9.53	9.37
Loan Amount 10,000.00 Pre-Pay Per Month		19.70	19.38	19.07	18.75
Loan Amount 15,000.00 Pre-Pay Per Month		29.56	29.08	28.60	28.12
Loan Amount 20,000.00 Pre-Pay Per Month		39.41	38.77	38.13	37.49
Loan Amount 25,000.00 Pre-Pay Per Month		49.26	48.46	47.66	46.87
Loan Amount 50,000.00 Pre-Pay Per Month		98.52	96.92	95.33	93.73
Loan Amount 75,000.00 Pre-Pay Per Month		147.78	145.39	142.99	140.60
Loan Amount 100,000.00 Pre-Pay Per Month		197.03	193.85	190.66	187.47
Loan Amount 125,000.00 Pre-Pay Per Month		246.29	242.31	238.32	234.33
Loan Amount 150,000.00 Pre-Pay Per Month		295.55	290.77	285.99	281.20
Loan Amount 175,000.00 Pre-Pay Per Month		344.81	339.24	333.65	328.07
Loan Amount 200,000.00 Pre-Pay Per Month		394.07	387.70	381.32	374.93
Loan Amount 225,000.00 Pre-Pay Per Month		443.33	436.16	428.98	421.80
Loan Amount 250,000.00 Pre-Pay Per Month		492.58	484.62	476.65	468.67
Loan Amount 275,000.00 Pre-Pay Per Month		541.84	533.09	524.31	515.53
Loan Amount 300,000.00 Pre-Pay Per Month		591.10	581.55	571.98	562.40
Loan Amount 325,000.00 Pre-Pay Per Month		640.36	630.01	619.64	609.27
Loan Amount 350,000.00 Pre-Pay Per Month		689.62	678.47	667.31	656.13
Loan Amount 375,000.00 Pre-Pay Per Month		738.88	726.94	714.97	703.00
Loan Amount 400,000.00 Pre-Pay Per Month		788.13	775.40	762.64	749.87
Loan Amount 450,000.00 Pre-Pay Per Month		886.65	872.32	857.97	843.60

10%

When Your Mortgage Will Be Paid
TABLE B

A 15 Year Mortgage Will Be Paid In 12½ Years If You Pre-Pay The Following:

		INTEREST RATES			
		10%	10¼%	10½%	10¾%
Loan Amount Pre-Pay Per Month	$ 1,000.00	.96	.95	.94	.94
Loan Amount Pre-Pay Per Month	2,000.00	1.92	1.90	1.89	1.87
Loan Amount Pre-Pay Per Month	3,000.00	2.87	2.85	2.83	2.81
Loan Amount Pre-Pay Per Month	4,000.00	3.83	3.80	3.77	3.75
Loan Amount Pre-Pay Per Month	5,000.00	4.79	4.75	4.72	4.68
Loan Amount Pre-Pay Per Month	10,000.00	9.58	9.51	9.44	9.36
Loan Amount Pre-Pay Per Month	15,000.00	14.37	14.26	14.15	14.04
Loan Amount Pre-Pay Per Month	20,000.00	19.16	19.02	18.87	18.73
Loan Amount Pre-Pay Per Month	25,000.00	23.95	23.77	23.59	23.41
Loan Amount Pre-Pay Per Month	50,000.00	47.90	47.54	47.18	46.81
Loan Amount Pre-Pay Per Month	75,000.00	71.85	71.31	70.77	70.22
Loan Amount Pre-Pay Per Month	100,000.00	95.79	95.08	94.36	93.63
Loan Amount Pre-Pay Per Month	125,000.00	119.74	118.85	117.95	117.03
Loan Amount Pre-Pay Per Month	150,000.00	143.69	142.62	141.54	140.44
Loan Amount Pre-Pay Per Month	175,000.00	167.64	166.40	165.13	163.85
Loan Amount Pre-Pay Per Month	200,000.00	191.59	190.17	188.72	187.26
Loan Amount Pre-Pay Per Month	225,000.00	215.54	213.94	212.31	210.66
Loan Amount Pre-Pay Per Month	250,000.00	239.49	237.71	235.90	234.07
Loan Amount Pre-Pay Per Month	275,000.00	263.44	261.48	259.49	257.48
Loan Amount Pre-Pay Per Month	300,000.00	287.38	285.25	283.08	280.88
Loan Amount Pre-Pay Per Month	325,000.00	311.33	309.02	306.67	304.29
Loan Amount Pre-Pay Per Month	350,000.00	335.28	332.79	330.26	327.70
Loan Amount Pre-Pay Per Month	375,000.00	359.23	356.56	353.85	351.10
Loan Amount Pre-Pay Per Month	400,000.00	383.18	380.33	377.44	374.51
Loan Amount Pre-Pay Per Month	450,000.00	431.08	427.87	424.62	421.32

10% When Your Mortgage Will Be Paid
TABLE B

A 15 Year Mortgage Will Be Paid In 10 Years If You Pre-Pay The Following:

		INTEREST RATES			
		10%	10¼%	10½%	10¾%
Loan Amount Pre-Pay Per Month	$ 1,000.00	2.47	2.45	2.44	2.42
Loan Amount Pre-Pay Per Month	2,000.00	4.94	4.91	4.88	4.85
Loan Amount Pre-Pay Per Month	3,000.00	7.41	7.36	7.32	7.27
Loan Amount Pre-Pay Per Month	4,000.00	9.88	9.82	9.76	9.70
Loan Amount Pre-Pay Per Month	5,000.00	12.35	12.27	12.20	12.12
Loan Amount Pre-Pay Per Month	10,000.00	24.69	24.54	24.40	24.24
Loan Amount Pre-Pay Per Month	15,000.00	37.04	36.82	36.59	36.37
Loan Amount Pre-Pay Per Month	20,000.00	49.38	49.09	48.79	48.49
Loan Amount Pre-Pay Per Month	25,000.00	61.73	61.36	60.99	60.61
Loan Amount Pre-Pay Per Month	50,000.00	123.45	122.72	121.98	121.22
Loan Amount Pre-Pay Per Month	75,000.00	185.18	184.08	182.96	181.83
Loan Amount Pre-Pay Per Month	100,000.00	246.90	245.44	243.95	242.44
Loan Amount Pre-Pay Per Month	125,000.00	308.63	306.80	304.94	303.05
Loan Amount Pre-Pay Per Month	150,000.00	370.35	368.16	365.93	363.66
Loan Amount Pre-Pay Per Month	175,000.00	432.08	429.52	426.91	424.27
Loan Amount Pre-Pay Per Month	200,000.00	493.80	490.88	487.90	484.88
Loan Amount Pre-Pay Per Month	225,000.00	555.53	552.24	548.89	545.49
Loan Amount Pre-Pay Per Month	250,000.00	617.26	613.60	609.88	606.10
Loan Amount Pre-Pay Per Month	275,000.00	678.98	674.96	670.87	666.71
Loan Amount Pre-Pay Per Month	300,000.00	740.71	736.32	731.85	727.32
Loan Amount Pre-Pay Per Month	325,000.00	802.43	797.68	792.84	787.93
Loan Amount Pre-Pay Per Month	350,000.00	864.16	859.04	853.83	848.54
Loan Amount Pre-Pay Per Month	375,000.00	925.88	920.40	914.82	909.15
Loan Amount Pre-Pay Per Month	400,000.00	987.61	981.76	975.80	969.76
Loan Amount Pre-Pay Per Month	450,000.00	1,111.06	1,104.48	1,097.78	1,090.97

10% When Your Mortgage Will Be Paid
TABLE B

A 15 Year Mortgage Will Be Paid In 7½ Years If You Pre-Pay The Following:

		INTEREST RATES			
		10%	10¼%	10½%	10¾%
Loan Amount	$ 1,000.00				
Pre-Pay Per Month		5.09	5.07	5.05	5.02
Loan Amount	2,000.00				
Pre-Pay Per Month		10.18	10.14	10.09	10.05
Loan Amount	3,000.00				
Pre-Pay Per Month		15.28	15.21	15.14	15.07
Loan Amount	4,000.00				
Pre-Pay Per Month		20.37	20.28	20.19	20.09
Loan Amount	5,000.00				
Pre-Pay Per Month		25.46	25.35	25.23	25.12
Loan Amount	10,000.00				
Pre-Pay Per Month		50.92	50.69	50.47	50.23
Loan Amount	15,000.00				
Pre-Pay Per Month		76.38	76.04	75.70	75.35
Loan Amount	20,000.00				
Pre-Pay Per Month		101.84	101.39	100.93	100.47
Loan Amount	25,000.00				
Pre-Pay Per Month		127.30	126.74	126.17	125.58
Loan Amount	50,000.00				
Pre-Pay Per Month		254.59	253.47	252.33	251.17
Loan Amount	75,000.00				
Pre-Pay Per Month		381.89	380.21	378.50	376.75
Loan Amount	100,000.00				
Pre-Pay Per Month		509.19	506.95	504.66	502.34
Loan Amount	125,000.00				
Pre-Pay Per Month		636.48	633.68	630.83	627.92
Loan Amount	150,000.00				
Pre-Pay Per Month		763.78	760.42	756.99	753.50
Loan Amount	175,000.00				
Pre-Pay Per Month		891.08	887.15	883.16	879.09
Loan Amount	200,000.00				
Pre-Pay Per Month		1,018.37	1,013.89	1,009.32	1,004.67
Loan Amount	225,000.00				
Pre-Pay Per Month		1,145.67	1,140.63	1,135.49	1,130.26
Loan Amount	250,000.00				
Pre-Pay Per Month		1,272.97	1,267.36	1,261.65	1,255.84
Loan Amount	275,000.00				
Pre-Pay Per Month		1,400.27	1,394.10	1,387.82	1,381.42
Loan Amount	300,000.00				
Pre-Pay Per Month		1,527.56	1,520.84	1,513.98	1,507.01
Loan Amount	325,000.00				
Pre-Pay Per Month		1,654.86	1,647.57	1,640.15	1,632.59
Loan Amount	350,000.00				
Pre-Pay Per Month		1,782.16	1,774.31	1,766.31	1,758.18
Loan Amount	375,000.00				
Pre-Pay Per Month		1,909.45	1,901.04	1,892.48	1,883.76
Loan Amount	400,000.00				
Pre-Pay Per Month		2,036.75	2,027.78	2,018.64	2,009.35
Loan Amount	450,000.00				
Pre-Pay Per Month		2,291.34	2,281.25	2,270.97	2,260.51

11% When Your Mortgage Will Be Paid
TABLE B

A 30 Year Mortgage Will Be Paid In 25 Years If You Pre-Pay The Following:

		INTEREST RATES			
		11%	11¼%	11½%	11¾%
Loan Amount Pre-Pay Per Month	$ 1,000.00	.28	.27	.26	.25
Loan Amount Pre-Pay Per Month	2,000.00	.56	.54	.52	.51
Loan Amount Pre-Pay Per Month	3,000.00	.83	.81	.79	.76
Loan Amount Pre-Pay Per Month	4,000.00	1.11	1.08	1.05	1.02
Loan Amount Pre-Pay Per Month	5,000.00	1.39	1.35	1.31	1.27
Loan Amount Pre-Pay Per Month	10,000.00	2.78	2.70	2.62	2.54
Loan Amount Pre-Pay Per Month	15,000.00	4.17	4.05	3.93	3.81
Loan Amount Pre-Pay Per Month	20,000.00	5.56	5.40	5.24	5.08
Loan Amount Pre-Pay Per Month	25,000.00	6.95	6.74	·6.54	6.35
Loan Amount Pre-Pay Per Month	50,000.00	13.89	13.49	13.09	12.69
Loan Amount Pre-Pay Per Month	75,000.00	20.84	20.23	19.63	19.04
Loan Amount Pre-Pay Per Month	100,000.00	27.79	26.98	26.18	25.39
Loan Amount Pre-Pay Per Month	125,000.00	34.74	33.72	32.72	31.74
Loan Amount Pre-Pay Per Month	150,000.00	41.68	40.47	39.27	38.08
Loan Amount Pre-Pay Per Month	175,000.00	48.63	47.21	45.81	44.43
Loan Amount Pre-Pay Per Month	200,000.00	55.58	53.96	52.36	50.78
Loan Amount Pre-Pay Per Month	225,000.00	62.53	60.70	58.90	57.12
Loan Amount Pre-Pay Per Month	250,000.00	69.47	67.45	65.44	63.47
Loan Amount Pre-Pay Per Month	275,000.00	76.42	74.19	71.99	69.82
Loan Amount Pre-Pay Per Month	300,000.00	83.37	80.93	78.53	76.17
Loan Amount Pre-Pay Per Month	325,000.00	90.32	87.68	85.08	82.51
Loan Amount Pre-Pay Per Month	350,000.00	97.26	94.42	91.62	88.86
Loan Amount Pre-Pay Per Month	375,000.00	104.21	101.17	98.17	95.21
Loan Amount Pre-Pay Per Month	400,000.00	111.16	107.91	104.71	101.55
Loan Amount Pre-Pay Per Month	450,000.00	125.05	121.40	117.80	114.25

When Your Mortgage Will Be Paid
TABLE B

A 30 Year Mortgage Will Be Paid In 20 Years If You Pre-Pay The Following:

		INTEREST RATES			
		11%	11¼%	11½%	11¾%
Loan Amount Pre-Pay Per Month	$ 1,000.00	.80	.78	.76	.74
Loan Amount Pre-Pay Per Month	2,000.00	1.60	1.56	1.52	1.49
Loan Amount Pre-Pay Per Month	3,000.00	2.40	2.34	2.28	2.23
Loan Amount Pre-Pay Per Month	4,000.00	3.19	3.12	3.05	2.97
Loan Amount Pre-Pay Per Month	5,000.00	3.99	3.90	3.81	3.71
Loan Amount Pre-Pay Per Month	10,000.00	7.99	7.80	7.61	7.43
Loan Amount Pre-Pay Per Month	15,000.00	11.98	11.70	11.42	11.14
Loan Amount Pre-Pay Per Month	20,000.00	15.97	15.60	15.23	14.86
Loan Amount Pre-Pay Per Month	25,000.00	19.97	19.50	19.03	18.57
Loan Amount Pre-Pay Per Month	50,000.00	39.93	39.00	38.07	37.15
Loan Amount Pre-Pay Per Month	75,000.00	59.90	58.50	57.10	55.72
Loan Amount Pre-Pay Per Month	100,000.00	79.86	77.99	76.14	74.30
Loan Amount Pre-Pay Per Month	125,000.00	99.83	97.49	95.17	92.87
Loan Amount Pre-Pay Per Month	150,000.00	119.80	116.99	114.21	111.45
Loan Amount Pre-Pay Per Month	175,000.00	139.76	136.49	133.24	130.02
Loan Amount Pre-Pay Per Month	200,000.00	159.73	155.99	152.28	148.59
Loan Amount Pre-Pay Per Month	225,000.00	179.70	175.49	171.31	167.17
Loan Amount Pre-Pay Per Month	250,000.00	199.66	194.99	190.35	185.74
Loan Amount Pre-Pay Per Month	275,000.00	219.63	214.49	209.38	204.32
Loan Amount Pre-Pay Per Month	300,000.00	239.59	233.98	228.41	222.89
Loan Amount Pre-Pay Per Month	325,000.00	259.56	253.48	247.45	241.47
Loan Amount Pre-Pay Per Month	350,000.00	279.53	272.98	266.48	260.04
Loan Amount Pre-Pay Per Month	375,000.00	299.49	292.48	285.52	278.61
Loan Amount Pre-Pay Per Month	400,000.00	319.46	311.98	304.55	297.19
Loan Amount Pre-Pay Per Month	450,000.00	359.39	350.98	342.62	334.34

When Your Mortgage Will Be Paid
TABLE B

A 30 Year Mortgage Will Be Paid In 15 Years If You Pre-Pay The Following:

		INTEREST RATES			
		11%	11¼%	11½%	11¾%
Loan Amount **Pre-Pay Per Month**	$ 1,000.00	1.84	1.81	1.78	1.75
Loan Amount **Pre-Pay Per Month**	2,000.00	3.69	3.62	3.56	3.49
Loan Amount **Pre-Pay Per Month**	3,000.00	5.53	5.43	5.34	5.24
Loan Amount **Pre-Pay Per Month**	4,000.00	7.37	7.24	7.12	6.99
Loan Amount **Pre-Pay Per Month**	5,000.00	9.21	9.05	8.89	8.74
Loan Amount **Pre-Pay Per Month**	10,000.00	18.43	18.11	17.79	17.47
Loan Amount **Pre-Pay Per Month**	15,000.00	27.64	27.16	26.68	26.21
Loan Amount **Pre-Pay Per Month**	20,000.00	36.85	36.22	35.58	34.94
Loan Amount **Pre-Pay Per Month**	25,000.00	46.07	45.27	44.47	43.68
Loan Amount **Pre-Pay Per Month**	50,000.00	92.14	90.54	88.95	87.36
Loan Amount **Pre-Pay Per Month**	75,000.00	138.21	135.81	133.42	131.04
Loan Amount **Pre-Pay Per Month**	100,000.00	184.27	181.08	177.90	174.72
Loan Amount **Pre-Pay Per Month**	125,000.00	230.34	226.35	222.37	218.40
Loan Amount **Pre-Pay Per Month**	150,000.00	276.41	271.62	266.85	262.08
Loan Amount **Pre-Pay Per Month**	175,000.00	322.48	316.90	311.32	305.76
Loan Amount **Pre-Pay Per Month**	200,000.00	368.55	362.17	355.80	349.44
Loan Amount **Pre-Pay Per Month**	225,000.00	414.62	407.44	400.27	393.12
Loan Amount **Pre-Pay Per Month**	250,000.00	460.68	452.71	444.75	436.80
Loan Amount **Pre-Pay Per Month**	275,000.00	506.75	497.98	489.22	480.48
Loan Amount **Pre-Pay Per Month**	300,000.00	552.82	543.25	533.70	524.16
Loan Amount **Pre-Pay Per Month**	325,000.00	598.89	588.52	578.17	567.85
Loan Amount **Pre-Pay Per Month**	350,000.00	644.96	633.79	622.64	611.53
Loan Amount **Pre-Pay Per Month**	375,000.00	691.03	679.06	667.12	655.21
Loan Amount **Pre-Pay Per Month**	400,000.00	737.09	724.33	711.59	698.89
Loan Amount **Pre-Pay Per Month**	450,000.00	829.23	814.87	800.54	786.25

11% When Your Mortgage Will Be Paid
TABLE B

A 15 Year Mortgage Will Be Paid In 12½ Years If You Pre-Pay The Following:

		INTEREST RATES			
		11%	11¼%	11½%	11¾%
Loan Amount Pre-Pay Per Month	$ 1,000.00	.93	.92	.91	.91
Loan Amount Pre-Pay Per Month	2,000.00	1.86	1.84	1.83	1.81
Loan Amount Pre-Pay Per Month	3,000.00	2.79	2.76	2.74	2.72
Loan Amount Pre-Pay Per Month	4,000.00	3.72	3.69	3.65	3.62
Loan Amount Pre-Pay Per Month	5,000.00	4.64	4.61	4.57	4.53
Loan Amount Pre-Pay Per Month	10,000.00	9.29	9.21	9.14	9.06
Loan Amount Pre-Pay Per Month	15,000.00	13.93	13.82	13.71	13.59
Loan Amount Pre-Pay Per Month	20,000.00	18.58	18.43	18.27	18.12
Loan Amount Pre-Pay Per Month	25,000.00	23.22	23.03	22.84	22.65
Loan Amount Pre-Pay Per Month	50,000.00	46.44	46.07	45.68	45.30
Loan Amount Pre-Pay Per Month	75,000.00	69.66	69.10	68.53	67.95
Loan Amount Pre-Pay Per Month	100,000.00	92.88	92.13	91.37	90.60
Loan Amount Pre-Pay Per Month	125,000.00	116.11	115.16	114.21	113.25
Loan Amount Pre-Pay Per Month	150,000.00	139.33	138.20	137.05	135.90
Loan Amount Pre-Pay Per Month	175,000.00	162.55	161.23	159.90	158.55
Loan Amount Pre-Pay Per Month	200,000.00	185.77	184.26	182.74	181.20
Loan Amount Pre-Pay Per Month	225,000.00	208.99	207.30	205.58	203.85
Loan Amount Pre-Pay Per Month	250,000.00	232.21	230.33	228.42	226.50
Loan Amount Pre-Pay Per Month	275,000.00	255.43	253.36	251.27	249.15
Loan Amount Pre-Pay Per Month	300,000.00	278.65	276.40	274.11	271.80
Loan Amount Pre-Pay Per Month	325,000.00	301.88	299.43	296.95	294.45
Loan Amount Pre-Pay Per Month	350,000.00	325.10	322.46	319.79	317.10
Loan Amount Pre-Pay Per Month	375,000.00	348.32	345.49	342.64	339.75
Loan Amount Pre-Pay Per Month	400,000.00	371.54	368.53	365.48	362.40
Loan Amount Pre-Pay Per Month	450,000.00	417.98	414.59	411.16	407.70

118

11%   When Your Mortgage Will Be Paid
TABLE B

A 15 Year Mortgage Will Be Paid In 10 Years If You Pre-Pay The Following:

		INTEREST RATES			
		11%	11¼%	11½%	11¾%
Loan Amount **Pre-Pay Per Month**	$ 1,000.00	2.41	2.39	2.38	2.36
Loan Amount **Pre-Pay Per Month**	2,000.00	4.82	4.79	4.76	4.72
Loan Amount **Pre-Pay Per Month**	3,000.00	7.23	7.18	7.13	7.08
Loan Amount **Pre-Pay Per Month**	4,000.00	9.64	9.57	9.51	9.45
Loan Amount **Pre-Pay Per Month**	5,000.00	12.05	11.97	11.89	11.81
Loan Amount **Pre-Pay Per Month**	10,000.00	24.09	23.93	23.78	23.62
Loan Amount **Pre-Pay Per Month**	15,000.00	36.14	35.90	35.66	35.42
Loan Amount **Pre-Pay Per Month**	20,000.00	48.18	47.87	47.55	47.23
Loan Amount **Pre-Pay Per Month**	25,000.00	60.23	59.84	59.44	59.04
Loan Amount **Pre-Pay Per Month**	50,000.00	120.45	119.67	118.88	118.08
Loan Amount **Pre-Pay Per Month**	75,000.00	180.68	179.51	178.32	177.12
Loan Amount **Pre-Pay Per Month**	100,000.00	240.90	239.34	237.76	236.16
Loan Amount **Pre-Pay Per Month**	125,000.00	301.13	299.18	297.21	295.20
Loan Amount **Pre-Pay Per Month**	150,000.00	361.35	359.02	356.65	354.24
Loan Amount **Pre-Pay Per Month**	175,000.00	421.58	418.85	416.09	413.29
Loan Amount **Pre-Pay Per Month**	200,000.00	481.81	478.69	475.53	472.33
Loan Amount **Pre-Pay Per Month**	225,000.00	542.03	538.53	534.97	531.37
Loan Amount **Pre-Pay Per Month**	250,000.00	602.26	598.36	594.41	590.41
Loan Amount **Pre-Pay Per Month**	275,000.00	662.48	658.20	653.85	649.45
Loan Amount **Pre-Pay Per Month**	300,000.00	722.71	718.03	713.29	708.49
Loan Amount **Pre-Pay Per Month**	325,000.00	782.94	777.87	772.74	767.53
Loan Amount **Pre-Pay Per Month**	350,000.00	843.16	837.71	832.18	826.57
Loan Amount **Pre-Pay Per Month**	375,000.00	903.39	897.54	891.62	885.61
Loan Amount **Pre-Pay Per Month**	400,000.00	963.61	957.38	951.06	944.65
Loan Amount **Pre-Pay Per Month**	450,000.00	1,084.06	1,077.05	1,069.94	1,062.73

11%   When Your Mortgage Will Be Paid
TABLE B

A 15 Year Mortgage Will Be Paid In 7½ Years If You Pre-Pay The Following:

		INTEREST RATES			
		11%	11¼%	11½%	11¾%
Loan Amount Pre-Pay Per Month	$ 1,000.00	5.00	4.98	4.95	4.93
Loan Amount Pre-Pay Per Month	2,000.00	10.00	9.95	9.90	9.85
Loan Amount Pre-Pay Per Month	3,000.00	15.00	14.93	14.85	14.78
Loan Amount Pre-Pay Per Month	4,000.00	20.00	19.90	19.81	19.71
Loan Amount Pre-Pay Per Month	5,000.00	25.00	24.88	24.76	24.63
Loan Amount Pre-Pay Per Month	10,000.00	50.00	49.76	49.51	49.27
Loan Amount Pre-Pay Per Month	15,000.00	75.00	74.64	74.27	73.90
Loan Amount Pre-Pay Per Month	20,000.00	99.99	99.51	99.03	98.53
Loan Amount Pre-Pay Per Month	25,000.00	124.99	124.39	123.78	123.16
Loan Amount Pre-Pay Per Month	50,000.00	249.99	248.78	247.56	246.33
Loan Amount Pre-Pay Per Month	75,000.00	374.98	373.18	371.35	369.49
Loan Amount Pre-Pay Per Month	100,000.00	499.97	497.57	495.13	492.65
Loan Amount Pre-Pay Per Month	125,000.00	624.97	621.96	618.91	615.81
Loan Amount Pre-Pay Per Month	150,000.00	749.96	746.35	742.69	738.98
Loan Amount Pre-Pay Per Month	175,000.00	874.95	870.75	866.47	862.14
Loan Amount Pre-Pay Per Month	200,000.00	999.94	995.14	990.26	985.30
Loan Amount Pre-Pay Per Month	225,000.00	1,124.94	1,119.53	1,114.04	1,108.47
Loan Amount Pre-Pay Per Month	250,000.00	1,249.93	1,243.92	1,237.82	1,231.63
Loan Amount Pre-Pay Per Month	275,000.00	1,374.92	1,368.32	1,361.60	1,354.79
Loan Amount Pre-Pay Per Month	300,000.00	1,499.92	1,492.71	1,485.39	1,477.95
Loan Amount Pre-Pay Per Month	325,000.00	1,624.91	1,617.10	1,609.17	1,601.12
Loan Amount Pre-Pay Per Month	350,000.00	1,749.90	1,741.49	1,732.95	1,724.28
Loan Amount Pre-Pay Per Month	375,000.00	1,874.90	1,865.88	1,856.73	1,847.44
Loan Amount Pre-Pay Per Month	400,000.00	1,999.89	1,990.28	1,980.51	1,970.60
Loan Amount Pre-Pay Per Month	450,000.00	2,249.87	2,239.06	2,228.08	2,216.93

When Your Mortgage Will Be Paid
TABLE B

A 30 Year Mortgage Will Be Paid In 25 Years If You Pre-Pay The Following:

		INTEREST RATES		
		12%	12¼%	12½%	12¾%
Loan Amount $ 1,000.00 Pre-Pay Per Month		.25	.24	.23	.22
Loan Amount 2,000.00 Pre-Pay Per Month		.49	.48	.46	.45
Loan Amount 3,000.00 Pre-Pay Per Month		.74	.72	.69	.67
Loan Amount 4,000.00 Pre-Pay Per Month		.98	.95	.92	.89
Loan Amount 5,000.00 Pre-Pay Per Month		1.23	1.19	1.15	1.12
Loan Amount 10,000.00 Pre-Pay Per Month		2.46	2.38	2.31	2.24
Loan Amount 15,000.00 Pre-Pay Per Month		3.69	3.58	3.46	3.35
Loan Amount 20,000.00 Pre-Pay Per Month		4.92	4.77	4.62	4.47
Loan Amount 25,000.00 Pre-Pay Per Month		6.15	5.96	5.77	5.59
Loan Amount 50,000.00 Pre-Pay Per Month		12.31	11.92	11.55	11.18
Loan Amount 75,000.00 Pre-Pay Per Month		18.46	17.89	17.32	16.77
Loan Amount 100,000.00 Pre-Pay Per Month		24.61	23.85	23.10	22.36
Loan Amount 125,000.00 Pre-Pay Per Month		30.76	29.81	28.87	27.95
Loan Amount 150,000.00 Pre-Pay Per Month		36.92	35.77	34.64	33.54
Loan Amount 175,000.00 Pre-Pay Per Month		43.07	41.73	40.42	39.13
Loan Amount 200,000.00 Pre-Pay Per Month		49.22	47.69	46.19	44.72
Loan Amount 225,000.00 Pre-Pay Per Month		55.38	53.66	51.97	50.31
Loan Amount 250,000.00 Pre-Pay Per Month		61.53	59.62	57.74	55.90
Loan Amount 275,000.00 Pre-Pay Per Month		67.68	65.58	63.52	61.49
Loan Amount 300,000.00 Pre-Pay Per Month		73.83	71.54	69.29	67.08
Loan Amount 325,000.00 Pre-Pay Per Month		79.99	77.50	75.06	72.67
Loan Amount 350,000.00 Pre-Pay Per Month		86.14	83.47	80.84	78.26
Loan Amount 375,000.00 Pre-Pay Per Month		92.29	89.43	86.61	83.85
Loan Amount 400,000.00 Pre-Pay Per Month		98.45	95.39	92.39	89.44
Loan Amount 450,000.00 Pre-Pay Per Month		110.75	107.31	103.93	100.62

12% When Your Mortgage Will Be Paid
TABLE B

A 30 Year Mortgage Will Be Paid In 20 Years If You Pre-Pay The Following:

		INTEREST RATES			
		12%	12¼%	12½%	12¾%
Loan Amount Pre-Pay Per Month	$ 1,000.00	.72	.71	.69	.67
Loan Amount Pre-Pay Per Month	2,000.00	1.45	1.41	1.38	1.34
Loan Amount Pre-Pay Per Month	3,000.00	2.17	2.12	2.07	2.01
Loan Amount Pre-Pay Per Month	4,000.00	2.90	2.83	2.76	2.68
Loan Amount Pre-Pay Per Month	5,000.00	3.62	3.53	3.44	3.36
Loan Amount Pre-Pay Per Month	10,000.00	7.25	7.07	6.89	6.71
Loan Amount Pre-Pay Per Month	15,000.00	10.87	10.60	10.33	10.07
Loan Amount Pre-Pay Per Month	20,000.00	14.49	14.13	13.78	13.42
Loan Amount Pre-Pay Per Month	25,000.00	18.12	17.67	17.22	16.78
Loan Amount Pre-Pay Per Month	50,000.00	36.24	35.33	34.44	33.56
Loan Amount Pre-Pay Per Month	75,000.00	54.36	53.00	51.66	50.34
Loan Amount Pre-Pay Per Month	100,000.00	72.47	70.67	68.88	67.12
Loan Amount Pre-Pay Per Month	125,000.00	90.59	88.34	86.10	83.90
Loan Amount Pre-Pay Per Month	150,000.00	108.71	106.00	103.32	100.68
Loan Amount Pre-Pay Per Month	175,000.00	126.83	123.67	120.54	117.46
Loan Amount Pre-Pay Per Month	200,000.00	144.95	141.34	137.77	134.24
Loan Amount Pre-Pay Per Month	225,000.00	163.07	159.00	154.99	151.02
Loan Amount Pre-Pay Per Month	250,000.00	181.18	176.67	172.21	167.80
Loan Amount Pre-Pay Per Month	275,000.00	199.30	194.34	189.43	184.58
Loan Amount Pre-Pay Per Month	300,000.00	217.42	212.00	206.65	201.36
Loan Amount Pre-Pay Per Month	325,000.00	235.54	229.67	223.87	218.13
Loan Amount Pre-Pay Per Month	350,000.00	253.66	247.34	241.09	234.91
Loan Amount Pre-Pay Per Month	375,000.00	271.78	265.01	258.31	251.69
Loan Amount Pre-Pay Per Month	400,000.00	289.89	282.67	275.53	268.47
Loan Amount Pre-Pay Per Month	450,000.00	326.13	318.01	309.97	302.03

12%   When Your Mortgage Will Be Paid
TABLE B

A 30 Year Mortgage Will Be Paid In 15 Years If You Pre-Pay The Following:

		INTEREST RATES			
		12%	12¼%	12½%	12¾%
Loan Amount Pre-Pay Per Month	$ 1,000.00	1.72	1.68	1.65	1.62
Loan Amount Pre-Pay Per Month	2,000.00	3.43	3.37	3.31	3.24
Loan Amount Pre-Pay Per Month	3,000.00	5.15	5.05	4.96	4.86
Loan Amount Pre-Pay Per Month	4,000.00	6.86	6.74	6.61	6.49
Loan Amount Pre-Pay Per Month	5,000.00	8.58	8.42	8.26	8.11
Loan Amount Pre-Pay Per Month	10,000.00	17.16	16.84	16.53	16.21
Loan Amount Pre-Pay Per Month	15,000.00	25.73	25.26	24.79	24.32
Loan Amount Pre-Pay Per Month	20,000.00	34.31	33.68	33.05	32.43
Loan Amount Pre-Pay Per Month	25,000.00	42.89	42.10	41.32	40.54
Loan Amount Pre-Pay Per Month	50,000.00	85.78	84.20	82.63	81.07
Loan Amount Pre-Pay Per Month	75,000.00	128.67	126.30	123.95	121.61
Loan Amount Pre-Pay Per Month	100,000.00	171.56	168.40	165.26	162.14
Loan Amount Pre-Pay Per Month	125,000.00	214.44	210.50	206.58	202.68
Loan Amount Pre-Pay Per Month	150,000.00	257.33	252.60	247.90	243.22
Loan Amount Pre-Pay Per Month	175,000.00	300.22	294.70	289.21	283.75
Loan Amount Pre-Pay Per Month	200,000.00	343.11	336.80	330.53	324.29
Loan Amount Pre-Pay Per Month	225,000.00	386.00	378.91	371.84	364.82
Loan Amount Pre-Pay Per Month	250,000.00	428.89	421.01	413.16	405.36
Loan Amount Pre-Pay Per Month	275,000.00	471.78	463.11	454.48	445.90
Loan Amount Pre-Pay Per Month	300,000.00	514.67	505.21	495.79	486.43
Loan Amount Pre-Pay Per Month	325,000.00	557.56	547.31	537.11	526.97
Loan Amount Pre-Pay Per Month	350,000.00	600.44	589.41	578.43	567.50
Loan Amount Pre-Pay Per Month	375,000.00	643.33	631.51	619.74	608.04
Loan Amount Pre-Pay Per Month	400,000.00	686.22	673.61	661.06	648.58
Loan Amount Pre-Pay Per Month	450,000.00	772.00	757.81	743.69	729.65

12%   When Your Mortgage Will Be Paid
TABLE B

A 15 Year Mortgage Will Be Paid In 12½ Years If You Pre-Pay The Following:

		INTEREST RATES			
		12%	12¼%	12½%	12¾%
Loan Amount Pre-Pay Per Month	$ 1,000.00	.90	.89	.88	.87
Loan Amount Pre-Pay Per Month	2,000.00	1.80	1.78	1.76	1.75
Loan Amount Pre-Pay Per Month	3,000.00	2.69	2.67	2.65	2.62
Loan Amount Pre-Pay Per Month	4,000.00	3.59	3.56	3.53	3.50
Loan Amount Pre-Pay Per Month	5,000.00	4.49	4.45	4.41	4.37
Loan Amount Pre-Pay Per Month	10,000.00	8.98	8.90	8.82	8.74
Loan Amount Pre-Pay Per Month	15,000.00	13.47	13.35	13.24	13.12
Loan Amount Pre-Pay Per Month	20,000.00	17.96	17.81	17.65	17.49
Loan Amount Pre-Pay Per Month	25,000.00	22.45	22.26	22.06	21.86
Loan Amount Pre-Pay Per Month	50,000.00	44.91	44.52	44.12	43.72
Loan Amount Pre-Pay Per Month	75,000.00	67.36	66.77	66.18	65.58
Loan Amount Pre-Pay Per Month	100,000.00	89.82	89.03	88.24	87.44
Loan Amount Pre-Pay Per Month	125,000.00	112.27	111.29	110.30	109.29
Loan Amount Pre-Pay Per Month	150,000.00	134.73	133.55	132.36	131.15
Loan Amount Pre-Pay Per Month	175,000.00	157.18	155.81	154.42	153.01
Loan Amount Pre-Pay Per Month	200,000.00	179.64	178.06	176.47	174.87
Loan Amount Pre-Pay Per Month	225,000.00	202.09	200.32	198.53	196.73
Loan Amount Pre-Pay Per Month	250,000.00	224.55	222.58	220.59	218.59
Loan Amount Pre-Pay Per Month	275,000.00	247.00	244.84	242.65	240.45
Loan Amount Pre-Pay Per Month	300,000.00	269.46	267.10	264.71	262.31
Loan Amount Pre-Pay Per Month	325,000.00	291.91	289.35	286.77	284.16
Loan Amount Pre-Pay Per Month	350,000.00	314.37	311.61	308.83	306.02
Loan Amount Pre-Pay Per Month	375,000.00	336.82	333.87	330.89	327.88
Loan Amount Pre-Pay Per Month	400,000.00	359.28	356.13	352.95	349.74
Loan Amount Pre-Pay Per Month	450,000.00	404.19	400.65	397.07	393.46

12%

When Your Mortgage Will Be Paid
TABLE B

A 15 Year Mortgage Will Be Paid In 10 Years If You Pre-Pay The Following:

Loan Amount / Pre-Pay Per Month	12%	12¼%	12½%	12¾%
$ 1,000.00	2.35	2.33	2.31	2.30
2,000.00	4.69	4.66	4.62	4.59
3,000.00	7.04	6.99	6.94	6.89
4,000.00	9.38	9.32	9.25	9.18
5,000.00	11.73	11.64	11.56	11.48
10,000.00	23.45	23.29	23.12	22.96
15,000.00	35.18	34.93	34.69	34.43
20,000.00	46.91	46.58	46.25	45.91
25,000.00	58.64	58.22	57.81	57.39
50,000.00	117.27	116.45	115.62	114.78
75,000.00	175.91	174.67	173.43	172.17
100,000.00	234.54	232.90	231.24	229.56
125,000.00	293.18	291.12	289.05	286.95
150,000.00	351.81	349.35	346.86	344.34
175,000.00	410.45	407.57	404.67	401.73
200,000.00	469.08	465.80	462.48	459.12
225,000.00	527.72	524.02	520.29	516.51
250,000.00	586.35	582.25	578.10	573.90
275,000.00	644.99	640.47	635.91	631.29
300,000.00	703.62	698.70	693.72	688.68
325,000.00	762.26	756.92	751.53	746.07
350,000.00	820.89	815.15	809.34	803.46
375,000.00	879.53	873.37	867.15	860.85
400,000.00	938.17	931.60	924.96	918.24
450,000.00	1,055.44	1,048.05	1,040.58	1,033.02

12%

When Your Mortgage Will Be Paid
TABLE B

A 15 Year Mortgage Will Be Paid In 7½ Years If You Pre-Pay The Following:

		INTEREST RATES			
		12%	**12¼%**	**12½%**	**12¾%**
Loan Amount	**$ 1,000.00**				
Pre-Pay Per Month		4.90	4.88	4.85	4.82
Loan Amount	**2,000.00**				
Pre-Pay Per Month		9.80	9.75	9.70	9.65
Loan Amount	**3,000.00**				
Pre-Pay Per Month		14.70	14.63	14.55	14.47
Loan Amount	**4,000.00**				
Pre-Pay Per Month		19.61	19.50	19.40	19.30
Loan Amount	**5,000.00**				
Pre-Pay Per Month		24.51	24.38	24.25	24.12
Loan Amount	**10,000.00**				
Pre-Pay Per Month		49.01	48.76	48.50	48.24
Loan Amount	**15,000.00**				
Pre-Pay Per Month		73.52	73.14	72.75	72.36
Loan Amount	**20,000.00**				
Pre-Pay Per Month		98.03	97.52	97.00	96.48
Loan Amount	**25,000.00**				
Pre-Pay Per Month		122.53	121.90	121.25	120.60
Loan Amount	**50,000.00**				
Pre-Pay Per Month		245.07	243.80	242.50	241.20
Loan Amount	**75,000.00**				
Pre-Pay Per Month		367.60	365.69	363.76	361.80
Loan Amount	**100,000.00**				
Pre-Pay Per Month		490.14	487.59	485.01	482.39
Loan Amount	**125,000.00**				
Pre-Pay Per Month		612.67	609.49	606.26	602.99
Loan Amount	**150,000.00**				
Pre-Pay Per Month		735.21	731.39	727.51	723.59
Loan Amount	**175,000.00**				
Pre-Pay Per Month		857.74	853.28	848.77	844.19
Loan Amount	**200,000.00**				
Pre-Pay Per Month		980.28	975.18	970.02	964.79
Loan Amount	**225,000.00**				
Pre-Pay Per Month		1,102.81	1,097.08	1,091.27	1,085.39
Loan Amount	**250,000.00**				
Pre-Pay Per Month		1,225.35	1,218.98	1,212.52	1,205.99
Loan Amount	**275,000.00**				
Pre-Pay Per Month		1,347.88	1,340.87	1,333.77	1,326.59
Loan Amount	**300,000.00**				
Pre-Pay Per Month		1,470.41	1,462.77	1,455.03	1,447.18
Loan Amount	**325,000.00**				
Pre-Pay Per Month		1,592.95	1,584.67	1,576.28	1,567.78
Loan Amount	**350,000.00**				
Pre-Pay Per Month		1,715.48	1,706.57	1,697.53	1,688.38
Loan Amount	**375,000.00**				
Pre-Pay Per Month		1,838.02	1,828.46	1,818.78	1,808.98
Loan Amount	**400,000.00**				
Pre-Pay Per Month		1,960.55	1,950.36	1,940.04	1,929.58
Loan Amount	**450,000.00**				
Pre-Pay Per Month		2,205.62	2,194.16	2,182.54	2,170.78

13% When Your Mortgage Will Be Paid
TABLE B

A 30 Year Mortgage Will Be Paid In 25 Years If You Pre-Pay The Following:

		INTEREST RATES			
		13%	13¼%	13½%	13¾%
Loan Amount Pre-Pay Per Month	$ 1,000.00	.22	.21	.20	.20
Loan Amount Pre-Pay Per Month	2,000.00	.43	.42	.40	.39
Loan Amount Pre-Pay Per Month	3,000.00	.65	.63	.61	.59
Loan Amount Pre-Pay Per Month	4,000.00	.87	.84	.81	.78
Loan Amount Pre-Pay Per Month	5,000.00	1.08	1.05	1.01	.98
Loan Amount Pre-Pay Per Month	10,000.00	2.16	2.09	2.02	1.96
Loan Amount Pre-Pay Per Month	15,000.00	3.25	3.14	3.03	2.93
Loan Amount Pre-Pay Per Month	20,000.00	4.33	4.19	4.05	3.91
Loan Amount Pre-Pay Per Month	25,000.00	5.41	5.23	5.06	4.89
Loan Amount Pre-Pay Per Month	50,000.00	10.82	10.46	10.12	9.78
Loan Amount Pre-Pay Per Month	75,000.00	16.23	15.70	15.17	14.67
Loan Amount Pre-Pay Per Month	100,000.00	21.64	20.93	20.23	19.55
Loan Amount Pre-Pay Per Month	125,000.00	27.04	26.16	25.29	24.44
Loan Amount Pre-Pay Per Month	150,000.00	32.45	31.39	30.35	29.33
Loan Amount Pre-Pay Per Month	175,000.00	37.86	36.62	35.41	34.22
Loan Amount Pre-Pay Per Month	200,000.00	43.27	41.85	40.47	39.11
Loan Amount Pre-Pay Per Month	225,000.00	48.68	47.09	45.52	44.00
Loan Amount Pre-Pay Per Month	250,000.00	54.09	52.32	50.58	48.88
Loan Amount Pre-Pay Per Month	275,000.00	59.50	57.55	55.64	53.77
Loan Amount Pre-Pay Per Month	300,000.00	64.91	62.78	60.70	58.66
Loan Amount Pre-Pay Per Month	325,000.00	70.32	68.01	65.76	63.55
Loan Amount Pre-Pay Per Month	350,000.00	75.73	73.24	70.81	68.44
Loan Amount Pre-Pay Per Month	375,000.00	81.13	78.48	75.87	73.33
Loan Amount Pre-Pay Per Month	400,000.00	86.54	83.71	80.93	78.21
Loan Amount Pre-Pay Per Month	450,000.00	97.36	94.17	91.05	87.99

13%   When Your Mortgage Will Be Paid
TABLE B

A 30 Year Mortgage Will Be Paid In 20 Years If You Pre-Pay The Following:

			INTEREST RATES		
		13%	13¼%	13½%	13¾%
Loan Amount Pre-Pay Per Month	$ 1,000.00	.65	.64	.62	.60
Loan Amount Pre-Pay Per Month	2,000.00	1.31	1.27	1.24	1.21
Loan Amount Pre-Pay Per Month	3,000.00	1.96	1.91	1.86	1.81
Loan Amount Pre-Pay Per Month	4,000.00	2.62	2.55	2.48	2.41
Loan Amount Pre-Pay Per Month	5,000.00	3.27	3.18	3.10	3.01
Loan Amount Pre-Pay Per Month	10,000.00	6.54	6.37	6.20	6.03
Loan Amount Pre-Pay Per Month	15,000.00	9.81	9.55	9.29	9.04
Loan Amount Pre-Pay Per Month	20,000.00	13.08	12.73	12.39	12.06
Loan Amount Pre-Pay Per Month	25,000.00	16.34	15.91	15.49	15.07
Loan Amount Pre-Pay Per Month	50,000.00	32.69	31.83	30.98	30.15
Loan Amount Pre-Pay Per Month	75,000.00	49.03	47.74	46.47	45.22
Loan Amount Pre-Pay Per Month	100,000.00	65.38	63.66	61.96	60.29
Loan Amount Pre-Pay Per Month	125,000.00	81.72	79.57	77.45	75.37
Loan Amount Pre-Pay Per Month	150,000.00	98.06	95.49	92.94	90.44
Loan Amount Pre-Pay Per Month	175,000.00	114.41	111.40	108.43	105.51
Loan Amount Pre-Pay Per Month	200,000.00	130.75	127.31	123.93	120.59
Loan Amount Pre-Pay Per Month	225,000.00	147.10	143.23	139.42	135.66
Loan Amount Pre-Pay Per Month	250,000.00	163.44	159.14	154.91	150.73
Loan Amount Pre-Pay Per Month	275,000.00	179.78	175.06	170.40	165.81
Loan Amount Pre-Pay Per Month	300,000.00	196.13	190.97	185.89	180.88
Loan Amount Pre-Pay Per Month	325,000.00	212.47	206.89	201.38	195.95
Loan Amount Pre-Pay Per Month	350,000.00	228.82	222.80	216.87	211.02
Loan Amount Pre-Pay Per Month	375,000.00	245.16	238.71	232.36	226.10
Loan Amount Pre-Pay Per Month	400,000.00	261.50	254.63	247.85	241.17
Loan Amount Pre-Pay Per Month	450,000.00	294.19	286.46	278.83	271.32

13% When Your Mortgage Will Be Paid
TABLE B

A 30 Year Mortgage Will Be Paid In 15 Years If You Pre-Pay The Following:

		INTEREST RATES		
		13%	**13¼%**	**13½%**	**13¾%**
Loan Amount $ 1,000.00 Pre-Pay Per Month	1.59	1.56	1.53	1.50
Loan Amount 2,000.00 Pre-Pay Per Month	3.18	3.12	3.06	3.00
Loan Amount 3,000.00 Pre-Pay Per Month	4.77	4.68	4.59	4.50
Loan Amount 4,000.00 Pre-Pay Per Month	6.36	6.24	6.12	5.99
Loan Amount 5,000.00 Pre-Pay Per Month	7.95	7.80	7.65	7.49
Loan Amount 10,000.00 Pre-Pay Per Month	15.90	15.60	15.29	14.99
Loan Amount 15,000.00 Pre-Pay Per Month	23.86	23.39	22.94	22.48
Loan Amount 20,000.00 Pre-Pay Per Month	31.81	31.19	30.58	29.97
Loan Amount 25,000.00 Pre-Pay Per Month	39.76	38.99	38.23	37.47
Loan Amount 50,000.00 Pre-Pay Per Month	79.52	77.98	76.45	74.94
Loan Amount 75,000.00 Pre-Pay Per Month	119.28	116.97	114.68	112.41
Loan Amount 100,000.00 Pre-Pay Per Month	159.04	155.96	152.91	149.87
Loan Amount 125,000.00 Pre-Pay Per Month	198.80	194.95	191.13	187.34
Loan Amount 150,000.00 Pre-Pay Per Month	238.56	233.94	229.36	224.81
Loan Amount 175,000.00 Pre-Pay Per Month	278.32	272.94	267.59	262.28
Loan Amount 200,000.00 Pre-Pay Per Month	318.09	311.93	305.81	299.75
Loan Amount 225,000.00 Pre-Pay Per Month	357.85	350.92	344.04	337.22
Loan Amount 250,000.00 Pre-Pay Per Month	397.61	389.91	382.27	374.69
Loan Amount 275,000.00 Pre-Pay Per Month	437.37	428.90	420.49	412.16
Loan Amount 300,000.00 Pre-Pay Per Month	477.13	467.89	458.72	449.62
Loan Amount 325,000.00 Pre-Pay Per Month	516.89	506.88	496.95	487.09
Loan Amount 350,000.00 Pre-Pay Per Month	556.65	545.87	535.17	524.56
Loan Amount 375,000.00 Pre-Pay Per Month	596.41	584.86	573.40	562.03
Loan Amount 400,000.00 Pre-Pay Per Month	636.17	623.85	611.63	599.50
Loan Amount 450,000.00 Pre-Pay Per Month	715.69	701.83	688.08	674.44

13% When Your Mortgage Will Be Paid
TABLE B

A 15 Year Mortgage Will Be Paid In 12½ Years If You Pre-Pay The Following:

		INTEREST RATES			
		13%	13¼%	13½%	13¾%
Loan Amount Pre-Pay Per Month	$ 1,000.00	.87	.86	.85	.84
Loan Amount Pre-Pay Per Month	2,000.00	1.73	1.72	1.70	1.68
Loan Amount Pre-Pay Per Month	3,000.00	2.60	2.57	2.55	2.52
Loan Amount Pre-Pay Per Month	4,000.00	3.47	3.43	3.40	3.37
Loan Amount Pre-Pay Per Month	5,000.00	4.33	4.29	4.25	4.21
Loan Amount Pre-Pay Per Month	10,000.00	8.66	8.58	8.50	8.42
Loan Amount Pre-Pay Per Month	15,000.00	12.99	12.87	12.75	12.62
Loan Amount Pre-Pay Per Month	20,000.00	17.33	17.16	17.00	16.83
Loan Amount Pre-Pay Per Month	25,000.00	21.66	21.45	21.25	21.04
Loan Amount Pre-Pay Per Month	50,000.00	43.31	42.91	42.50	42.08
Loan Amount Pre-Pay Per Month	75,000.00	64.97	64.36	63.74	63.12
Loan Amount Pre-Pay Per Month	100,000.00	86.63	85.81	84.99	84.16
Loan Amount Pre-Pay Per Month	125,000.00	108.28	107.26	106.24	105.20
Loan Amount Pre-Pay Per Month	150,000.00	129.94	128.72	127.49	126.25
Loan Amount Pre-Pay Per Month	175,000.00	151.60	150.17	148.73	147.29
Loan Amount Pre-Pay Per Month	200,000.00	173.25	171.62	169.98	168.33
Loan Amount Pre-Pay Per Month	225,000.00	194.91	193.08	191.23	189.37
Loan Amount Pre-Pay Per Month	250,000.00	216.57	214.53	212.48	210.41
Loan Amount Pre-Pay Per Month	275,000.00	238.22	235.98	233.72	231.45
Loan Amount Pre-Pay Per Month	300,000.00	259.88	257.43	254.97	252.49
Loan Amount Pre-Pay Per Month	325,000.00	281.54	278.89	276.22	273.53
Loan Amount Pre-Pay Per Month	350,000.00	303.19	300.34	297.47	294.57
Loan Amount Pre-Pay Per Month	375,000.00	324.85	321.79	318.71	315.61
Loan Amount Pre-Pay Per Month	400,000.00	346.51	343.24	339.96	336.65
Loan Amount Pre-Pay Per Month	450,000.00	389.82	386.15	382.46	378.74

13%

When Your Mortgage Will Be Paid
TABLE B

A 15 Year Mortgage Will Be Paid In 10 Years If You Pre-Pay The Following:

		INTEREST RATES			
		13%	13¼%	13½%	13¾%
Loan Amount **$ 1,000.00** Pre-Pay Per Month		2.28	2.26	2.24	2.23
Loan Amount **2,000.00** Pre-Pay Per Month		4.56	4.52	4.49	4.45
Loan Amount **3,000.00** Pre-Pay Per Month		6.84	6.78	6.73	6.68
Loan Amount **4,000.00** Pre-Pay Per Month		9.11	9.05	8.98	8.91
Loan Amount **5,000.00** Pre-Pay Per Month		11.39	11.31	11.22	11.13
Loan Amount **10,000.00** Pre-Pay Per Month		22.79	22.62	22.44	22.27
Loan Amount **15,000.00** Pre-Pay Per Month		34.18	33.92	33.66	33.40
Loan Amount **20,000.00** Pre-Pay Per Month		45.57	45.23	44.88	44.54
Loan Amount **25,000.00** Pre-Pay Per Month		56.97	56.54	56.11	55.67
Loan Amount **50,000.00** Pre-Pay Per Month		113.93	113.08	112.21	111.34
Loan Amount **75,000.00** Pre-Pay Per Month		170.90	169.61	168.32	167.01
Loan Amount **100,000.00** Pre-Pay Per Month		227.87	226.15	224.42	222.68
Loan Amount **125,000.00** Pre-Pay Per Month		284.83	282.69	280.53	278.35
Loan Amount **150,000.00** Pre-Pay Per Month		341.80	339.23	336.64	334.02
Loan Amount **175,000.00** Pre-Pay Per Month		398.76	395.77	392.74	389.69
Loan Amount **200,000.00** Pre-Pay Per Month		455.73	452.31	448.85	445.36
Loan Amount **225,000.00** Pre-Pay Per Month		512.70	508.84	504.95	501.03
Loan Amount **250,000.00** Pre-Pay Per Month		569.66	565.38	561.06	556.70
Loan Amount **275,000.00** Pre-Pay Per Month		626.63	621.92	617.17	612.37
Loan Amount **300,000.00** Pre-Pay Per Month		683.60	678.46	673.27	668.04
Loan Amount **325,000.00** Pre-Pay Per Month		740.56	735.00	729.38	723.71
Loan Amount **350,000.00** Pre-Pay Per Month		797.53	791.53	785.49	779.38
Loan Amount **375,000.00** Pre-Pay Per Month		854.49	848.07	841.59	835.05
Loan Amount **400,000.00** Pre-Pay Per Month		911.46	904.61	897.70	890.72
Loan Amount **450,000.00** Pre-Pay Per Month		1,025.39	1,017.69	1,009.91	1,002.06

13%   When Your Mortgage Will Be Paid
TABLE B

A 15 Year Mortgage Will Be Paid In 7½ Years If You Pre-Pay The Following:

		INTEREST RATES			
		13%	13¼%	13½%	13¾%
Loan Amount Pre-Pay Per Month	$ 1,000.00	4.80	4.77	4.74	4.72
Loan Amount Pre-Pay Per Month	2,000.00	9.59	9.54	9.49	9.43
Loan Amount Pre-Pay Per Month	3,000.00	14.39	14.31	14.23	14.15
Loan Amount Pre-Pay Per Month	4,000.00	19.19	19.08	18.97	18.87
Loan Amount Pre-Pay Per Month	5,000.00	23.99	23.85	23.72	23.58
Loan Amount Pre-Pay Per Month	10,000.00	47.97	47.71	47.44	47.16
Loan Amount Pre-Pay Per Month	15,000.00	71.96	71.56	71.15	70.74
Loan Amount Pre-Pay Per Month	20,000.00	95.95	95.41	94.87	94.33
Loan Amount Pre-Pay Per Month	25,000.00	119.94	119.27	118.59	117.91
Loan Amount Pre-Pay Per Month	50,000.00	239.87	238.54	237.18	235.82
Loan Amount Pre-Pay Per Month	75,000.00	359.81	357.80	355.77	353.72
Loan Amount Pre-Pay Per Month	100,000.00	479.75	477.07	474.37	471.63
Loan Amount Pre-Pay Per Month	125,000.00	599.69	596.34	592.96	589.54
Loan Amount Pre-Pay Per Month	150,000.00	719.62	715.61	711.55	707.45
Loan Amount Pre-Pay Per Month	175,000.00	839.56	834.88	830.14	825.35
Loan Amount Pre-Pay Per Month	200,000.00	959.50	954.14	948.73	943.26
Loan Amount Pre-Pay Per Month	225,000.00	1,079.43	1,073.41	1,067.32	1,061.17
Loan Amount Pre-Pay Per Month	250,000.00	1,199.37	1,192.68	1,185.91	1,179.08
Loan Amount Pre-Pay Per Month	275,000.00	1,319.31	1,311.95	1,304.51	1,296.98
Loan Amount Pre-Pay Per Month	300,000.00	1,439.25	1,431.22	1,423.10	1,414.89
Loan Amount Pre-Pay Per Month	325,000.00	1,559.18	1,550.48	1,541.69	1,532.80
Loan Amount Pre-Pay Per Month	350,000.00	1,679.12	1,669.75	1,660.28	1,650.71
Loan Amount Pre-Pay Per Month	375,000.00	1,799.06	1,789.02	1,778.87	1,768.61
Loan Amount Pre-Pay Per Month	400,000.00	1,918.99	1,908.29	1,897.46	1,886.52
Loan Amount Pre-Pay Per Month	450,000.00	2,158.87	2,146.82	2,134.64	2,122.34

14%

When Your Mortgage Will Be Paid
TABLE B

A 30 Year Mortgage Will Be Paid In 25 Years If You Pre-Pay The Following:

		INTEREST RATES			
		14%	14¼%	14½%	14¾%
Loan Amount **Pre-Pay Per Month**	$ 1,000.00	.19	.18	.18	.17
Loan Amount **Pre-Pay Per Month**	2,000.00	.38	.36	.35	.34
Loan Amount **Pre-Pay Per Month**	3,000.00	.57	.55	.53	.51
Loan Amount **Pre-Pay Per Month**	4,000.00	.76	.73	.70	.68
Loan Amount **Pre-Pay Per Month**	5,000.00	.94	.91	.88	.85
Loan Amount **Pre-Pay Per Month**	10,000.00	1.89	1.82	1.76	1.70
Loan Amount **Pre-Pay Per Month**	15,000.00	2.83	2.74	2.64	2.55
Loan Amount **Pre-Pay Per Month**	20,000.00	3.78	3.65	3.52	3.40
Loan Amount **Pre-Pay Per Month**	25,000.00	4.72	4.56	4.40	4.25
Loan Amount **Pre-Pay Per Month**	50,000.00	9.44	9.12	8.80	8.49
Loan Amount **Pre-Pay Per Month**	75,000.00	14.17	13.68	13.21	12.74
Loan Amount **Pre-Pay Per Month**	100,000.00	18.89	18.24	17.61	16.99
Loan Amount **Pre-Pay Per Month**	125,000.00	23.61	22.80	22.01	21.24
Loan Amount **Pre-Pay Per Month**	150,000.00	28.33	27.36	26.41	25.48
Loan Amount **Pre-Pay Per Month**	175,000.00	33.06	31.92	30.81	29.73
Loan Amount **Pre-Pay Per Month**	200,000.00	37.78	36.48	35.21	33.98
Loan Amount **Pre-Pay Per Month**	225,000.00	42.50	41.04	39.62	38.23
Loan Amount **Pre-Pay Per Month**	250,000.00	47.22	45.60	44.02	42.47
Loan Amount **Pre-Pay Per Month**	275,000.00	51.95	50.16	48.42	46.72
Loan Amount **Pre-Pay Per Month**	300,000.00	56.67	54.72	52.82	50.97
Loan Amount **Pre-Pay Per Month**	325,000.00	61.39	59.28	57.22	55.21
Loan Amount **Pre-Pay Per Month**	350,000.00	66.11	63.84	61.62	59.46
Loan Amount **Pre-Pay Per Month**	375,000.00	70.83	68.40	66.03	63.71
Loan Amount **Pre-Pay Per Month**	400,000.00	75.56	72.96	70.43	67.96
Loan Amount **Pre-Pay Per Month**	450,000.00	85.00	82.08	79.23	76.45

14%

When Your Mortgage Will Be Paid
TABLE B

A 30 Year Mortgage Will Be Paid In 20 Years If You Pre-Pay The Following:

Loan Amount / Pre-Pay Per Month	INTEREST RATES			
	14%	14¼%	14½%	14¾%
Loan Amount $ 1,000.00 Pre-Pay Per Month	.59	.57	.55	.54
Loan Amount 2,000.00 Pre-Pay Per Month	1.17	1.14	1.11	1.08
Loan Amount 3,000.00 Pre-Pay Per Month	1.76	1.71	1.66	1.62
Loan Amount 4,000.00 Pre-Pay Per Month	2.35	2.28	2.22	2.16
Loan Amount 5,000.00 Pre-Pay Per Month	2.93	2.85	2.77	2.69
Loan Amount 10,000.00 Pre-Pay Per Month	5.86	5.70	5.54	5.39
Loan Amount 15,000.00 Pre-Pay Per Month	8.80	8.55	8.32	8.08
Loan Amount 20,000.00 Pre-Pay Per Month	11.73	11.41	11.09	10.78
Loan Amount 25,000.00 Pre-Pay Per Month	14.66	14.26	13.86	13.47
Loan Amount 50,000.00 Pre-Pay Per Month	29.32	28.52	27.72	26.94
Loan Amount 75,000.00 Pre-Pay Per Month	43.99	42.77	41.58	40.41
Loan Amount 100,000.00 Pre-Pay Per Month	58.65	57.03	55.44	53.88
Loan Amount 125,000.00 Pre-Pay Per Month	73.31	71.29	69.30	67.35
Loan Amount 150,000.00 Pre-Pay Per Month	87.97	85.55	83.16	80.82
Loan Amount 175,000.00 Pre-Pay Per Month	102.64	99.81	97.02	94.29
Loan Amount 200,000.00 Pre-Pay Per Month	117.30	114.06	110.88	107.76
Loan Amount 225,000.00 Pre-Pay Per Month	131.96	128.32	124.74	121.23
Loan Amount 250,000.00 Pre-Pay Per Month	146.62	142.58	138.60	134.70
Loan Amount 275,000.00 Pre-Pay Per Month	161.28	156.84	152.47	148.17
Loan Amount 300,000.00 Pre-Pay Per Month	175.95	171.10	166.33	161.64
Loan Amount 325,000.00 Pre-Pay Per Month	190.61	185.35	180.19	175.11
Loan Amount 350,000.00 Pre-Pay Per Month	205.27	199.61	194.05	188.58
Loan Amount 375,000.00 Pre-Pay Per Month	219.93	213.87	207.91	202.05
Loan Amount 400,000.00 Pre-Pay Per Month	234.60	228.13	221.77	215.52
Loan Amount 450,000.00 Pre-Pay Per Month	263.92	256.64	249.49	242.46

14% When Your Mortgage Will Be Paid
TABLE B

A 30 Year Mortgage Will Be Paid In 15 Years If You Pre-Pay The Following:

		INTEREST RATES			
		14%	**14¼%**	**14½%**	**14¾%**
Loan Amount Pre-Pay Per Month	$ 1,000.00	.19	.18	.18	.17
Loan Amount Pre-Pay Per Month	2,000.00	.38	.36	.35	.34
Loan Amount Pre-Pay Per Month	3,000.00	.57	.55	.53	.51
Loan Amount Pre-Pay Per Month	4,000.00	.76	.73	.70	.68
Loan Amount Pre-Pay Per Month	5,000.00	.94	.91	.88	.85
Loan Amount Pre-Pay Per Month	10,000.00	1.89	1.82	1.76	1.70
Loan Amount Pre-Pay Per Month	15,000.00	2.83	2.74	2.64	2.55
Loan Amount Pre-Pay Per Month	20,000.00	3.78	3.65	3.52	3.40
Loan Amount Pre-Pay Per Month	25,000.00	4.72	4.56	4.40	4.25
Loan Amount Pre-Pay Per Month	50,000.00	9.44	9.12	8.80	8.49
Loan Amount Pre-Pay Per Month	75,000.00	14.17	13.68	13.21	12.74
Loan Amount Pre-Pay Per Month	100,000.00	18.89	18.24	17.61	16.99
Loan Amount Pre-Pay Per Month	125,000.00	23.61	22.80	22.01	21.24
Loan Amount Pre-Pay Per Month	150,000.00	28.33	27.36	26.41	25.48
Loan Amount Pre-Pay Per Month	175,000.00	33.06	31.92	30.81	29.73
Loan Amount Pre-Pay Per Month	200,000.00	37.78	36.48	35.21	33.98
Loan Amount Pre-Pay Per Month	225,000.00	42.50	41.04	39.62	38.23
Loan Amount Pre-Pay Per Month	250,000.00	47.22	45.60	44.02	42.47
Loan Amount Pre-Pay Per Month	275,000.00	51.95	50.16	48.42	46.72
Loan Amount Pre-Pay Per Month	300,000.00	56.67	54.72	52.82	50.97
Loan Amount Pre-Pay Per Month	325,000.00	61.39	59.28	57.22	55.21
Loan Amount Pre-Pay Per Month	350,000.00	66.11	63.84	61.62	59.46
Loan Amount Pre-Pay Per Month	375,000.00	70.83	68.40	66.03	63.71
Loan Amount Pre-Pay Per Month	400,000.00	75.56	72.96	70.43	67.96
Loan Amount Pre-Pay Per Month	450,000.00	85.00	82.08	79.23	76.45

135

When Your Mortgage Will Be Paid
TABLE B

A 15 Year Mortgage Will Be Paid In 12½ Years If You Pre-Pay The Following:

		INTEREST RATES			
		14%	14¼%	14½%	14¾%
Loan Amount Pre-Pay Per Month	$ 1,000.00	.83	.82	.82	.81
Loan Amount Pre-Pay Per Month	2,000.00	1.67	1.65	1.63	1.62
Loan Amount Pre-Pay Per Month	3,000.00	2.50	2.47	2.45	2.42
Loan Amount Pre-Pay Per Month	4,000.00	3.33	3.30	3.27	3.23
Loan Amount Pre-Pay Per Month	5,000.00	4.17	4.12	4.08	4.04
Loan Amount Pre-Pay Per Month	10,000.00	8.33	8.25	8.17	8.08
Loan Amount Pre-Pay Per Month	15,000.00	12.50	12.37	12.25	12.12
Loan Amount Pre-Pay Per Month	20,000.00	16.67	16.50	16.33	16.16
Loan Amount Pre-Pay Per Month	25,000.00	20.83	20.62	20.41	20.20
Loan Amount Pre-Pay Per Month	50,000.00	41.67	41.25	40.83	40.40
Loan Amount Pre-Pay Per Month	75,000.00	62.50	61.87	61.24	60.61
Loan Amount Pre-Pay Per Month	100,000.00	83.33	82.50	81.65	80.81
Loan Amount Pre-Pay Per Month	125,000.00	104.16	103.12	102.07	101.01
Loan Amount Pre-Pay Per Month	150,000.00	125.00	123.74	122.48	121.21
Loan Amount Pre-Pay Per Month	175,000.00	145.83	144.37	142.90	141.42
Loan Amount Pre-Pay Per Month	200,000.00	166.66	164.99	163.31	161.62
Loan Amount Pre-Pay Per Month	225,000.00	187.50	185.61	183.72	181.82
Loan Amount Pre-Pay Per Month	250,000.00	208.33	206.24	204.14	202.02
Loan Amount Pre-Pay Per Month	275,000.00	229.16	226.86	224.55	222.23
Loan Amount Pre-Pay Per Month	300,000.00	249.99	247.49	244.96	242.43
Loan Amount Pre-Pay Per Month	325,000.00	270.83	268.11	265.38	262.63
Loan Amount Pre-Pay Per Month	350,000.00	291.66	288.73	285.79	282.83
Loan Amount Pre-Pay Per Month	375,000.00	312.49	309.36	306.20	303.04
Loan Amount Pre-Pay Per Month	400,000.00	333.33	329.98	326.62	323.24
Loan Amount Pre-Pay Per Month	450,000.00	374.99	371.23	367.44	363.64

14% When Your Mortgage Will Be Paid
TABLE B

A 15 Year Mortgage Will Be Paid In 10 Years If You Pre-Pay The Following:

		INTEREST RATES			
		14%	14¼%	14½%	14¾%
Loan Amount $ 1,000.00 Pre-Pay Per Month		2.21	2.19	2.17	2.16
Loan Amount 2,000.00 Pre-Pay Per Month		4.42	4.38	4.35	4.31
Loan Amount 3,000.00 Pre-Pay Per Month		6.63	6.57	6.52	6.47
Loan Amount 4,000.00 Pre-Pay Per Month		8.84	8.77	8.69	8.62
Loan Amount 5,000.00 Pre-Pay Per Month		11.05	10.96	10.87	10.78
Loan Amount 10,000.00 Pre-Pay Per Month		22.09	21.92	21.74	21.56
Loan Amount 15,000.00 Pre-Pay Per Month		33.14	32.87	32.61	32.34
Loan Amount 20,000.00 Pre-Pay Per Month		44.18	43.83	43.47	43.11
Loan Amount 25,000.00 Pre-Pay Per Month		55.23	54.79	54.34	53.89
Loan Amount 50,000.00 Pre-Pay Per Month		110.46	109.58	108.68	107.79
Loan Amount 75,000.00 Pre-Pay Per Month		165.69	164.36	163.03	161.68
Loan Amount 100,000.00 Pre-Pay Per Month		220.92	219.15	217.37	215.57
Loan Amount 125,000.00 Pre-Pay Per Month		276.15	273.94	271.71	269.46
Loan Amount 150,000.00 Pre-Pay Per Month		331.38	328.73	326.05	323.36
Loan Amount 175,000.00 Pre-Pay Per Month		386.62	383.52	380.39	377.25
Loan Amount 200,000.00 Pre-Pay Per Month		441.85	438.30	434.73	431.14
Loan Amount 225,000.00 Pre-Pay Per Month		497.08	493.09	489.08	485.03
Loan Amount 250,000.00 Pre-Pay Per Month		552.31	547.88	543.42	538.93
Loan Amount 275,000.00 Pre-Pay Per Month		607.54	602.67	597.76	592.82
Loan Amount 300,000.00 Pre-Pay Per Month		662.77	657.45	652.10	646.71
Loan Amount 325,000.00 Pre-Pay Per Month		718.00	712.24	706.44	700.60
Loan Amount 350,000.00 Pre-Pay Per Month		773.23	767.03	760.78	754.50
Loan Amount 375,000.00 Pre-Pay Per Month		828.46	821.82	815.13	808.39
Loan Amount 400,000.00 Pre-Pay Per Month		883.69	876.61	869.47	862.28
Loan Amount 450,000.00 Pre-Pay Per Month		994.15	986.18	978.15	970.07

14%

When Your Mortgage Will Be Paid
TABLE B

A 15 Year Mortgage Will Be Paid In 7½ Years If You Pre-Pay The Following:

		INTEREST RATES			
		14%	14¼%	14½%	14¾%
Loan Amount Pre-Pay Per Month	$ 1,000.00	4.69	4.66	4.63	4.60
Loan Amount Pre-Pay Per Month	2,000.00	9.38	9.32	9.27	9.21
Loan Amount Pre-Pay Per Month	3,000.00	14.07	13.98	13.90	13.81
Loan Amount Pre-Pay Per Month	4,000.00	18.75	18.64	18.53	18.42
Loan Amount Pre-Pay Per Month	5,000.00	23.44	23.30	23.16	23.02
Loan Amount Pre-Pay Per Month	10,000.00	46.89	46.61	46.33	46.04
Loan Amount Pre-Pay Per Month	15,000.00	70.33	69.91	69.49	69.06
Loan Amount Pre-Pay Per Month	20,000.00	93.77	93.22	92.65	92.08
Loan Amount Pre-Pay Per Month	25,000.00	117.22	116.52	115.82	115.11
Loan Amount Pre-Pay Per Month	50,000.00	234.43	233.04	231.63	230.21
Loan Amount Pre-Pay Per Month	75,000.00	351.65	349.56	347.45	345.32
Loan Amount Pre-Pay Per Month	100,000.00	468.87	466.08	463.26	460.42
Loan Amount Pre-Pay Per Month	125,000.00	586.08	582.60	579.08	575.53
Loan Amount Pre-Pay Per Month	150,000.00	703.30	699.12	694.89	690.63
Loan Amount Pre-Pay Per Month	175,000.00	820.52	815.64	810.71	805.74
Loan Amount Pre-Pay Per Month	200,000.00	937.74	932.16	926.53	920.85
Loan Amount Pre-Pay Per Month	225,000.00	1,054.95	1,048.68	1,042.34	1,035.95
Loan Amount Pre-Pay Per Month	250,000.00	1,172.17	1,165.20	1,158.16	1,151.06
Loan Amount Pre-Pay Per Month	275,000.00	1,289.39	1,281.71	1,273.97	1,266.16
Loan Amount Pre-Pay Per Month	300,000.00	1,406.60	1,398.23	1,389.79	1,381.27
Loan Amount Pre-Pay Per Month	325,000.00	1,523.82	1,514.75	1,505.60	1,496.37
Loan Amount Pre-Pay Per Month	350,000.00	1,641.04	1,631.27	1,621.42	1,611.48
Loan Amount Pre-Pay Per Month	375,000.00	1,758.25	1,747.79	1,737.24	1,726.59
Loan Amount Pre-Pay Per Month	400,000.00	1,875.47	1,864.31	1,853.05	1,841.69
Loan Amount Pre-Pay Per Month	450,000.00	2,109.90	2,097.35	2,084.68	2,071.90

15%

When Your Mortgage Will Be Paid
TABLE B

A 30 Year Mortgage Will Be Paid In 25 Years If You Pre-Pay The Following:

		INTEREST RATES			
		15%	**15¼%**	**15½%**	**15¾%**
Loan Amount Pre-Pay Per Month	$ 1,000.00	.16	.16	.15	.15
Loan Amount Pre-Pay Per Month	2,000.00	.33	.32	.30	.29
Loan Amount Pre-Pay Per Month	3,000.00	.49	.47	.46	.44
Loan Amount Pre-Pay Per Month	4,000.00	.66	.63	.61	.59
Loan Amount Pre-Pay Per Month	5,000.00	.82	.79	.76	.73
Loan Amount Pre-Pay Per Month	10,000.00	1.64	1.58	1.52	1.47
Loan Amount Pre-Pay Per Month	15,000.00	2.46	2.37	2.28	2.20
Loan Amount Pre-Pay Per Month	20,000.00	3.28	3.16	3.05	2.93
Loan Amount Pre-Pay Per Month	25,000.00	4.10	3.95	3.81	3.67
Loan Amount Pre-Pay Per Month	50,000.00	8.19	7.90	7.61	7.34
Loan Amount Pre-Pay Per Month	75,000.00	12.29	11.85	11.42	11.00
Loan Amount Pre-Pay Per Month	100,000.00	16.39	15.80	15.23	14.67
Loan Amount Pre-Pay Per Month	125,000.00	20.48	19.75	19.04	18.34
Loan Amount Pre-Pay Per Month	150,000.00	24.58	23.70	22.84	22.01
Loan Amount Pre-Pay Per Month	175,000.00	28.68	27.65	26.65	25.68
Loan Amount Pre-Pay Per Month	200,000.00	32.77	31.60	30.46	29.34
Loan Amount Pre-Pay Per Month	225,000.00	36.87	35.55	34.26	33.01
Loan Amount Pre-Pay Per Month	250,000.00	40.97	39.50	38.07	36.68
Loan Amount Pre-Pay Per Month	275,000.00	45.06	43.45	41.88	40.35
Loan Amount Pre-Pay Per Month	300,000.00	49.16	47.40	45.68	44.02
Loan Amount Pre-Pay Per Month	325,000.00	53.26	51.35	49.49	47.69
Loan Amount Pre-Pay Per Month	350,000.00	57.35	55.30	53.30	51.35
Loan Amount Pre-Pay Per Month	375,000.00	61.45	59.25	57.11	55.02
Loan Amount Pre-Pay Per Month	400,000.00	65.55	63.20	60.91	58.69
Loan Amount Pre-Pay Per Month	450,000.00	73.74	71.10	68.53	66.03

15% When Your Mortgage Will Be Paid
TABLE B

A 30 Year Mortgage Will Be Paid In 20 Years If You Pre-Pay The Following:

	INTEREST RATES			
	15%	15¼%	15½%	15¾%
Loan Amount $ 1,000.00 Pre-Pay Per Month	.52	.51	.49	.48
Loan Amount 2,000.00 Pre-Pay Per Month	1.05	1.02	.99	.96
Loan Amount 3,000.00 Pre-Pay Per Month	1.57	1.53	1.48	1.44
Loan Amount 4,000.00 Pre-Pay Per Month	2.09	2.03	1.97	1.92
Loan Amount 5,000.00 Pre-Pay Per Month	2.62	2.54	2.47	2.40
Loan Amount 10,000.00 Pre-Pay Per Month	5.23	5.08	4.94	4.79
Loan Amount 15,000.00 Pre-Pay Per Month	7.85	7.63	7.40	7.19
Loan Amount 20,000.00 Pre-Pay Per Month	10.47	10.17	9.87	9.58
Loan Amount 25,000.00 Pre-Pay Per Month	13.09	12.71	12.34	11.98
Loan Amount 50,000.00 Pre-Pay Per Month	26.17	25.42	24.68	23.96
Loan Amount 75,000.00 Pre-Pay Per Month	39.26	38.13	37.02	35.94
Loan Amount 100,000.00 Pre-Pay Per Month	52.35	50.84	49.36	47.92
Loan Amount 125,000.00 Pre-Pay Per Month	65.43	63.55	61.70	59.90
Loan Amount 150,000.00 Pre-Pay Per Month	78.52	76.26	74.05	71.87
Loan Amount 175,000.00 Pre-Pay Per Month	91.60	88.97	86.39	83.85
Loan Amount 200,000.00 Pre-Pay Per Month	104.69	101.68	98.73	95.83
Loan Amount 225,000.00 Pre-Pay Per Month	117.78	114.39	111.07	107.81
Loan Amount 250,000.00 Pre-Pay Per Month	130.86	127.10	123.41	119.79
Loan Amount 275,000.00 Pre-Pay Per Month	143.95	139.81	135.75	131.77
Loan Amount 300,000.00 Pre-Pay Per Month	157.04	152.52	148.09	143.75
Loan Amount 325,000.00 Pre-Pay Per Month	170.12	165.23	160.43	155.73
Loan Amount 350,000.00 Pre-Pay Per Month	183.21	177.94	172.77	167.71
Loan Amount 375,000.00 Pre-Pay Per Month	196.30	190.65	185.11	179.69
Loan Amount 400,000.00 Pre-Pay Per Month	209.38	203.36	197.46	191.67
Loan Amount 450,000.00 Pre-Pay Per Month	235.56	228.78	222.14	215.62

15%   When Your Mortgage Will Be Paid
TABLE B

A 30 Year Mortgage Will Be Paid In 15 Years If You Pre-Pay The Following:

		INTEREST RATES			
		15%	15¼%	15½%	15¾%
Loan Amount	**$ 1,000.00**				
Pre-Pay Per Month		1.35	1.32	1.29	1.27
Loan Amount	**2,000.00**				
Pre-Pay Per Month		2.70	2.65	2.59	2.53
Loan Amount	**3,000.00**				
Pre-Pay Per Month		4.05	3.97	3.88	3.80
Loan Amount	**4,000.00**				
Pre-Pay Per Month		5.41	5.29	5.18	5.07
Loan Amount	**5,000.00**				
Pre-Pay Per Month		6.76	6.61	6.47	6.33
Loan Amount	**10,000.00**				
Pre-Pay Per Month		13.51	13.23	12.95	12.67
Loan Amount	**15,000.00**				
Pre-Pay Per Month		20.27	19.84	19.42	19.00
Loan Amount	**20,000.00**				
Pre-Pay Per Month		27.03	26.46	25.89	25.34
Loan Amount	**25,000.00**				
Pre-Pay Per Month		33.79	33.07	32.37	31.67
Loan Amount	**50,000.00**				
Pre-Pay Per Month		67.57	66.15	64.74	63.35
Loan Amount	**75,000.00**				
Pre-Pay Per Month		101.36	99.22	97.11	95.02
Loan Amount	**100,000.00**				
Pre-Pay Per Month		135.14	132.29	129.47	126.69
Loan Amount	**125,000.00**				
Pre-Pay Per Month		168.93	165.36	161.84	158.36
Loan Amount	**150,000.00**				
Pre-Pay Per Month		202.71	198.44	194.21	190.04
Loan Amount	**175,000.00**				
Pre-Pay Per Month		236.50	231.51	226.58	221.71
Loan Amount	**200,000.00**				
Pre-Pay Per Month		270.29	264.58	258.95	253.38
Loan Amount	**225,000.00**				
Pre-Pay Per Month		304.07	297.66	291.32	285.05
Loan Amount	**250,000.00**				
Pre-Pay Per Month		337.86	330.73	323.68	316.73
Loan Amount	**275,000.00**				
Pre-Pay Per Month		371.64	363.80	356.05	348.40
Loan Amount	**300,000.00**				
Pre-Pay Per Month		405.43	396.87	388.42	380.07
Loan Amount	**325,000.00**				
Pre-Pay Per Month		439.22	429.95	420.79	411.74
Loan Amount	**350,000.00**				
Pre-Pay Per Month		473.00	463.02	453.16	443.42
Loan Amount	**375,000.00**				
Pre-Pay Per Month		506.79	496.09	485.53	475.09
Loan Amount	**400,000.00**				
Pre-Pay Per Month		540.57	529.16	517.89	506.76
Loan Amount	**450,000.00**				
Pre-Pay Per Month		608.14	595.31	582.63	570.11

15%

When Your Mortgage Will Be Paid
TABLE B

A 15 Year Mortgage Will Be Paid In 12½ Years If You Pre-Pay The Following:

		INTEREST RATES			
		15%	15¼%	15½%	15¾%
Loan Amount Pre-Pay Per Month	$ 1,000.00	y .80	.79	.78	.77
Loan Amount Pre-Pay Per Month	2,000.00	1.60	1.58	1.57	1.55
Loan Amount Pre-Pay Per Month	3,000.00	2.40	2.37	2.35	2.32
Loan Amount Pre-Pay Per Month	4,000.00	3.20	3.16	3.13	3.10
Loan Amount Pre-Pay Per Month	5,000.00	4.00	3.96	3.91	3.87
Loan Amount Pre-Pay Per Month	10,000.00	8.00	7.91	7.83	7.74
Loan Amount Pre-Pay Per Month	15,000.00	11.99	11.87	11.74	11.61
Loan Amount Pre-Pay Per Month	20,000.00	15.99	15.82	15.65	15.48
Loan Amount Pre-Pay Per Month	25,000.00	19.99	19.78	19.56	19.35
Loan Amount Pre-Pay Per Month	50,000.00	39.98	39.55	39.13	38.70
Loan Amount Pre-Pay Per Month	75,000.00	59.97	59.33	58.69	58.05
Loan Amount Pre-Pay Per Month	100,000.00	79.96	79.11	78.26	77.40
Loan Amount Pre-Pay Per Month	125,000.00	99.95	98.89	97.82	96.75
Loan Amount Pre-Pay Per Month	150,000.00	119.94	118.66	117.38	116.10
Loan Amount Pre-Pay Per Month	175,000.00	139.93	138.44	136.95	135.45
Loan Amount Pre-Pay Per Month	200,000.00	159.92	158.22	156.51	154.80
Loan Amount Pre-Pay Per Month	225,000.00	179.91	178.00	176.08	174.15
Loan Amount Pre-Pay Per Month	250,000.00	199.90	197.77	195.64	193.50
Loan Amount Pre-Pay Per Month	275,000.00	219.89	217.55	215.20	212.85
Loan Amount Pre-Pay Per Month	300,000.00	239.88	237.33	234.77	232.20
Loan Amount Pre-Pay Per Month	325,000.00	259.87	257.11	254.33	251.55
Loan Amount Pre-Pay Per Month	350,000.00	279.86	276.88	273.89	270.90
Loan Amount Pre-Pay Per Month	375,000.00	299.86	296.66	293.46	290.25
Loan Amount Pre-Pay Per Month	400,000.00	319.85	316.44	313.02	309.60
Loan Amount Pre-Pay Per Month	450,000.00	359.83	355.99	352.15	348.30

When Your Mortgage Will Be Paid
TABLE B

A 15 Year Mortgage Will Be Paid In 10 Years If You Pre-Pay The Following:

		INTEREST RATES			
		15%	**15¼%**	**15½%**	**15¾%**
Loan Amount	$ 1,000.00				
Pre-Pay Per Month		2.14	2.12	2.10	2.08
Loan Amount	2,000.00				
Pre-Pay Per Month		4.28	4.24	4.20	4.17
Loan Amount	3,000.00				
Pre-Pay Per Month		6.41	6.36	6.30	6.25
Loan Amount	4,000.00				
Pre-Pay Per Month		8.55	8.48	8.40	8.33
Loan Amount	5,000.00				
Pre-Pay Per Month		10.69	10.60	10.51	10.41
Loan Amount	10,000.00				
Pre-Pay Per Month		21.38	21.19	21.01	20.83
Loan Amount	15,000.00				
Pre-Pay Per Month		32.06	31.79	31.52	31.24
Loan Amount	20,000.00				
Pre-Pay Per Month		42.75	42.39	42.02	41.66
Loan Amount	25,000.00				
Pre-Pay Per Month		53.44	52.99	52.53	52.07
Loan Amount	50,000.00				
Pre-Pay Per Month		106.88	105.97	105.06	104.14
Loan Amount	75,000.00				
Pre-Pay Per Month		160.32	158.96	157.59	156.21
Loan Amount	100,000.00				
Pre-Pay Per Month		213.76	211.94	210.12	208.28
Loan Amount	125,000.00				
Pre-Pay Per Month		267.20	264.93	262.64	260.35
Loan Amount	150,000.00				
Pre-Pay Per Month		320.64	317.92	315.17	312.42
Loan Amount	175,000.00				
Pre-Pay Per Month		374.08	370.90	367.70	364.48
Loan Amount	200,000.00				
Pre-Pay Per Month		427.52	423.89	420.23	416.55
Loan Amount	225,000.00				
Pre-Pay Per Month		480.97	476.87	472.76	468.62
Loan Amount	250,000.00				
Pre-Pay Per Month		534.41	529.86	525.29	520.69
Loan Amount	275,000.00				
Pre-Pay Per Month		587.85	582.85	577.82	572.76
Loan Amount	300,000.00				
Pre-Pay Per Month		641.29	635.83	630.35	624.83
Loan Amount	325,000.00				
Pre-Pay Per Month		694.73	688.82	682.87	676.90
Loan Amount	350,000.00				
Pre-Pay Per Month		748.17	741.80	735.40	728.97
Loan Amount	375,000.00				
Pre-Pay Per Month		801.61	794.79	787.93	781.04
Loan Amount	400,000.00				
Pre-Pay Per Month		855.05	847.77	840.46	833.11
Loan Amount	450,000.00				
Pre-Pay Per Month		961.93	953.75	945.52	937.25

15%

When Your Mortgage Will Be Paid
TABLE B

A 15 Year Mortgage Will Be Paid In 7½ Years If You Pre-Pay The Following:

		INTEREST RATES			
		15%	15¼%	15½%	15¾%
Loan Amount Pre-Pay Per Month	$ 1,000.00	4.58	4.55	4.52	4.49
Loan Amount Pre-Pay Per Month	2,000.00	9.15	9.09	9.04	8.98
Loan Amount Pre-Pay Per Month	3,000.00	13.73	13.64	13.55	13.47
Loan Amount Pre-Pay Per Month	4,000.00	18.30	18.19	18.07	17.95
Loan Amount Pre-Pay Per Month	5,000.00	22.88	22.73	22.59	22.44
Loan Amount Pre-Pay Per Month	10,000.00	45.76	45.47	45.18	44.88
Loan Amount Pre-Pay Per Month	15,000.00	68.63	68.20	67.76	67.33
Loan Amount Pre-Pay Per Month	20,000.00	91.51	90.93	90.35	89.77
Loan Amount Pre-Pay Per Month	25,000.00	114.39	113.67	112.94	112.21
Loan Amount Pre-Pay Per Month	50,000.00	228.78	227.34	225.88	224.42
Loan Amount Pre-Pay Per Month	75,000.00	343.17	341.00	338.82	336.63
Loan Amount Pre-Pay Per Month	100,000.00	457.56	454.67	451.76	448.83
Loan Amount Pre-Pay Per Month	125,000.00	571.95	568.34	564.71	561.04
Loan Amount Pre-Pay Per Month	150,000.00	686.34	682.01	677.65	673.25
Loan Amount Pre-Pay Per Month	175,000.00	800.73	795.68	790.59	785.46
Loan Amount Pre-Pay Per Month	200,000.00	915.12	909.34	903.53	897.67
Loan Amount Pre-Pay Per Month	225,000.00	1,029.51	1,023.01	1,016.47	1,009.88
Loan Amount Pre-Pay Per Month	250,000.00	1,143.90	1,136.68	1,129.41	1,122.09
Loan Amount Pre-Pay Per Month	275,000.00	1,258.29	1,250.35	1,242.35	1,234.30
Loan Amount Pre-Pay Per Month	300,000.00	1,372.68	1,364.02	1,355.29	1,346.50
Loan Amount Pre-Pay Per Month	325,000.00	1,487.07	1,477.69	1,468.23	1,458.71
Loan Amount Pre-Pay Per Month	350,000.00	1,601.46	1,591.35	1,581.17	1,570.92
Loan Amount Pre-Pay Per Month	375,000.00	1,715.85	1,705.02	1,694.12	1,683.13
Loan Amount Pre-Pay Per Month	400,000.00	1,830.24	1,818.69	1,807.06	1,795.34
Loan Amount Pre-Pay Per Month	450,000.00	2,059.02	2,046.03	2,032.94	2,019.76

16% When Your Mortgage Will Be Paid
TABLE B

A 30 Year Mortgage Will Be Paid In 25 Years If You Pre-Pay The Following:

	INTEREST RATES			
	16%	16¼%	16½%	16¾%
Loan Amount $ 1,000.00 **Pre-Pay Per Month**	.14	.14	.13	.13
Loan Amount 2,000.00 **Pre-Pay Per Month**	.28	.27	.26	.25
Loan Amount 3,000.00 **Pre-Pay Per Month**	.42	.41	.39	.38
Loan Amount 4,000.00 **Pre-Pay Per Month**	.57	.54	.52	.50
Loan Amount 5,000.00 **Pre-Pay Per Month**	.71	.68	.65	.63
Loan Amount 10,000.00 **Pre-Pay Per Month**	1.41	1.36	1.31	1.26
Loan Amount 15,000.00 **Pre-Pay Per Month**	2.12	2.04	1.96	1.89
Loan Amount 20,000.00 **Pre-Pay Per Month**	2.83	2.72	2.62	2.52
Loan Amount 25,000.00 **Pre-Pay Per Month**	3.53	3.40	3.27	3.15
Loan Amount 50,000.00 **Pre-Pay Per Month**	7.07	6.80	6.55	6.30
Loan Amount 75,000.00 **Pre-Pay Per Month**	10.60	10.20	9.82	9.45
Loan Amount 100,000.00 **Pre-Pay Per Month**	14.13	13.61	13.10	12.60
Loan Amount 125,000.00 **Pre-Pay Per Month**	17.66	17.01	16.37	15.75
Loan Amount 150,000.00 **Pre-Pay Per Month**	21.20	20.41	19.64	18.90
Loan Amount 175,000.00 **Pre-Pay Per Month**	24.73	23.81	22.92	22.05
Loan Amount 200,000.00 **Pre-Pay Per Month**	28.26	27.21	26.19	25.20
Loan Amount 225,000.00 **Pre-Pay Per Month**	31.80	30.61	29.47	28.35
Loan Amount 250,000.00 **Pre-Pay Per Month**	35.33	34.02	32.74	31.50
Loan Amount 275,000.00 **Pre-Pay Per Month**	38.86	37.42	36.02	34.65
Loan Amount 300,000.00 **Pre-Pay Per Month**	42.40	40.82	39.29	37.80
Loan Amount 325,000.00 **Pre-Pay Per Month**	45.93	44.22	42.56	40.95
Loan Amount 350,000.00 **Pre-Pay Per Month**	49.46	47.62	45.84	44.11
Loan Amount 375,000.00 **Pre-Pay Per Month**	52.99	51.02	49.11	47.26
Loan Amount 400,000.00 **Pre-Pay Per Month**	56.53	54.43	52.39	50.41
Loan Amount 450,000.00 **Pre-Pay Per Month**	63.59	61.23	58.93	56.71

16% When Your Mortgage Will Be Paid
TABLE B

A 30 Year Mortgage Will Be Paid In 20 Years If You Pre-Pay The Following:

		INTEREST RATES			
		16%	16¼%	16½%	16¾%
Loan Amount $ 1,000.00 Pre-Pay Per Month		.46	.45	.44	.42
Loan Amount 2,000.00 Pre-Pay Per Month		.93	.90	.88	.85
Loan Amount 3,000.00 Pre-Pay Per Month		1.39	1.35	1.31	1.27
Loan Amount 4,000.00 Pre-Pay Per Month		1.86	1.80	1.75	1.70
Loan Amount 5,000.00 Pre-Pay Per Month		2.32	2.26	2.19	2.12
Loan Amount 10,000.00 Pre-Pay Per Month		4.65	4.51	4.38	4.24
Loan Amount 15,000.00 Pre-Pay Per Month		6.97	6.77	6.56	6.36
Loan Amount 20,000.00 Pre-Pay Per Month		9.30	9.02	8.75	8.48
Loan Amount 25,000.00 Pre-Pay Per Month		11.62	11.28	10.94	10.61
Loan Amount 50,000.00 Pre-Pay Per Month		23.25	22.56	21.88	21.21
Loan Amount 75,000.00 Pre-Pay Per Month		34.87	33.83	32.81	31.82
Loan Amount 100,000.00 Pre-Pay Per Month		46.50	45.11	43.75	42.42
Loan Amount 125,000.00 Pre-Pay Per Month		58.12	56.39	54.69	53.03
Loan Amount 150,000.00 Pre-Pay Per Month		69.75	67.67	65.63	63.64
Loan Amount 175,000.00 Pre-Pay Per Month		81.37	78.94	76.57	74.24
Loan Amount 200,000.00 Pre-Pay Per Month		93.00	90.22	87.51	84.85
Loan Amount 225,000.00 Pre-Pay Per Month		104.62	101.50	98.44	95.45
Loan Amount 250,000.00 Pre-Pay Per Month		116.25	112.78	109.38	106.06
Loan Amount 275,000.00 Pre-Pay Per Month		127.87	124.05	120.32	116.67
Loan Amount 300,000.00 Pre-Pay Per Month		139.50	135.33	131.26	127.27
Loan Amount 325,000.00 Pre-Pay Per Month		151.12	146.61	142.20	137.88
Loan Amount 350,000.00 Pre-Pay Per Month		162.75	157.89	153.13	148.48
Loan Amount 375,000.00 Pre-Pay Per Month		174.37	169.17	164.07	159.09
Loan Amount 400,000.00 Pre-Pay Per Month		186.00	180.44	175.01	169.70
Loan Amount 450,000.00 Pre-Pay Per Month		209.25	203.00	196.89	190.91

16% When Your Mortgage Will Be Paid
TABLE B

A 30 Year Mortgage Will Be Paid In 15 Years If You Pre-Pay The Following:

	INTEREST RATES			
	16%	16¼%	16½%	16¾%
Loan Amount $ 1,000.00 **Pre-Pay Per Month**	1.24	1.21	1.19	1.16
Loan Amount 2,000.00 **Pre-Pay Per Month**	2.48	2.42	2.37	2.32
Loan Amount 3,000.00 **Pre-Pay Per Month**	3.72	3.64	3.56	3.48
Loan Amount 4,000.00 **Pre-Pay Per Month**	4.96	4.85	4.74	4.64
Loan Amount 5,000.00 **Pre-Pay Per Month**	6.20	6.06	5.93	5.80
Loan Amount 10,000.00 **Pre-Pay Per Month**	12.39	12.12	11.86	11.59
Loan Amount 15,000.00 **Pre-Pay Per Month**	18.59	18.19	17.78	17.39
Loan Amount 20,000.00 **Pre-Pay Per Month**	24.79	24.25	23.71	23.19
Loan Amount 25,000.00 **Pre-Pay Per Month**	30.99	30.31	29.64	28.98
Loan Amount 50,000.00 **Pre-Pay Per Month**	61.97	60.62	59.28	57.96
Loan Amount 75,000.00 **Pre-Pay Per Month**	92.96	90.93	88.92	86.94
Loan Amount 100,000.00 **Pre-Pay Per Month**	123.94	121.23	118.56	115.93
Loan Amount 125,000.00 **Pre-Pay Per Month**	154.93	151.54	148.20	144.91
Loan Amount 150,000.00 **Pre-Pay Per Month**	185.92	181.85	177.84	173.89
Loan Amount 175,000.00 **Pre-Pay Per Month**	216.90	212.16	207.48	202.87
Loan Amount 200,000.00 **Pre-Pay Per Month**	247.89	242.47	237.12	231.85
Loan Amount 225,000.00 **Pre-Pay Per Month**	278.87	272.78	266.76	260.83
Loan Amount 250,000.00 **Pre-Pay Per Month**	309.86	303.08	296.40	289.81
Loan Amount 275,000.00 **Pre-Pay Per Month**	340.85	333.39	326.04	318.80
Loan Amount 300,000.00 **Pre-Pay Per Month**	371.83	363.70	355.68	347.78
Loan Amount 325,000.00 **Pre-Pay Per Month**	402.82	394.01	385.32	376.76
Loan Amount 350,000.00 **Pre-Pay Per Month**	433.80	424.32	414.96	405.74
Loan Amount 375,000.00 **Pre-Pay Per Month**	464.79	454.63	444.60	434.72
Loan Amount 400,000.00 **Pre-Pay Per Month**	495.77	484.93	474.24	463.70
Loan Amount 450,000.00 **Pre-Pay Per Month**	557.75	545.55	533.52	521.66

16%

When Your Mortgage Will Be Paid
TABLE B

A 15 Year Mortgage Will Be Paid In 12½ Years If You Pre-Pay The Following:

		INTEREST RATES			
		16%	16¼%	16½%	16¾%
Loan Amount	$ 1,000.00				
Pre-Pay Per Month		.77	.76	.75	.74
Loan Amount	2,000.00				
Pre-Pay Per Month		1.53	1.51	1.50	1.48
Loan Amount	3,000.00				
Pre-Pay Per Month		2.30	2.27	2.24	2.22
Loan Amount	4,000.00				
Pre-Pay Per Month		3.06	3.03	2.99	2.96
Loan Amount	5,000.00				
Pre-Pay Per Month		3.83	3.78	3.74	3.70
Loan Amount	10,000.00				
Pre-Pay Per Month		7.65	7.57	7.48	7.40
Loan Amount	15,000.00				
Pre-Pay Per Month		11.48	11.35	11.22	11.09
Loan Amount	20,000.00				
Pre-Pay Per Month		15.31	15.14	14.96	14.79
Loan Amount	25,000.00				
Pre-Pay Per Month		19.14	18.92	18.70	18.49
Loan Amount	50,000.00				
Pre-Pay Per Month		38.27	37.84	37.41	36.98
Loan Amount	75,000.00				
Pre-Pay Per Month		57.41	56.76	56.11	55.47
Loan Amount	100,000.00				
Pre-Pay Per Month		76.54	75.68	74.82	73.96
Loan Amount	125,000.00				
Pre-Pay Per Month		95.68	94.60	93.52	92.44
Loan Amount	150,000.00				
Pre-Pay Per Month		114.81	113.52	112.23	110.93
Loan Amount	175,000.00				
Pre-Pay Per Month		133.95	132.44	130.93	129.42
Loan Amount	200,000.00				
Pre-Pay Per Month		153.08	151.36	149.64	147.91
Loan Amount	225,000.00				
Pre-Pay Per Month		172.22	170.28	168.34	166.40
Loan Amount	250,000.00				
Pre-Pay Per Month		191.35	189.20	187.05	184.89
Loan Amount	275,000.00				
Pre-Pay Per Month		210.49	208.12	205.75	203.38
Loan Amount	300,000.00				
Pre-Pay Per Month		229.62	227.04	224.46	221.87
Loan Amount	325,000.00				
Pre-Pay Per Month		248.76	245.96	243.16	240.36
Loan Amount	350,000.00				
Pre-Pay Per Month		267.89	264.88	261.86	258.84
Loan Amount	375,000.00				
Pre-Pay Per Month		287.03	283.80	280.57	277.33
Loan Amount	400,000.00				
Pre-Pay Per Month		306.16	302.72	299.27	295.82
Loan Amount	450,000.00				
Pre-Pay Per Month		344.43	340.56	336.68	332.80

16% When Your Mortgage Will Be Paid
TABLE B

A 15 Year Mortgage Will Be Paid In 10 Years If You Pre-Pay The Following:

		INTEREST RATES			
		16%	16¼%	16½%	16¾%
Loan Amount $ 1,000.00 Pre-Pay Per Month		2.06	2.05	2.03	2.01
Loan Amount 2,000.00 Pre-Pay Per Month		4.13	4.09	4.05	4.02
Loan Amount 3,000.00 Pre-Pay Per Month		6.19	6.14	6.08	6.03
Loan Amount 4,000.00 Pre-Pay Per Month		8.26	8.18	8.11	8.03
Loan Amount 5,000.00 Pre-Pay Per Month		10.32	10.23	10.14	10.04
Loan Amount 10,000.00 Pre-Pay Per Month		20.64	20.46	20.27	20.08
Loan Amount 15,000.00 Pre-Pay Per Month		30.96	30.69	30.41	30.13
Loan Amount 20,000.00 Pre-Pay Per Month		41.29	40.92	40.54	40.17
Loan Amount 25,000.00 Pre-Pay Per Month		51.61	51.14	50.68	50.21
Loan Amount 50,000.00 Pre-Pay Per Month		103.22	102.29	101.36	100.42
Loan Amount 75,000.00 Pre-Pay Per Month		154.82	153.43	152.04	150.63
Loan Amount 100,000.00 Pre-Pay Per Month		206.43	204.58	202.71	200.85
Loan Amount 125,000.00 Pre-Pay Per Month		258.04	255.72	253.39	251.06
Loan Amount 150,000.00 Pre-Pay Per Month		309.65	306.86	304.07	301.27
Loan Amount 175,000.00 Pre-Pay Per Month		361.25	358.01	354.75	351.48
Loan Amount 200,000.00 Pre-Pay Per Month		412.86	409.15	405.43	401.69
Loan Amount 225,000.00 Pre-Pay Per Month		464.47	460.30	456.11	451.90
Loan Amount 250,000.00 Pre-Pay Per Month		516.08	511.44	506.79	502.12
Loan Amount 275,000.00 Pre-Pay Per Month		567.68	562.58	557.46	552.33
Loan Amount 300,000.00 Pre-Pay Per Month		619.29	613.73	608.14	602.54
Loan Amount 325,000.00 Pre-Pay Per Month		670.90	664.87	658.82	652.75
Loan Amount 350,000.00 Pre-Pay Per Month		722.51	716.02	709.50	702.96
Loan Amount 375,000.00 Pre-Pay Per Month		774.11	767.16	760.18	753.17
Loan Amount 400,000.00 Pre-Pay Per Month		825.72	818.30	810.86	803.38
Loan Amount 450,000.00 Pre-Pay Per Month		928.94	920.59	912.21	903.81

16%   When Your Mortgage Will Be Paid
TABLE B

A 15 Year Mortgage Will Be Paid In 7½ Years If You Pre-Pay The Following:

	INTEREST RATES			
	16%	16¼%	16½%	16¾%
Loan Amount $ 1,000.00 **Pre-Pay Per Month**	4.46	4.43	4.40	4.37
Loan Amount 2,000.00 **Pre-Pay Per Month**	8.92	8.86	8.80	8.74
Loan Amount 3,000.00 **Pre-Pay Per Month**	13.38	13.29	13.20	13.11
Loan Amount 4,000.00 **Pre-Pay Per Month**	17.84	17.72	17.60	17.48
Loan Amount 5,000.00 **Pre-Pay Per Month**	22.29	22.15	22.00	21.85
Loan Amount 10,000.00 **Pre-Pay Per Month**	44.59	44.29	43.99	43.69
Loan Amount 15,000.00 **Pre-Pay Per Month**	66.88	66.44	65.99	65.54
Loan Amount 20,000.00 **Pre-Pay Per Month**	89.18	88.58	87.99	87.39
Loan Amount 25,000.00 **Pre-Pay Per Month**	111.47	110.73	109.98	109.23
Loan Amount 50,000.00 **Pre-Pay Per Month**	222.94	221.46	219.97	218.46
Loan Amount 75,000.00 **Pre-Pay Per Month**	334.41	332.19	329.95	327.70
Loan Amount 100,000.00 **Pre-Pay Per Month**	445.89	442.92	439.93	436.93
Loan Amount 125,000.00 **Pre-Pay Per Month**	557.36	553.65	549.92	546.16
Loan Amount 150,000.00 **Pre-Pay Per Month**	668.83	664.38	659.90	655.39
Loan Amount 175,000.00 **Pre-Pay Per Month**	780.30	775.11	769.88	764.63
Loan Amount 200,000.00 **Pre-Pay Per Month**	891.77	885.84	879.86	873.86
Loan Amount 225,000.00 **Pre-Pay Per Month**	1,003.24	996.57	989.85	983.09
Loan Amount 250,000.00 **Pre-Pay Per Month**	1,114.71	1,107.29	1,099.83	1,092.32
Loan Amount 275,000.00 **Pre-Pay Per Month**	1,226.19	1,218.02	1,209.81	1,201.56
Loan Amount 300,000.00 **Pre-Pay Per Month**	1,337.66	1,328.75	1,319.80	1,310.79
Loan Amount 325,000.00 **Pre-Pay Per Month**	1,449.13	1,439.48	1,429.78	1,420.02
Loan Amount 350,000.00 **Pre-Pay Per Month**	1,560.60	1,550.21	1,539.76	1,529.25
Loan Amount 375,000.00 **Pre-Pay Per Month**	1,672.07	1,660.94	1,649.75	1,638.48
Loan Amount 400,000.00 **Pre-Pay Per Month**	1,783.54	1,771.67	1,759.73	1,747.72
Loan Amount 450,000.00 **Pre-Pay Per Month**	2,006.49	1,993.13	1,979.69	1,966.18

17%

When Your Mortgage Will Be Paid
TABLE B

A 30 Year Mortgage Will Be Paid In 25 Years If You Pre-Pay The Following:

		INTEREST RATES			
		17%	17¼%	17½%	17¾%
Loan Amount Pre-Pay Per Month	$ 1,000.00	.12	.12	.11	.11
Loan Amount Pre-Pay Per Month	2,000.00	.24	.23	.22	.22
Loan Amount Pre-Pay Per Month	3,000.00	.36	.35	.34	.32
Loan Amount Pre-Pay Per Month	4,000.00	.48	.47	.45	.43
Loan Amount Pre-Pay Per Month	5,000.00	.61	.58	.56	.54
Loan Amount Pre-Pay Per Month	10,000.00	1.21	1.17	1.12	1.08
Loan Amount Pre-Pay Per Month	15,000.00	1.82	1.75	1.68	1.62
Loan Amount Pre-Pay Per Month	20,000.00	2.42	2.33	2.24	2.15
Loan Amount Pre-Pay Per Month	25,000.00	3.03	2.91	2.80	2.69
Loan Amount Pre-Pay Per Month	50,000.00	6.06	5.83	5.60	5.38
Loan Amount Pre-Pay Per Month	75,000.00	9.09	8.74	8.40	8.08
Loan Amount Pre-Pay Per Month	100,000.00	12.12	11.66	11.20	10.77
Loan Amount Pre-Pay Per Month	125,000.00	15.15	14.57	14.01	13.46
Loan Amount Pre-Pay Per Month	150,000.00	18.18	17.48	16.81	16.15
Loan Amount Pre-Pay Per Month	175,000.00	21.21	20.40	19.61	18.84
Loan Amount Pre-Pay Per Month	200,000.00	24.24	23.31	22.41	21.54
Loan Amount Pre-Pay Per Month	225,000.00	27.27	26.23	25.21	24.23
Loan Amount Pre-Pay Per Month	250,000.00	30.30	29.14	28.01	26.92
Loan Amount Pre-Pay Per Month	275,000.00	33.33	32.05	30.81	29.61
Loan Amount Pre-Pay Per Month	300,000.00	36.36	34.97	33.61	32.30
Loan Amount Pre-Pay Per Month	325,000.00	39.39	37.88	36.41	34.99
Loan Amount Pre-Pay Per Month	350,000.00	42.42	40.79	39.22	37.69
Loan Amount Pre-Pay Per Month	375,000.00	45.45	43.71	42.02	40.38
Loan Amount Pre-Pay Per Month	400,000.00	48.48	46.62	44.82	43.07
Loan Amount Pre-Pay Per Month	450,000.00	54.55	52.45	50.42	48.45

17%　When Your Mortgage Will Be Paid
TABLE B

A 30 Year Mortgage Will Be Paid In 20 Years If You Pre-Pay The Following:

		INTEREST RATES			
		17%	17¼%	17½%	17¾%
Loan Amount Pre-Pay Per Month	$ 1,000.00	.41	.40	.39	.37
Loan Amount Pre-Pay Per Month	2,000.00	.82	.80	.77	.75
Loan Amount Pre-Pay Per Month	3,000.00	1.23	1.20	1.16	1.12
Loan Amount Pre-Pay Per Month	4,000.00	1.65	1.59	1.54	1.50
Loan Amount Pre-Pay Per Month	5,000.00	2.06	1.99	1.93	1.87
Loan Amount Pre-Pay Per Month	10,000.00	4.11	3.99	3.86	3.74
Loan Amount Pre-Pay Per Month	15,000.00	6.17	5.98	5.79	5.61
Loan Amount Pre-Pay Per Month	20,000.00	8.23	7.97	7.72	7.48
Loan Amount Pre-Pay Per Month	25,000.00	10.28	9.96	9.65	9.35
Loan Amount Pre-Pay Per Month	50,000.00	20.56	19.93	19.31	18.70
Loan Amount Pre-Pay Per Month	75,000.00	30.84	29.89	28.96	28.06
Loan Amount Pre-Pay Per Month	100,000.00	41.13	39.86	38.62	37.41
Loan Amount Pre-Pay Per Month	125,000.00	51.41	49.82	48.27	46.76
Loan Amount Pre-Pay Per Month	150,000.00	61.69	59.78	57.93	56.11
Loan Amount Pre-Pay Per Month	175,000.00	71.97	69.75	67.58	65.46
Loan Amount Pre-Pay Per Month	200,000.00	82.25	79.71	77.23	74.81
Loan Amount Pre-Pay Per Month	225,000.00	92.53	89.68	86.89	84.17
Loan Amount Pre-Pay Per Month	250,000.00	102.81	99.64	96.54	93.52
Loan Amount Pre-Pay Per Month	275,000.00	113.09	109.60	106.20	102.87
Loan Amount Pre-Pay Per Month	300,000.00	123.38	119.57	115.85	112.22
Loan Amount Pre-Pay Per Month	325,000.00	133.66	129.53	125.50	121.57
Loan Amount Pre-Pay Per Month	350,000.00	143.94	139.50	135.16	130.92
Loan Amount Pre-Pay Per Month	375,000.00	154.22	149.46	144.81	140.28
Loan Amount Pre-Pay Per Month	400,000.00	164.50	159.42	154.47	149.63
Loan Amount Pre-Pay Per Month	450,000.00	185.06	179.35	173.78	168.33

17%

When Your Mortgage Will Be Paid
TABLE B

A 30 Year Mortgage Will Be Paid In 15 Years If You Pre-Pay The Following:

		INTEREST RATES			
		17%	17¼%	17½%	17¾%
Loan Amount	$ 1,000.00				
Pre-Pay Per Month		1.13	1.11	1.08	1.06
Loan Amount	2,000.00				
Pre-Pay Per Month		2.27	2.22	2.17	2.12
Loan Amount	3,000.00				
Pre-Pay Per Month		3.40	3.32	3.25	3.17
Loan Amount	4,000.00				
Pre-Pay Per Month		4.53	4.43	4.33	4.23
Loan Amount	5,000.00				
Pre-Pay Per Month		5.67	5.54	5.41	5.29
Loan Amount	10,000.00				
Pre-Pay Per Month		11.33	11.08	10.83	10.58
Loan Amount	15,000.00				
Pre-Pay Per Month		17.00	16.62	16.24	15.87
Loan Amount	20,000.00				
Pre-Pay Per Month		22.67	22.15	21.65	21.15
Loan Amount	25,000.00				
Pre-Pay Per Month		28.33	27.69	27.06	26.44
Loan Amount	50,000.00				
Pre-Pay Per Month		56.66	55.39	54.13	52.89
Loan Amount	75,000.00				
Pre-Pay Per Month		85.00	83.08	81.19	79.33
Loan Amount	100,000.00				
Pre-Pay Per Month		113.33	110.77	108.25	105.77
Loan Amount	125,000.00				
Pre-Pay Per Month		141.66	138.46	135.32	132.22
Loan Amount	150,000.00				
Pre-Pay Per Month		169.99	166.16	162.38	158.66
Loan Amount	175,000.00				
Pre-Pay Per Month		198.33	193.85	189.44	185.11
Loan Amount	200,000.00				
Pre-Pay Per Month		226.66	221.54	216.51	211.55
Loan Amount	225,000.00				
Pre-Pay Per Month		254.99	249.24	243.57	237.99
Loan Amount	250,000.00				
Pre-Pay Per Month		283.32	276.93	270.63	264.44
Loan Amount	275,000.00				
Pre-Pay Per Month		311.65	304.62	297.70	290.88
Loan Amount	300,000.00				
Pre-Pay Per Month		339.99	332.31	324.76	317.32
Loan Amount	325,000.00				
Pre-Pay Per Month		368.32	360.01	351.82	343.77
Loan Amount	350,000.00				
Pre-Pay Per Month		396.65	387.70	378.89	370.21
Loan Amount	375,000.00				
Pre-Pay Per Month		424.98	415.39	405.95	396.65
Loan Amount	400,000.00				
Pre-Pay Per Month		453.32	443.09	433.01	423.10
Loan Amount	450,000.00				
Pre-Pay Per Month		509.98	498.47	487.14	475.98

153

17%   When Your Mortgage Will Be Paid
TABLE B

A 15 Year Mortgage Will Be Paid In 12½ Years If You Pre-Pay The Following:

	INTEREST RATES			
	17%	**17¼%**	**17½%**	**17¾%**
Loan Amount $ 1,000.00 **Pre-Pay Per Month**	.73	.72	.71	.71
Loan Amount 2,000.00 **Pre-Pay Per Month**	1.46	1.44	1.43	1.41
Loan Amount 3,000.00 **Pre-Pay Per Month**	2.19	2.17	2.14	2.12
Loan Amount 4,000.00 **Pre-Pay Per Month**	2.92	2.89	2.85	2.82
Loan Amount 5,000.00 **Pre-Pay Per Month**	3.65	3.61	3.57	3.53
Loan Amount 10,000.00 **Pre-Pay Per Month**	7.31	7.22	7.14	7.05
Loan Amount 15,000.00 **Pre-Pay Per Month**	10.96	10.83	10.70	10.58
Loan Amount 20,000.00 **Pre-Pay Per Month**	14.62	14.45	14.27	14.10
Loan Amount 25,000.00 **Pre-Pay Per Month**	18.27	18.06	17.84	17.63
Loan Amount 50,000.00 **Pre-Pay Per Month**	36.55	36.11	35.68	35.25
Loan Amount 75,000.00 **Pre-Pay Per Month**	54.82	54.17	53.52	52.88
Loan Amount 100,000.00 **Pre-Pay Per Month**	73.09	72.23	71.37	70.50
Loan Amount 125,000.00 **Pre-Pay Per Month**	91.37	90.29	89.21	88.13
Loan Amount 150,000.00 **Pre-Pay Per Month**	109.64	108.34	107.05	105.75
Loan Amount 175,000.00 **Pre-Pay Per Month**	127.91	126.40	124.89	123.38
Loan Amount 200,000.00 **Pre-Pay Per Month**	146.18	144.46	142.73	141.00
Loan Amount 225,000.00 **Pre-Pay Per Month**	164.46	162.51	160.57	158.63
Loan Amount 250,000.00 **Pre-Pay Per Month**	182.73	180.57	178.41	176.26
Loan Amount 275,000.00 **Pre-Pay Per Month**	201.00	198.63	196.25	193.88
Loan Amount 300,000.00 **Pre-Pay Per Month**	219.28	216.69	214.10	211.51
Loan Amount 325,000.00 **Pre-Pay Per Month**	237.55	234.74	231.94	229.13
Loan Amount 350,000.00 **Pre-Pay Per Month**	255.82	252.80	249.78	246.76
Loan Amount 375,000.00 **Pre-Pay Per Month**	274.10	270.86	267.62	264.38
Loan Amount 400,000.00 **Pre-Pay Per Month**	292.37	288.92	285.46	282.01
Loan Amount 450,000.00 **Pre-Pay Per Month**	328.92	325.03	321.14	317.26

When Your Mortgage Will Be Paid
TABLE B

A 15 Year Mortgage Will Be Paid In 10 Years If You Pre-Pay The Following:

		INTEREST RATES			
		17%	17¼%	17½%	17¾%
Loan Amount **Pre-Pay Per Month**	$ 1,000.00	1.99	1.97	1.95	1.93
Loan Amount **Pre-Pay Per Month**	2,000.00	3.98	3.94	3.90	3.87
Loan Amount **Pre-Pay Per Month**	3,000.00	5.97	5.91	5.86	5.80
Loan Amount **Pre-Pay Per Month**	4,000.00	7.96	7.88	7.81	7.73
Loan Amount **Pre-Pay Per Month**	5,000.00	9.95	9.85	9.76	9.67
Loan Amount **Pre-Pay Per Month**	10,000.00	19.90	19.71	19.52	19.33
Loan Amount **Pre-Pay Per Month**	15,000.00	29.85	29.56	29.28	29.00
Loan Amount **Pre-Pay Per Month**	20,000.00	39.79	39.42	39.04	38.66
Loan Amount **Pre-Pay Per Month**	25,000.00	49.74	49.27	48.80	48.33
Loan Amount **Pre-Pay Per Month**	50,000.00	99.49	98.55	97.60	96.66
Loan Amount **Pre-Pay Per Month**	75,000.00	149.23	147.82	146.41	144.99
Loan Amount **Pre-Pay Per Month**	100,000.00	198.97	197.09	195.21	193.32
Loan Amount **Pre-Pay Per Month**	125,000.00	248.72	246.37	244.01	241.65
Loan Amount **Pre-Pay Per Month**	150,000.00	298.46	295.64	292.81	289.98
Loan Amount **Pre-Pay Per Month**	175,000.00	348.20	344.91	341.62	338.31
Loan Amount **Pre-Pay Per Month**	200,000.00	397.94	394.19	390.42	386.64
Loan Amount **Pre-Pay Per Month**	225,000.00	447.69	443.46	439.22	434.97
Loan Amount **Pre-Pay Per Month**	250,000.00	497.43	492.73	488.02	483.30
Loan Amount **Pre-Pay Per Month**	275,000.00	547.17	542.01	536.83	531.63
Loan Amount **Pre-Pay Per Month**	300,000.00	596.92	591.28	585.63	579.97
Loan Amount **Pre-Pay Per Month**	325,000.00	646.66	640.55	634.43	628.30
Loan Amount **Pre-Pay Per Month**	350,000.00	696.40	689.83	683.23	676.63
Loan Amount **Pre-Pay Per Month**	375,000.00	746.15	739.10	732.04	724.96
Loan Amount **Pre-Pay Per Month**	400,000.00	795.89	788.37	780.84	773.29
Loan Amount **Pre-Pay Per Month**	450,000.00	895.38	886.92	878.44	869.95

17%

When Your Mortgage Will Be Paid
TABLE B

A 15 Year Mortgage Will Be Paid In 7½ Years If You Pre-Pay The Following:

		INTEREST RATES			
		17%	17¼%	17½%	17¾%
Loan Amount	**$ 1,000.00**				
Pre-Pay Per Month		4.34	4.31	4.28	4.25
Loan Amount	**2,000.00**				
Pre-Pay Per Month		8.68	8.62	8.56	8.50
Loan Amount	**3,000.00**				
Pre-Pay Per Month		13.02	12.93	12.83	12.74
Loan Amount	**4,000.00**				
Pre-Pay Per Month		17.36	17.24	17.11	16.99
Loan Amount	**5,000.00**				
Pre-Pay Per Month		21.70	21.54	21.39	21.24
Loan Amount	**10,000.00**				
Pre-Pay Per Month		43.39	43.09	42.78	42.48
Loan Amount	**15,000.00**				
Pre-Pay Per Month		65.09	64.63	64.17	63.71
Loan Amount	**20,000.00**				
Pre-Pay Per Month		86.78	86.18	85.57	84.95
Loan Amount	**25,000.00**				
Pre-Pay Per Month		108.48	107.72	106.96	106.19
Loan Amount	**50,000.00**				
Pre-Pay Per Month		216.96	215.44	213.91	212.38
Loan Amount	**75,000.00**				
Pre-Pay Per Month		325.43	323.16	320.87	318.57
Loan Amount	**100,000.00**				
Pre-Pay Per Month		433.91	430.88	427.83	424.77
Loan Amount	**125,000.00**				
Pre-Pay Per Month		542.39	538.60	534.78	530.96
Loan Amount	**150,000.00**				
Pre-Pay Per Month		650.87	646.31	641.74	637.15
Loan Amount	**175,000.00**				
Pre-Pay Per Month		759.34	754.03	748.70	743.34
Loan Amount	**200,000.00**				
Pre-Pay Per Month		867.82	861.75	855.66	849.53
Loan Amount	**225,000.00**				
Pre-Pay Per Month		976.30	969.47	962.61	955.72
Loan Amount	**250,000.00**				
Pre-Pay Per Month		1,084.78	1,077.19	1,069.57	1,061.92
Loan Amount	**275,000.00**				
Pre-Pay Per Month		1,193.25	1,184.91	1,176.53	1,168.11
Loan Amount	**300,000.00**				
Pre-Pay Per Month		1,301.73	1,292.63	1,283.48	1,274.30
Loan Amount	**325,000.00**				
Pre-Pay Per Month		1,410.21	1,400.35	1,390.44	1,380.49
Loan Amount	**350,000.00**				
Pre-Pay Per Month		1,518.69	1,508.07	1,497.40	1,486.68
Loan Amount	**375,000.00**				
Pre-Pay Per Month		1,627.16	1,615.79	1,604.35	1,592.87
Loan Amount	**400,000.00**				
Pre-Pay Per Month		1,735.64	1,723.50	1,711.31	1,699.07
Loan Amount	**450,000.00**				
Pre-Pay Per Month		1,952.60	1,938.94	1,925.23	1,911.45

Table C

Figuring Out Your Monthly Mortgage Payment

TABLE C
(Amount Necessary to Amortize a Loan)

AMOUNT OF LOAN	TERM OF LOAN				
	1 Year	2 Years	3 Years	4 Years	5 Years
$ 50.00	$ 4.33	$ 2.24	$ 1.54	$ 1.20	$ .99
100.00	8.65	4.48	3.09	2.39	1.98
200.00	7.31	8.95	6.18	4.79	3.96
300.00	25.96	13.43	9.26	7.18	5.94
400.00	34.61	17.91	12.35	9.58	7.92
500.00	43.26	22.39	15.44	11.97	9.90
1,000.00	86.53	44.77	30.88	23.95	19.80
2,000.00	173.05	89.55	61.75	47.89	39.60
3,000.00	259.58	134.32	92.63	71.84	59.40
4,000.00	346.11	179.09	123.51	95.78	79.20
5,000.00	432.63	223.86	154.39	119.73	99.01
10,000.00	865.27	447.73	308.77	239.46	198.01
15,000.00	1,297.90	671.59	463.16	359.19	297.02
20,000.00	1,730.53	895.45	617.54	478.92	396.02
25,000.00	2,163.17	1,119.31	771.93	598.66	495.03
30,000.00	2,595.80	1,343.18	926.31	718.39	594.04
35,000.00	3,028.44	1,567.04	1,080.70	838.12	693.04
40,000.00	3,461.07	1,790.90	1,235.08	957.85	792.05
45,000.00	3,893.70	2,014.77	1,389.47	1,077.58	891.05
50,000.00	4,326.34	2,238.63	1,543.85	1,197.31	990.06
55,000.00	4,758.97	2,462.49	1,698.24	1,317.04	1,089.07
60,000.00	5,191.60	2,686.35	1,852.63	1,436.77	1,188.07
65,000.00	5,624.24	2,910.22	2,007.01	1,556.51	1,287.08
70,000.00	6,056.87	3,134.08	2,161.40	1,676.24	1,386.08
75,000.00	6,489.51	3,357.94	2,315.78	1,795.97	1,485.09
80,000.00	6,922.14	3,581.81	2,470.17	1,915.70	1,584.10
85,000.00	7,354.77	3,805.67	2,624.55	2,035.43	1,683.10
90,000.00	7,787.41	4,029.53	2,778.94	2,155.16	1,782.11
95,000.00	8,220.04	4,253.40	2,933.32	2,274.89	1,881.11
100,000.00	8,652.67	4,477.26	3,087.71	2,394.62	1,980.12
110,000.00	9,517.94	4,924.98	3,396.48	2,634.09	2,178.13
120,000.00	10,383.21	5,372.71	3,705.25	2,873.55	2,376.14
130,000.00	11,248.48	5,820.44	4,014.02	3,113.01	2,574.16
140,000.00	12,113.74	6,268.16	4,322.79	3,352.47	2,772.17
150,000.00	12,979.01	6,715.89	4,631.56	3,591.94	2,970.18
160,000.00	13,844.28	7,163.61	4,940.34	3,831.40	3,168.19
170,000.00	14,709.55	7,611.34	5,249.11	4,070.86	3,366.20
180,000.00	15,574.81	8,059.06	5,557.88	4,310.32	3,564.22
190,000.00	16,440.08	8,506.79	5,866.65	4,549.79	3,762.23
200,000.00	17,305.35	8,954.52	6,175.42	4,789.25	3,960.24
225,000.00	19,468.52	10,073.83	6,947.35	5,387.91	4,455.27
250,000.00	21,631.69	11,193.14	7,719.27	5,986.56	4,950.30
275,000.00	23,794.86	12,312.46	8,491.20	6,585.22	5,445.33
300,000.00	25,958.02	13,431.77	9,263.13	7,183.87	5,940.36
350,000.00	30,284.36	15,670.40	10,806.98	8,381.19	6,930.42
400,000.00	34,610.70	17,909.03	12,350.84	9,578.50	7,920.48
450,000.00	38,937.04	20,147.66	13,894.69	10,775.81	8,910.54
500,000.00	43,263.37	22,386.29	15,438.55	11,973.12	9,900.60

Monthly Mortgage Payment   7%

TABLE C

(Amount Necessary to Amortize a Loan)

| TERM OF LOAN | | | | | AMOUNT |
10 Years	15 Years	20 Years	25 Years	30 Years	OF LOAN
$ .58	$ .45	$ .39	$ .35	$ .33	$ 50.00
1.16	.90	.78	.71	.67	100.00
2.32	1.80	1.55	1.41	1.33	200.00
3.48	2.70	2.33	2.12	2.00	300.00
4.64	3.60	3.10	2.83	2.66	400.00
5.81	4.49	3.88	3.53	3.33	500.00
11.61	8.99	7.75	7.07	6.65	1,000.00
23.22	17.98	15.51	14.14	13.31	2,000.00
34.83	26.96	23.26	21.20	19.96	3,000.00
46.44	35.95	31.01	28.27	26.61	4,000.00
58.05	44.94	38.76	35.34	33.27	5,000.00
116.11	89.88	77.53	70.68	66.53	10,000.00
174.16	134.82	116.29	106.02	99.80	15,000.00
232.22	179.77	155.06	141.36	133.06	20,000.00
290.27	224.71	193.82	176.69	166.33	25,000.00
348.33	269.65	232.59	212.03	199.59	30,000.00
406.38	314.59	271.35	247.37	232.86	35,000.00
464.43	359.53	310.12	282.71	266.12	40,000.00
522.49	404.47	348.88	318.05	299.39	45,000.00
580.54	449.41	387.65	353.39	332.65	50,000.00
638.60	494.36	426.41	388.73	365.92	55,000.00
696.65	539.30	465.18	424.07	399.18	60,000.00
754.71	584.24	503.94	459.41	432.45	65,000.00
812.76	629.18	542.71	494.75	465.71	70,000.00
870.81	674.12	581.47	530.08	498.98	75,000.00
928.87	719.06	620.24	565.42	532.24	80,000.00
986.92	764.00	659.00	600.76	565.51	85,000.00
1,044.98	808.95	697.77	636.10	598.77	90,000.00
1,103.03	853.89	736.53	671.44	632.04	95,000.00
1,161.08	898.83	775.30	706.78	665.30	100,000.00
1,277.19	988.71	852.83	777.46	731.83	110,000.00
1,393.30	1,078.59	930.36	848.14	798.36	120,000.00
1,509.41	1,168.48	1,007.89	918.81	864.89	130,000.00
1,625.52	1,258.36	1,085.42	989.49	931.42	140,000.00
1,741.63	1,348.24	1,162.95	1,060.17	997.95	150,000.00
1,857.74	1,438.13	1,240.48	1,130.85	1,064.48	160,000.00
1,973.84	1,528.01	1,318.01	1,201.52	1,131.01	170,000.00
2,089.95	1,617.89	1,395.54	1,272.20	1,197.54	180,000.00
2,206.06	1,707.77	1,473.07	1,342.88	1,264.07	190,000.00
2,322.17	1,797.66	1,550.60	1,413.56	1,330.60	200,000.00
2,612.44	2,022.36	1,744.42	1,590.25	1,496.93	225,000.00
2,902.71	2,247.07	1,938.25	1,766.95	1,663.26	250,000.00
3,192.98	2,471.78	2,132.07	1,943.64	1,829.58	275,000.00
3,483.25	2,696.48	2,325.90	2,120.34	1,995.91	300,000.00
4,063.80	3,145.90	2,713.55	2,473.73	2,328.56	350,000.00
4,644.34	3,595.31	3,101.20	2,827.12	2,661.21	400,000.00
5,224.88	4,044.73	3,488.85	3,180.51	2,993.86	450,000.00
5,805.42	4,494.14	3,876.49	3,533.90	3,326.51	500,000.00

7¼%

TABLE C

(Amount Necessary to Amortize a Loan)

AMOUNT OF LOAN	TERM OF LOAN 1 Year	2 Years	3 Years	4 Years	5 Years
$ 50.00	$ 4.33	$ 2.24	$ 1.55	$ 1.20	$ 1.00
100.00	8.66	4.49	3.10	2.41	1.99
200.00	17.33	8.98	6.20	4.81	3.98
300.00	25.99	13.47	9.30	7.22	5.98
400.00	34.66	17.95	12.40	9.62	7.97
500.00	43.32	22.44	15.50	12.03	9.96
1,000.00	86.64	44.89	30.99	24.06	19.92
2,000.00	173.28	89.77	61.98	48.12	39.84
3,000.00	259.93	134.66	92.97	72.19	59.76
4,000.00	346.57	179.54	123.97	96.25	79.68
5,000.00	433.21	224.43	154.96	120.31	99.60
10,000.00	866.42	448.86	309.92	240.62	199.19
15,000.00	1,299.63	673.29	464.87	360.94	298.79
20,000.00	1,732.84	897.72	619.83	481.25	398.39
25,000.00	2,166.05	1,122.15	774.79	601.56	497.98
30,000.00	2,599.26	1,346.58	929.75	721.87	597.58
35,000.00	3,032.47	1,571.01	1,084.70	842.18	697.18
40,000.00	3,465.68	1,795.44	1,239.66	962.50	796.77
45,000.00	3,898.89	2,019.87	1,394.62	1,082.81	896.37
50,000.00	4,332.10	2,244.30	1,549.58	1,203.12	995.97
55,000.00	4,765.31	2,468.73	1,704.53	1,323.43	1,095.56
60,000.00	5,198.52	2,693.16	1,859.49	1,443.74	1,195.16
65,000.00	5,631.73	2,917.59	2,014.45	1,564.06	1,294.76
70,000.00	6,064.94	3,142.02	2,169.41	1,684.37	1,394.36
75,000.00	6,498.15	3,366.45	2,324.36	1,804.68	1,493.95
80,000.00	6,931.36	3,590.88	2,479.32	1,924.99	1,593.55
85,000.00	7,364.57	3,815.31	2,634.28	2,045.30	1,693.15
90,000.00	7,797.78	4,039.74	2,789.24	2,165.62	1,792.74
95,000.00	8,230.99	4,264.17	2,944.20	2,285.93	1,892.34
100,000.00	8,664.20	4,488.60	3,099.15	2,406.24	1,991.94
110,000.00	9,530.62	4,937.46	3,409.07	2,646.86	2,191.13
120,000.00	10,397.04	5,386.32	3,718.98	2,887.49	2,390.32
130,000.00	11,263.47	5,835.18	4,028.90	3,128.11	2,589.52
140,000.00	12,129.89	6,284.04	4,338.81	3,368.74	2,788.71
150,000.00	12,996.31	6,732.90	4,648.73	3,609.36	2,987.90
160,000.00	13,862.73	7,181.76	4,958.64	3,849.98	3,187.10
170,000.00	14,729.15	7,630.62	5,268.56	4,090.61	3,386.29
180,000.00	15,595.57	8,079.48	5,578.48	4,331.23	3,585.49
190,000.00	16,461.99	8,528.34	5,888.39	4,571.86	3,784.68
200,000.00	17,328.41	8,977.20	6,198.31	4,812.48	3,983.87
225,000.00	19,494.46	10,099.35	6,973.09	5,414.04	4,481.86
250,000.00	21,660.51	11,221.50	7,747.88	6,015.60	4,979.84
275,000.00	23,826.56	12,343.65	8,522.67	6,617.16	5,477.82
300,000.00	25,992.61	13,465.80	9,297.46	7,218.72	5,975.81
350,000.00	30,324.71	15,710.10	10,847.04	8,421.84	6,971.78
400,000.00	34,656.82	17,954.40	12,396.61	9,624.96	7,967.74
450,000.00	38,988.92	20,198.70	13,946.19	10,828.08	8,963.71
500,000.00	43,321.02	22,443.00	15,495.76	12,031.20	9,959.68

Monthly Mortgage Payment

TABLE C

(Amount Necessary to Amortize a Loan)

10 Years	15 Years	TERM OF LOAN 20 Years	25 Years	30 Years	AMOUNT OF LOAN
$ .59	$ .46	$ .40	$ .36	$ .34	$ 50.00
1.17	.91	.79	.72	.68	100.00
2.35	1.83	1.58	1.45	1.36	200.00
3.52	2.74	2.37	2.17	2.05	300.00
4.70	3.65	3.16	2.89	2.73	400.00
5.87	4.56	3.95	3.61	3.41	500.00
11.74	9.13	7.90	7.23	6.82	1,000.00
23.48	18.26	15.81	14.46	13.64	2,000.00
35.22	27.39	23.71	21.68	20.47	3,000.00
46.96	36.51	31.62	28.91	27.29	4,000.00
58.70	45.64	39.52	36.14	34.11	5,000.00
117.40	91.29	79.04	72.28	68.22	10,000.00
176.10	136.93	118.56	108.42	102.33	15,000.00
234.80	182.57	158.08	144.56	136.44	20,000.00
293.50	228.22	197.59	180.70	170.54	25,000.00
352.20	273.86	237.11	216.84	204.65	30,000.00
410.90	319.50	276.63	252.98	238.76	35,000.00
469.60	365.15	316.15	289.12	272.87	40,000.00
528.30	410.79	355.67	325.26	306.98	45,000.00
587.01	456.43	395.19	361.40	341.09	50,000.00
645.71	502.07	434.71	397.54	375.20	55,000.00
704.41	547.72	474.23	433.68	409.31	60,000.00
763.11	593.36	513.74	469.82	443.41	65,000.00
821.81	639.00	553.26	505.96	477.52	70,000.00
880.51	684.65	592.78	542.11	511.63	75,000.00
939.21	730.29	632.30	578.25	545.74	80,000.00
997.91	775.93	671.82	614.39	579.85	85,000.00
1,056.61	821.58	711.34	650.53	613.96	90,000.00
1,115.31	867.22	750.86	686.67	648.07	95,000.00
1,174.01	912.86	790.38	722.81	682.18	100,000.00
1,291.41	1,004.15	869.41	795.09	750.39	110,000.00
1,408.81	1,095.44	948.45	867.37	818.61	120,000.00
1,526.21	1,186.72	1,027.49	939.65	886.83	130,000.00
1,643.61	1,278.01	1,106.53	1,011.93	955.05	140,000.00
1,761.02	1,369.29	1,185.56	1,084.21	1,023.26	150,000.00
1,878.42	1,460.58	1,264.60	1,156.49	1,091.48	160,000.00
1,995.82	1,551.87	1,343.64	1,228.77	1,159.70	170,000.00
2,113.22	1,643.15	1,422.68	1,301.05	1,227.92	180,000.00
2,230.62	1,734.44	1,501.71	1,373.33	1,296.13	190,000.00
2,348.02	1,825.73	1,580.75	1,445.61	1,364.35	200,000.00
2,641.52	2,053.94	1,778.35	1,626.32	1,534.90	225,000.00
2,935.03	2,282.16	1,975.94	1,807.02	1,705.44	250,000.00
3,228.53	2,510.37	2,173.53	1,987.72	1,875.98	275,000.00
3,522.03	2,738.59	2,371.13	2,168.42	2,046.53	300,000.00
4,109.04	3,195.02	2,766.32	2,529.82	2,387.62	350,000.00
4,696.04	3,651.45	3,161.50	2,891.23	2,728.71	400,000.00
5,283.05	4,107.88	3,556.69	3,252.63	3,069.79	450,000.00
5,870.05	4,564.31	3,951.88	3,614.03	3,410.88	500,000.00

7½%

TABLE C

(Amount Necessary to Amortize a Loan)

AMOUNT OF LOAN	TERM OF LOAN 1 Year	2 Years	3 Years	4 Years	5 Years
$ 50.00	$ 4.34	$ 2.25	$ 1.56	$ 1.21	$ 1.00
100.00	8.68	4.50	3.11	2.42	2.00
200.00	17.35	9.00	6.22	4.84	4.01
300.00	26.03	13.50	9.33	7.25	6.01
400.00	34.70	18.00	12.44	9.67	8.02
500.00	43.38	22.50	15.55	12.09	10.02
1,000.00	86.76	45.00	31.11	24.18	20.04
2,000.00	173.51	90.00	62.21	48.36	40.08
3,000.00	260.27	135.00	93.32	72.54	60.11
4,000.00	347.03	180.00	124.42	96.72	80.15
5,000.00	433.79	225.00	155.53	120.89	100.19
10,000.00	867.57	450.00	311.06	241.79	200.38
15,000.00	1,301.36	674.99	466.59	362.68	300.57
20,000.00	1,735.15	899.99	622.12	483.58	400.76
25,000.00	2,168.94	1,124.99	777.66	604.47	500.95
30,000.00	2,602.72	1,349.99	933.19	725.37	601.14
35,000.00	3,036.51	1,574.99	1,088.72	846.26	701.33
40,000.00	3,470.30	1,799.98	1,244.25	967.16	801.52
45,000.00	3,904.08	2,024.98	1,399.78	1,088.05	901.71
50,000.00	4,337.87	2,249.98	1,555.31	1,208.95	1,001.90
55,000.00	4,771.66	2,474.98	1,710.84	1,329.84	1,102.09
60,000.00	5,205.45	2,699.98	1,866.37	1,450.73	1,202.28
65,000.00	5,639.23	2,924.97	2,021.90	1,571.63	1,302.47
70,000.00	6,073.02	3,149.97	2,177.44	1,692.52	1,402.66
75,000.00	6,506.81	3,374.97	2,332.97	1,813.42	1,502.85
80,000.00	6,940.59	3,599.97	2,488.50	1,934.31	1,603.04
85,000.00	7,374.38	3,824.97	2,644.03	2,055.21	1,703.23
90,000.00	7,808.17	4,049.96	2,799.56	2,176.10	1,803.42
95,000.00	8,241.95	4,274.96	2,955.09	2,297.00	1,903.61
100,000.00	8,675.74	4,499.96	3,110.62	2,417.89	2,003.79
110,000.00	9,543.32	4,949.96	3,421.68	2,659.68	2,204.17
120,000.00	10,410.89	5,399.95	3,732.75	2,901.47	2,404.55
130,000.00	11,278.46	5,849.95	4,043.81	3,143.26	2,604.93
140,000.00	12,146.04	6,299.94	4,354.87	3,385.05	2,805.31
150,000.00	13,013.61	6,749.94	4,665.93	3,626.84	3,005.69
160,000.00	13,881.19	7,199.93	4,976.99	3,868.62	3,206.07
170,000.00	14,748.76	7,649.93	5,288.06	4,110.41	3,406.45
180,000.00	15,616.34	8,099.93	5,599.12	4,352.20	3,606.83
190,000.00	16,483.91	8,549.92	5,910.18	4,593.99	3,807.21
200,000.00	17,351.48	8,999.92	6,221.24	4,835.78	4,007.59
225,000.00	19,520.42	10,124.91	6,998.90	5,440.25	4,508.54
250,000.00	21,689.35	11,249.90	7,776.55	6,044.73	5,009.49
275,000.00	23,858.29	12,374.89	8,554.21	6,649.20	5,510.44
300,000.00	26,027.23	13,499.88	9,331.87	7,253.67	6,011.38
350,000.00	30,365.10	15,749.86	10,887.18	8,462.62	7,013.28
400,000.00	34,702.97	17,999.84	12,442.49	9,671.56	8,015.18
450,000.00	39,040.84	20,249.82	13,997.80	10,880.51	9,017.08
500,000.00	43,378.71	22,499.80	15,553.11	12,089.45	10,018.97

Monthly Mortgage Payment 7½%

TABLE C

(Amount Necessary to Amortize a Loan)

10 Years	15 Years	TERM OF LOAN 20 Years	25 Years	30 Years	AMOUNT OF LOAN
$ .59	$ .46	$ .40	$ .37	$ .35	$ 50.00
1.19	.93	.81	.74	.70	100.00
2.37	1.85	1.61	1.48	1.40	200.00
3.56	2.78	2.42	2.22	2.10	300.00
4.75	3.71	3.22	2.96	2.80	400.00
5.94	4.64	4.03	3.69	3.50	500.00
11.87	9.27	8.06	7.39	6.99	1,000.00
23.74	18.54	16.11	14.78	13.98	2,000.00
35.61	27.81	24.17	22.17	20.98	3,000.00
47.48	37.08	32.22	29.56	27.97	4,000.00
59.35	46.35	40.28	36.95	34.96	5,000.00
118.70	92.70	80.56	73.90	69.92	10,000.00
178.05	139.05	120.84	110.85	104.88	15,000.00
237.40	185.40	161.12	147.80	139.84	20,000.00
296.75	231.75	201.40	184.75	174.80	25,000.00
356.11	278.10	241.68	221.70	209.76	30,000.00
415.46	324.45	281.96	258.65	244.73	35,000.00
474.81	370.80	322.24	295.60	279.69	40,000.00
534.16	417.16	362.52	332.55	314.65	45,000.00
593.51	463.51	402.80	369.50	349.61	50,000.00
652.86	509.86	443.08	406.45	384.57	55,000.00
712.21	556.21	483.36	443.39	419.53	60,000.00
771.56	602.56	523.64	480.34	454.49	65,000.00
830.91	648.91	563.92	517.29	489.45	70,000.00
890.26	695.26	604.19	554.24	524.41	75,000.00
949.61	741.61	644.47	591.19	559.37	80,000.00
1,008.97	787.96	684.75	628.14	594.33	85,000.00
1,068.32	834.31	725.03	665.09	629.29	90,000.00
1,127.67	880.66	765.31	702.04	664.25	95,000.00
1,187.02	927.01	805.59	738.99	699.21	100,000.00
1,305.72	1,019.71	886.15	812.89	769.14	110,000.00
1,424.42	1,112.41	966.71	886.79	839.06	120,000.00
1,543.12	1,205.12	1,047.27	960.69	908.98	130,000.00
1,661.82	1,297.82	1,127.83	1,034.59	978.90	140,000.00
1,780.53	1,390.52	1,208.39	1,108.49	1,048.82	150,000.00
1,899.23	1,483.22	1,288.95	1,182.39	1,118.74	160,000.00
2,017.93	1,575.92	1,369.51	1,256.29	1,188.66	170,000.00
2,136.63	1,668.62	1,450.07	1,330.18	1,258.59	180,000.00
2,255.33	1,761.32	1,530.63	1,404.08	1,328.51	190,000.00
2,374.04	1,854.02	1,611.19	1,477.98	1,398.43	200,000.00
2,670.79	2,085.78	1,812.58	1,662.73	1,573.23	225,000.00
2,967.54	2,317.53	2,013.98	1,847.48	1,748.04	250,000.00
3,264.30	2,549.28	2,215.38	2,032.23	1,922.84	275,000.00
3,561.05	2,781.04	2,416.78	2,216.97	2,097.64	300,000.00
4,154.56	3,244.54	2,819.58	2,586.47	2,447.25	350,000.00
4,748.07	3,708.05	3,222.37	2,955.96	2,796.86	400,000.00
5,341.58	4,171.56	3,625.17	3,325.46	3,146.47	450,000.00
5,935.09	4,635.06	4,027.97	3,694.96	3,496.07	500,000.00

Figuring Out Your

TABLE C
(Amount Necessary to Amortize a Loan)

AMOUNT OF LOAN	TERM OF LOAN				
	1 Year	2 Years	3 Years	4 Years	5 Years
$ 50.00	$ 4.34	$ 2.26	$ 1.56	$ 1.21	$ 1.01
100.00	8.69	4.51	3.12	2.43	2.02
200.00	17.37	9.02	6.24	4.86	4.03
300.00	26.06	13.53	9.37	7.29	6.05
400.00	34.75	18.05	12.49	9.72	8.06
500.00	43.44	22.56	15.61	12.15	10.08
1,000.00	86.87	45.11	31.22	24.30	20.16
2,000.00	173.75	90.23	62.44	48.59	40.31
3,000.00	260.62	135.34	93.66	72.89	60.47
4,000.00	347.49	180.45	124.88	97.18	80.63
5,000.00	434.36	225.57	156.11	121.48	100.78
10,000.00	868.73	451.13	312.21	242.96	201.57
15,000.00	1,303.09	676.70	468.32	364.44	302.35
20,000.00	1,737.46	902.27	624.42	485.91	403.14
25,000.00	2,171.82	1,127.83	780.53	607.39	503.92
30,000.00	2,606.19	1,353.40	936.63	728.87	604.71
35,000.00	3,040.55	1,578.97	1,092.74	850.35	705.49
40,000.00	3,474.92	1,804.53	1,248.85	971.83	806.28
45,000.00	3,909.28	2,030.10	1,404.95	1,093.31	907.06
50,000.00	4,343.64	2,255.67	1,561.06	1,214.79	1,007.85
55,000.00	4,778.01	2,481.23	1,717.16	1,336.27	1,108.63
60,000.00	5,212.37	2,706.80	1,873.27	1,457.74	1,209.42
65,000.00	5,646.74	2,932.37	2,029.38	1,579.22	1,310.20
70,000.00	6,081.10	3,157.93	2,185.48	1,700.70	1,410.99
75,000.00	6,515.47	3,383.50	2,341.59	1,822.18	1,511.77
80,000.00	6,949.83	3,609.07	2,497.69	1,943.66	1,612.56
85,000.00	7,384.19	3,834.64	2,653.80	2,065.14	1,713.34
90,000.00	7,818.56	4,060.20	2,809.90	2,186.62	1,814.13
95,000.00	8,252.92	4,285.77	2,966.01	2,308.10	1,914.91
100,000.00	8,687.29	4,511.34	3,122.12	2,429.57	2,015.70
110,000.00	9,556.02	4,962.47	3,434.33	2,672.53	2,217.27
120,000.00	10,424.75	5,413.60	3,746.54	2,915.49	2,418.84
130,000.00	11,293.47	5,864.74	4,058.75	3,158.45	2,620.40
140,000.00	12,162.20	6,315.87	4,370.96	3,401.40	2,821.97
150,000.00	13,030.93	6,767.00	4,683.17	3,644.36	3,023.54
160,000.00	13,899.66	7,218.14	4,995.39	3,887.32	3,225.11
170,000.00	14,768.39	7,669.27	5,307.60	4,130.28	3,426.68
180,000.00	15,637.12	8,120.40	5,619.81	4,373.23	3,628.25
190,000.00	16,505.85	8,571.54	5,932.02	4,616.19	3,829.82
200,000.00	17,374.58	9,022.67	6,244.23	4,859.15	4,031.39
225,000.00	19,546.40	10,150.51	7,024.76	5,466.54	4,535.32
250,000.00	21,718.22	11,278.34	7,805.29	6,073.94	5,039.24
275,000.00	23,890.04	12,406.17	8,585.82	6,681.33	5,543.16
300,000.00	26,061.86	13,534.01	9,366.35	7,288.72	6,047.09
350,000.00	30,405.51	15,789.67	10,927.41	8,503.51	7,054.94
400,000.00	34,749.15	18,045.34	12,488.47	9,718.30	8,062.78
450,000.00	39,092.80	20,301.01	14,049.52	10,933.08	9,070.63
500,000.00	43,436.44	22,556.68	15,610.58	12,147.87	10,078.48

Monthly Mortgage Payment

TABLE C

(Amount Necessary to Amortize a Loan)

10 Years	15 Years	TERM OF LOAN 20 Years	25 Years	30 Years	AMOUNT OF LOAN
$ .60	$ .47	$ .41	$ .38	$ .36	$ 50.00
1.20	.94	.82	.76	.72	100.00
2.40	1.88	1.64	1.51	1.43	200.00
3.60	2.82	2.46	2.27	2.15	300.00
4.80	3.77	3.28	3.02	2.87	400.00
6.00	4.71	4.10	3.78	3.58	500.00
12.00	9.41	8.21	7.55	7.16	1,000.00
24.00	18.83	16.42	15.11	14.33	2,000.00
36.00	28.24	24.63	22.66	21.49	3,000.00
48.00	37.65	32.84	30.21	28.66	4,000.00
60.01	47.06	41.05	37.77	35.82	5,000.00
120.01	94.13	82.09	75.53	71.64	10,000.00
180.02	141.19	123.14	113.30	107.46	15,000.00
240.02	188.26	164.19	151.07	143.28	20,000.00
300.03	235.32	205.24	188.83	179.10	25,000.00
360.03	282.38	246.28	226.60	214.92	30,000.00
420.04	329.45	287.33	264.37	250.74	35,000.00
480.04	376.51	328.38	302.13	286.56	40,000.00
540.05	423.57	369.43	339.90	322.39	45,000.00
600.05	470.64	410.47	377.66	358.21	50,000.00
660.06	517.70	451.52	415.43	394.03	55,000.00
720.06	564.77	492.57	453.20	429.85	60,000.00
780.07	611.83	533.62	490.96	465.67	65,000.00
840.07	658.89	574.66	528.73	501.49	70,000.00
900.08	705.96	615.71	566.50	537.31	75,000.00
960.09	753.02	656.76	604.26	573.13	80,000.00
1,020.09	800.08	697.81	642.03	608.95	85,000.00
1,080.10	847.15	738.85	679.80	644.77	90,000.00
1,140.10	894.21	779.90	717.56	680.59	95,000.00
1,200.11	941.28	820.95	755.33	716.41	100,000.00
1,320.12	1,035.40	903.04	830.86	788.05	110,000.00
1,440.13	1,129.53	985.14	906.39	859.69	120,000.00
1,560.14	1,223.66	1,067.23	981.93	931.34	130,000.00
1,680.15	1,317.79	1,149.33	1,057.46	1,002.98	140,000.00
1,800.16	1,411.91	1,231.42	1,132.99	1,074.62	150,000.00
1,920.17	1,506.04	1,313.52	1,208.53	1,146.26	160,000.00
2,040.18	1,600.17	1,395.61	1,284.06	1,217.90	170,000.00
2,160.19	1,694.30	1,477.71	1,359.59	1,289.54	180,000.00
2,280.20	1,788.42	1,559.80	1,435.12	1,361.18	190,000.00
2,400.21	1,882.55	1,641.90	1,510.66	1,432.82	200,000.00
2,700.24	2,117.87	1,847.13	1,699.49	1,611.93	225,000.00
3,000.27	2,353.19	2,052.37	1,888.32	1,791.03	250,000.00
3,300.29	2,588.51	2,257.61	2,077.15	1,970.13	275,000.00
3,600.32	2,823.83	2,462.85	2,265.99	2,149.24	300,000.00
4,200.37	3,294.47	2,873.32	2,643.65	2,507.44	350,000.00
4,800.43	3,765.10	3,283.79	3,021.32	2,865.65	400,000.00
5,400.48	4,235.74	3,694.27	3,398.98	3,223.86	450,000.00
6,000.53	4,706.38	4,104.74	3,776.64	3,582.06	500,000.00

Figuring Out Your

TABLE C

(Amount Necessary to Amortize a Loan)

AMOUNT OF LOAN	TERM OF LOAN 1 Year	2 Years	3 Years	4 Years	5 Years
$ 50.00	$ 4.35	$ 2.26	$ 1.57	$ 1.22	$ 1.01
100.00	8.70	4.52	3.13	2.44	2.03
200.00	17.40	9.05	6.27	4.88	4.06
300.00	26.10	13.57	9.40	7.32	6.08
400.00	34.80	18.09	12.53	9.77	8.11
500.00	43.49	22.61	15.67	12.21	10.14
1,000.00	86.99	45.23	31.34	24.41	20.28
2,000.00	173.98	90.45	62.67	48.83	40.55
3,000.00	260.97	135.68	94.01	73.24	60.83
4,000.00	347.95	180.91	125.35	97.65	81.11
5,000.00	434.94	226.14	156.68	122.06	101.38
10,000.00	869.88	452.27	313.36	244.13	202.76
15,000.00	1,304.83	678.41	470.05	366.19	304.15
20,000.00	1,739.77	904.55	626.73	488.26	405.53
25,000.00	2,174.71	1,130.68	783.41	610.32	506.91
30,000.00	2,609.65	1,356.82	940.09	732.39	608.29
35,000.00	3,044.60	1,582.96	1,096.77	854.45	709.67
40,000.00	3,479.54	1,809.09	1,253.45	976.52	811.06
45,000.00	3,914.48	2,035.23	1,410.14	1,098.58	912.44
50,000.00	4,349.42	2,261.36	1,566.82	1,220.65	1,013.82
55,000.00	4,784.36	2,487.50	1,723.50	1,342.71	1,115.20
60,000.00	5,219.31	2,713.64	1,880.18	1,464.78	1,216.58
65,000.00	5,654.25	2,939.77	2,036.86	1,586.84	1,317.97
70,000.00	6,089.19	3,165.91	2,193.55	1,708.90	1,419.35
75,000.00	6,524.13	3,392.05	2,350.23	1,830.97	1,520.73
80,000.00	6,959.07	3,618.18	2,506.91	1,953.03	1,622.11
85,000.00	7,394.02	3,844.32	2,663.59	2,075.10	1,723.49
90,000.00	7,828.96	4,070.46	2,820.27	2,197.16	1,824.88
95,000.00	8,263.90	4,296.59	2,976.95	2,319.23	1,926.26
100,000.00	8,698.84	4,522.73	3,133.64	2,441.29	2,027.64
110,000.00	9,568.73	4,975.00	3,447.00	2,685.42	2,230.40
120,000.00	10,438.61	5,427.27	3,760.36	2,929.55	2,433.17
130,000.00	11,308.50	5,879.55	4,073.73	3,173.68	2,635.93
140,000.00	12,178.38	6,331.82	4,387.09	3,417.81	2,838.70
150,000.00	13,048.26	6,784.09	4,700.45	3,661.94	3,041.46
160,000.00	13,918.15	7,236.37	5,013.82	3,906.07	3,244.22
170,000.00	14,788.03	7,688.64	5,327.18	4,150.20	3,446.99
180,000.00	15,657.92	8,140.91	5,640.55	4,394.33	3,649.75
190,000.00	16,527.80	8,593.19	5,953.91	4,638.46	3,852.51
200,000.00	17,397.69	9,045.46	6,267.27	4,882.58	4,055.28
225,000.00	19,572.40	10,176.14	7,050.68	5,492.91	4,562.19
250,000.00	21,747.11	11,306.82	7,834.09	6,103.23	5,069.10
275,000.00	23,921.82	12,437.51	8,617.50	6,713.55	5,576.01
300,000.00	26,096.53	13,568.19	9,400.91	7,323.88	6,082.92
350,000.00	30,445.95	15,829.55	10,967.73	8,544.52	7,096.74
400,000.00	34,795.37	18,090.92	12,534.55	9,765.17	8,110.56
450,000.00	39,144.79	20,352.28	14,101.36	10,985.82	9,124.38
500,000.00	43,494.21	22,613.65	15,668.18	12,206.46	10,138.20

Monthly Mortgage Payment

8%

TABLE C

(Amount Necessary to Amortize a Loan)

		TERM OF LOAN			AMOUNT OF LOAN
10 Years	15 Years	20 Years	25 Years	30 Years	
$ .61	$ .48	$ .42	$ .39	$ .37	$ 50.00
1.21	.96	.84	.77	.73	100.00
2.43	1.91	1.67	1.54	1.47	200.00
3.64	2.87	2.51	2.32	2.20	300.00
4.85	3.82	3.35	3.09	2.94	400.00
6.07	4.78	4.18	3.86	3.67	500.00
12.13	9.56	8.36	7.72	7.34	1,000.00
24.27	19.11	16.73	15.44	14.68	2,000.00
36.40	28.67	25.09	23.15	22.01	3,000.00
48.53	38.23	33.46	30.87	29.35	4,000.00
60.66	47.78	41.82	38.59	36.69	5,000.00
121.33	95.57	83.64	77.18	73.38	10,000.00
181.99	143.35	125.47	115.77	110.06	15,000.00
242.66	191.13	167.29	154.36	146.75	20,000.00
303.32	238.91	209.11	192.95	183.44	25,000.00
363.98	286.70	250.93	231.54	220.13	30,000.00
424.65	334.48	292.75	270.14	256.82	35,000.00
485.31	382.26	334.58	308.73	293.51	40,000.00
545.97	430.04	376.40	347.32	330.19	45,000.00
606.64	477.83	418.22	385.91	366.88	50,000.00
667.30	525.61	460.04	424.50	403.57	55,000.00
727.97	573.39	501.86	463.09	440.26	60,000.00
788.63	621.17	543.69	501.68	476.95	65,000.00
849.29	668.96	585.51	540.27	513.64	70,000.00
909.96	716.74	627.33	578.86	550.32	75,000.00
970.62	764.52	669.15	617.45	587.01	80,000.00
1,031.28	812.30	710.97	656.04	623.70	85,000.00
1,091.95	860.09	752.80	694.63	660.39	90,000.00
1,152.61	907.87	794.62	733.23	697.08	95,000.00
1,213.28	955.65	836.44	771.82	733.76	100,000.00
1,334.60	1,051.22	920.08	849.00	807.14	110,000.00
1,455.93	1,146.78	1,003.73	926.18	880.52	120,000.00
1,577.26	1,242.35	1,087.37	1,003.36	953.89	130,000.00
1,698.59	1,337.91	1,171.02	1,080.54	1,027.27	140,000.00
1,819.91	1,433.48	1,254.66	1,157.72	1,100.65	150,000.00
1,941.24	1,529.04	1,338.30	1,234.91	1,174.02	160,000.00
2,062.57	1,624.61	1,421.95	1,312.09	1,247.40	170,000.00
2,183.90	1,720.17	1,505.59	1,389.27	1,320.78	180,000.00
2,305.22	1,815.74	1,589.24	1,466.45	1,394.15	190,000.00
2,426.55	1,911.30	1,672.88	1,543.63	1,467.53	200,000.00
2,729.87	2,150.22	1,881.99	1,736.59	1,650.97	225,000.00
3,033.19	2,389.13	2,091.10	1,929.54	1,834.41	250,000.00
3,336.51	2,628.04	2,300.21	2,122.49	2,017.85	275,000.00
3,639.83	2,866.96	2,509.32	2,315.45	2,201.29	300,000.00
4,246.47	3,344.78	2,927.54	2,701.36	2,568.18	350,000.00
4,853.10	3,822.61	3,345.76	3,087.26	2,935.06	400,000.00
5,459.74	4,300.43	3,763.98	3,473.17	3,301.94	450,000.00
6,066.38	4,778.26	4,182.20	3,859.08	3,668.82	500,000.00

TABLE C

(Amount Necessary to Amortize a Loan)

AMOUNT OF LOAN	TERM OF LOAN 1 Year	2 Years	3 Years	4 Years	5 Years
$ 50.00	$ 4.36	$ 2.27	$ 1.57	$ 1.23	$ 1.02
100.00	8.71	4.53	3.15	2.45	2.04
200.00	17.42	9.07	6.29	4.91	4.08
300.00	26.13	13.60	9.44	7.36	6.12
400.00	34.84	18.14	12.58	9.81	8.16
500.00	43.55	22.67	15.73	12.27	10.20
1,000.00	87.10	45.34	31.45	24.53	20.40
2,000.00	174.21	90.68	62.90	49.06	40.79
3,000.00	261.31	136.02	94.36	73.59	61.19
4,000.00	348.42	181.37	125.81	98.12	81.59
5,000.00	435.52	226.71	157.26	122.65	101.98
10,000.00	871.04	453.41	314.52	245.30	203.96
15,000.00	1,306.56	680.12	471.78	367.96	305.94
20,000.00	1,742.08	906.83	629.04	490.61	407.93
25,000.00	2,177.60	1,133.53	786.30	613.26	509.91
30,000.00	2,613.12	1,360.24	943.55	735.91	611.89
35,000.00	3,048.64	1,586.95	1,100.81	858.57	713.87
40,000.00	3,484.16	1,813.66	1,258.07	981.22	815.85
45,000.00	3,919.68	2,040.36	1,415.33	1,103.87	917.83
50,000.00	4,355.20	2,267.07	1,572.59	1,226.52	1,019.81
55,000.00	4,790.72	2,493.78	1,729.85	1,349.17	1,121.79
60,000.00	5,226.24	2,720.48	1,887.11	1,471.83	1,223.78
65,000.00	5,661.76	2,947.19	2,044.37	1,594.48	1,325.76
70,000.00	6,097.28	3,173.90	2,201.63	1,717.13	1,427.74
75,000.00	6,532.80	3,400.60	2,358.89	1,839.78	1,529.72
80,000.00	6,968.33	3,627.31	2,516.15	1,962.44	1,631.70
85,000.00	7,403.85	3,854.02	2,673.40	2,085.09	1,733.68
90,000.00	7,839.37	4,080.73	2,830.66	2,207.74	1,835.66
95,000.00	8,274.89	4,307.43	2,987.92	2,330.39	1,937.64
100,000.00	8,710.41	4,534.14	3,145.18	2,453.04	2,039.63
110,000.00	9,581.45	4,987.55	3,459.70	2,698.35	2,243.59
120,000.00	10,452.49	5,440.97	3,774.22	2,943.65	2,447.55
130,000.00	11,323.53	5,894.38	4,088.74	3,188.96	2,651.51
140,000.00	12,194.57	6,347.80	4,403.26	3,434.26	2,855.48
150,000.00	13,065.61	6,801.21	4,717.77	3,679.57	3,059.44
160,000.00	13,936.65	7,254.62	5,032.29	3,924.87	3,263.40
170,000.00	14,807.69	7,708.04	5,346.81	4,170.18	3,467.36
180,000.00	15,678.73	8,161.45	5,661.33	4,415.48	3,671.33
190,000.00	16,549.77	8,614.87	5,975.85	4,660.78	3,875.29
200,000.00	17,420.81	9,068.28	6,290.36	4,906.09	4,079.25
225,000.00	19,598.41	10,201.81	7,076.66	5,519.35	4,589.16
250,000.00	21,776.02	11,335.35	7,862.96	6,132.61	5,099.06
275,000.00	23,953.62	12,468.88	8,649.25	6,745.87	5,608.97
300,000.00	26,131.22	13,602.42	9,435.55	7,359.13	6,118.88
350,000.00	30,486.42	15,869.49	11,008.14	8,585.66	7,138.69
400,000.00	34,841.63	18,136.56	12,580.73	9,812.18	8,158.50
450,000.00	39,196.83	20,403.63	14,153.32	11,038.70	9,178.31
500,000.00	43,552.03	22,670.70	15,725.91	12,265.22	10,198.13

Monthly Mortgage Payment

TABLE C

(Amount Necessary to Amortize a Loan)

10 Years	15 Years	TERM OF LOAN 20 Years	25 Years	30 Years	AMOUNT OF LOAN
$ .61	$ .49	$ .43	$ .39	$ .38	$ 50.00
1.23	.97	.85	.79	.75	100.00
2.45	1.94	1.70	1.58	1.50	200.00
3.68	2.91	2.56	2.37	2.25	300.00
4.91	3.88	3.41	3.15	3.01	400.00
6.13	4.85	4.26	3.94	3.76	500.00
12.27	9.70	8.52	7.88	7.51	1,000.00
24.53	19.40	17.04	15.77	15.03	2,000.00
36.80	29.10	25.56	23.65	22.54	3,000.00
49.06	38.81	34.08	31.54	30.05	4,000.00
61.33	48.51	42.60	39.42	37.56	5,000.00
122.65	97.01	85.21	78.85	75.13	10,000.00
183.98	145.52	127.81	118.27	112.69	15,000.00
245.31	194.03	170.41	157.69	150.25	20,000.00
306.63	242.54	213.02	197.11	187.82	25,000.00
367.96	291.04	255.62	236.54	225.38	30,000.00
429.28	339.55	298.22	275.96	262.94	35,000.00
490.61	388.06	340.83	315.38	300.51	40,000.00
551.94	436.56	383.43	354.80	338.07	45,000.00
613.26	485.07	426.03	394.23	375.63	50,000.00
674.59	533.58	468.64	433.65	413.20	55,000.00
735.92	582.08	511.24	473.07	450.76	60,000.00
797.24	630.59	553.84	512.49	488.32	65,000.00
858.57	679.10	596.45	551.92	525.89	70,000.00
919.89	727.61	639.05	591.34	563.45	75,000.00
981.22	776.11	681.65	630.76	601.01	80,000.00
1,042.55	824.62	724.26	670.18	638.58	85,000.00
1,103.87	873.13	766.86	709.61	676.14	90,000.00
1,165.20	921.63	809.46	749.03	713.70	95,000.00
1,226.53	970.14	852.07	788.45	751.27	100,000.00
1,349.18	1,067.15	937.27	867.30	826.39	110,000.00
1,471.83	1,164.17	1,022.48	946.14	901.52	120,000.00
1,594.48	1,261.18	1,107.69	1,024.99	976.65	130,000.00
1,717.14	1,358.20	1,192.89	1,103.83	1,051.77	140,000.00
1,839.79	1,455.21	1,278.10	1,182.68	1,126.90	150,000.00
1,962.44	1,552.22	1,363.31	1,261.52	1,202.03	160,000.00
2,085.09	1,649.24	1,448.51	1,340.37	1,277.15	170,000.00
2,207.75	1,746.25	1,533.72	1,419.21	1,352.28	180,000.00
2,330.40	1,843.27	1,618.92	1,498.06	1,427.41	190,000.00
2,453.05	1,940.28	1,704.13	1,576.90	1,502.53	200,000.00
2,759.68	2,182.82	1,917.15	1,774.01	1,690.35	225,000.00
3,066.32	2,425.35	2,130.16	1,971.13	1,878.17	250,000.00
3,372.95	2,667.89	2,343.18	2,168.24	2,065.98	275,000.00
3,679.58	2,910.42	2,556.20	2,365.35	2,253.80	300,000.00
4,292.84	3,395.49	2,982.23	2,759.58	2,629.43	350,000.00
4,906.11	3,880.56	3,408.26	3,153.80	3,005.07	400,000.00
5,519.37	4,365.63	3,834.30	3,548.03	3,380.70	450,000.00
6,132.63	4,850.70	4,260.33	3,942.25	3,756.33	500,000.00

TABLE C

(Amount Necessary to Amortize a Loan)

AMOUNT OF LOAN	TERM OF LOAN 1 Year	2 Years	3 Years	4 Years	5 Years
$ 50.00	$ 4.36	$ 2.27	$ 1.58	$ 1.23	$ 1.03
100.00	8.72	4.55	3.16	2.46	2.05
200.00	17.44	9.09	6.31	4.93	4.10
300.00	26.17	13.64	9.47	7.39	6.15
400.00	34.89	18.18	12.63	9.86	8.21
500.00	43.61	22.73	15.78	12.32	10.26
1,000.00	87.22	45.46	31.57	24.65	20.52
2,000.00	174.44	90.91	63.14	49.30	41.03
3,000.00	261.66	136.37	94.70	73.94	61.55
4,000.00	348.88	181.82	126.27	98.59	82.07
5,000.00	436.10	227.28	157.84	123.24	102.58
10,000.00	872.20	454.56	315.68	246.48	205.17
15,000.00	1,308.30	681.84	473.51	369.72	307.75
20,000.00	1,744.40	909.11	631.35	492.97	410.33
25,000.00	2,180.49	1,136.39	789.19	616.21	512.91
30,000.00	2,616.59	1,363.67	947.03	739.45	615.50
35,000.00	3,052.69	1,590.95	1,104.86	862.69	718.08
40,000.00	3,488.79	1,818.23	1,262.70	985.93	820.66
45,000.00	3,924.89	2,045.51	1,420.54	1,109.17	923.24
50,000.00	4,360.99	2,272.78	1,578.38	1,232.42	1,025.83
55,000.00	4,797.09	2,500.06	1,736.21	1,355.66	1,128.41
60,000.00	5,233.19	2,727.34	1,894.05	1,478.90	1,230.99
65,000.00	5,669.29	2,954.62	2,051.89	1,602.14	1,333.57
70,000.00	6,105.38	3,181.90	2,209.73	1,725.38	1,436.16
75,000.00	6,541.48	3,409.18	2,367.57	1,848.62	1,538.74
80,000.00	6,977.58	3,636.45	2,525.40	1,971.86	1,641.32
85,000.00	7,413.68	3,863.73	2,683.24	2,095.11	1,743.91
90,000.00	7,849.78	4,091.01	2,841.08	2,218.35	1,846.49
95,000.00	8,285.88	4,318.29	2,998.92	2,341.59	1,949.07
100,000.00	8,721.98	4,545.57	3,156.75	2,464.83	2,051.65
110,000.00	9,594.18	5,000.12	3,472.43	2,711.31	2,256.82
120,000.00	10,466.37	5,454.68	3,788.10	2,957.80	2,461.98
130,000.00	11,338.57	5,909.24	4,103.78	3,204.28	2,667.15
140,000.00	12,210.77	6,363.79	4,419.46	3,450.76	2,872.31
150,000.00	13,082.97	6,818.35	4,735.13	3,697.25	3,077.48
160,000.00	13,955.17	7,272.91	5,050.81	3,943.73	3,282.65
170,000.00	14,827.36	7,727.46	5,366.48	4,190.21	3,487.81
180,000.00	15,699.56	8,182.02	5,682.16	4,436.69	3,692.98
190,000.00	16,571.76	8,636.58	5,997.83	4,683.18	3,898.14
200,000.00	17,443.96	9,091.13	6,313.51	4,929.66	4,103.31
225,000.00	19,624.45	10,227.53	7,102.70	5,545.87	4,616.22
250,000.00	21,804.95	11,363.92	7,891.88	6,162.08	5,129.13
275,000.00	23,985.44	12,500.31	8,681.07	6,778.28	5,642.05
300,000.00	26,165.93	13,636.70	9,470.26	7,394.49	6,154.96
350,000.00	30,526.92	15,909.49	11,048.64	8,626.91	7,180.79
400,000.00	34,887.91	18,182.27	12,627.01	9,859.32	8,206.61
450,000.00	39,248.90	20,455.05	14,205.39	11,091.74	9,232.44
500,000.00	43,609.89	22,727.84	15,783.77	12,324.15	10,258.27

Monthly Mortgage Payment

8½%

TABLE C

(Amount Necessary to Amortize a Loan)

		TERM OF LOAN			AMOUNT
10 Years	15 Years	20 Years	25 Years	30 Years	OF LOAN
$ .62	$ .49	$ .43	$ .40	$ .38	$ 50.00
1.24	.98	.87	.81	.77	100.00
2.48	1.97	1.74	1.61	1.54	200.00
3.72	2.95	2.60	2.42	2.31	300.00
4.96	3.94	3.47	3.22	3.08	400.00
6.20	4.92	4.34	4.03	3.84	500.00
12.40	9.85	8.68	8.05	7.69	1,000.00
24.80	19.69	17.36	16.10	15.38	2,000.00
37.20	29.54	26.03	24.16	23.07	3,000.00
49.59	39.39	34.71	32.21	30.76	4,000.00
61.99	49.24	43.39	40.26	38.45	5,000.00
123.99	98.47	86.78	80.52	76.89	10,000.00
185.98	147.71	130.17	120.78	115.34	15,000.00
247.97	196.95	173.56	161.05	153.78	20,000.00
309.96	246.18	216.96	201.31	192.23	25,000.00
371.96	295.42	260.35	241.57	230.67	30,000.00
433.95	344.66	303.74	281.83	269.12	35,000.00
495.94	393.90	347.13	322.09	307.57	40,000.00
557.94	443.13	390.52	362.35	346.01	45,000.00
619.93	492.37	433.91	402.61	384.46	50,000.00
681.92	541.61	477.30	442.87	422.90	55,000.00
743.91	590.84	520.69	483.14	461.35	60,000.00
805.91	640.08	564.09	523.40	499.79	65,000.00
867.90	689.32	607.48	563.66	538.24	70,000.00
929.89	738.55	650.87	603.92	576.69	75,000.00
991.89	787.79	694.26	644.18	615.13	80,000.00
1,053.88	837.03	737.65	684.44	653.58	85,000.00
1,115.87	886.27	781.04	724.70	692.02	90,000.00
1,177.86	935.50	824.43	764.97	730.47	95,000.00
1,239.86	984.74	867.82	805.23	768.91	100,000.00
1,363.84	1,083.21	954.61	885.75	845.80	110,000.00
1,487.83	1,181.69	1,041.39	966.27	922.70	120,000.00
1,611.81	1,280.16	1,128.17	1,046.80	999.59	130,000.00
1,735.80	1,378.64	1,214.95	1,127.32	1,076.48	140,000.00
1,859.79	1,477.11	1,301.73	1,207.84	1,153.37	150,000.00
1,983.77	1,575.58	1,388.52	1,288.36	1,230.26	160,000.00
2,107.76	1,674.06	1,475.30	1,368.89	1,307.15	170,000.00
2,231.74	1,772.53	1,562.08	1,449.41	1,384.04	180,000.00
2,355.73	1,871.01	1,648.86	1,529.93	1,460.94	190,000.00
2,479.71	1,969.48	1,735.65	1,610.45	1,537.83	200,000.00
2,789.68	2,215.66	1,952.60	1,811.76	1,730.06	225,000.00
3,099.64	2,461.85	2,169.56	2,013.07	1,922.28	250,000.00
3,409.61	2,708.03	2,386.51	2,214.37	2,114.51	275,000.00
3,719.57	2,954.22	2,603.47	2,415.68	2,306.74	300,000.00
4,339.50	3,446.59	3,037.38	2,818.29	2,691.20	350,000.00
4,959.43	3,938.96	3,471.29	3,220.91	3,075.65	400,000.00
5,579.36	4,431.33	3,905.20	3,623.52	3,460.11	450,000.00
6,199.28	4,923.70	4,339.12	4,026.14	3,844.57	500,000.00

TABLE C
(Amount Necessary to Amortize a Loan)

AMOUNT OF LOAN	TERM OF LOAN				
	1 Year	2 Years	3 Years	4 Years	5 Years
$ 50.00	$ 4.37	$ 2.28	$ 1.58	$ 1.24	$ 1.03
100.00	8.73	4.56	3.17	2.48	2.06
200.00	17.47	9.11	6.34	4.95	4.13
300.00	26.20	13.67	9.51	7.43	6.19
400.00	34.93	18.23	12.67	9.91	8.25
500.00	43.67	22.79	15.84	12.38	10.32
1,000.00	87.34	45.57	31.68	24.77	20.64
2,000.00	174.67	91.14	63.37	49.53	41.27
3,000.00	262.01	136.71	95.05	74.30	61.91
4,000.00	349.34	182.28	126.73	99.07	82.55
5,000.00	436.68	227.85	158.42	123.83	103.19
10,000.00	873.36	455.70	316.84	247.67	206.37
15,000.00	1,310.03	683.55	475.25	371.50	309.56
20,000.00	1,746.71	911.40	633.67	495.33	412.74
25,000.00	2,183.39	1,139.25	792.09	619.16	515.93
30,000.00	2,620.07	1,367.10	950.51	743.00	619.12
35,000.00	3,056.75	1,594.95	1,108.92	866.83	722.30
40,000.00	3,493.42	1,822.80	1,267.34	990.66	825.49
45,000.00	3,930.10	2,050.66	1,425.76	1,114.49	928.68
50,000.00	4,366.78	2,278.51	1,584.18	1,238.33	1,031.86
55,000.00	4,803.46	2,506.36	1,742.59	1,362.16	1,135.05
60,000.00	5,240.14	2,734.21	1,901.01	1,485.99	1,238.23
65,000.00	5,676.81	2,962.06	2,059.43	1,609.82	1,341.42
70,000.00	6,113.49	3,189.91	2,217.85	1,733.66	1,444.61
75,000.00	6,550.17	3,417.76	2,376.26	1,857.49	1,547.79
80,000.00	6,986.85	3,645.61	2,534.68	1,981.32	1,650.98
85,000.00	7,423.52	3,873.46	2,693.10	2,105.15	1,754.16
90,000.00	7,860.20	4,101.31	2,851.52	2,228.99	1,857.35
95,000.00	8,296.88	4,329.16	3,009.93	2,352.82	1,960.54
100,000.00	8,733.56	4,557.01	3,168.35	2,476.65	2,063.72
110,000.00	9,606.91	5,012.71	3,485.19	2,724.32	2,270.10
120,000.00	10,480.27	5,468.41	3,802.02	2,971.98	2,476.47
130,000.00	11,353.63	5,924.12	4,118.86	3,219.65	2,682.84
140,000.00	12,226.98	6,379.82	4,435.69	3,467.31	2,889.21
150,000.00	13,100.34	6,835.52	4,752.53	3,714.98	3,095.58
160,000.00	13,973.69	7,291.22	5,069.36	3,962.64	3,301.96
170,000.00	14,847.05	7,746.92	5,386.20	4,210.31	3,508.33
180,000.00	15,720.41	8,202.62	5,703.03	4,457.97	3,714.70
190,000.00	16,593.76	8,658.32	6,019.87	4,705.64	3,921.07
200,000.00	17,467.12	9,114.02	6,336.70	4,953.30	4,127.45
225,000.00	19,650.51	10,253.28	7,128.79	5,572.46	4,643.38
250,000.00	21,833.90	11,392.53	7,920.88	6,191.63	5,159.31
275,000.00	24,017.29	12,531.78	8,712.96	6,810.79	5,675.24
300,000.00	26,200.68	13,671.04	9,505.05	7,429.95	6,191.17
350,000.00	30,567.46	15,949.54	11,089.23	8,668.28	7,223.03
400,000.00	34,934.23	18,228.05	12,673.40	9,906.60	8,254.89
450,000.00	39,301.01	20,506.56	14,257.58	11,144.93	9,286.75
500,000.00	43,667.79	22,785.06	15,841.75	12,383.25	10,318.62

Monthly Mortgage Payment

TABLE C

(Amount Necessary to Amortize a Loan)

10 Years	15 Years	TERM OF LOAN 20 Years	25 Years	30 Years	AMOUNT OF LOAN
$ .63	$ .50	$ .44	$ .41	$ .39	$ 50.00
1.25	1.00	.88	.82	.79	100.00
2.51	2.00	1.77	1.64	1.57	200.00
3.76	3.00	2.65	2.47	2.36	300.00
5.01	4.00	3.53	3.29	3.15	400.00
6.27	5.00	4.42	4.11	3.93	500.00
12.53	9.99	8.84	8.22	7.87	1,000.00
25.07	19.99	17.67	16.44	15.73	2,000.00
37.60	29.98	26.51	24.66	23.60	3,000.00
50.13	39.98	35.35	32.89	31.47	4,000.00
62.66	49.97	44.19	41.11	39.34	5,000.00
125.33	99.94	88.37	82.21	78.67	10,000.00
187.99	149.92	132.56	123.32	118.01	15,000.00
250.65	199.89	176.74	164.43	157.34	20,000.00
313.32	249.86	220.93	205.54	196.68	25,000.00
375.98	299.83	265.11	246.64	236.01	30,000.00
438.64	349.81	309.30	287.75	275.35	35,000.00
501.31	399.78	353.48	328.86	314.68	40,000.00
563.97	449.75	397.67	369.96	354.02	45,000.00
626.63	499.72	441.86	411.07	393.35	50,000.00
689.30	549.70	486.04	452.18	432.69	55,000.00
751.96	599.67	530.23	493.29	472.02	60,000.00
814.62	649.64	574.41	534.39	511.36	65,000.00
877.29	699.61	618.60	575.50	550.69	70,000.00
939.95	749.59	662.78	616.61	590.03	75,000.00
1,002.61	799.56	706.97	657.71	629.36	80,000.00
1,065.28	849.53	751.15	698.82	668.70	85,000.00
1,127.94	899.50	795.34	739.93	708.03	90,000.00
1,190.60	949.48	839.53	781.04	747.37	95,000.00
1,253.27	999.45	883.71	822.14	786.70	100,000.00
1,378.59	1,099.39	972.08	904.36	865.37	110,000.00
1,503.92	1,199.34	1,060.45	986.57	944.04	120,000.00
1,629.25	1,299.28	1,148.82	1,068.79	1,022.71	130,000.00
1,754.57	1,399.23	1,237.19	1,151.00	1,101.38	140,000.00
1,879.90	1,499.17	1,325.57	1,233.22	1,180.05	150,000.00
2,005.23	1,599.12	1,413.94	1,315.43	1,258.72	160,000.00
2,130.55	1,699.06	1,502.31	1,397.64	1,337.39	170,000.00
2,255.88	1,799.01	1,590.68	1,479.86	1,416.06	180,000.00
2,381.21	1,898.95	1,679.05	1,562.07	1,494.73	190,000.00
2,506.54	1,998.90	1,767.42	1,644.29	1,573.40	200,000.00
2,819.85	2,248.76	1,988.35	1,849.82	1,770.08	225,000.00
3,133.17	2,498.62	2,209.28	2,055.36	1,966.75	250,000.00
3,446.49	2,748.48	2,430.20	2,260.89	2,163.43	275,000.00
3,759.80	2,998.35	2,651.13	2,466.43	2,360.10	300,000.00
4,386.44	3,498.07	3,092.99	2,877.50	2,753.45	350,000.00
5,013.07	3,997.79	3,534.84	3,288.57	3,146.80	400,000.00
5,639.70	4,497.52	3,976.70	3,699.65	3,540.15	450,000.00
6,266.34	4,997.24	4,418.55	4,110.72	3,933.50	500,000.00

TABLE C
(Amount Necessary to Amortize a Loan)

AMOUNT OF LOAN	1 Year	2 Years	3 Years	4 Years	5 Years
$ 50.00	$ 4.37	$ 2.28	$ 1.59	$ 1.24	$ 1.04
100.00	8.75	4.57	3.18	2.49	2.08
200.00	17.49	9.14	6.36	4.98	4.15
300.00	26.24	13.71	9.54	7.47	6.23
400.00	34.98	18.27	12.72	9.95	8.30
500.00	43.73	22.84	15.90	12.44	10.38
1,000.00	87.45	45.68	31.80	24.89	20.76
2,000.00	174.90	91.37	63.60	49.77	41.52
3,000.00	262.35	137.05	95.40	74.66	62.28
4,000.00	349.81	182.74	127.20	99.54	83.03
5,000.00	437.26	228.42	159.00	124.43	103.79
10,000.00	874.51	456.85	318.00	248.85	207.58
15,000.00	1,311.77	685.27	477.00	373.28	311.38
20,000.00	1,749.03	913.69	635.99	497.70	415.17
25,000.00	2,186.29	1,142.12	794.99	622.13	518.96
30,000.00	2,623.54	1,370.54	953.99	746.55	622.75
35,000.00	3,060.80	1,598.97	1,112.99	870.98	726.54
40,000.00	3,498.06	1,827.39	1,271.99	995.40	830.33
45,000.00	3,935.32	2,055.81	1,430.99	1,119.83	934.13
50,000.00	4,372.57	2,284.24	1,589.99	1,244.25	1,037.92
55,000.00	4,809.83	2,512.66	1,748.99	1,368.68	1,141.71
60,000.00	5,247.09	2,741.08	1,907.98	1,493.10	1,245.50
65,000.00	5,684.35	2,969.51	2,066.98	1,617.53	1,349.29
70,000.00	6,121.60	3,197.93	2,225.98	1,741.95	1,453.08
75,000.00	6,558.86	3,426.36	2,384.98	1,866.38	1,556.88
80,000.00	6,996.12	3,654.78	2,543.98	1,990.80	1,660.67
85,000.00	7,433.38	3,883.20	2,702.98	2,115.23	1,764.46
90,000.00	7,870.63	4,111.63	2,861.98	2,239.65	1,868.25
95,000.00	8,307.89	4,340.05	3,020.97	2,364.08	1,972.04
100,000.00	8,745.15	4,568.47	3,179.97	2,488.50	2,075.84
110,000.00	9,619.66	5,025.32	3,497.97	2,737.35	2,283.42
120,000.00	10,494.18	5,482.17	3,815.97	2,986.21	2,491.00
130,000.00	11,368.69	5,939.02	4,133.97	3,235.06	2,698.59
140,000.00	12,243.21	6,395.86	4,451.96	3,483.91	2,906.17
150,000.00	13,117.72	6,852.71	4,769.96	3,732.76	3,113.75
160,000.00	13,992.24	7,309.56	5,087.96	3,981.61	3,321.34
170,000.00	14,866.75	7,766.41	5,405.95	4,230.46	3,528.92
180,000.00	15,741.27	8,223.25	5,723.95	4,479.31	3,736.50
190,000.00	16,615.78	8,680.10	6,041.95	4,728.16	3,944.09
200,000.00	17,490.30	9,136.95	6,359.95	4,977.01	4,151.67
225,000.00	19,676.58	10,279.07	7,154.94	5,599.13	4,670.63
250,000.00	21,862.87	11,421.19	7,949.93	6,221.26	5,189.59
275,000.00	24,049.16	12,563.30	8,744.93	6,843.39	5,708.55
300,000.00	26,235.44	13,705.42	9,539.92	7,465.51	6,227.51
350,000.00	30,608.02	15,989.66	11,129.91	8,709.76	7,265.42
400,000.00	34,980.59	18,273.90	12,719.89	9,954.02	8,303.34
450,000.00	39,353.16	20,558.13	14,309.88	11,198.27	9,341.26
500,000.00	43,725.74	22,842.37	15,899.87	12,442.52	10,379.18

Monthly Mortgage Payment 9%

TABLE C

(Amount Necessary to Amortize a Loan)

10 Years	15 Years	20 Years	25 Years	30 Years	AMOUNT OF LOAN
$ .63	$ .51	$ .45	$ .42	$ .40	$ 50.00
1.27	1.01	.90	.84	.80	100.00
2.53	2.03	1.80	1.68	1.61	200.00
3.80	3.04	2.70	2.52	2.41	300.00
5.07	4.06	3.60	3.36	3.22	400.00
6.33	5.07	4.50	4.20	4.02	500.00
12.67	10.14	9.00	8.39	8.05	1,000.00
25.34	20.29	17.99	16.78	16.09	2,000.00
38.00	30.43	26.99	25.18	24.14	3,000.00
50.67	40.57	35.99	33.57	32.18	4,000.00
63.34	50.71	44.99	41.96	40.23	5,000.00
126.68	101.43	89.97	83.92	80.46	10,000.00
190.01	152.14	134.96	125.88	120.69	15,000.00
253.35	202.85	179.95	167.84	160.92	20,000.00
316.69	253.57	224.93	209.80	201.16	25,000.00
380.03	304.28	269.92	251.76	241.39	30,000.00
443.37	354.99	314.90	293.72	281.62	35,000.00
506.70	405.71	359.89	335.68	321.85	40,000.00
570.04	456.42	404.88	377.64	362.08	45,000.00
633.38	507.13	449.86	419.60	402.31	50,000.00
696.72	557.85	494.85	461.56	442.54	55,000.00
760.05	608.56	539.84	503.52	482.77	60,000.00
823.39	659.27	584.82	545.48	523.00	65,000.00
886.73	709.99	629.81	587.44	563.24	70,000.00
950.07	760.70	674.79	629.40	603.47	75,000.00
1,013.41	811.41	719.78	671.36	643.70	80,000.00
1,076.74	862.13	764.77	713.32	683.93	85,000.00
1,140.08	912.84	809.75	755.28	724.16	90,000.00
1,203.42	963.55	854.74	797.24	764.39	95,000.00
1,266.76	1,014.27	899.73	839.20	804.62	100,000.00
1,393.43	1,115.69	989.70	923.12	885.08	110,000.00
1,520.11	1,217.12	1,079.67	1,007.04	965.55	120,000.00
1,646.79	1,318.55	1,169.64	1,090.96	1,046.01	130,000.00
1,773.46	1,419.97	1,259.62	1,174.87	1,126.47	140,000.00
1,900.14	1,521.40	1,349.59	1,258.79	1,206.93	150,000.00
2,026.81	1,622.83	1,439.56	1,342.71	1,287.40	160,000.00
2,153.49	1,724.25	1,529.53	1,426.63	1,367.86	170,000.00
2,280.16	1,825.68	1,619.51	1,510.55	1,448.32	180,000.00
2,406.84	1,927.11	1,709.48	1,594.47	1,528.78	190,000.00
2,533.52	2,028.53	1,799.45	1,678.39	1,609.25	200,000.00
2,850.20	2,282.10	2,024.38	1,888.19	1,810.40	225,000.00
3,166.89	2,535.67	2,249.31	2,097.99	2,011.56	250,000.00
3,483.58	2,789.23	2,474.25	2,307.79	2,212.71	275,000.00
3,800.27	3,042.80	2,699.18	2,517.59	2,413.87	300,000.00
4,433.65	3,549.93	3,149.04	2,937.19	2,816.18	350,000.00
5,067.03	4,057.07	3,598.90	3,356.79	3,218.49	400,000.00
5,700.41	4,564.20	4,048.77	3,776.38	3,620.80	450,000.00
6,333.79	5,071.33	4,498.63	4,195.98	4,023.11	500,000.00

9¼%

Figuring Out Your

TABLE C

(Amount Necessary to Amortize a Loan)

AMOUNT OF LOAN	1 Year	2 Years	3 Years	4 Years	5 Years
$ 50.00	$ 4.38	$ 2.29	$ 1.60	$ 1.25	$ 1.04
100.00	8.76	4.58	3.19	2.50	2.09
200.00	17.51	9.16	6.38	5.00	4.18
300.00	26.27	13.74	9.57	7.50	6.26
400.00	35.03	18.32	12.77	10.00	8.35
500.00	43.78	22.90	15.96	12.50	10.44
1,000.00	87.57	45.80	31.92	25.00	20.88
2,000.00	175.13	91.60	63.83	50.01	41.76
3,000.00	262.70	137.40	95.75	75.01	62.64
4,000.00	350.27	183.20	127.66	100.02	83.52
5,000.00	437.84	229.00	159.58	125.02	104.40
10,000.00	875.67	458.00	319.16	250.04	208.80
15,000.00	1,313.51	686.99	478.74	375.06	313.20
20,000.00	1,751.35	915.99	638.32	500.08	417.60
25,000.00	2,189.19	1,144.99	797.91	625.10	522.00
30,000.00	2,627.02	1,373.99	957.49	750.12	626.40
35,000.00	3,064.86	1,602.98	1,117.07	875.14	730.80
40,000.00	3,502.70	1,831.98	1,276.65	1,000.16	835.20
45,000.00	3,940.54	2,060.98	1,436.23	1,125.18	939.60
50,000.00	4,378.37	2,289.98	1,595.81	1,250.20	1,043.99
55,000.00	4,816.21	2,518.97	1,755.39	1,375.22	1,148.39
60,000.00	5,254.05	2,747.97	1,914.97	1,500.24	1,252.79
65,000.00	5,691.88	2,976.97	2,074.55	1,625.25	1,357.19
70,000.00	6,129.72	3,205.97	2,234.13	1,750.27	1,461.59
75,000.00	6,567.56	3,434.96	2,393.72	1,875.29	1,565.99
80,000.00	7,005.40	3,663.96	2,553.30	2,000.31	1,670.39
85,000.00	7,443.23	3,892.96	2,712.88	2,125.33	1,774.79
90,000.00	7,881.07	4,121.96	2,872.46	2,250.35	1,879.19
95,000.00	8,318.91	4,350.96	3,032.04	2,375.37	1,983.59
100,000.00	8,756.75	4,579.95	3,191.62	2,500.39	2,087.99
110,000.00	9,632.42	5,037.95	3,510.78	2,750.43	2,296.79
120,000.00	10,508.09	5,495.94	3,829.95	3,000.47	2,505.59
130,000.00	11,383.77	5,953.94	4,149.11	3,250.51	2,714.39
140,000.00	12,259.44	6,411.93	4,468.27	3,500.55	2,923.19
150,000.00	13,135.12	6,869.93	4,787.43	3,750.59	3,131.98
160,000.00	14,010.79	7,327.93	5,106.59	4,000.63	3,340.78
170,000.00	14,886.47	7,785.92	5,425.76	4,250.67	3,549.58
180,000.00	15,762.14	8,243.92	5,744.92	4,500.71	3,758.38
190,000.00	16,637.82	8,701.91	6,064.08	4,750.74	3,967.18
200,000.00	17,513.49	9,159.91	6,383.24	5,000.78	4,175.98
225,000.00	19,702.68	10,304.89	7,181.15	5,625.88	4,697.98
250,000.00	21,891.86	11,449.88	7,979.05	6,250.98	5,219.97
275,000.00	24,081.05	12,594.87	8,776.96	6,876.08	5,741.97
300,000.00	26,270.24	13,739.86	9,574.86	7,501.18	6,263.97
350,000.00	30,648.61	16,029.84	11,170.67	8,751.37	7,307.96
400,000.00	35,026.98	18,319.81	12,766.49	10,001.57	8,351.96
450,000.00	39,405.35	20,609.79	14,362.30	11,251.76	9,395.95
500,000.00	43,783.73	22,899.77	15,958.11	12,501.96	10,439.95

176

Monthly Mortgage Payment

9¼%

TABLE C

(Amount Necessary to Amortize a Loan)

10 Years	15 Years	TERM OF LOAN 20 Years	25 Years	30 Years	AMOUNT OF LOAN
$ .64	$ .51	$ .46	$ .43	$ .41	$ 50.00
1.28	1.03	.92	.86	.82	100.00
2.56	2.06	1.83	1.71	1.65	200.00
3.84	3.09	2.75	2.57	2.47	300.00
5.12	4.12	3.66	3.43	3.29	400.00
6.40	5.15	4.58	4.28	4.11	500.00
12.80	10.29	9.16	8.56	8.23	1,000.00
25.61	20.58	18.32	17.13	16.45	2,000.00
38.41	30.88	27.48	25.69	24.68	3,000.00
51.21	41.17	36.63	34.26	32.91	4,000.00
64.02	51.46	45.79	42.82	41.13	5,000.00
128.03	102.92	91.59	85.64	82.27	10,000.00
192.05	154.38	137.38	128.46	123.40	15,000.00
256.07	205.84	183.17	171.28	164.54	20,000.00
320.08	257.30	228.97	214.10	205.67	25,000.00
384.10	308.76	274.76	256.91	246.80	30,000.00
448.11	360.22	320.55	299.73	287.94	35,000.00
512.13	411.68	366.35	342.55	329.07	40,000.00
576.15	463.14	412.14	385.37	370.20	45,000.00
640.16	514.60	457.93	428.19	411.34	50,000.00
704.18	566.06	503.73	471.01	452.47	55,000.00
768.20	617.52	549.52	513.83	493.61	60,000.00
832.21	668.97	595.31	556.65	534.74	65,000.00
896.23	720.43	641.11	599.47	575.87	70,000.00
960.25	771.89	686.90	642.29	617.01	75,000.00
1,024.26	823.35	732.69	685.11	658.14	80,000.00
1,088.28	874.81	778.49	727.92	699.27	85,000.00
1,152.29	926.27	824.28	770.74	740.41	90,000.00
1,216.31	977.73	870.07	813.56	781.54	95,000.00
1,280.33	1,029.19	915.87	856.38	822.68	100,000.00
1,408.36	1,132.11	1,007.45	942.02	904.94	110,000.00
1,536.39	1,235.03	1,099.04	1,027.66	987.21	120,000.00
1,664.43	1,337.95	1,190.63	1,113.30	1,069.48	130,000.00
1,792.46	1,440.87	1,282.21	1,198.93	1,151.75	140,000.00
1,920.49	1,543.79	1,373.80	1,284.57	1,234.01	150,000.00
2,048.52	1,646.71	1,465.39	1,370.21	1,316.28	160,000.00
2,176.56	1,749.63	1,556.97	1,455.85	1,398.55	170,000.00
2,304.59	1,852.55	1,648.56	1,541.49	1,480.82	180,000.00
2,432.62	1,955.47	1,740.15	1,627.13	1,563.08	190,000.00
2,560.65	2,058.38	1,831.73	1,712.76	1,645.35	200,000.00
2,880.74	2,315.68	2,060.70	1,926.86	1,851.02	225,000.00
3,200.82	2,572.98	2,289.67	2,140.95	2,056.69	250,000.00
3,520.90	2,830.28	2,518.63	2,355.05	2,262.36	275,000.00
3,840.98	3,087.58	2,747.60	2,569.15	2,468.03	300,000.00
4,481.15	3,602.17	3,205.53	2,997.34	2,879.36	350,000.00
5,121.31	4,116.77	3,663.47	3,425.53	3,290.70	400,000.00
5,761.47	4,631.37	4,121.40	3,853.72	3,702.04	450,000.00
6,401.64	5,145.96	4,579.33	4,281.91	4,113.38	500,000.00

9½%

Figuring Out Your

TABLE C

(Amount Necessary to Amortize a Loan)

AMOUNT OF LOAN	TERM OF LOAN				
	1 Year	2 Years	3 Years	4 Years	5 Years
$ 50.00	$ 4.38	$ 2.30	$ 1.60	$ 1.26	$ 1.05
100.00	8.77	4.59	3.20	2.51	2.10
200.00	17.54	9.18	6.41	5.02	4.20
300.00	26.31	13.77	9.61	7.54	6.30
400.00	35.07	18.37	12.81	10.05	8.40
500.00	43.84	22.96	16.02	12.56	10.50
1,000.00	87.68	45.91	32.03	25.12	21.00
2,000.00	175.37	91.83	64.07	50.25	42.00
3,000.00	263.05	137.74	96.10	75.37	63.01
4,000.00	350.73	183.66	128.13	100.49	84.01
5,000.00	438.42	229.57	160.16	125.62	105.01
10,000.00	876.84	459.14	320.33	251.23	210.02
15,000.00	1,315.25	688.72	480.49	376.85	315.03
20,000.00	1,753.67	918.29	640.66	502.46	420.04
25,000.00	2,192.09	1,147.86	800.82	628.08	525.05
30,000.00	2,630.51	1,377.43	960.99	753.69	630.06
35,000.00	3,068.92	1,607.01	1,121.15	879.31	735.07
40,000.00	3,507.34	1,836.58	1,281.32	1,004.93	840.07
45,000.00	3,945.76	2,066.15	1,441.48	1,130.54	945.08
50,000.00	4,384.18	2,295.72	1,601.65	1,256.16	1,050.09
55,000.00	4,822.59	2,525.30	1,761.81	1,381.77	1,155.10
60,000.00	5,261.01	2,754.87	1,921.98	1,507.39	1,260.11
65,000.00	5,699.43	2,984.44	2,082.14	1,633.00	1,365.12
70,000.00	6,137.85	3,214.01	2,242.31	1,758.62	1,470.13
75,000.00	6,576.26	3,443.59	2,402.47	1,884.24	1,575.14
80,000.00	7,014.68	3,673.16	2,562.64	2,009.85	1,680.15
85,000.00	7,453.10	3,902.73	2,722.80	2,135.47	1,785.16
90,000.00	7,891.52	4,132.30	2,882.97	2,261.08	1,890.17
95,000.00	8,329.93	4,361.88	3,043.13	2,386.70	1,995.18
100,000.00	8,768.35	4,591.45	3,203.29	2,512.31	2,100.19
110,000.00	9,645.19	5,050.59	3,523.62	2,763.55	2,310.20
120,000.00	10,522.02	5,509.74	3,843.95	3,014.78	2,520.22
130,000.00	11,398.86	5,968.88	4,164.28	3,266.01	2,730.24
140,000.00	12,275.69	6,428.03	4,484.61	3,517.24	2,940.26
150,000.00	13,152.53	6,887.17	4,804.94	3,768.47	3,150.28
160,000.00	14,029.36	7,346.32	5,125.27	4,019.70	3,360.30
170,000.00	14,906.20	7,805.46	5,445.60	4,270.93	3,570.32
180,000.00	15,783.03	8,264.61	5,765.93	4,522.16	3,780.34
190,000.00	16,659.87	8,723.75	6,086.26	4,773.40	3,990.35
200,000.00	17,536.70	9,182.90	6,406.59	5,024.63	4,200.37
225,000.00	19,728.79	10,330.76	7,207.41	5,652.71	4,725.42
250,000.00	21,920.88	11,478.62	8,008.24	6,280.78	5,250.47
275,000.00	24,112.97	12,626.49	8,809.06	6,908.86	5,775.51
300,000.00	26,305.05	13,774.35	9,609.88	7,536.94	6,300.56
350,000.00	30,689.23	16,070.07	11,211.53	8,793.10	7,350.65
400,000.00	35,073.40	18,365.80	12,813.18	10,049.25	8,400.74
450,000.00	39,457.58	20,661.52	14,414.83	11,305.41	9,450.84
500,000.00	43,841.76	22,957.25	16,016.47	12,561.57	10,500.93

Monthly Mortgage Payment

 9½%

TABLE C
(Amount Necessary to Amortize a Loan)

| TERM OF LOAN | | | | | AMOUNT OF LOAN |
10 Years	15 Years	20 Years	25 Years	30 Years	
$ .65	$ .52	$ .47	$ .44	$ .42	$ 50.00
1.29	1.04	.93	.87	.84	100.00
2.59	2.09	1.86	1.75	1.68	200.00
3.88	3.13	2.80	2.62	2.52	300.00
5.18	4.18	3.73	3.49	3.36	400.00
6.47	5.22	4.66	4.37	4.20	500.00
12.94	10.44	9.32	8.74	8.41	1,000.00
25.88	20.88	18.64	17.47	16.82	2,000.00
38.82	31.33	27.96	26.21	25.23	3,000.00
51.76	41.77	37.29	34.95	33.63	4,000.00
64.70	52.21	46.61	43.68	42.04	5,000.00
129.40	104.42	93.21	87.37	84.09	10,000.00
194.10	156.63	139.82	131.05	126.13	15,000.00
258.80	208.84	186.43	174.74	168.17	20,000.00
323.49	261.06	233.03	218.42	210.21	25,000.00
388.19	313.27	279.64	262.11	252.26	30,000.00
452.89	365.48	326.25	305.79	294.30	35,000.00
517.59	417.69	372.85	349.48	336.34	40,000.00
582.29	469.90	419.46	393.16	378.38	45,000.00
646.99	522.11	466.07	436.85	420.43	50,000.00
711.69	574.32	512.67	480.53	462.47	55,000.00
776.39	626.53	559.28	524.22	504.51	60,000.00
841.08	678.75	605.89	567.90	546.56	65,000.00
905.78	730.96	652.49	611.59	588.60	70,000.00
970.48	783.17	699.10	655.27	630.64	75,000.00
1,035.18	835.38	745.70	698.96	672.68	80,000.00
1,099.88	887.59	792.31	742.64	714.73	85,000.00
1,164.58	939.80	838.92	786.33	756.77	90,000.00
1,229.28	992.01	885.52	830.01	798.81	95,000.00
1,293.98	1,044.22	932.13	873.70	840.85	100,000.00
1,423.37	1,148.65	1,025.34	961.07	924.94	110,000.00
1,552.77	1,253.07	1,118.56	1,048.44	1,009.03	120,000.00
1,682.17	1,357.49	1,211.77	1,135.81	1,093.11	130,000.00
1,811.57	1,461.91	1,304.98	1,223.18	1,177.20	140,000.00
1,940.96	1,566.34	1,398.20	1,310.54	1,261.28	150,000.00
2,070.36	1,670.76	1,491.41	1,397.91	1,345.37	160,000.00
2,199.76	1,775.18	1,584.62	1,485.28	1,429.45	170,000.00
2,329.16	1,879.60	1,677.84	1,572.65	1,513.54	180,000.00
2,458.55	1,984.03	1,771.05	1,660.02	1,597.62	190,000.00
2,587.95	2,088.45	1,864.26	1,747.39	1,681.71	200,000.00
2,911.45	2,349.51	2,097.30	1,965.82	1,891.92	225,000.00
3,234.94	2,610.56	2,330.33	2,184.24	2,102.14	250,000.00
3,558.43	2,871.62	2,563.36	2,402.67	2,312.35	275,000.00
3,881.93	3,132.67	2,796.39	2,621.09	2,522.56	300,000.00
4,528.91	3,654.79	3,262.46	3,057.94	2,942.99	350,000.00
5,175.90	4,176.90	3,728.52	3,494.79	3,363.42	400,000.00
5,822.89	4,699.01	4,194.59	3,931.63	3,783.84	450,000.00
6,469.88	5,221.12	4,660.66	4,368.48	4,204.27	500,000.00

179

9¾% **Figuring Out Your**

TABLE C
(Amount Necessary to Amortize a Loan)

AMOUNT OF LOAN	TERM OF LOAN				
	1 Year	2 Years	3 Years	4 Years	5 Years
$ 50.00	$ 4.39	$ 2.30	$ 1.61	$ 1.26	$ 1.06
100.00	8.78	4.60	3.21	2.52	2.11
200.00	17.56	9.21	6.43	5.05	4.22
300.00	26.34	13.81	9.64	7.57	6.34
400.00	35.12	18.41	12.86	10.10	8.45
500.00	43.90	23.01	16.07	12.62	10.56
1,000.00	87.80	46.03	32.15	25.24	21.12
2,000.00	175.60	92.06	64.30	50.49	42.25
3,000.00	263.40	138.09	96.45	75.73	63.37
4,000.00	351.20	184.12	128.60	100.97	84.50
5,000.00	439.00	230.15	160.75	126.21	105.62
10,000.00	878.00	460.30	321.50	252.43	211.24
15,000.00	1,316.99	690.44	482.25	378.64	316.86
20,000.00	1,755.99	920.59	643.00	504.85	422.48
25,000.00	2,194.99	1,150.74	803.75	631.07	528.11
30,000.00	2,633.99	1,380.89	964.50	757.28	633.73
35,000.00	3,072.99	1,611.04	1,125.25	883.49	739.35
40,000.00	3,511.99	1,841.18	1,286.00	1,009.71	844.97
45,000.00	3,950.98	2,071.33	1,446.75	1,135.92	950.59
50,000.00	4,389.98	2,301.48	1,607.50	1,262.13	1,056.21
55,000.00	4,828.98	2,531.63	1,768.25	1,388.35	1,161.83
60,000.00	5,267.98	2,761.78	1,929.00	1,514.56	1,267.45
65,000.00	5,706.98	2,991.93	2,089.75	1,640.77	1,373.08
70,000.00	6,145.98	3,222.07	2,250.50	1,766.99	1,478.70
75,000.00	6,584.97	3,452.22	2,411.25	1,893.20	1,584.32
80,000.00	7,023.97	3,682.37	2,572.00	2,019.42	1,689.94
85,000.00	7,462.97	3,912.52	2,732.74	2,145.63	1,795.56
90,000.00	7,901.97	4,142.67	2,893.49	2,271.84	1,901.18
95,000.00	8,340.97	4,372.81	3,054.24	2,398.06	2,006.80
100,000.00	8,779.97	4,602.96	3,214.99	2,524.27	2,112.42
110,000.00	9,657.96	5,063.26	3,536.49	2,776.70	2,323.67
120,000.00	10,535.96	5,523.55	3,857.99	3,029.12	2,534.91
130,000.00	11,413.96	5,983.85	4,179.49	3,281.55	2,746.15
140,000.00	12,291.95	6,444.15	4,500.99	3,533.98	2,957.39
150,000.00	13,169.95	6,904.44	4,822.49	3,786.40	3,168.64
160,000.00	14,047.95	7,364.74	5,143.99	4,038.83	3,379.88
170,000.00	14,925.94	7,825.04	5,465.49	4,291.26	3,591.12
180,000.00	15,803.94	8,285.33	5,786.99	4,543.68	3,802.36
190,000.00	16,681.93	8,745.63	6,108.49	4,796.11	4,013.61
200,000.00	17,559.93	9,205.92	6,429.99	5,048.54	4,224.85
225,000.00	19,754.92	10,356.67	7,233.74	5,679.61	4,752.95
250,000.00	21,949.91	11,507.41	8,037.49	6,310.67	5,281.06
275,000.00	24,144.91	12,658.15	8,841.23	6,941.74	5,809.17
300,000.00	26,339.90	13,808.89	9,644.98	7,572.81	6,337.27
350,000.00	30,729.88	16,110.37	11,252.48	8,834.94	7,393.49
400,000.00	35,119.86	18,411.85	12,859.98	10,097.08	8,449.70
450,000.00	39,509.85	20,713.33	14,467.47	11,359.21	9,505.91
500,000.00	43,899.83	23,014.81	16,074.97	12,621.35	10,562.12

180

Monthly Mortgage Payment 9¾%

TABLE C

(Amount Necessary to Amortize a Loan)

10 Years	15 Years	TERM OF LOAN 20 Years	25 Years	30 Years	AMOUNT OF LOAN
$ .65	$ .53	$ .47	$ .45	$ .43	$ 50.00
1.31	1.06	.95	.89	.86	100.00
2.62	2.12	1.90	1.78	1.72	200.00
3.92	3.18	2.85	2.67	2.58	300.00
5.23	4.24	3.79	3.56	3.44	400.00
6.54	5.30	4.74	4.46	4.30	500.00
13.08	10.59	9.49	8.91	8.59	1,000.00
26.15	21.19	18.97	17.82	17.18	2,000.00
39.23	31.78	28.46	26.73	25.77	3,000.00
52.31	42.37	37.94	35.65	34.37	4,000.00
65.39	52.97	47.43	44.56	42.96	5,000.00
130.77	105.94	94.85	89.11	85.92	10,000.00
196.16	158.90	142.28	133.67	128.87	15,000.00
261.54	211.87	189.70	178.23	171.83	20,000.00
326.93	264.84	237.13	222.78	214.79	25,000.00
392.31	317.81	284.56	267.34	257.75	30,000.00
457.70	370.78	331.98	311.90	300.70	35,000.00
523.08	423.75	379.41	356.45	343.66	40,000.00
588.47	476.71	426.83	401.01	386.62	45,000.00
653.85	529.68	474.26	445.57	429.58	50,000.00
719.24	582.65	521.68	490.13	472.53	55,000.00
784.62	635.62	569.11	534.68	515.49	60,000.00
850.01	688.59	616.54	579.24	558.45	65,000.00
915.39	741.55	663.96	623.80	601.41	70,000.00
980.78	794.52	711.39	668.35	644.37	75,000.00
1,046.16	847.49	758.81	712.91	687.32	80,000.00
1,111.55	900.46	806.24	757.47	730.28	85,000.00
1,176.93	953.43	853.67	802.02	773.24	90,000.00
1,242.32	1,006.39	901.09	846.58	816.20	95,000.00
1,307.70	1,059.36	948.52	891.14	859.15	100,000.00
1,438.47	1,165.30	1,043.37	980.25	945.07	110,000.00
1,569.24	1,271.24	1,138.22	1,069.36	1,030.99	120,000.00
1,700.01	1,377.17	1,233.07	1,158.48	1,116.90	130,000.00
1,830.78	1,483.11	1,327.92	1,247.59	1,202.82	140,000.00
1,961.55	1,589.04	1,422.78	1,336.71	1,288.73	150,000.00
2,092.32	1,694.98	1,517.63	1,425.82	1,374.65	160,000.00
2,223.09	1,800.92	1,612.48	1,514.93	1,460.56	170,000.00
2,353.86	1,906.85	1,707.33	1,604.05	1,546.48	180,000.00
2,484.63	2,012.79	1,802.18	1,693.16	1,632.39	190,000.00
2,615.40	2,118.73	1,897.03	1,782.27	1,718.31	200,000.00
2,942.33	2,383.57	2,134.16	2,005.06	1,933.10	225,000.00
3,269.26	2,648.41	2,371.29	2,227.84	2,147.89	250,000.00
3,596.18	2,913.25	2,608.42	2,450.63	2,362.67	275,000.00
3,923.11	3,178.09	2,845.55	2,673.41	2,577.46	300,000.00
4,576.96	3,707.77	3,319.81	3,118.98	3,007.04	350,000.00
5,230.81	4,237.45	3,794.07	3,564.55	3,436.62	400,000.00
5,884.66	4,767.13	4,268.33	4,010.12	3,866.19	450,000.00
6,538.51	5,296.81	4,742.58	4,455.69	4,295.77	500,000.00

TABLE C

(Amount Necessary to Amortize a Loan)

AMOUNT OF LOAN	TERM OF LOAN				
	1 Year	2 Years	3 Years	4 Years	5 Years
$ 50.00	$ 4.40	$ 2.31	$ 1.61	$ 1.27	$ 1.06
100.00	8.79	4.61	3.23	2.54	2.12
200.00	17.58	9.23	6.45	5.07	4.25
300.00	26.37	13.84	9.68	7.61	6.37
400.00	35.17	18.46	12.91	10.15	8.50
500.00	43.96	23.07	16.13	12.68	10.62
1,000.00	87.92	46.14	32.27	25.36	21.25
2,000.00	175.83	92.29	64.53	50.73	42.49
3,000.00	263.75	138.43	96.80	76.09	63.74
4,000.00	351.66	184.58	129.07	101.45	84.99
5,000.00	439.58	230.72	161.34	126.81	106.24
10,000.00	879.16	461.45	322.67	253.63	212.47
15,000.00	1,318.74	692.17	484.01	380.44	318.71
20,000.00	1,758.32	922.90	645.34	507.25	424.94
25,000.00	2,197.90	1,153.62	806.68	634.06	531.18
30,000.00	2,637.48	1,384.35	968.02	760.88	637.41
35,000.00	3,077.06	1,615.07	1,129.35	887.69	743.65
40,000.00	3,516.64	1,845.80	1,290.69	1,014.50	849.88
45,000.00	3,956.21	2,076.52	1,452.02	1,141.32	956.12
50,000.00	4,395.79	2,307.25	1,613.36	1,268.13	1,062.35
55,000.00	4,835.37	2,537.97	1,774.70	1,394.94	1,168.59
60,000.00	5,274.95	2,768.70	1,936.03	1,521.76	1,274.82
65,000.00	5,714.53	2,999.42	2,097.37	1,648.57	1,381.06
70,000.00	6,154.11	3,230.14	2,258.70	1,775.38	1,487.29
75,000.00	6,593.69	3,460.87	2,420.04	1,902.19	1,593.53
80,000.00	7,033.27	3,691.59	2,581.37	2,029.01	1,699.76
85,000.00	7,472.85	3,922.32	2,742.71	2,155.82	1,806.00
90,000.00	7,912.43	4,153.04	2,904.05	2,282.63	1,912.23
95,000.00	8,352.01	4,383.77	3,065.38	2,409.45	2,018.47
100,000.00	8,791.59	4,614.49	3,226.72	2,536.26	2,124.70
110,000.00	9,670.75	5,075.94	3,549.39	2,789.88	2,337.17
120,000.00	10,549.91	5,537.39	3,872.06	3,043.51	2,549.65
130,000.00	11,429.07	5,998.84	4,194.73	3,297.14	2,762.12
140,000.00	12,308.22	6,460.29	4,517.41	3,550.76	2,974.59
150,000.00	13,187.38	6,921.74	4,840.08	3,804.39	3,187.06
160,000.00	14,066.54	7,383.19	5,162.75	4,058.01	3,399.53
170,000.00	14,945.70	7,844.64	5,485.42	4,311.64	3,612.00
180,000.00	15,824.86	8,306.09	5,808.09	4,565.27	3,824.47
190,000.00	16,704.02	8,767.54	6,130.77	4,818.89	4,036.94
200,000.00	17,583.18	9,228.99	6,453.44	5,072.52	4,249.41
225,000.00	19,781.07	10,382.61	7,260.12	5,706.58	4,780.59
250,000.00	21,978.97	11,536.23	8,066.80	6,340.65	5,311.76
275,000.00	24,176.87	12,689.85	8,873.48	6,974.71	5,842.94
300,000.00	26,374.77	13,843.48	9,680.16	7,608.78	6,374.11
350,000.00	30,770.56	16,150.72	11,293.52	8,876.90	7,436.47
400,000.00	35,166.35	18,457.97	12,906.87	10,145.03	8,498.82
450,000.00	39,562.15	20,765.22	14,520.23	11,413.16	9,561.17
500,000.00	43,957.94	23,072.46	16,133.59	12,681.29	10,623.52

Monthly Mortgage Payment   10%

TABLE C

(Amount Necessary to Amortize a Loan)

10 Years	15 Years	TERM OF LOAN 20 Years	25 Years	30 Years	AMOUNT OF LOAN
$ .66	$ .54	$ .48	$ .45	$ .44	$ 50.00
1.32	1.07	.97	.91	.88	100.00
2.64	2.15	1.93	1.82	1.76	200.00
3.96	3.22	2.90	2.73	2.63	300.00
5.29	4.30	3.86	3.63	3.51	400.00
6.61	5.37	4.83	4.54	4.39	500.00
13.22	10.75	9.65	9.09	8.78	1,000.00
26.43	21.49	19.30	18.17	17.55	2,000.00
39.65	32.24	28.95	27.26	26.33	3,000.00
52.86	42.98	38.60	36.35	35.10	4,000.00
66.08	53.73	48.25	45.44	43.88	5,000.00
132.15	107.46	96.50	90.87	87.76	10,000.00
198.23	161.19	144.75	136.31	131.64	15,000.00
264.30	214.92	193.00	181.74	175.51	20,000.00
330.38	268.65	241.26	227.18	219.39	25,000.00
396.45	322.38	289.51	272.61	263.27	30,000.00
462.53	376.11	337.76	318.05	307.15	35,000.00
528.60	429.84	386.01	363.48	351.03	40,000.00
594.68	483.57	434.26	408.92	394.91	45,000.00
660.75	537.30	482.51	454.35	438.79	50,000.00
726.83	591.03	530.76	499.79	482.66	55,000.00
792.90	644.76	579.01	545.22	526.54	60,000.00
858.98	698.49	627.26	590.66	570.42	65,000.00
925.06	752.22	675.52	636.09	614.30	70,000.00
991.13	805.95	723.77	681.53	658.18	75,000.00
1,057.21	859.68	772.02	726.96	702.06	80,000.00
1,123.28	913.41	820.27	772.40	745.94	85,000.00
1,189.36	967.14	868.52	817.83	789.81	90,000.00
1,255.43	1,020.87	916.77	863.27	833.69	95,000.00
1,321.51	1,074.61	965.02	908.70	877.57	100,000.00
1,453.66	1,182.07	1,061.52	999.57	965.33	110,000.00
1,585.81	1,289.53	1,158.03	1,090.44	1,053.09	120,000.00
1,717.96	1,396.99	1,254.53	1,181.31	1,140.84	130,000.00
1,850.11	1,504.45	1,351.03	1,272.18	1,228.60	140,000.00
1,982.26	1,611.91	1,447.53	1,363.05	1,316.36	150,000.00
2,114.41	1,719.37	1,544.03	1,453.92	1,404.11	160,000.00
2,246.56	1,826.83	1,640.54	1,544.79	1,491.87	170,000.00
2,378.71	1,934.29	1,737.04	1,635.66	1,579.63	180,000.00
2,510.86	2,041.75	1,833.54	1,726.53	1,667.39	190,000.00
2,643.01	2,149.21	1,930.04	1,817.40	1,755.14	200,000.00
2,973.39	2,417.86	2,171.30	2,044.58	1,974.54	225,000.00
3,303.77	2,686.51	2,412.55	2,271.75	2,193.93	250,000.00
3,634.15	2,955.16	2,653.81	2,498.93	2,413.32	275,000.00
3,964.52	3,223.82	2,895.06	2,726.10	2,632.71	300,000.00
4,625.28	3,761.12	3,377.58	3,180.45	3,071.50	350,000.00
5,286.03	4,298.42	3,860.09	3,634.80	3,510.29	400,000.00
5,946.78	4,835.72	4,342.60	4,089.15	3,949.07	450,000.00
6,607.54	5,373.03	4,825.11	4,543.50	4,387.86	500,000.00

10¼%

Figuring Out Your

TABLE C

(Amount Necessary to Amortize a Loan)

AMOUNT OF LOAN	TERM OF LOAN				
	1 Year	2 Years	3 Years	4 Years	5 Years
$ 50.00	$ 4.40	$ 2.31	$ 1.62	$ 1.27	$ 1.07
100.00	8.80	4.63	3.24	2.55	2.14
200.00	17.61	9.25	6.48	5.10	4.27
300.00	26.41	13.88	9.72	7.64	6.41
400.00	35.21	18.50	12.95	10.19	8.55
500.00	44.02	23.13	16.19	12.74	10.69
1,000.00	88.03	46.26	32.38	25.48	21.37
2,000.00	176.06	92.52	64.77	50.97	42.74
3,000.00	264.10	138.78	97.15	76.45	64.11
4,000.00	352.13	185.04	129.54	101.93	85.48
5,000.00	440.16	231.30	161.92	127.41	106.85
10,000.00	880.32	462.60	323.85	254.83	213.70
15,000.00	1,320.48	693.91	485.77	382.24	320.55
20,000.00	1,760.64	925.21	647.69	509.66	427.41
25,000.00	2,200.81	1,156.51	809.62	637.07	534.26
30,000.00	2,640.97	1,387.81	971.54	764.48	641.11
35,000.00	3,081.13	1,619.11	1,133.46	891.90	747.96
40,000.00	3,521.29	1,850.42	1,295.39	1,019.31	854.81
45,000.00	3,961.45	2,081.72	1,457.31	1,146.73	961.66
50,000.00	4,401.61	2,313.02	1,619.23	1,274.14	1,068.51
55,000.00	4,841.77	2,544.32	1,781.16	1,401.55	1,175.36
60,000.00	5,281.93	2,775.62	1,943.08	1,528.97	1,282.22
65,000.00	5,722.09	3,006.93	2,105.00	1,656.38	1,389.07
70,000.00	6,162.25	3,238.23	2,266.93	1,783.80	1,495.92
75,000.00	6,602.42	3,469.53	2,428.85	1,911.21	1,602.77
80,000.00	7,042.58	3,700.83	2,590.78	2,038.63	1,709.62
85,000.00	7,482.74	3,932.13	2,752.70	2,166.04	1,816.47
90,000.00	7,922.90	4,163.44	2,914.62	2,293.45	1,923.32
95,000.00	8,363.06	4,394.74	3,076.55	2,420.87	2,030.18
100,000.00	8,803.22	4,626.04	3,238.47	2,548.28	2,137.03
110,000.00	9,683.54	5,088.64	3,562.32	2,803.11	2,350.73
120,000.00	10,563.86	5,551.25	3,886.16	3,057.94	2,564.43
130,000.00	11,444.19	6,013.85	4,210.01	3,312.77	2,778.13
140,000.00	12,324.51	6,476.46	4,533.86	3,567.59	2,991.84
150,000.00	13,204.83	6,939.06	4,857.70	3,822.42	3,205.54
160,000.00	14,085.15	7,401.66	5,181.55	4,077.25	3,419.24
170,000.00	14,965.47	7,864.27	5,505.40	4,332.08	3,632.94
180,000.00	15,845.80	8,326.87	5,829.24	4,586.91	3,846.65
190,000.00	16,726.12	8,789.48	6,153.09	4,841.73	4,060.35
200,000.00	17,606.44	9,252.08	6,476.94	5,096.56	4,274.05
225,000.00	19,807.25	10,408.59	7,286.55	5,733.63	4,808.31
250,000.00	22,008.05	11,565.10	8,096.17	6,370.70	5,342.57
275,000.00	24,208.86	12,721.61	8,905.79	7,007.77	5,876.82
300,000.00	26,409.66	13,878.12	9,715.41	7,644.84	6,411.08
350,000.00	30,811.27	16,191.14	11,334.64	8,918.98	7,479.59
400,000.00	35,212.88	18,504.16	12,953.88	10,193.13	8,548.11
450,000.00	39,614.49	20,817.18	14,573.11	11,467.27	9,616.62
500,000.00	44,016.10	23,130.20	16,192.34	12,741.41	10,685.13

Monthly Mortgage Payment 10¼%

TABLE C

(Amount Necessary to Amortize a Loan)

10 Years	15 Years	TERM OF LOAN 20 Years	25 Years	30 Years	AMOUNT OF LOAN
$ .67	$ .54	$ .49	$ .46	$ .45	$ 50.00
1.34	1.09	.98	.93	.90	100.00
2.67	2.18	1.96	1.85	1.79	200.00
4.01	3.27	2.94	2.78	2.69	300.00
5.34	4.36	3.93	3.71	3.58	400.00
6.68	5.45	4.91	4.63	4.48	500.00
13.35	10.90	9.82	9.26	8.96	1,000.00
26.71	21.80	19.63	18.53	17.92	2,000.00
40.06	32.70	29.45	27.79	26.88	3,000.00
53.42	43.60	39.27	37.06	35.84	4,000.00
66.77	54.50	49.08	46.32	44.81	5,000.00
133.54	109.00	98.16	92.64	89.61	10,000.00
200.31	163.49	147.25	138.96	134.42	15,000.00
267.08	217.99	196.33	185.28	179.22	20,000.00
333.85	272.49	245.41	231.60	224.03	25,000.00
400.62	326.99	294.49	277.91	268.83	30,000.00
467.39	381.48	343.58	324.23	313.64	35,000.00
534.16	435.98	392.66	370.55	358.44	40,000.00
600.93	490.48	441.74	416.87	403.25	45,000.00
667.70	544.98	490.82	463.19	448.05	50,000.00
734.46	599.47	539.90	509.51	492.86	55,000.00
801.23	653.97	588.99	555.83	537.66	60,000.00
868.00	708.47	638.07	602.15	582.47	65,000.00
934.77	762.97	687.15	648.47	627.27	70,000.00
1,001.54	817.46	736.23	694.79	672.08	75,000.00
1,068.31	871.96	785.31	741.11	716.88	80,000.00
1,135.08	926.46	834.40	787.43	761.69	85,000.00
1,201.85	980.96	883.48	833.74	806.49	90,000.00
1,268.62	1,035.45	932.56	880.06	851.30	95,000.00
1,335.39	1,089.95	981.64	926.38	896.10	100,000.00
1,468.93	1,198.95	1,079.81	1,019.02	985.71	110,000.00
1,602.47	1,307.94	1,177.97	1,111.66	1,075.32	120,000.00
1,736.01	1,416.94	1,276.14	1,204.30	1,164.93	130,000.00
1,869.55	1,525.93	1,374.30	1,296.94	1,254.54	140,000.00
2,003.09	1,634.93	1,472.47	1,389.57	1,344.15	150,000.00
2,136.62	1,743.92	1,570.63	1,482.21	1,433.76	160,000.00
2,270.16	1,852.92	1,668.79	1,574.85	1,523.37	170,000.00
2,403.70	1,961.91	1,766.96	1,667.49	1,612.98	180,000.00
2,537.24	2,070.91	1,865.12	1,760.13	1,702.59	190,000.00
2,670.78	2,179.90	1,963.29	1,852.77	1,792.20	200,000.00
3,004.63	2,452.39	2,208.70	2,084.36	2,016.23	225,000.00
3,338.48	2,724.88	2,454.11	2,315.96	2,240.25	250,000.00
3,672.32	2,997.37	2,699.52	2,547.55	2,464.28	275,000.00
4,006.17	3,269.85	2,944.93	2,779.15	2,688.30	300,000.00
4,673.87	3,814.83	3,435.75	3,242.34	3,136.35	350,000.00
5,341.56	4,359.80	3,926.57	3,705.53	3,584.41	400,000.00
6,009.26	4,904.78	4,417.40	4,168.72	4,032.46	450,000.00
6,676.95	5,449.75	4,908.22	4,631.92	4,480.51	500,000.00

10½%   **Figuring Out Your**

TABLE C

(Amount Necessary to Amortize a Loan)

AMOUNT OF LOAN	TERM OF LOAN				
	1 Year	2 Years	3 Years	4 Years	5 Years
$ 50.00	$ 4.41	$ 2.32	$ 1.63	$ 1.28	$ 1.07
100.00	8.81	4.64	3.25	2.56	2.15
200.00	17.63	9.28	6.50	5.12	4.30
300.00	26.44	13.91	9.75	7.68	6.45
400.00	35.26	18.55	13.00	10.24	8.60
500.00	44.07	23.19	16.25	12.80	10.75
1,000.00	88.15	46.38	32.50	25.60	21.49
2,000.00	176.30	92.75	65.00	51.21	42.99
3,000.00	264.45	139.13	97.51	76.81	64.48
4,000.00	352.59	185.50	130.01	102.41	85.98
5,000.00	440.74	231.88	162.51	128.02	107.47
10,000.00	881.49	463.76	325.02	256.03	214.94
15,000.00	1,322.23	695.64	487.54	384.05	322.41
20,000.00	1,762.97	927.52	650.05	512.07	429.88
25,000.00	2,203.72	1,159.40	812.56	640.08	537.35
30,000.00	2,644.46	1,391.28	975.07	768.10	644.82
35,000.00	3,085.20	1,623.16	1,137.59	896.12	752.29
40,000.00	3,525.94	1,855.04	1,300.10	1,024.14	859.76
45,000.00	3,966.69	2,086.92	1,462.61	1,152.15	967.23
50,000.00	4,407.43	2,318.80	1,625.12	1,280.17	1,074.70
55,000.00	4,848.17	2,550.68	1,787.63	1,408.19	1,182.16
60,000.00	5,288.92	2,782.56	1,950.15	1,536.20	1,289.63
65,000.00	5,729.66	3,014.44	2,112.66	1,664.22	1,397.10
70,000.00	6,170.40	3,246.32	2,275.17	1,792.24	1,504.57
75,000.00	6,611.15	3,478.20	2,437.68	1,920.25	1,612.04
80,000.00	7,051.89	3,710.08	2,600.20	2,048.27	1,719.51
85,000.00	7,492.63	3,941.96	2,762.71	2,176.29	1,826.98
90,000.00	7,933.37	4,173.84	2,925.22	2,304.30	1,934.45
95,000.00	8,374.12	4,405.72	3,087.73	2,432.32	2,041.92
100,000.00	8,814.86	4,637.60	3,250.24	2,560.34	2,149.39
110,000.00	9,696.35	5,101.36	3,575.27	2,816.37	2,364.33
120,000.00	10,577.83	5,565.12	3,900.29	3,072.41	2,579.27
130,000.00	11,459.32	6,028.89	4,225.32	3,328.44	2,794.21
140,000.00	12,340.80	6,492.65	4,550.34	3,584.47	3,009.15
150,000.00	13,222.29	6,956.41	4,875.37	3,840.51	3,224.09
160,000.00	14,103.78	7,420.17	5,200.39	4,096.54	3,439.02
170,000.00	14,985.26	7,883.93	5,525.42	4,352.57	3,653.96
180,000.00	15,866.75	8,347.69	5,850.44	4,608.61	3,868.90
190,000.00	16,748.23	8,811.45	6,175.46	4,864.64	4,083.84
200,000.00	17,629.72	9,275.21	6,500.49	5,120.68	4,298.78
225,000.00	19,833.44	10,434.61	7,313.05	5,760.76	4,836.13
250,000.00	22,037.15	11,594.01	8,125.61	6,400.84	5,373.48
275,000.00	24,240.87	12,753.41	8,938.17	7,040.93	5,910.82
300,000.00	26,444.58	13,912.81	9,750.73	7,681.01	6,448.17
350,000.00	30,852.01	16,231.61	11,375.86	8,961.18	7,522.87
400,000.00	35,259.44	18,550.42	13,000.98	10,241.35	8,597.56
450,000.00	39,666.87	20,869.22	14,626.10	11,521.52	9,672.26
500,000.00	44,074.30	23,188.02	16,251.22	12,801.69	10,746.95

Monthly Mortgage Payment 10½%

TABLE C

(Amount Necessary to Amortize a Loan)

10 Years	15 Years	TERM OF LOAN 20 Years	25 Years	30 Years	AMOUNT OF LOAN
$ .67	$ .55	$ .50	$ .47	$ .46	$ 50.00
1.35	1.11	1.00	.94	.91	100.00
2.70	2.21	2.00	1.89	1.83	200.00
4.05	3.32	3.00	2.83	2.74	300.00
5.40	4.42	3.99	3.78	3.66	400.00
6.75	5.53	4.99	4.72	4.57	500.00
13.49	11.05	9.98	9.44	9.15	1,000.00
26.99	22.11	19.97	18.88	18.29	2,000.00
40.48	33.16	29.95	28.33	27.44	3,000.00
53.97	44.22	39.94	37.77	36.59	4,000.00
67.47	55.27	49.92	47.21	45.74	5,000.00
134.93	110.54	99.84	94.42	91.47	10,000.00
202.40	165.81	149.76	141.63	137.21	15,000.00
269.87	221.08	199.68	188.84	182.95	20,000.00
337.34	276.35	249.59	236.05	228.68	25,000.00
404.80	331.62	299.51	283.25	274.42	30,000.00
472.27	386.89	349.43	330.46	320.16	35,000.00
539.74	442.16	399.35	377.67	365.90	40,000.00
607.21	497.43	449.27	424.88	411.63	45,000.00
674.67	552.70	499.19	472.09	457.37	50,000.00
742.14	607.97	549.11	519.30	503.11	55,000.00
809.61	663.24	599.03	566.51	548.84	60,000.00
877.08	718.51	648.95	613.72	594.58	65,000.00
944.54	773.78	698.87	660.93	640.32	70,000.00
1,012.01	829.05	748.78	708.14	686.05	75,000.00
1,079.48	884.32	798.70	755.35	731.79	80,000.00
1,146.95	939.59	848.62	802.55	777.53	85,000.00
1,214.41	994.86	898.54	849.76	823.27	90,000.00
1,281.88	1,050.13	948.46	896.97	869.00	95,000.00
1,349.35	1,105.40	998.38	944.18	914.74	100,000.00
1,484.28	1,215.94	1,098.22	1,038.60	1,006.21	110,000.00
1,619.22	1,326.48	1,198.06	1,133.02	1,097.69	120,000.00
1,754.15	1,437.02	1,297.89	1,227.44	1,189.16	130,000.00
1,889.09	1,547.56	1,397.73	1,321.85	1,280.64	140,000.00
2,024.02	1,658.10	1,497.57	1,416.27	1,372.11	150,000.00
2,158.96	1,768.64	1,597.41	1,510.69	1,463.58	160,000.00
2,293.89	1,879.18	1,697.25	1,605.11	1,555.06	170,000.00
2,428.83	1,989.72	1,797.08	1,699.53	1,646.53	180,000.00
2,563.76	2,100.26	1,896.92	1,793.95	1,738.00	190,000.00
2,698.70	2,210.80	1,996.76	1,888.36	1,829.48	200,000.00
3,036.04	2,487.15	2,246.35	2,124.41	2,058.16	225,000.00
3,373.37	2,763.50	2,495.95	2,360.45	2,286.85	250,000.00
3,710.71	3,039.85	2,745.54	2,596.50	2,515.53	275,000.00
4,048.05	3,316.20	2,995.14	2,832.55	2,744.22	300,000.00
4,722.72	3,868.90	3,494.33	3,304.64	3,201.59	350,000.00
5,397.40	4,421.60	3,993.52	3,776.73	3,658.96	400,000.00
6,072.07	4,974.30	4,492.71	4,248.82	4,116.33	450,000.00
6,746.75	5,526.99	4,991.90	4,720.91	4,573.70	500,000.00

10¾% Figuring Out Your

TABLE C
(Amount Necessary to Amortize a Loan)

AMOUNT OF LOAN	TERM OF LOAN 1 Year	2 Years	3 Years	4 Years	5 Years
$ 50.00	$ 4.41	$ 2.32	$ 1.63	$ 1.29	$ 1.08
100.00	8.83	4.65	3.26	2.57	2.16
200.00	17.65	9.30	6.52	5.14	4.32
300.00	26.48	13.95	9.79	7.72	6.49
400.00	35.31	18.60	13.05	10.29	8.65
500.00	44.13	23.25	16.31	12.86	10.81
1,000.00	88.27	46.49	32.62	25.72	21.62
2,000.00	176.53	92.98	65.24	51.45	43.24
3,000.00	264.80	139.48	97.86	77.17	64.85
4,000.00	353.06	185.97	130.48	102.90	86.47
5,000.00	441.33	232.46	163.10	128.62	108.09
10,000.00	882.65	464.92	326.20	257.24	216.18
15,000.00	1,323.98	697.38	489.31	385.86	324.27
20,000.00	1,765.30	929.84	652.41	514.49	432.36
25,000.00	2,206.63	1,162.30	815.51	643.11	540.45
30,000.00	2,647.95	1,394.76	978.61	771.73	648.54
35,000.00	3,089.28	1,627.21	1,141.72	900.35	756.63
40,000.00	3,530.60	1,859.67	1,304.82	1,028.97	864.72
45,000.00	3,971.93	2,092.13	1,467.92	1,157.59	972.81
50,000.00	4,413.25	2,324.59	1,631.02	1,286.21	1,080.90
55,000.00	4,854.58	2,557.05	1,794.12	1,414.84	1,188.99
60,000.00	5,295.91	2,789.51	1,957.23	1,543.46	1,297.08
65,000.00	5,737.23	3,021.97	2,120.33	1,672.08	1,405.17
70,000.00	6,178.56	3,254.43	2,283.43	1,800.70	1,513.26
75,000.00	6,619.88	3,486.89	2,446.53	1,929.32	1,621.35
80,000.00	7,061.21	3,719.35	2,609.64	2,057.94	1,729.44
85,000.00	7,502.53	3,951.81	2,772.74	2,186.56	1,837.53
90,000.00	7,943.86	4,184.27	2,935.84	2,315.19	1,945.62
95,000.00	8,385.18	4,416.73	3,098.94	2,443.81	2,053.71
100,000.00	8,826.51	4,649.19	3,262.05	2,572.43	2,161.80
110,000.00	9,709.16	5,114.10	3,588.25	2,829.67	2,377.97
120,000.00	10,591.81	5,579.02	3,914.45	3,086.91	2,594.15
130,000.00	11,474.46	6,043.94	4,240.66	3,344.16	2,810.33
140,000.00	12,357.11	6,508.86	4,566.86	3,601.40	3,026.51
150,000.00	13,239.76	6,973.78	4,893.07	3,858.64	3,242.69
160,000.00	14,122.41	7,438.70	5,219.27	4,115.89	3,458.87
170,000.00	15,005.06	7,903.62	5,545.48	4,373.13	3,675.05
180,000.00	15,887.72	8,368.53	5,871.68	4,630.37	3,891.23
190,000.00	16,770.37	8,833.45	6,197.89	4,887.61	4,107.41
200,000.00	17,653.02	9,298.37	6,524.09	5,144.86	4,323.59
225,000.00	19,859.64	10,460.67	7,339.60	5,787.96	4,864.04
250,000.00	22,066.27	11,622.96	8,155.11	6,431.07	5,404.49
275,000.00	24,272.90	12,785.26	8,970.62	7,074.18	5,944.94
300,000.00	26,479.53	13,947.56	9,786.14	7,717.28	6,485.39
350,000.00	30,892.78	16,272.15	11,417.16	9,003.50	7,566.28
400,000.00	35,306.04	18,596.74	13,048.18	10,289.71	8,647.18
450,000.00	39,719.29	20,921.33	14,679.20	11,575.93	9,728.08
500,000.00	44,132.54	23,245.93	16,310.23	12,862.14	10,808.98

Monthly Mortgage Payment

TABLE C
(Amount Necessary to Amortize a Loan)

| TERM OF LOAN | | | | | AMOUNT OF LOAN |
10 Years	15 Years	20 Years	25 Years	30 Years	
$ .68	$ .56	$ .51	$ .48	$ .47	$ 50.00
1.36	1.12	1.02	.96	.93	100.00
2.73	2.24	2.03	1.92	1.87	200.00
4.09	3.36	3.05	2.89	2.80	300.00
5.45	4.48	4.06	3.85	3.73	400.00
6.82	5.60	5.08	4.81	4.67	500.00
13.63	11.21	10.15	9.62	9.33	1,000.00
27.27	22.42	20.30	19.24	18.67	2,000.00
40.90	33.63	30.46	28.86	28.00	3,000.00
54.54	44.84	40.61	38.48	37.34	4,000.00
68.17	56.05	50.76	48.10	46.67	5,000.00
136.34	112.09	101.52	96.21	93.35	10,000.00
204.51	168.14	152.28	144.31	140.02	15,000.00
272.68	224.19	203.05	192.42	186.70	20,000.00
340.85	280.24	253.81	240.52	233.37	25,000.00
409.02	336.28	304.57	288.63	280.04	30,000.00
477.19	392.33	355.33	336.73	326.72	35,000.00
545.35	448.38	406.09	384.84	373.39	40,000.00
613.52	504.43	456.85	432.94	420.07	45,000.00
681.69	560.47	507.61	481.05	466.74	50,000.00
749.86	616.52	558.38	529.15	513.41	55,000.00
818.03	672.57	609.14	577.26	560.09	60,000.00
886.20	728.62	659.90	625.36	606.76	65,000.00
954.37	784.66	710.66	673.46	653.44	70,000.00
1,022.54	840.71	761.42	721.57	700.11	75,000.00
1,090.71	896.76	812.18	769.67	746.79	80,000.00
1,158.88	952.81	862.94	817.78	793.46	85,000.00
1,227.05	1,008.85	913.71	865.88	840.13	90,000.00
1,295.22	1,064.90	964.47	913.99	886.81	95,000.00
1,363.39	1,120.95	1,015.23	962.09	933.48	100,000.00
1,499.73	1,233.04	1,116.75	1,058.30	1,026.83	110,000.00
1,636.06	1,345.14	1,218.27	1,154.51	1,120.18	120,000.00
1,772.40	1,457.23	1,319.80	1,250.72	1,213.53	130,000.00
1,908.74	1,569.33	1,421.32	1,346.93	1,306.87	140,000.00
2,045.08	1,681.42	1,522.84	1,443.14	1,400.22	150,000.00
2,181.42	1,793.52	1,624.37	1,539.35	1,493.57	160,000.00
2,317.76	1,905.61	1,725.89	1,635.56	1,586.92	170,000.00
2,454.10	2,017.71	1,827.41	1,731.77	1,680.27	180,000.00
2,590.43	2,129.80	1,928.94	1,827.98	1,773.61	190,000.00
2,726.77	2,241.90	2,030.46	1,924.19	1,866.96	200,000.00
3,067.62	2,522.13	2,284.27	2,164.71	2,100.33	225,000.00
3,408.47	2,802.37	2,538.07	2,405.23	2,333.70	250,000.00
3,749.31	3,082.61	2,791.88	2,645.75	2,567.07	275,000.00
4,090.16	3,362.84	3,045.69	2,886.28	2,800.44	300,000.00
4,771.85	3,923.32	3,553.30	3,367.32	3,267.18	350,000.00
5,453.55	4,483.79	4,060.92	3,848.37	3,733.93	400,000.00
6,135.24	5,044.27	4,568.53	4,329.42	4,200.67	450,000.00
6,816.93	5,604.74	5,076.14	4,810.46	4,667.41	500,000.00

TABLE C
(Amount Necessary to Amortize a Loan)

AMOUNT OF LOAN	TERM OF LOAN				
	1 Year	2 Years	3 Years	4 Years	5 Years
$ 50.00	$ 4.42	$ 2.33	$ 1.64	$ 1.29	$ 1.09
100.00	8.84	4.66	3.27	2.58	2.17
200.00	17.68	9.32	6.55	5.17	4.35
300.00	26.51	13.98	9.82	7.75	6.52
400.00	35.35	18.64	13.10	10.34	8.70
500.00	44.19	23.30	16.37	12.92	10.87
1,000.00	88.38	46.61	32.74	25.85	21.74
2,000.00	176.76	93.22	65.48	51.69	43.48
3,000.00	265.14	139.82	98.22	77.54	65.23
4,000.00	353.53	186.43	130.95	103.38	86.97
5,000.00	441.91	233.04	163.69	129.23	108.71
10,000.00	883.82	466.08	327.39	258.46	217.42
15,000.00	1,325.72	699.12	491.08	387.68	326.14
20,000.00	1,767.63	932.16	654.77	516.91	434.85
25,000.00	2,209.54	1,165.20	818.47	646.14	543.56
30,000.00	2,651.45	1,398.24	982.16	775.37	652.27
35,000.00	3,093.36	1,631.27	1,145.86	904.59	760.98
40,000.00	3,535.27	1,864.31	1,309.55	1,033.82	869.70
45,000.00	3,977.17	2,097.35	1,473.24	1,163.05	978.41
50,000.00	4,419.08	2,330.39	1,636.94	1,292.28	1,087.12
55,000.00	4,860.99	2,563.43	1,800.63	1,421.50	1,195.83
60,000.00	5,302.90	2,796.47	1,964.32	1,550.73	1,304.55
65,000.00	5,744.81	3,029.51	2,128.02	1,679.96	1,413.26
70,000.00	6,186.72	3,262.55	2,291.71	1,809.19	1,521.97
75,000.00	6,628.62	3,495.59	2,455.40	1,938.41	1,630.68
80,000.00	7,070.53	3,728.63	2,619.10	2,067.64	1,739.39
85,000.00	7,512.44	3,961.67	2,782.79	2,196.87	1,848.11
90,000.00	7,954.35	4,194.71	2,946.48	2,326.10	1,956.82
95,000.00	8,396.26	4,427.74	3,110.18	2,455.32	2,065.53
100,000.00	8,838.17	4,660.78	3,273.87	2,584.55	2,174.24
110,000.00	9,721.98	5,126.86	3,601.26	2,843.01	2,391.67
120,000.00	10,605.80	5,592.94	3,928.65	3,101.46	2,609.09
130,000.00	11,489.62	6,059.02	4,256.03	3,359.92	2,826.51
140,000.00	12,373.43	6,525.10	4,583.42	3,618.37	3,043.94
150,000.00	13,257.25	6,991.18	4,910.81	3,876.83	3,261.36
160,000.00	14,141.07	7,457.25	5,238.19	4,135.28	3,478.79
170,000.00	15,024.88	7,923.33	5,565.58	4,393.74	3,696.21
180,000.00	15,908.70	8,389.41	5,892.97	4,652.19	3,913.64
190,000.00	16,792.52	8,855.49	6,220.36	4,910.65	4,131.06
200,000.00	17,676.33	9,321.57	6,547.74	5,169.10	4,348.48
225,000.00	19,885.87	10,486.76	7,366.21	5,815.24	4,892.05
250,000.00	22,095.41	11,651.96	8,184.68	6,461.38	5,435.61
275,000.00	24,304.96	12,817.16	9,003.15	7,107.52	5,979.17
300,000.00	26,514.50	13,982.35	9,821.62	7,753.66	6,522.73
350,000.00	30,933.58	16,312.74	11,458.55	9,045.93	7,609.85
400,000.00	35,352.66	18,643.14	13,095.49	10,338.21	8,696.97
450,000.00	39,771.75	20,973.53	14,732.42	11,630.49	9,784.09
500,000.00	44,190.83	23,303.92	16,369.36	12,922.76	10,871.21

Monthly Mortgage Payment 11%

TABLE C

(Amount Necessary to Amortize a Loan)

10 Years	15 Years	TERM OF LOAN 20 Years	25 Years	30 Years	AMOUNT OF LOAN
$ .69	$ .57	$ .52	$ .49	$ .48	$ 50.00
1.38	1.14	1.03	.98	.95	100.00
2.76	2.27	2.06	1.96	1.90	200.00
4.13	3.41	3.10	2.94	2.86	300.00
5.51	4.55	4.13	3.92	3.81	400.00
6.89	5.68	5.16	4.90	4.76	500.00
13.78	11.37	10.32	9.80	9.52	1,000.00
27.55	22.73	20.64	19.60	19.05	2,000.00
41.33	34.10	30.97	29.40	28.57	3,000.00
55.10	45.46	41.29	39.20	38.09	4,000.00
68.88	56.83	51.61	49.01	47.62	5,000.00
137.75	113.66	103.22	98.01	95.23	10,000.00
206.63	170.49	154.83	147.02	142.85	15,000.00
275.50	227.32	206.44	196.02	190.46	20,000.00
344.38	284.15	258.05	245.03	238.08	25,000.00
413.25	340.98	309.66	294.03	285.70	30,000.00
482.13	397.81	361.27	343.04	333.31	35,000.00
551.00	454.64	412.88	392.05	380.93	40,000.00
619.88	511.47	464.48	441.05	428.55	45,000.00
688.75	568.30	516.09	490.06	476.16	50,000.00
757.63	625.13	567.70	539.06	523.78	55,000.00
826.50	681.96	619.31	588.07	571.39	60,000.00
895.38	738.79	670.92	637.07	619.01	65,000.00
964.25	795.62	722.53	686.08	666.63	70,000.00
1,033.13	852.45	774.14	735.08	714.24	75,000.00
1,102.00	909.28	825.75	784.09	761.86	80,000.00
1,170.88	966.11	877.36	833.10	809.47	85,000.00
1,239.75	1,022.94	928.97	882.10	857.09	90,000.00
1,308.63	1,079.77	980.58	931.11	904.71	95,000.00
1,377.50	1,136.60	1,032.19	980.11	952.32	100,000.00
1,515.25	1,250.26	1,135.41	1,078.12	1,047.56	110,000.00
1,653.00	1,363.92	1,238.63	1,176.14	1,142.79	120,000.00
1,790.75	1,477.58	1,341.84	1,274.15	1,238.02	130,000.00
1,928.50	1,591.24	1,445.06	1,372.16	1,333.25	140,000.00
2,066.25	1,704.90	1,548.28	1,470.17	1,428.49	150,000.00
2,204.00	1,818.56	1,651.50	1,568.18	1,523.72	160,000.00
2,341.75	1,932.21	1,754.72	1,666.19	1,618.95	170,000.00
2,479.50	2,045.87	1,857.94	1,764.20	1,714.18	180,000.00
2,617.25	2,159.53	1,961.16	1,862.21	1,809.41	190,000.00
2,755.00	2,273.19	2,064.38	1,960.23	1,904.65	200,000.00
3,099.38	2,557.34	2,322.42	2,205.25	2,142.73	225,000.00
3,443.75	2,841.49	2,580.47	2,450.28	2,380.81	250,000.00
3,788.13	3,125.64	2,838.52	2,695.31	2,618.89	275,000.00
4,132.50	3,409.79	3,096.57	2,940.34	2,856.97	300,000.00
4,821.25	3,978.09	3,612.66	3,430.40	3,333.13	350,000.00
5,510.00	4,546.39	4,128.75	3,920.45	3,809.29	400,000.00
6,198.75	5,114.69	4,644.85	4,410.51	4,285.46	450,000.00
6,887.50	5,682.98	5,160.94	4,900.57	4,761.62	500,000.00

11¼% Figuring Out Your

TABLE C
(Amount Necessary to Amortize a Loan)

AMOUNT OF LOAN	TERM OF LOAN				
	1 Year	2 Years	3 Years	4 Years	5 Years
$ 50.00	$ 4.42	$ 2.34	$ 1.64	$ 1.30	$ 1.09
100.00	8.85	4.67	3.29	2.60	2.19
200.00	17.70	9.34	6.57	5.19	4.37
300.00	26.55	14.02	9.86	7.79	6.56
400.00	35.40	18.69	13.14	10.39	8.75
500.00	44.25	23.36	16.43	12.98	10.93
1,000.00	88.50	46.72	32.86	25.97	21.87
2,000.00	177.00	93.45	65.71	51.93	43.73
3,000.00	265.49	140.17	98.57	77.90	65.60
4,000.00	353.99	186.90	131.43	103.87	87.47
5,000.00	442.49	233.62	164.29	129.84	109.34
10,000.00	884.98	467.24	328.57	259.67	218.67
15,000.00	1,327.47	700.86	492.86	389.51	328.01
20,000.00	1,769.97	934.48	657.14	519.34	437.35
25,000.00	2,212.46	1,168.10	821.43	649.18	546.68
30,000.00	2,654.95	1,401.72	985.72	779.01	656.02
35,000.00	3,097.44	1,635.34	1,150.00	908.85	765.36
40,000.00	3,539.93	1,868.96	1,314.29	1,038.68	874.69
45,000.00	3,982.42	2,102.58	1,478.58	1,168.52	984.03
50,000.00	4,424.92	2,336.20	1,642.86	1,298.35	1,093.37
55,000.00	4,867.41	2,569.82	1,807.15	1,428.19	1,202.70
60,000.00	5,309.90	2,803.44	1,971.43	1,558.03	1,312.04
65,000.00	5,752.39	3,037.06	2,135.72	1,687.86	1,421.38
70,000.00	6,194.88	3,270.68	2,300.01	1,817.70	1,530.71
75,000.00	6,637.37	3,504.30	2,464.29	1,947.53	1,640.05
80,000.00	7,079.87	3,737.92	2,628.58	2,077.37	1,749.38
85,000.00	7,522.36	3,971.54	2,792.86	2,207.20	1,858.72
90,000.00	7,964.85	4,205.16	2,957.15	2,337.04	1,968.06
95,000.00	8,407.34	4,438.78	3,121.44	2,466.87	2,077.39
100,000.00	8,849.83	4,672.40	3,285.72	2,596.71	2,186.73
110,000.00	9,734.81	5,139.64	3,614.30	2,856.38	2,405.40
120,000.00	10,619.80	5,606.88	3,942.87	3,116.05	2,624.08
130,000.00	11,504.78	6,074.12	4,271.44	3,375.72	2,842.75
140,000.00	12,389.76	6,541.36	4,600.01	3,635.39	3,061.42
150,000.00	13,274.75	7,008.60	4,928.59	3,895.06	3,280.10
160,000.00	14,159.73	7,475.84	5,257.16	4,154.74	3,498.77
170,000.00	15,044.71	7,943.08	5,585.73	4,414.41	3,717.44
180,000.00	15,929.70	8,410.32	5,914.30	4,674.08	3,936.12
190,000.00	16,814.68	8,877.56	6,242.87	4,933.75	4,154.79
200,000.00	17,699.66	9,344.80	6,571.45	5,193.42	4,373.46
225,000.00	19,912.12	10,512.90	7,392.88	5,842.60	4,920.14
250,000.00	22,124.58	11,681.00	8,214.31	6,491.77	5,466.83
275,000.00	24,337.04	12,849.10	9,035.74	7,140.95	6,013.51
300,000.00	26,549.49	14,017.20	9,857.17	7,790.13	6,560.19
350,000.00	30,974.41	16,353.40	11,500.03	9,088.48	7,653.56
400,000.00	35,399.33	18,689.60	13,142.89	10,386.84	8,746.92
450,000.00	39,824.24	21,025.80	14,785.76	11,685.19	9,840.29
500,000.00	44,249.16	23,362.00	16,428.62	12,983.55	10,933.65

Monthly Mortgage Payment   11¼%

TABLE C

(Amount Necessary to Amortize a Loan)

10 Years	15 Years	20 Years	25 Years	30 Years	AMOUNT OF LOAN
$ .70	$ .58	$ .52	$ .50	$ .49	$ 50.00
1.39	1.15	1.05	1.00	.97	100.00
2.78	2.30	2.10	2.00	1.94	200.00
4.18	3.46	3.15	2.99	2.91	300.00
5.57	4.61	4.20	3.99	3.89	400.00
6.96	5.76	5.25	4.99	4.86	500.00
13.92	11.52	10.49	9.98	9.71	1,000.00
27.83	23.05	20.99	19.96	19.43	2,000.00
41.75	34.57	31.48	29.95	29.14	3,000.00
55.67	46.09	41.97	39.93	38.85	4,000.00
69.58	57.62	52.46	49.91	48.56	5,000.00
139.17	115.23	104.93	99.82	97.13	10,000.00
208.75	172.85	157.39	149.74	145.69	15,000.00
278.34	230.47	209.85	199.65	194.25	20,000.00
347.92	288.09	262.31	249.56	242.82	25,000.00
417.51	345.70	314.78	299.47	291.38	30,000.00
487.09	403.32	367.24	349.38	339.94	35,000.00
556.68	460.94	419.70	399.30	388.50	40,000.00
626.26	518.56	472.17	449.21	437.07	45,000.00
695.84	576.17	524.63	499.12	485.63	50,000.00
765.43	633.79	577.09	549.03	534.19	55,000.00
835.01	691.41	629.55	598.94	582.76	60,000.00
904.60	749.02	682.02	648.86	631.32	65,000.00
974.18	806.64	734.48	698.77	679.88	70,000.00
1,043.77	864.26	786.94	748.68	728.45	75,000.00
1,113.35	921.88	839.40	798.59	777.01	80,000.00
1,182.94	979.49	891.87	848.50	825.57	85,000.00
1,252.52	1,037.11	944.33	898.42	874.14	90,000.00
1,322.10	1,094.73	996.79	948.33	922.70	95,000.00
1,391.69	1,152.34	1,049.26	998.24	971.26	100,000.00
1,530.86	1,267.58	1,154.18	1,098.06	1,068.39	110,000.00
1,670.03	1,382.81	1,259.11	1,197.89	1,165.51	120,000.00
1,809.20	1,498.05	1,364.03	1,297.71	1,262.64	130,000.00
1,948.37	1,613.28	1,468.96	1,397.54	1,359.77	140,000.00
2,087.53	1,728.52	1,573.88	1,497.36	1,456.89	150,000.00
2,226.70	1,843.75	1,678.81	1,597.18	1,554.02	160,000.00
2,365.87	1,958.99	1,783.74	1,697.01	1,651.14	170,000.00
2,505.04	2,074.22	1,888.66	1,796.83	1,748.27	180,000.00
2,644.21	2,189.45	1,993.59	1,896.66	1,845.40	190,000.00
2,783.38	2,304.69	2,098.51	1,996.48	1,942.52	200,000.00
3,131.30	2,592.78	2,360.83	2,246.04	2,185.34	225,000.00
3,479.22	2,880.86	2,623.14	2,495.60	2,428.15	250,000.00
3,827.15	3,168.95	2,885.45	2,745.16	2,670.97	275,000.00
4,175.07	3,457.03	3,147.77	2,994.72	2,913.78	300,000.00
4,870.91	4,033.21	3,672.40	3,493.84	3,399.41	350,000.00
5,566.76	4,609.38	4,197.02	3,992.96	3,885.05	400,000.00
6,262.60	5,185.55	4,721.65	4,492.08	4,370.68	450,000.00
6,958.45	5,761.72	5,246.28	4,991.20	4,856.31	500,000.00

11½%   Figuring Out Your

TABLE C
(Amount Necessary to Amortize a Loan)

AMOUNT OF LOAN	TERM OF LOAN				
	1 Year	2 Years	3 Years	4 Years	5 Years
$ 50.00	$ 4.43	$ 2.34	$ 1.65	$ 1.30	$ 1.10
100.00	8.86	4.68	3.30	2.61	2.20
200.00	17.72	9.37	6.60	5.22	4.40
300.00	26.58	14.05	9.89	7.83	6.60
400.00	35.45	18.74	13.19	10.44	8.80
500.00	44.31	23.42	16.49	13.04	11.00
1,000.00	88.62	46.84	32.98	26.09	21.99
2,000.00	177.23	93.68	65.95	52.18	43.99
3,000.00	265.85	140.52	98.93	78.27	65.98
4,000.00	354.46	187.36	131.90	104.36	87.97
5,000.00	443.08	234.20	164.88	130.45	109.96
10,000.00	886.15	468.40	329.76	260.89	219.93
15,000.00	1,329.23	702.60	494.64	391.34	329.89
20,000.00	1,772.30	936.81	659.52	521.78	439.85
25,000.00	2,215.38	1,171.01	824.40	652.23	549.82
30,000.00	2,658.45	1,405.21	989.28	782.67	659.78
35,000.00	3,101.53	1,639.41	1,154.16	913.12	769.74
40,000.00	3,544.60	1,873.61	1,319.04	1,043.56	879.70
45,000.00	3,987.68	2,107.81	1,483.92	1,174.01	989.67
50,000.00	4,430.75	2,342.02	1,648.80	1,304.45	1,099.63
55,000.00	4,873.83	2,576.22	1,813.68	1,434.90	1,209.59
60,000.00	5,316.90	2,810.42	1,978.56	1,565.34	1,319.56
65,000.00	5,759.98	3,044.62	2,143.44	1,695.79	1,429.52
70,000.00	6,203.05	3,278.82	2,308.32	1,826.23	1,539.48
75,000.00	6,646.13	3,513.02	2,473.20	1,956.68	1,649.45
80,000.00	7,089.20	3,747.23	2,638.08	2,087.12	1,759.41
85,000.00	7,532.28	3,981.43	2,802.96	2,217.57	1,869.37
90,000.00	7,975.35	4,215.63	2,967.84	2,348.01	1,979.33
95,000.00	8,418.43	4,449.83	3,132.72	2,478.46	2,089.30
100,000.00	8,861.51	4,684.03	3,297.60	2,608.90	2,199.26
110,000.00	9,747.66	5,152.43	3,627.36	2,869.79	2,419.19
120,000.00	10,633.81	5,620.84	3,957.12	3,130.68	2,639.11
130,000.00	11,519.96	6,089.24	4,286.88	3,391.57	2,859.04
140,000.00	12,406.11	6,557.64	4,616.64	3,652.46	3,078.97
150,000.00	13,292.26	7,026.05	4,946.40	3,913.35	3,298.89
160,000.00	14,178.41	7,494.45	5,276.16	4,174.24	3,518.82
170,000.00	15,064.56	7,962.85	5,605.92	4,435.13	3,738.74
180,000.00	15,950.71	8,431.26	5,935.68	4,696.02	3,958.67
190,000.00	16,836.86	8,899.66	6,265.44	4,956.91	4,178.60
200,000.00	17,723.01	9,368.06	6,595.20	5,217.80	4,398.52
225,000.00	19,938.39	10,539.07	7,419.60	5,870.03	4,948.34
250,000.00	22,153.76	11,710.08	8,244.00	6,522.25	5,498.15
275,000.00	24,369.14	12,881.09	9,068.40	7,174.48	6,047.97
300,000.00	26,584.52	14,052.09	9,892.80	7,826.70	6,597.78
350,000.00	31,015.27	16,394.11	11,541.60	9,131.15	7,697.41
400,000.00	35,446.02	18,736.13	13,190.40	10,435.60	8,797.04
450,000.00	39,876.77	21,078.14	14,839.20	11,740.05	9,896.67
500,000.00	44,307.53	23,420.16	16,488.00	13,044.50	10,996.30

Monthly Mortgage Payment 11½%

TABLE C
(Amount Necessary to Amortize a Loan)

10 Years	15 Years	TERM OF LOAN 20 Years	25 Years	30 Years	AMOUNT OF LOAN
$ .70	$ .58	$ .53	$ .51	$ .50	$ 50.00
1.41	1.17	1.07	1.02	.99	100.00
2.81	2.34	2.13	2.03	1.98	200.00
4.22	3.50	3.20	3.05	2.97	300.00
5.62	4.67	4.27	4.07	3.96	400.00
7.03	5.84	5.33	5.08	4.95	500.00
14.06	11.68	10.66	10.16	9.90	1,000.00
28.12	23.36	21.33	20.33	19.81	2,000.00
42.18	35.05	31.99	30.49	29.71	3,000.00
56.24	46.73	42.66	40.66	39.61	4,000.00
70.30	58.41	53.32	50.82	49.51	5,000.00
140.60	116.82	106.64	101.65	99.03	10,000.00
210.89	175.23	159.96	152.47	148.54	15,000.00
281.19	233.64	213.29	203.29	198.06	20,000.00
351.49	292.05	266.61	254.12	247.57	25,000.00
421.79	350.46	319.93	304.94	297.09	30,000.00
492.08	408.87	373.25	355.76	346.60	35,000.00
562.38	467.28	426.57	406.59	396.12	40,000.00
632.68	525.69	479.89	457.41	445.63	45,000.00
702.98	584.09	533.21	508.23	495.15	50,000.00
773.27	642.50	586.54	559.06	544.66	55,000.00
843.57	700.91	639.86	609.88	594.17	60,000.00
913.87	759.32	693.18	660.70	643.69	65,000.00
984.17	817.73	746.50	711.53	693.20	70,000.00
1,054.47	876.14	799.82	762.35	742.72	75,000.00
1,124.76	934.55	853.14	813.18	792.23	80,000.00
1,195.06	992.96	906.47	864.00	841.75	85,000.00
1,265.36	1,051.37	959.79	914.82	891.26	90,000.00
1,335.66	1,109.78	1,013.11	965.65	940.78	95,000.00
1,405.95	1,168.19	1,066.43	1,016.47	990.29	100,000.00
1,546.55	1,285.01	1,173.07	1,118.12	1,089.32	110,000.00
1,687.15	1,401.83	1,279.72	1,219.76	1,188.35	120,000.00
1,827.74	1,518.65	1,386.36	1,321.41	1,287.38	130,000.00
1,968.34	1,635.47	1,493.00	1,423.06	1,386.41	140,000.00
2,108.93	1,752.28	1,599.64	1,524.70	1,485.44	150,000.00
2,249.53	1,869.10	1,706.29	1,626.35	1,584.47	160,000.00
2,390.12	1,985.92	1,812.93	1,728.00	1,683.50	170,000.00
2,530.72	2,102.74	1,919.57	1,829.64	1,782.52	180,000.00
2,671.31	2,219.56	2,026.22	1,931.29	1,881.55	190,000.00
2,811.91	2,336.38	2,132.86	2,032.94	1,980.58	200,000.00
3,163.40	2,628.43	2,399.47	2,287.06	2,228.16	225,000.00
3,514.89	2,920.47	2,666.07	2,541.17	2,475.73	250,000.00
3,866.37	3,212.52	2,932.68	2,795.29	2,723.30	275,000.00
4,217.86	3,504.57	3,199.29	3,049.41	2,970.87	300,000.00
4,920.84	4,088.66	3,732.50	3,557.64	3,466.02	350,000.00
5,623.82	4,672.76	4,265.72	4,065.88	3,961.17	400,000.00
6,326.79	5,256.85	4,798.93	4,574.11	4,456.31	450,000.00
7,029.77	5,840.95	5,332.15	5,082.34	4,951.46	500,000.00

11¾% Figuring Out Your

TABLE C
(Amount Necessary to Amortize a Loan)

AMOUNT OF LOAN	TERM OF LOAN				
	1 Year	2 Years	3 Years	4 Years	5 Years
$ 50.00	$ .71	$ .59	$ .54	$ .52	$ .50
100.00	1.42	1.18	1.08	1.03	1.01
200.00	2.84	2.37	2.17	2.07	2.02
300.00	4.26	3.55	3.25	3.10	3.03
400.00	5.68	4.74	4.33	4.14	4.04
500.00	7.10	5.92	5.42	5.17	5.05
1,000.00	14.20	11.84	10.84	10.35	10.09
2,000.00	28.41	23.68	21.67	20.70	20.19
3,000.00	42.61	35.52	32.51	31.04	30.28
4,000.00	56.81	47.37	43.35	41.39	40.38
5,000.00	71.01	59.21	54.19	51.74	50.47
10,000.00	142.03	118.41	108.37	103.48	100.94
15,000.00	213.04	177.62	162.56	155.22	151.41
20,000.00	284.06	236.83	216.74	206.96	201.88
25,000.00	355.07	296.03	270.93	258.70	252.35
30,000.00	426.09	355.24	325.11	310.44	302.82
35,000.00	497.10	414.45	379.30	362.18	353.29
40,000.00	568.12	473.65	433.48	413.92	403.76
45,000.00	639.13	532.86	487.67	465.66	454.23
50,000.00	710.15	592.07	541.85	517.40	504.70
55,000.00	781.16	651.27	596.04	569.14	555.18
60,000.00	852.18	710.48	650.22	620.88	605.65
65,000.00	923.19	769.69	704.41	672.62	656.12
70,000.00	994.21	828.89	758.59	724.36	706.59
75,000.00	1,065.22	888.10	812.78	776.10	757.06
80,000.00	1,136.24	947.31	866.97	827.84	807.53
85,000.00	1,207.25	1,006.51	921.15	879.58	858.00
90,000.00	1,278.27	1,065.72	975.34	931.32	908.47
95,000.00	1,349.28	1,124.92	1,029.52	983.06	958.94
100,000.00	1,420.29	1,184.13	1,083.71	1,034.80	1,009.41
110,000.00	1,562.32	1,302.54	1,192.08	1,138.28	1,110.35
120,000.00	1,704.35	1,420.96	1,300.45	1,241.76	1,211.29
130,000.00	1,846.38	1,539.37	1,408.82	1,345.24	1,312.23
140,000.00	1,988.41	1,657.78	1,517.19	1,448.72	1,413.17
150,000.00	2,130.44	1,776.20	1,625.56	1,552.20	1,514.11
160,000.00	2,272.47	1,894.61	1,733.93	1,655.68	1,615.06
170,000.00	2,414.50	2,013.02	1,842.30	1,759.16	1,716.00
180,000.00	2,556.53	2,131.44	1,950.67	1,862.64	1,816.94
190,000.00	2,698.56	2,249.85	2,059.04	1,966.12	1,917.88
200,000.00	2,840.59	2,368.26	2,167.41	2,069.60	2,018.82
225,000.00	3,195.66	2,664.30	2,438.34	2,328.30	2,271.17
250,000.00	3,550.74	2,960.33	2,709.27	2,587.00	2,523.52
275,000.00	3,905.81	3,256.36	2,980.19	2,845.70	2,775.88
300,000.00	4,260.88	3,552.39	3,251.12	3,104.39	3,028.23
350,000.00	4,971.03	4,144.46	3,792.97	3,621.79	3,532.93
400,000.00	5,681.18	4,736.53	4,334.83	4,139.19	4,037.64
450,000.00	6,391.33	5,328.59	4,876.68	4,656.59	4,542.34
500,000.00	7,101.47	5,920.66	5,418.54	5,173.99	5,047.05

Monthly Mortgage Payment 11¾%

TABLE C

(Amount Necessary to Amortize a Loan)

10 Years	15 Years	TERM OF LOAN 20 Years	25 Years	30 Years	AMOUNT OF LOAN
$ .71	$ .59	$ .54	$ .52	$ .50	$ 50.00
1.42	1.18	1.08	1.03	1.01	100.00
2.84	2.37	2.17	2.07	2.02	200.00
4.26	3.55	3.25	3.10	3.03	300.00
5.68	4.74	4.33	4.14	4.04	400.00
7.10	5.92	5.42	5.17	5.05	500.00
14.20	11.84	10.84	10.35	10.09	1,000.00
28.41	23.68	21.67	20.70	20.19	2,000.00
42.61	35.52	32.51	31.04	30.28	3,000.00
56.81	47.37	43.35	41.39	40.38	4,000.00
71.01	59.21	54.19	51.74	50.47	5,000.00
142.03	118.41	108.37	103.48	100.94	10,000.00
213.04	177.62	162.56	155.22	151.41	15,000.00
284.06	236.83	216.74	206.96	201.88	20,000.00
355.07	296.03	270.93	258.70	252.35	25,000.00
426.09	355.24	325.11	310.44	302.82	30,000.00
497.10	414.45	379.30	362.18	353.29	35,000.00
568.12	473.65	433.48	413.92	403.76	40,000.00
639.13	532.86	487.67	465.66	454.23	45,000.00
710.15	592.07	541.85	517.40	504.70	50,000.00
781.16	651.27	596.04	569.14	555.18	55,000.00
852.18	710.48	650.22	620.88	605.65	60,000.00
923.19	769.69	704.41	672.62	656.12	65,000.00
994.21	828.89	758.59	724.36	706.59	70,000.00
1,065.22	888.10	812.78	776.10	757.06	75,000.00
1,136.24	947.31	866.97	827.84	807.53	80,000.00
1,207.25	1,006.51	921.15	879.58	858.00	85,000.00
1,278.27	1,065.72	975.34	931.32	908.47	90,000.00
1,349.28	1,124.92	1,029.52	983.06	958.94	95,000.00
1,420.29	1,184.13	1,083.71	1,034.80	1,009.41	100,000.00
1,562.32	1,302.54	1,192.08	1,138.28	1,110.35	110,000.00
1,704.35	1,420.96	1,300.45	1,241.76	1,211.29	120,000.00
1,846.38	1,539.37	1,408.82	1,345.24	1,312.23	130,000.00
1,988.41	1,657.78	1,517.19	1,448.72	1,413.17	140,000.00
2,130.44	1,776.20	1,625.56	1,552.20	1,514.11	150,000.00
2,272.47	1,894.61	1,733.93	1,655.68	1,615.06	160,000.00
2,414.50	2,013.02	1,842.30	1,759.16	1,716.00	170,000.00
2,556.53	2,131.44	1,950.67	1,862.64	1,816.94	180,000.00
2,698.56	2,249.85	2,059.04	1,966.12	1,917.88	190,000.00
2,840.59	2,368.26	2,167.41	2,069.60	2,018.82	200,000.00
3,195.66	2,664.30	2,438.34	2,328.30	2,271.17	225,000.00
3,550.74	2,960.33	2,709.27	2,587.00	2,523.52	250,000.00
3,905.81	3,256.36	2,980.19	2,845.70	2,775.88	275,000.00
4,260.88	3,552.39	3,251.12	3,104.39	3,028.23	300,000.00
4,971.03	4,144.46	3,792.97	3,621.79	3,532.93	350,000.00
5,681.18	4,736.53	4,334.83	4,139.19	4,037.64	400,000.00
6,391.33	5,328.59	4,876.68	4,656.59	4,542.34	450,000.00
7,101.47	5,920.66	5,418.54	5,173.99	5,047.05	500,000.00

197

12%

Figuring Out Your

TABLE C
(Amount Necessary to Amortize a Loan)

AMOUNT OF LOAN	TERM OF LOAN 1 Year	2 Years	3 Years	4 Years	5 Years
$ 50.00	$ 4.44	$ 2.35	$ 1.66	$ 1.32	$ 1.11
100.00	8.88	4.71	3.32	2.63	2.22
200.00	17.77	9.41	6.64	5.27	4.45
300.00	26.65	14.12	9.96	7.90	6.67
400.00	35.54	18.83	13.29	10.53	8.90
500.00	44.42	23.54	16.61	13.17	11.12
1,000.00	88.85	47.07	33.21	26.33	22.24
2,000.00	177.70	94.15	66.43	52.67	44.49
3,000.00	266.55	141.22	99.64	79.00	66.73
4,000.00	355.40	188.29	132.86	105.34	88.98
5,000.00	444.24	235.37	166.07	131.67	111.22
10,000.00	888.49	470.73	332.14	263.34	222.44
15,000.00	1,332.73	706.10	498.21	395.01	333.67
20,000.00	1,776.98	941.47	664.29	526.68	444.89
25,000.00	2,221.22	1,176.84	830.36	658.35	556.11
30,000.00	2,665.46	1,412.20	996.43	790.02	667.33
35,000.00	3,109.71	1,647.57	1,162.50	921.68	778.56
40,000.00	3,553.95	1,882.94	1,328.57	1,053.35	889.78
45,000.00	3,998.20	2,118.31	1,494.64	1,185.02	1,001.00
50,000.00	4,442.44	2,353.67	1,660.72	1,316.69	1,112.22
55,000.00	4,886.68	2,589.04	1,826.79	1,448.36	1,223.44
60,000.00	5,330.93	2,824.41	1,992.86	1,580.03	1,334.67
65,000.00	5,775.17	3,059.78	2,158.93	1,711.70	1,445.89
70,000.00	6,219.42	3,295.14	2,325.00	1,843.37	1,557.11
75,000.00	6,663.66	3,530.51	2,491.07	1,975.04	1,668.33
80,000.00	7,107.90	3,765.88	2,657.14	2,106.71	1,779.56
85,000.00	7,552.15	4,001.25	2,823.22	2,238.38	1,890.78
90,000.00	7,996.39	4,236.61	2,989.29	2,370.05	2,002.00
95,000.00	8,440.63	4,471.98	3,155.36	2,501.71	2,113.22
100,000.00	8,884.88	4,707.35	3,321.43	2,633.38	2,224.44
110,000.00	9,773.37	5,178.08	3,653.57	2,896.72	2,446.89
120,000.00	10,661.85	5,648.82	3,985.72	3,160.06	2,669.33
130,000.00	11,550.34	6,119.55	4,317.86	3,423.40	2,891.78
140,000.00	12,438.83	6,590.29	4,650.00	3,686.74	3,114.22
150,000.00	13,327.32	7,061.02	4,982.15	3,950.08	3,336.67
160,000.00	14,215.81	7,531.76	5,314.29	4,213.41	3,559.11
170,000.00	15,104.29	8,002.49	5,646.43	4,476.75	3,781.56
180,000.00	15,992.78	8,473.23	5,978.58	4,740.09	4,004.00
190,000.00	16,881.27	8,943.96	6,310.72	5,003.43	4,226.45
200,000.00	17,769.76	9,414.69	6,642.86	5,266.77	4,448.89
225,000.00	19,990.98	10,591.53	7,473.22	5,925.11	5,005.00
250,000.00	22,212.20	11,768.37	8,303.58	6,583.46	5,561.11
275,000.00	24,433.42	12,945.20	9,133.94	7,241.80	6,117.22
300,000.00	26,654.64	14,122.04	9,964.29	7,900.15	6,673.33
350,000.00	31,097.08	16,475.72	11,625.01	9,216.84	7,785.56
400,000.00	35,539.52	18,829.39	13,285.72	10,533.53	8,897.78
450,000.00	39,981.95	21,183.06	14,946.44	11,850.23	10,010.00
500,000.00	44,424.39	23,536.74	16,607.15	13,166.92	11,122.22

Monthly Mortgage Payment 12%

TABLE C

(Amount Necessary to Amortize a Loan)

10 Years	15 Years	20 Years	25 Years	30 Years	AMOUNT OF LOAN
$ .72	$ .60	$ .55	$ .53	$ .51	$ 50.00
1.43	1.20	1.10	1.05	1.03	100.00
2.87	2.40	2.20	2.11	2.06	200.00
4.30	3.60	3.30	3.16	3.09	300.00
5.74	4.80	4.40	4.21	4.11	400.00
7.17	6.00	5.51	5.27	5.14	500.00
14.35	12.00	11.01	10.53	10.29	1,000.00
28.69	24.00	22.02	21.06	20.57	2,000.00
43.04	36.01	33.03	31.60	30.86	3,000.00
57.39	48.01	44.04	42.13	41.14	4,000.00
71.74	60.01	55.05	52.66	51.43	5,000.00
143.47	120.02	110.11	105.32	102.86	10,000.00
215.21	180.03	165.16	157.98	154.29	15,000.00
286.94	240.03	220.22	210.64	205.72	20,000.00
358.68	300.04	275.27	263.31	257.15	25,000.00
430.41	360.05	330.33	315.97	308.58	30,000.00
502.15	420.06	385.38	368.63	360.01	35,000.00
573.88	480.07	440.43	421.29	411.45	40,000.00
645.62	540.08	495.49	473.95	462.88	45,000.00
717.35	600.08	550.54	526.61	514.31	50,000.00
789.09	660.09	605.60	579.27	565.74	55,000.00
860.83	720.10	660.65	631.93	617.17	60,000.00
932.56	780.11	715.71	684.60	668.60	65,000.00
1,004.30	840.12	770.76	737.26	720.03	70,000.00
1,076.03	900.13	825.81	789.92	771.46	75,000.00
1,147.77	960.13	880.87	842.58	822.89	80,000.00
1,219.50	1,020.14	935.92	895.24	874.32	85,000.00
1,291.24	1,080.15	990.98	947.90	925.75	90,000.00
1,362.97	1,140.16	1,046.03	1,000.56	977.18	95,000.00
1,434.71	1,200.17	1,101.09	1,053.22	1,028.61	100,000.00
1,578.18	1,320.18	1,211.19	1,158.55	1,131.47	110,000.00
1,721.65	1,440.20	1,321.30	1,263.87	1,234.34	120,000.00
1,865.12	1,560.22	1,431.41	1,369.19	1,337.20	130,000.00
2,008.59	1,680.24	1,541.52	1,474.51	1,440.06	140,000.00
2,152.06	1,800.25	1,651.63	1,579.84	1,542.92	150,000.00
2,295.54	1,920.27	1,761.74	1,685.16	1,645.78	160,000.00
2,439.01	2,040.29	1,871.85	1,790.48	1,748.64	170,000.00
2,582.48	2,160.30	1,981.96	1,895.80	1,851.50	180,000.00
2,725.95	2,280.32	2,092.06	2,001.13	1,954.36	190,000.00
2,869.42	2,400.34	2,202.17	2,106.45	2,057.23	200,000.00
3,228.10	2,700.38	2,477.44	2,369.75	2,314.38	225,000.00
3,586.77	3,000.42	2,752.72	2,633.06	2,571.53	250,000.00
3,945.45	3,300.46	3,027.99	2,896.37	2,828.68	275,000.00
4,304.13	3,600.50	3,303.26	3,159.67	3,085.84	300,000.00
5,021.48	4,200.59	3,853.80	3,686.28	3,600.14	350,000.00
5,738.84	4,800.67	4,404.34	4,212.90	4,114.45	400,000.00
6,456.19	5,400.76	4,954.89	4,739.51	4,628.76	450,000.00
7,173.55	6,000.84	5,505.43	5,266.12	5,143.06	500,000.00

12¼%   Figuring Out Your

TABLE C
(Amount Necessary to Amortize a Loan)

AMOUNT OF LOAN	TERM OF LOAN				
	1 Year	2 Years	3 Years	4 Years	5 Years
$ 50.00	$ 4.45	$ 2.36	$ 1.67	$ 1.32	$ 1.12
100.00	8.90	4.72	3.33	2.65	2.24
200.00	17.79	9.44	6.67	5.29	4.47
300.00	26.69	14.16	10.00	7.94	6.71
400.00	35.59	18.88	13.33	10.58	8.95
500.00	44.48	23.60	16.67	13.23	11.19
1,000.00	88.97	47.19	33.33	26.46	22.37
2,000.00	177.93	94.38	66.67	52.91	44.74
3,000.00	266.90	141.57	100.00	79.37	67.11
4,000.00	355.86	188.76	133.34	105.83	89.48
5,000.00	444.83	235.95	166.67	132.28	111.85
10,000.00	889.66	471.90	333.34	264.57	223.71
15,000.00	1,334.49	707.85	500.01	396.85	335.56
20,000.00	1,779.32	943.81	666.68	529.14	447.42
25,000.00	2,224.14	1,179.76	833.35	661.42	559.27
30,000.00	2,668.97	1,415.71	1,000.02	793.70	671.13
35,000.00	3,113.80	1,651.66	1,166.68	925.99	782.98
40,000.00	3,558.63	1,887.61	1,333.35	1,058.27	894.84
45,000.00	4,003.46	2,123.56	1,500.02	1,190.55	1,006.69
50,000.00	4,448.29	2,359.52	1,666.69	1,322.84	1,118.55
55,000.00	4,893.12	2,595.47	1,833.36	1,455.12	1,230.40
60,000.00	5,337.95	2,831.42	2,000.03	1,587.41	1,342.26
65,000.00	5,782.78	3,067.37	2,166.70	1,719.69	1,454.11
70,000.00	6,227.60	3,303.32	2,333.37	1,851.97	1,565.97
75,000.00	6,672.43	3,539.27	2,500.04	1,984.26	1,677.82
80,000.00	7,117.26	3,775.22	2,666.71	2,116.54	1,789.68
85,000.00	7,562.09	4,011.18	2,833.38	2,248.82	1,901.53
90,000.00	8,006.92	4,247.13	3,000.05	2,381.11	2,013.39
95,000.00	8,451.75	4,483.08	3,166.71	2,513.39	2,125.24
100,000.00	8,896.58	4,719.03	3,333.38	2,645.68	2,237.10
110,000.00	9,786.24	5,190.93	3,666.72	2,910.24	2,460.81
120,000.00	10,675.89	5,662.84	4,000.06	3,174.81	2,684.52
130,000.00	11,565.55	6,134.74	4,333.40	3,439.38	2,908.23
140,000.00	12,455.21	6,606.64	4,666.74	3,703.95	3,131.94
150,000.00	13,344.87	7,078.55	5,000.08	3,968.51	3,355.65
160,000.00	14,234.53	7,550.45	5,333.41	4,233.08	3,579.36
170,000.00	15,124.18	8,022.35	5,666.75	4,497.65	3,803.07
180,000.00	16,013.84	8,494.25	6,000.09	4,762.22	4,026.78
190,000.00	16,903.50	8,966.16	6,333.43	5,026.78	4,250.49
200,000.00	17,793.16	9,438.06	6,666.77	5,291.35	4,474.20
225,000.00	20,017.30	10,617.82	7,500.11	5,952.77	5,033.47
250,000.00	22,241.45	11,797.58	8,333.46	6,614.19	5,592.75
275,000.00	24,465.59	12,977.33	9,166.81	7,275.61	6,152.02
300,000.00	26,689.73	14,157.09	10,000.15	7,937.03	6,711.30
350,000.00	31,138.02	16,516.61	11,666.84	9,259.86	7,829.85
400,000.00	35,586.31	18,876.12	13,333.54	10,582.70	8,948.39
450,000.00	40,034.60	21,235.64	15,000.23	11,905.54	10,066.94
500,000.00	44,482.89	23,595.15	16,666.92	13,228.38	11,185.49

Monthly Mortgage Payment

TABLE C

(Amount Necessary to Amortize a Loan)

TERM OF LOAN					AMOUNT
10 Years	15 Years	20 Years	25 Years	30 Years	OF LOAN
$ .72	$ .61	$ .56	$ .54	$ .52	$ 50.00
1.45	1.22	1.12	1.07	1.05	100.00
2.90	2.43	2.24	2.14	2.10	200.00
4.35	3.65	3.36	3.22	3.14	300.00
5.80	4.87	4.47	4.29	4.19	400.00
7.25	6.08	5.59	5.36	5.24	500.00
14.49	12.16	11.19	10.72	10.48	1,000.00
28.98	24.33	22.37	21.43	20.96	2,000.00
43.48	36.49	33.56	32.15	31.44	3,000.00
57.97	48.65	44.74	42.87	41.92	4,000.00
72.46	60.81	55.93	53.59	52.39	5,000.00
144.92	121.63	111.86	107.17	104.79	10,000.00
217.38	182.44	167.78	160.76	157.18	15,000.00
289.84	243.26	223.71	214.35	209.58	20,000.00
362.30	304.07	279.64	267.94	261.97	25,000.00
434.76	364.89	335.57	321.52	314.37	30,000.00
507.22	425.70	391.50	375.11	366.76	35,000.00
579.68	486.52	447.43	428.70	419.16	40,000.00
652.14	547.33	503.35	482.28	471.55	45,000.00
724.60	608.15	559.28	535.87	523.95	50,000.00
797.06	668.96	615.21	589.46	576.34	55,000.00
869.52	729.78	671.14	643.05	628.74	60,000.00
941.98	790.59	727.07	696.63	681.13	65,000.00
1,014.44	851.41	783.00	750.22	733.53	70,000.00
1,086.90	912.22	838.92	803.81	785.92	75,000.00
1,159.36	973.04	894.85	857.40	838.32	80,000.00
1,231.82	1,033.85	950.78	910.98	890.71	85,000.00
1,304.28	1,094.67	1,006.71	964.57	943.11	90,000.00
1,376.74	1,155.48	1,062.64	1,018.16	995.50	95,000.00
1,449.20	1,216.30	1,118.56	1,071.74	1,047.90	100,000.00
1,594.12	1,337.93	1,230.42	1,178.92	1,152.69	110,000.00
1,739.04	1,459.56	1,342.28	1,286.09	1,257.48	120,000.00
1,883.96	1,581.19	1,454.13	1,393.27	1,362.27	130,000.00
2,028.88	1,702.82	1,565.99	1,500.44	1,467.06	140,000.00
2,173.80	1,824.45	1,677.85	1,607.62	1,571.84	150,000.00
2,318.72	1,946.08	1,789.70	1,714.79	1,676.63	160,000.00
2,463.64	2,067.71	1,901.56	1,821.96	1,781.42	170,000.00
2,608.56	2,189.34	2,013.42	1,929.14	1,886.21	180,000.00
2,753.48	2,310.97	2,125.27	2,036.31	1,991.00	190,000.00
2,898.40	2,432.60	2,237.13	2,143.49	2,095.79	200,000.00
3,260.70	2,736.67	2,516.77	2,411.42	2,357.77	225,000.00
3,623.00	3,040.75	2,796.41	2,679.36	2,619.74	250,000.00
3,985.30	3,344.82	3,076.05	2,947.30	2,881.72	275,000.00
4,347.60	3,648.90	3,355.69	3,215.23	3,143.69	300,000.00
5,072.20	4,257.05	3,914.98	3,751.10	3,667.64	350,000.00
5,796.79	4,865.19	4,474.26	4,286.98	4,191.59	400,000.00
6,521.39	5,473.34	5,033.54	4,822.85	4,715.53	450,000.00
7,245.99	6,081.49	5,592.82	5,358.72	5,239.48	500,000.00

12½%

Figuring Out Your

TABLE C
(Amount Necessary to Amortize a Loan)

AMOUNT OF LOAN	TERM OF LOAN				
	1 Year	2 Years	3 Years	4 Years	5 Years
$ 50.00	$ 4.45	$ 2.37	$ 1.67	$ 1.33	$ 1.12
100.00	8.91	4.73	3.35	2.66	2.25
200.00	17.82	9.46	6.69	5.32	4.50
300.00	26.72	14.19	10.04	7.97	6.75
400.00	35.63	18.92	13.38	10.63	9.00
500.00	44.54	23.65	16.73	13.29	11.25
1,000.00	89.08	47.31	33.45	26.58	22.50
2,000.00	178.17	94.61	66.91	53.16	45.00
3,000.00	267.25	141.92	100.36	79.74	67.49
4,000.00	356.33	189.23	133.81	106.32	89.99
5,000.00	445.41	236.54	167.27	132.90	112.49
10,000.00	890.83	473.07	334.54	265.80	224.98
15,000.00	1,336.24	709.61	501.80	398.70	337.47
20,000.00	1,781.66	946.15	669.07	531.60	449.96
25,000.00	2,227.07	1,182.68	836.34	664.50	562.45
30,000.00	2,672.49	1,419.22	1,003.61	797.40	674.94
35,000.00	3,117.90	1,655.76	1,170.88	930.30	787.43
40,000.00	3,563.31	1,892.29	1,338.15	1,063.20	899.92
45,000.00	4,008.73	2,128.83	1,505.41	1,196.10	1,012.41
50,000.00	4,454.14	2,365.37	1,672.68	1,329.00	1,124.90
55,000.00	4,899.56	2,601.90	1,839.95	1,461.90	1,237.39
60,000.00	5,344.97	2,838.44	2,007.22	1,594.80	1,349.88
65,000.00	5,790.39	3,074.98	2,174.49	1,727.70	1,462.37
70,000.00	6,235.80	3,311.51	2,341.75	1,860.60	1,574.86
75,000.00	6,681.21	3,548.05	2,509.02	1,993.50	1,687.35
80,000.00	7,126.63	3,784.58	2,676.29	2,126.40	1,799.84
85,000.00	7,572.04	4,021.12	2,843.56	2,259.30	1,912.32
90,000.00	8,017.46	4,257.66	3,010.83	2,392.20	2,024.81
95,000.00	8,462.87	4,494.19	3,178.09	2,525.10	2,137.30
100,000.00	8,908.29	4,730.73	3,345.36	2,658.00	2,249.79
110,000.00	9,799.11	5,203.80	3,679.90	2,923.80	2,474.77
120,000.00	10,689.94	5,676.88	4,014.44	3,189.60	2,699.75
130,000.00	11,580.77	6,149.95	4,348.97	3,455.40	2,924.73
140,000.00	12,471.60	6,623.02	4,683.51	3,721.20	3,149.71
150,000.00	13,362.43	7,096.10	5,018.04	3,987.00	3,374.69
160,000.00	14,253.26	7,569.17	5,352.58	4,252.80	3,599.67
170,000.00	15,144.09	8,042.24	5,687.12	4,518.60	3,824.65
180,000.00	16,034.92	8,515.32	6,021.65	4,784.40	4,049.63
190,000.00	16,925.74	8,988.39	6,356.19	5,050.20	4,274.61
200,000.00	17,816.57	9,461.46	6,690.73	5,316.00	4,499.59
225,000.00	20,043.64	10,644.14	7,527.07	5,980.50	5,062.04
250,000.00	22,270.72	11,826.83	8,363.41	6,645.00	5,624.48
275,000.00	24,497.79	13,009.51	9,199.75	7,309.50	6,186.93
300,000.00	26,724.86	14,192.19	10,036.09	7,974.00	6,749.38
350,000.00	31,179.00	16,557.56	11,708.77	9,303.00	7,874.28
400,000.00	35,633.15	18,922.92	13,381.45	10,632.00	8,999.18
450,000.00	40,087.29	21,288.29	15,054.13	11,961.00	10,124.07
500,000.00	44,541.43	23,653.65	16,726.81	13,290.00	11,248.97

Monthly Mortgage Payment 12½%

TABLE C

(Amount Necessary to Amortize a Loan)

10 Years	15 Years	TERM OF LOAN 20 Years	25 Years	30 Years	AMOUNT OF LOAN
$ .73	$ .62	$ .57	$ .55	$ .53	$ 50.00
1.46	1.23	1.14	1.09	1.07	100.00
2.93	2.47	2.27	2.18	2.13	200.00
4.39	3.70	3.41	3.27	3.20	300.00
5.86	4.93	4.54	4.36	4.27	400.00
7.32	6.16	5.68	5.45	5.34	500.00
14.64	12.33	11.36	10.90	10.67	1,000.00
29.28	24.65	22.72	21.81	21.35	2,000.00
43.91	36.98	34.08	32.71	32.02	3,000.00
58.55	49.30	45.45	43.61	42.69	4,000.00
73.19	61.63	56.81	54.52	53.36	5,000.00
146.38	123.25	113.61	109.04	106.73	10,000.00
219.56	184.88	170.42	163.55	160.09	15,000.00
292.75	246.50	227.23	218.07	213.45	20,000.00
365.94	308.13	284.04	272.59	266.81	25,000.00
439.13	369.76	340.84	327.11	320.18	30,000.00
512.32	431.38	397.65	381.62	373.54	35,000.00
585.50	493.01	454.46	436.14	426.90	40,000.00
658.69	554.63	511.26	490.66	480.27	45,000.00
731.88	616.26	568.07	545.18	533.63	50,000.00
805.07	677.89	624.88	599.69	586.99	55,000.00
878.26	739.51	681.68	654.21	640.35	60,000.00
951.45	801.14	738.49	708.73	693.72	65,000.00
1,024.63	862.77	795.30	763.25	747.08	70,000.00
1,097.82	924.39	852.11	817.77	800.44	75,000.00
1,171.01	986.02	908.91	872.28	853.81	80,000.00
1,244.20	1,047.64	965.72	926.80	907.17	85,000.00
1,317.39	1,109.27	1,022.53	981.32	960.53	90,000.00
1,390.57	1,170.90	1,079.33	1,035.84	1,013.89	95,000.00
1,463.76	1,232.52	1,136.14	1,090.35	1,067.26	100,000.00
1,610.14	1,355.77	1,249.75	1,199.39	1,173.98	110,000.00
1,756.51	1,479.03	1,363.37	1,308.42	1,280.71	120,000.00
1,902.89	1,602.28	1,476.98	1,417.46	1,387.44	130,000.00
2,049.27	1,725.53	1,590.60	1,526.50	1,494.16	140,000.00
2,195.64	1,848.78	1,704.21	1,635.53	1,600.89	150,000.00
2,342.02	1,972.04	1,817.82	1,744.57	1,707.61	160,000.00
2,488.39	2,095.29	1,931.44	1,853.60	1,814.34	170,000.00
2,634.77	2,218.54	2,045.05	1,962.64	1,921.06	180,000.00
2,781.15	2,341.79	2,158.67	2,071.67	2,027.79	190,000.00
2,927.52	2,465.04	2,272.28	2,180.71	2,134.52	200,000.00
3,293.46	2,773.17	2,556.32	2,453.30	2,401.33	225,000.00
3,659.40	3,081.31	2,840.35	2,725.89	2,668.14	250,000.00
4,025.34	3,389.44	3,124.39	2,998.47	2,934.96	275,000.00
4,391.29	3,697.57	3,408.42	3,271.06	3,201.77	300,000.00
5,123.17	4,313.83	3,976.49	3,816.24	3,735.40	350,000.00
5,855.05	4,930.09	4,544.56	4,361.42	4,269.03	400,000.00
6,586.93	5,546.35	5,112.63	4,906.59	4,802.66	450,000.00
7,318.81	6,162.61	5,680.70	5,451.77	5,336.29	500,000.00

12¾%   **Figuring Out Your**

TABLE C

(Amount Necessary to Amortize a Loan)

AMOUNT OF LOAN	TERM OF LOAN 1 Year	2 Years	3 Years	4 Years	5 Years
$ 50.00	$ 4.46	$ 2.37	$ 1.68	$ 1.34	$ 1.13
100.00	8.92	4.74	3.36	2.67	2.26
200.00	17.84	9.48	6.71	5.34	4.53
300.00	26.76	14.23	10.07	8.01	6.79
400.00	35.68	18.97	13.43	10.68	9.05
500.00	44.60	23.71	16.79	13.35	11.31
1,000.00	89.20	47.42	33.57	26.70	22.63
2,000.00	178.40	94.85	67.15	53.41	45.25
3,000.00	267.60	142.27	100.72	80.11	67.88
4,000.00	356.80	189.70	134.29	106.81	90.50
5,000.00	446.00	237.12	167.87	133.52	113.13
10,000.00	892.00	474.24	335.74	267.04	226.25
15,000.00	1,338.00	711.37	503.60	400.55	339.38
20,000.00	1,784.00	948.49	671.47	534.07	452.51
25,000.00	2,230.00	1,185.61	839.34	667.59	565.63
30,000.00	2,676.00	1,422.73	1,007.21	801.11	678.76
35,000.00	3,122.00	1,659.86	1,175.08	934.63	791.89
40,000.00	3,568.00	1,896.98	1,342.95	1,068.14	905.01
45,000.00	4,014.00	2,134.10	1,510.81	1,201.66	1,018.14
50,000.00	4,460.00	2,371.22	1,678.68	1,335.18	1,131.27
55,000.00	4,906.00	2,608.35	1,846.55	1,468.70	1,244.39
60,000.00	5,352.00	2,845.47	2,014.42	1,602.21	1,357.52
65,000.00	5,798.00	3,082.59	2,182.29	1,735.73	1,470.64
70,000.00	6,244.00	3,319.71	2,350.16	1,869.25	1,583.77
75,000.00	6,690.00	3,556.84	2,518.02	2,002.77	1,696.90
80,000.00	7,136.00	3,793.96	2,685.89	2,136.29	1,810.02
85,000.00	7,582.00	4,031.08	2,853.76	2,269.80	1,923.15
90,000.00	8,028.00	4,268.20	3,021.63	2,403.32	2,036.28
95,000.00	8,474.00	4,505.33	3,189.50	2,536.84	2,149.40
100,000.00	8,920.00	4,742.45	3,357.37	2,670.36	2,262.53
110,000.00	9,812.00	5,216.69	3,693.10	2,937.39	2,488.78
120,000.00	10,704.00	5,690.94	4,028.84	3,204.43	2,715.04
130,000.00	11,596.00	6,165.18	4,364.58	3,471.47	2,941.29
140,000.00	12,488.00	6,639.43	4,700.31	3,738.50	3,167.54
150,000.00	13,380.00	7,113.67	5,036.05	4,005.54	3,393.80
160,000.00	14,272.00	7,587.92	5,371.79	4,272.57	3,620.05
170,000.00	15,164.00	8,062.16	5,707.52	4,539.61	3,846.30
180,000.00	16,056.00	8,536.41	6,043.26	4,806.64	4,072.55
190,000.00	16,948.01	9,010.65	6,379.00	5,073.68	4,298.81
200,000.00	17,840.01	9,484.90	6,714.73	5,340.72	4,525.06
225,000.00	20,070.01	10,670.51	7,554.07	6,008.31	5,090.69
250,000.00	22,300.01	11,856.12	8,393.42	6,675.90	5,656.33
275,000.00	24,530.01	13,041.73	9,232.76	7,343.48	6,221.96
300,000.00	26,760.01	14,227.34	10,072.10	8,011.07	6,787.59
350,000.00	31,220.01	16,598.57	11,750.78	9,346.25	7,918.86
400,000.00	35,680.01	18,969.79	13,429.47	10,681.43	9,050.12
450,000.00	40,140.01	21,341.02	15,108.15	12,016.61	10,181.39
500,000.00	44,600.01	23,712.24	16,786.83	13,351.79	11,312.65

Monthly Mortgage Payment 12¾%

TABLE C

(Amount Necessary to Amortize a Loan)

10 Years	15 Years	TERM OF LOAN 20 Years	25 Years	30 Years	AMOUNT OF LOAN
$ .74	$ .62	$ .58	$ .55	$ .54	$ 50.00
1.48	1.25	1.15	1.11	1.09	100.00
2.96	2.50	2.31	2.22	2.17	200.00
4.44	3.75	3.46	3.33	3.26	300.00
5.91	5.00	4.62	4.44	4.35	400.00
7.39	6.24	5.77	5.55	5.43	500.00
14.78	12.49	11.54	11.09	10.87	1,000.00
29.57	24.98	23.08	22.18	21.73	2,000.00
44.35	37.47	34.61	33.27	32.60	3,000.00
59.14	49.95	46.15	44.36	43.47	4,000.00
73.92	62.44	57.69	55.45	54.33	5,000.00
147.84	124.88	115.38	110.91	108.67	10,000.00
221.76	187.33	173.07	166.36	163.00	15,000.00
295.68	249.77	230.76	221.81	217.34	20,000.00
369.60	312.21	288.45	277.26	271.67	25,000.00
443.52	374.65	346.14	332.72	326.01	30,000.00
517.44	437.09	403.83	388.17	380.34	35,000.00
591.36	499.53	461.52	443.62	434.68	40,000.00
665.28	561.98	519.22	499.07	489.01	45,000.00
739.20	624.42	576.91	554.53	543.35	50,000.00
813.12	686.86	634.60	609.98	597.68	55,000.00
887.04	749.30	692.29	665.43	652.02	60,000.00
960.96	811.74	749.98	720.88	706.35	65,000.00
1,034.88	874.19	807.67	776.34	760.69	70,000.00
1,108.80	936.63	865.36	831.79	815.02	75,000.00
1,182.72	999.07	923.05	887.24	869.35	80,000.00
1,256.64	1,061.51	980.74	942.69	923.69	85,000.00
1,330.56	1,123.95	1,038.43	998.15	978.02	90,000.00
1,404.48	1,186.40	1,096.12	1,053.60	1,032.36	95,000.00
1,478.40	1,248.84	1,153.81	1,109.05	1,086.69	100,000.00
1,626.24	1,373.72	1,269.19	1,219.96	1,195.36	110,000.00
1,774.08	1,498.60	1,384.57	1,330.86	1,304.03	120,000.00
1,921.92	1,623.49	1,499.96	1,441.77	1,412.70	130,000.00
2,069.76	1,748.37	1,615.34	1,552.67	1,521.37	140,000.00
2,217.60	1,873.26	1,730.72	1,663.58	1,630.04	150,000.00
2,365.44	1,998.14	1,846.10	1,774.48	1,738.71	160,000.00
2,513.28	2,123.02	1,961.48	1,885.39	1,847.38	170,000.00
2,661.12	2,247.91	2,076.86	1,996.29	1,956.05	180,000.00
2,808.96	2,372.79	2,192.24	2,107.20	2,064.72	190,000.00
2,956.80	2,497.67	2,307.62	2,218.10	2,173.39	200,000.00
3,326.40	2,809.88	2,596.08	2,495.37	2,445.06	225,000.00
3,696.00	3,122.09	2,884.53	2,772.63	2,716.73	250,000.00
4,065.59	3,434.30	3,172.98	3,049.89	2,988.41	275,000.00
4,435.19	3,746.51	3,461.43	3,327.16	3,260.08	300,000.00
5,174.39	4,370.93	4,038.34	3,881.68	3,803.43	350,000.00
5,913.59	4,995.35	4,615.25	4,436.21	4,346.77	400,000.00
6,652.79	5,619.77	5,192.15	4,990.74	4,890.12	450,000.00
7,391.99	6,244.18	5,769.06	5,545.26	5,433.47	500,000.00

TABLE C

(Amount Necessary to Amortize a Loan)

AMOUNT OF LOAN	TERM OF LOAN				
	1 Year	2 Years	3 Years	4 Years	5 Years
$ 50.00	$ 4.47	$ 2.38	$ 1.68	$ 1.34	$ 1.14
100.00	8.93	4.75	3.37	2.68	2.28
200.00	17.86	9.51	6.74	5.37	4.55
300.00	26.80	14.26	10.11	8.05	6.83
400.00	35.73	19.02	13.48	10.73	9.10
500.00	44.66	23.77	16.85	13.41	11.38
1,000.00	89.32	47.54	33.69	26.83	22.75
2,000.00	178.63	95.08	67.39	53.65	45.51
3,000.00	267.95	142.63	101.08	80.48	68.26
4,000.00	357.27	190.17	134.78	107.31	91.01
5,000.00	446.59	237.71	168.47	134.14	113.77
10,000.00	893.17	475.42	336.94	268.27	227.53
15,000.00	1,339.76	713.13	505.41	402.41	341.30
20,000.00	1,786.35	950.84	673.88	536.55	455.06
25,000.00	2,232.93	1,188.55	842.35	670.69	568.83
30,000.00	2,679.52	1,426.25	1,010.82	804.82	682.59
35,000.00	3,126.10	1,663.96	1,179.29	938.96	796.36
40,000.00	3,572.69	1,901.67	1,347.76	1,073.10	910.12
45,000.00	4,019.28	2,139.38	1,516.23	1,207.24	1,023.89
50,000.00	4,465.86	2,377.09	1,684.70	1,341.37	1,137.65
55,000.00	4,912.45	2,614.80	1,853.17	1,475.51	1,251.42
60,000.00	5,359.04	2,852.51	2,021.64	1,609.65	1,365.18
65,000.00	5,805.62	3,090.22	2,190.11	1,743.79	1,478.95
70,000.00	6,252.21	3,327.93	2,358.58	1,877.92	1,592.72
75,000.00	6,698.80	3,565.64	2,527.05	2,012.06	1,706.48
80,000.00	7,145.38	3,803.35	2,695.52	2,146.20	1,820.25
85,000.00	7,591.97	4,041.05	2,863.99	2,280.34	1,934.01
90,000.00	8,038.55	4,278.76	3,032.46	2,414.47	2,047.78
95,000.00	8,485.14	4,516.47	3,200.93	2,548.61	2,161.54
100,000.00	8,931.73	4,754.18	3,369.40	2,682.75	2,275.31
110,000.00	9,824.90	5,229.60	3,706.33	2,951.02	2,502.84
120,000.00	10,718.07	5,705.02	4,043.27	3,219.30	2,730.37
130,000.00	11,611.25	6,180.44	4,380.21	3,487.57	2,957.90
140,000.00	12,504.42	6,655.86	4,717.15	3,755.85	3,185.43
150,000.00	13,397.59	7,131.27	5,054.09	4,024.12	3,412.96
160,000.00	14,290.76	7,606.69	5,391.03	4,292.40	3,640.49
170,000.00	15,183.94	8,082.11	5,727.97	4,560.67	3,868.02
180,000.00	16,077.11	8,557.53	6,064.91	4,828.95	4,095.55
190,000.00	16,970.28	9,032.95	6,401.85	5,097.22	4,323.08
200,000.00	17,863.46	9,508.36	6,738.79	5,365.50	4,550.61
225,000.00	20,096.39	10,696.91	7,581.14	6,036.19	5,119.44
250,000.00	22,329.32	11,885.46	8,423.49	6,706.87	5,688.27
275,000.00	24,562.25	13,074.00	9,265.84	7,377.56	6,257.10
300,000.00	26,795.18	14,262.55	10,108.19	8,048.25	6,825.92
350,000.00	31,261.05	16,639.64	11,792.88	9,389.62	7,963.58
400,000.00	35,726.91	19,016.73	13,477.58	10,731.00	9,101.23
450,000.00	40,192.77	21,393.82	15,162.28	12,072.37	10,238.88
500,000.00	44,658.64	23,770.91	16,846.98	13,413.75	11,376.54

Monthly Mortgage Payment   13%

TABLE C

(Amount Necessary to Amortize a Loan)

10 Years	15 Years	TERM OF LOAN 20 Years	25 Years	30 Years	AMOUNT OF LOAN
$ .75	$ .63	$ .59	$ .56	$ .55	$ 50.00
1.49	1.27	1.17	1.13	1.11	100.00
2.99	2.53	2.34	2.26	2.21	200.00
4.48	3.80	3.51	3.38	3.32	300.00
5.97	5.06	4.69	4.51	4.42	400.00
7.47	6.33	5.86	5.64	5.53	500.00
14.93	12.65	11.72	11.28	11.06	1,000.00
29.86	25.30	23.43	22.56	22.12	2,000.00
44.79	37.96	35.15	33.84	33.19	3,000.00
59.72	50.61	46.86	45.11	44.25	4,000.00
74.66	63.26	58.58	56.39	55.31	5,000.00
149.31	126.52	117.16	112.78	110.62	10,000.00
223.97	189.79	175.74	169.18	165.93	15,000.00
298.62	253.05	234.32	225.57	221.24	20,000.00
373.28	316.31	292.89	281.96	276.55	25,000.00
447.93	379.57	351.47	338.35	331.86	30,000.00
522.59	442.83	410.05	394.74	387.17	35,000.00
597.24	506.10	468.63	451.13	442.48	40,000.00
671.90	569.36	527.21	507.53	497.79	45,000.00
746.55	632.62	585.79	563.92	553.10	50,000.00
821.21	695.88	644.37	620.31	608.41	55,000.00
895.86	759.15	702.95	676.70	663.72	60,000.00
970.52	822.41	761.52	733.09	719.03	65,000.00
1,045.18	885.67	820.10	789.48	774.34	70,000.00
1,119.83	948.93	878.68	845.88	829.65	75,000.00
1,194.49	1,012.19	937.26	902.27	884.96	80,000.00
1,269.14	1,075.46	995.84	958.66	940.27	85,000.00
1,343.80	1,138.72	1,054.42	1,015.05	995.58	90,000.00
1,418.45	1,201.98	1,113.00	1,071.44	1,050.89	95,000.00
1,493.11	1,265.24	1,171.58	1,127.84	1,106.20	100,000.00
1,642.42	1,391.77	1,288.73	1,240.62	1,216.82	110,000.00
1,791.73	1,518.29	1,405.89	1,353.40	1,327.44	120,000.00
1,941.04	1,644.81	1,523.05	1,466.19	1,438.06	130,000.00
2,090.35	1,771.34	1,640.21	1,578.97	1,548.68	140,000.00
2,239.66	1,897.86	1,757.36	1,691.75	1,659.30	150,000.00
2,388.97	2,024.39	1,874.52	1,804.54	1,769.92	160,000.00
2,538.28	2,150.91	1,991.68	1,917.32	1,880.54	170,000.00
2,687.59	2,277.44	2,108.84	2,030.10	1,991.16	180,000.00
2,836.90	2,403.96	2,225.99	2,142.89	2,101.78	190,000.00
2,986.21	2,530.48	2,343.15	2,255.67	2,212.40	200,000.00
3,359.49	2,846.79	2,636.05	2,537.63	2,488.95	225,000.00
3,732.77	3,163.11	2,928.94	2,819.59	2,765.50	250,000.00
4,106.05	3,479.42	3,221.83	3,101.55	3,042.05	275,000.00
4,479.32	3,795.73	3,514.73	3,383.51	3,318.60	300,000.00
5,225.88	4,428.35	4,100.51	3,947.42	3,871.70	350,000.00
5,972.43	5,060.97	4,686.30	4,511.34	4,424.80	400,000.00
6,718.98	5,693.59	5,272.09	5,075.26	4,977.90	450,000.00
7,465.54	6,326.21	5,857.88	5,639.18	5,531.00	500,000.00

13¼%   **Figuring Out Your**

TABLE C

(Amount Necessary to Amortize a Loan)

AMOUNT OF LOAN	TERM OF LOAN				
	1 Year	2 Years	3 Years	4 Years	5 Years
$ 50.00	$ 4.47	$ 2.38	$ 1.69	$ 1.35	$ 1.14
100.00	8.94	4.77	3.38	2.70	2.29
200.00	17.89	9.53	6.76	5.39	4.58
300.00	26.83	14.30	10.14	8.09	6.86
400.00	35.77	19.06	13.53	10.78	9.15
500.00	44.72	23.83	16.91	13.48	11.44
1,000.00	89.43	47.66	33.81	26.95	22.88
2,000.00	178.87	95.32	67.63	53.90	45.76
3,000.00	268.30	142.98	101.44	80.86	68.64
4,000.00	357.74	190.64	135.26	107.81	91.53
5,000.00	447.17	238.30	169.07	134.76	114.41
10,000.00	894.35	476.59	338.14	269.52	228.81
15,000.00	1,341.52	714.89	507.22	404.28	343.22
20,000.00	1,788.69	953.19	676.29	539.03	457.63
25,000.00	2,235.87	1,191.48	845.36	673.79	572.03
30,000.00	2,683.04	1,429.78	1,014.43	808.55	686.44
35,000.00	3,130.21	1,668.08	1,183.51	943.31	800.84
40,000.00	3,577.38	1,906.37	1,352.58	1,078.07	915.25
45,000.00	4,024.56	2,144.67	1,521.65	1,212.83	1,029.66
50,000.00	4,471.73	2,302.97	1,690.72	1,347.59	1,144.06
55,000.00	4,918.90	2,621.26	1,859.80	1,482.35	1,258.47
60,000.00	5,366.08	2,859.56	2,028.87	1,617.10	1,372.88
65,000.00	5,813.25	3,097.86	2,197.94	1,751.86	1,487.28
70,000.00	6,260.42	3,336.15	2,367.01	1,886.62	1,601.69
75,000.00	6,707.60	3,574.45	2,536.09	2,021.38	1,716.09
80,000.00	7,154.77	3,812.75	2,705.16	2,156.14	1,830.50
85,000.00	7,601.94	4,051.04	2,874.23	2,290.90	1,944.91
90,000.00	8,049.11	4,289.34	3,043.30	2,425.66	2,059.31
95,000.00	8,496.29	4,527.64	3,212.38	2,560.42	2,173.72
100,000.00	8,943.46	4,765.93	3,381.45	2,695.17	2,288.13
110,000.00	9,837.81	5,242.53	3,719.59	2,964.69	2,516.94
120,000.00	10,732.15	5,719.12	4,057.74	3,234.21	2,745.75
130,000.00	11,626.50	6,195.71	4,395.88	3,503.73	2,974.56
140,000.00	12,520.85	6,672.31	4,734.03	3,773.24	3,203.38
150,000.00	13,415.19	7,148.90	5,072.17	4,042.76	3,432.19
160,000.00	14,309.54	7,625.49	5,410.32	4,312.28	3,661.00
170,000.00	15,203.88	8,102.09	5,748.46	4,581.80	3,889.81
180,000.00	16,098.23	8,578.68	6,086.61	4,851.31	4,118.63
190,000.00	16,992.58	9,055.27	6,424.75	5,120.83	4,347.44
200,000.00	17,886.92	9,531.87	6,762.90	5,390.35	4,576.25
225,000.00	20,122.79	10,723.35	7,608.26	6,064.14	5,148.28
250,000.00	22,358.65	11,914.83	8,453.62	6,737.94	5,720.31
275,000.00	24,594.52	13,106.32	9,298.99	7,411.73	6,292.35
300,000.00	26,830.38	14,297.80	10,144.35	8,085.52	6,864.38
350,000.00	31,302.11	16,680.77	11,835.07	9,433.11	8,008.44
400,000.00	35,773.84	19,063.73	13,525.80	10,780.70	9,152.50
450,000.00	40,245.57	21,446.70	15,216.52	12,128.28	10,296.56
500,000.00	44,717.30	23,829.67	16,907.25	13,475.87	11,440.63

Monthly Mortgage Payment $13\frac{1}{4}\%$

TABLE C

(Amount Necessary to Amortize a Loan)

| | | TERM OF LOAN | | | AMOUNT |
10 Years	15 Years	20 Years	25 Years	30 Years	OF LOAN
$ .75	$ .64	$ .59	$ .57	$ .56	$ 50.00
1.51	1.28	1.19	1.15	1.13	100.00
3.02	2.56	2.38	2.29	2.25	200.00
4.52	3.85	3.57	3.44	3.38	300.00
6.03	5.13	4.76	4.59	4.50	400.00
7.54	6.41	5.95	5.73	5.63	500.00
15.08	12.82	11.89	11.47	11.26	1,000.00
30.16	25.63	23.79	22.93	22.52	2,000.00
45.24	38.45	35.68	34.40	33.77	3,000.00
60.32	51.27	47.58	45.87	45.03	4,000.00
75.39	64.09	59.47	57.34	56.29	5,000.00
150.79	128.17	118.94	114.67	112.58	10,000.00
226.18	192.26	178.41	172.01	168.87	15,000.00
301.58	256.35	237.89	229.34	225.15	20,000.00
376.97	320.43	297.36	286.68	281.44	25,000.00
452.37	384.52	356.83	344.01	337.73	30,000.00
527.76	448.61	416.30	401.35	394.02	35,000.00
603.16	512.69	475.77	458.68	450.31	40,000.00
678.55	576.78	535.24	516.02	506.60	45,000.00
753.94	640.87	594.72	573.35	562.89	50,000.00
829.34	704.96	654.19	630.69	619.18	55,000.00
904.73	769.04	713.66	688.02	675.46	60,000.00
980.13	833.13	773.13	745.36	731.75	65,000.00
1,055.52	897.22	832.60	802.69	788.04	70,000.00
1,130.92	961.30	892.07	860.03	844.33	75,000.00
1,206.31	1,025.39	951.54	917.36	900.62	80,000.00
1,281.71	1,089.48	1,011.02	974.70	956.91	85,000.00
1,357.10	1,153.56	1,070.49	1,032.03	1,013.20	90,000.00
1,432.49	1,217.65	1,129.96	1,089.37	1,069.48	95,000.00
1,507.89	1,281.74	1,189.43	1,146.70	1,125.77	100,000.00
1,658.68	1,409.91	1,308.37	1,261.37	1,238.35	110,000.00
1,809.47	1,538.08	1,427.32	1,376.04	1,350.93	120,000.00
1,960.26	1,666.26	1,546.26	1,490.71	1,463.51	130,000.00
2,111.04	1,794.43	1,665.20	1,605.38	1,576.08	140,000.00
2,261.83	1,922.60	1,784.15	1,720.05	1,688.66	150,000.00
2,412.62	2,050.78	1,903.09	1,834.72	1,801.24	160,000.00
2,563.41	2,178.95	2,022.03	1,949.39	1,913.81	170,000.00
2,714.20	2,307.13	2,140.98	2,064.06	2,026.39	180,000.00
2,864.99	2,435.30	2,259.92	2,178.73	2,138.97	190,000.00
3,015.78	2,563.47	2,378.86	2,293.40	2,251.55	200,000.00
3,392.75	2,883.91	2,676.22	2,580.08	2,532.99	225,000.00
3,769.72	3,204.34	2,973.58	2,866.75	2,814.43	250,000.00
4,146.70	3,524.78	3,270.93	3,153.43	3,095.88	275,000.00
4,523.67	3,845.21	3,568.29	3,440.10	3,377.32	300,000.00
5,277.61	4,486.08	4,163.01	4,013.45	3,940.21	350,000.00
6,031.56	5,126.95	4,757.72	4,586.80	4,503.09	400,000.00
6,785.50	5,767.81	5,352.44	5,160.15	5,065.98	450,000.00
7,539.45	6,408.68	5,947.15	5,733.50	5,628.87	500,000.00

13½%   Figuring Out Your

TABLE C
(Amount Necessary to Amortize a Loan)

AMOUNT OF LOAN	1 Year	2 Years	3 Years	4 Years	5 Years
$ 50.00	$ 4.48	$ 2.39	$ 1.70	$ 1.35	$ 1.15
100.00	8.96	4.78	3.39	2.71	2.30
200.00	17.91	9.56	6.79	5.42	4.60
300.00	26.87	14.33	10.18	8.12	6.90
400.00	35.82	19.11	13.57	10.83	9.20
500.00	44.78	23.89	16.97	13.54	11.50
1,000.00	89.55	47.78	33.94	27.08	23.01
2,000.00	179.10	95.55	67.87	54.15	46.02
3,000.00	268.66	143.33	101.81	81.23	69.03
4,000.00	358.21	191.11	135.74	108.31	92.04
5,000.00	447.76	238.89	169.68	135.38	115.05
10,000.00	895.52	477.77	339.35	270.76	230.10
15,000.00	1,343.28	716.66	509.03	406.14	345.15
20,000.00	1,791.04	955.54	678.71	541.53	460.20
25,000.00	2,238.80	1,194.43	848.38	676.91	575.25
30,000.00	2,686.56	1,433.31	1,018.06	812.29	690.30
35,000.00	3,134.32	1,672.20	1,187.74	947.67	805.34
40,000.00	3,582.08	1,911.08	1,357.41	1,083.05	920.39
45,000.00	4,029.84	2,149.97	1,527.09	1,218.43	1,035.44
50,000.00	4,477.60	2,388.85	1,696.76	1,353.82	1,150.49
55,000.00	4,925.36	2,627.74	1,866.44	1,489.20	1,265.54
60,000.00	5,373.12	2,866.62	2,036.12	1,624.58	1,380.59
65,000.00	5,820.88	3,105.51	2,205.79	1,759.96	1,495.64
70,000.00	6,268.64	3,344.39	2,375.47	1,895.34	1,610.69
75,000.00	6,716.40	3,583.28	2,545.15	2,030.72	1,725.74
80,000.00	7,164.16	3,822.16	2,714.82	2,166.11	1,840.79
85,000.00	7,611.92	4,061.05	2,884.50	2,301.49	1,955.84
90,000.00	8,059.68	4,299.93	3,054.18	2,436.87	2,070.89
95,000.00	8,507.44	4,538.82	3,223.85	2,572.25	2,185.94
100,000.00	8,955.20	4,777.70	3,393.53	2,707.63	2,300.98
110,000.00	9,850.72	5,255.47	3,732.88	2,978.40	2,531.08
120,000.00	10,746.24	5,733.24	4,072.23	3,249.16	2,761.18
130,000.00	11,641.76	6,211.01	4,411.59	3,519.92	2,991.28
140,000.00	12,537.28	6,688.78	4,750.94	3,790.69	3,221.38
150,000.00	13,432.80	7,166.55	5,090.29	4,061.45	3,451.48
160,000.00	14,328.32	7,644.32	5,429.65	4,332.21	3,681.58
170,000.00	15,223.84	8,122.09	5,769.00	4,602.97	3,911.67
180,000.00	16,119.36	8,599.86	6,108.35	4,873.74	4,141.77
190,000.00	17,014.89	9,077.63	6,447.70	5,144.50	4,371.87
200,000.00	17,910.41	9,555.40	6,787.06	5,415.26	4,601.97
225,000.00	20,149.21	10,749.83	7,635.44	6,092.17	5,177.22
250,000.00	22,388.01	11,944.25	8,483.82	6,769.08	5,752.46
275,000.00	24,626.81	13,138.68	9,332.20	7,445.99	6,327.71
300,000.00	26,865.61	14,333.10	10,180.59	8,122.90	6,902.95
350,000.00	31,343.21	16,721.96	11,877.35	9,476.71	8,053.45
400,000.00	35,820.81	19,110.81	13,574.11	10,830.53	9,203.94
450,000.00	40,298.41	21,499.66	15,270.88	12,184.35	10,354.43
500,000.00	44,776.01	23,888.51	16,967.64	13,538.16	11,504.92

Monthly Mortgage Payment 13½%

TABLE C

(Amount Necessary to Amortize a Loan)

10 Years	15 Years	TERM OF LOAN 20 Years	25 Years	30 Years	AMOUNT OF LOAN
$ .76	$ .65	$ .60	$ .58	$ .57	$ 50.00
1.52	1.30	1.21	1.17	1.15	100.00
3.05	2.60	2.41	2.33	2.29	200.00
4.57	3.89	3.62	3.50	3.44	300.00
6.09	5.19	4.83	4.66	4.58	400.00
7.61	6.49	6.04	5.83	5.73	500.00
15.23	12.98	12.07	11.66	11.45	1,000.00
30.45	25.97	24.15	23.31	22.91	2,000.00
45.68	38.95	36.22	34.97	34.36	3,000.00
60.91	51.93	48.29	46.63	45.82	4,000.00
76.14	64.92	60.37	58.28	57.27	5,000.00
152.27	129.83	120.74	116.56	114.54	10,000.00
228.41	194.75	181.11	174.85	171.81	15,000.00
304.55	259.66	241.47	233.13	229.08	20,000.00
380.69	324.58	301.84	291.41	286.35	25,000.00
456.82	389.50	362.21	349.69	343.62	30,000.00
532.96	454.41	422.58	407.98	400.89	35,000.00
609.10	519.33	482.95	466.26	458.16	40,000.00
685.23	584.24	543.32	524.54	515.44	45,000.00
761.37	649.16	603.69	582.82	572.71	50,000.00
837.51	714.08	664.06	641.10	629.98	55,000.00
913.65	778.99	724.42	699.39	687.25	60,000.00
989.78	843.91	784.79	757.67	744.52	65,000.00
1,065.92	908.82	845.16	815.95	801.79	70,000.00
1,142.06	973.74	905.53	874.23	859.06	75,000.00
1,218.19	1,038.65	965.90	932.52	916.33	80,000.00
1,294.33	1,103.57	1,026.27	990.80	973.60	85,000.00
1,370.47	1,168.49	1,086.64	1,049.08	1,030.87	90,000.00
1,446.61	1,233.40	1,147.01	1,107.36	1,088.14	95,000.00
1,522.74	1,298.32	1,207.37	1,165.64	1,145.41	100,000.00
1,675.02	1,428.15	1,328.11	1,282.21	1,259.95	110,000.00
1,827.29	1,557.98	1,448.85	1,398.77	1,374.49	120,000.00
1,979.57	1,687.81	1,569.59	1,515.34	1,489.04	130,000.00
2,131.84	1,817.65	1,690.32	1,631.90	1,603.58	140,000.00
2,284.11	1,947.48	1,811.06	1,748.47	1,718.12	150,000.00
2,436.39	2,077.31	1,931.80	1,865.03	1,832.66	160,000.00
2,588.66	2,207.14	2,052.54	1,981.60	1,947.20	170,000.00
2,740.94	2,336.97	2,173.27	2,098.16	2,061.74	180,000.00
2,893.21	2,466.81	2,294.01	2,214.73	2,176.28	190,000.00
3,045.49	2,596.64	2,414.75	2,331.29	2,290.82	200,000.00
3,426.17	2,921.22	2,716.59	2,622.70	2,577.18	225,000.00
3,806.86	3,245.80	3,018.44	2,914.11	2,863.53	250,000.00
4,187.54	3,570.38	3,320.28	3,205.52	3,149.88	275,000.00
4,568.23	3,894.96	3,622.12	3,496.93	3,436.24	300,000.00
5,329.60	4,544.11	4,225.81	4,079.76	4,008.94	350,000.00
6,090.97	5,193.27	4,829.50	4,662.58	4,581.65	400,000.00
6,852.34	5,842.43	5,433.19	5,245.40	5,154.35	450,000.00
7,613.71	6,491.59	6,036.87	5,828.22	5,727.06	500,000.00

TABLE C

(Amount Necessary to Amortize a Loan)

AMOUNT OF LOAN	TERM OF LOAN				
	1 Year	2 Years	3 Years	4 Years	5 Years
$ 50.00	$ 4.48	$ 2.39	$ 1.70	$ 1.36	$ 1.16
100.00	8.97	4.79	3.41	2.72	2.31
200.00	17.93	9.58	6.81	5.44	4.63
300.00	26.90	14.37	10.22	8.16	6.94
400.00	35.87	19.16	13.62	10.88	9.26
500.00	44.83	23.95	17.03	13.60	11.57
1,000.00	89.67	47.89	34.06	27.20	23.14
2,000.00	179.34	95.79	68.11	54.40	46.28
3,000.00	269.01	143.68	102.17	81.60	69.42
4,000.00	358.68	191.58	136.23	108.80	92.56
5,000.00	448.35	239.47	170.28	136.01	115.69
10,000.00	896.70	478.95	340.56	272.01	231.39
15,000.00	1,345.04	718.42	510.84	408.02	347.08
20,000.00	1,793.39	957.90	681.13	544.02	462.78
25,000.00	2,241.74	1,197.37	851.41	680.03	578.47
30,000.00	2,690.09	1,436.85	1,021.69	816.04	694.17
35,000.00	3,138.43	1,676.32	1,191.97	952.04	809.86
40,000.00	3,586.78	1,915.79	1,362.25	1,088.05	925.55
45,000.00	4,035.13	2,155.27	1,532.53	1,224.06	1,041.25
50,000.00	4,483.48	2,394.74	1,702.82	1,360.06	1,156.94
55,000.00	4,931.82	2,634.22	1,873.10	1,496.07	1,272.64
60,000.00	5,380.17	2,873.69	2,043.38	1,632.07	1,388.33
65,000.00	5,828.52	3,113.17	2,213.66	1,768.08	1,504.02
70,000.00	6,276.87	3,352.64	2,383.94	1,904.09	1,619.72
75,000.00	6,725.21	3,592.11	2,554.22	2,040.09	1,735.41
80,000.00	7,173.56	3,831.59	2,724.51	2,176.10	1,851.11
85,000.00	7,621.91	4,071.06	2,894.79	2,312.10	1,966.80
90,000.00	8,070.26	4,310.54	3,065.07	2,448.11	2,082.50
95,000.00	8,518.61	4,550.01	3,235.35	2,584.12	2,198.19
100,000.00	8,966.95	4,789.49	3,405.63	2,720.12	2,313.88
110,000.00	9,863.65	5,268.44	3,746.20	2,992.14	2,545.27
120,000.00	10,760.34	5,747.38	4,086.76	3,264.15	2,776.66
130,000.00	11,657.04	6,226.33	4,427.32	3,536.16	3,008.05
140,000.00	12,553.73	6,705.28	4,767.89	3,808.17	3,239.44
150,000.00	13,450.43	7,184.23	5,108.45	4,080.19	3,470.83
160,000.00	14,347.12	7,663.18	5,449.01	4,352.20	3,702.22
170,000.00	15,243.82	8,142.13	5,789.58	4,624.21	3,933.60
180,000.00	16,140.52	8,621.08	6,130.14	4,896.22	4,164.99
190,000.00	17,037.21	9,100.02	6,470.70	5,168.23	4,396.38
200,000.00	17,933.91	9,578.97	6,811.27	5,440.25	4,627.77
225,000.00	20,175.64	10,776.34	7,662.67	6,120.28	5,206.24
250,000.00	22,417.38	11,973.72	8,514.08	6,800.31	5,784.71
275,000.00	24,659.12	13,171.09	9,365.49	7,480.34	6,363.18
300,000.00	26,900.86	14,368.46	10,216.90	8,160.37	6,941.65
350,000.00	31,384.34	16,763.20	11,919.72	9,520.43	8,098.60
400,000.00	35,867.81	19,157.95	13,622.53	10,880.49	9,255.54
450,000.00	40,351.29	21,552.69	15,325.35	12,240.56	10,412.48
500,000.00	44,834.77	23,947.43	17,028.17	13,600.62	11,569.42

Monthly Mortgage Payment 13¾%

TABLE C
(Amount Necessary to Amortize a Loan)

10 Years	15 Years	TERM OF LOAN 20 Years	25 Years	30 Years	AMOUNT OF LOAN
$ .77	$ .66	$ .61	$ .59	$ .58	$ 50.00
1.54	1.31	1.23	1.18	1.17	100.00
3.08	2.63	2.45	2.37	2.33	200.00
4.61	3.94	3.68	3.55	3.50	300.00
6.15	5.26	4.90	4.74	4.66	400.00
7.69	6.57	6.13	5.92	5.83	500.00
15.38	13.15	12.25	11.85	11.65	1,000.00
30.75	26.30	24.51	23.69	23.30	2,000.00
46.13	39.45	36.76	35.54	34.95	3,000.00
61.51	52.60	49.02	47.39	46.60	4,000.00
76.88	65.75	61.27	59.23	58.26	5,000.00
153.77	131.50	122.54	118.47	116.51	10,000.00
230.65	197.25	183.81	177.70	174.77	15,000.00
307.53	263.00	245.08	236.93	233.02	20,000.00
384.42	328.75	306.35	296.17	291.28	25,000.00
461.30	394.50	367.62	355.40	349.53	30,000.00
538.18	460.25	428.89	414.63	407.79	35,000.00
615.07	525.99	490.16	473.87	466.05	40,000.00
691.95	591.74	551.43	533.10	524.30	45,000.00
768.83	657.49	612.70	592.33	582.56	50,000.00
845.72	723.24	673.97	651.57	640.81	55,000.00
922.60	788.99	735.24	710.80	699.07	60,000.00
999.48	854.74	796.51	770.03	757.32	65,000.00
1,076.37	920.49	857.78	829.27	815.58	70,000.00
1,153.25	986.24	919.05	888.50	873.83	75,000.00
1,230.13	1,051.99	980.32	947.73	932.09	80,000.00
1,307.02	1,117.74	1,041.59	1,006.97	990.35	85,000.00
1,383.90	1,183.49	1,102.86	1,066.20	1,048.60	90,000.00
1,460.78	1,249.24	1,164.14	1,125.43	1,106.86	95,000.00
1,537.67	1,314.99	1,225.41	1,184.67	1,165.11	100,000.00
1,691.43	1,446.49	1,347.95	1,303.13	1,281.62	110,000.00
1,845.20	1,577.98	1,470.49	1,421.60	1,398.14	120,000.00
1,998.97	1,709.48	1,593.03	1,540.07	1,514.65	130,000.00
2,152.74	1,840.98	1,715.57	1,658.53	1,631.16	140,000.00
2,306.50	1,972.48	1,838.11	1,777.00	1,747.67	150,000.00
2,460.27	2,103.98	1,960.65	1,895.47	1,864.18	160,000.00
2,614.04	2,235.48	2,083.19	2,013.93	1,980.69	170,000.00
2,767.80	2,366.98	2,205.73	2,132.40	2,097.20	180,000.00
2,921.57	2,498.48	2,328.27	2,250.87	2,213.71	190,000.00
3,075.34	2,629.97	2,450.81	2,369.33	2,330.23	200,000.00
3,459.75	2,958.72	2,757.16	2,665.50	2,621.50	225,000.00
3,844.17	3,287.47	3,063.51	2,961.66	2,912.78	250,000.00
4,228.59	3,616.21	3,369.86	3,257.83	3,204.06	275,000.00
4,613.00	3,944.96	3,676.22	3,554.00	3,495.34	300,000.00
5,381.84	4,602.46	4,288.92	4,146.33	4,077.89	350,000.00
6,150.67	5,259.95	4,901.62	4,738.66	4,660.45	400,000.00
6,919.51	5,917.44	5,514.32	5,331.00	5,243.01	450,000.00
7,688.34	6,574.94	6,127.03	5,923.33	5,825.56	500,000.00

TABLE C

(Amount Necessary to Amortize a Loan)

AMOUNT OF LOAN	TERM OF LOAN				
	1 Year	2 Years	3 Years	4 Years	5 Years
$ 50.00	$ 4.49	$ 2.40	$ 1.71	$ 1.37	$ 1.16
100.00	8.98	4.80	3.42	2.73	2.33
200.00	17.96	9.60	6.84	5.47	4.65
300.00	26.94	14.40	10.25	8.20	6.98
400.00	35.91	19.21	13.67	10.93	9.31
500.00	44.89	24.01	17.09	13.66	11.63
1,000.00	89.79	48.01	34.18	27.33	23.27
2,000.00	179.57	96.03	68.36	54.65	46.54
3,000.00	269.36	144.04	102.53	81.98	69.80
4,000.00	359.15	192.05	136.71	109.31	93.07
5,000.00	448.94	240.06	170.89	136.63	116.34
10,000.00	897.87	480.13	341.78	273.26	232.68
15,000.00	1,346.81	720.19	512.66	409.90	349.02
20,000.00	1,795.74	960.26	683.55	546.53	465.37
25,000.00	2,244.68	1,200.32	854.44	683.16	581.71
30,000.00	2,693.61	1,440.39	1,025.33	819.79	698.05
35,000.00	3,142.55	1,680.45	1,196.22	956.43	814.39
40,000.00	3,591.48	1,920.52	1,367.11	1,093.06	930.73
45,000.00	4,040.42	2,160.58	1,537.99	1,229.69	1,047.07
50,000.00	4,489.36	2,400.64	1,708.88	1,366.32	1,163.41
55,000.00	4,938.29	2,640.71	1,879.77	1,502.96	1,279.75
60,000.00	5,387.23	2,880.77	2,050.66	1,639.59	1,396.10
65,000.00	5,836.16	3,120.84	2,221.55	1,776.22	1,512.44
70,000.00	6,285.10	3,360.90	2,392.43	1,912.85	1,628.78
75,000.00	6,734.03	3,600.97	2,563.32	2,049.49	1,745.12
80,000.00	7,182.97	3,841.03	2,734.21	2,186.12	1,861.46
85,000.00	7,631.90	4,081.10	2,905.10	2,322.75	1,977.80
90,000.00	8,080.84	4,321.16	3,075.99	2,459.38	2,094.14
95,000.00	8,529.78	4,561.22	3,246.87	2,596.02	2,210.48
100,000.00	8,978.71	4,801.29	3,417.76	2,732.65	2,326.83
110,000.00	9,876.58	5,281.42	3,759.54	3,005.91	2,559.51
120,000.00	10,774.45	5,761.55	4,101.32	3,279.18	2,792.19
130,000.00	11,672.33	6,241.67	4,443.09	3,552.44	3,024.87
140,000.00	12,570.20	6,721.80	4,784.87	3,825.71	3,257.56
150,000.00	13,468.07	7,201.93	5,126.64	4,098.97	3,490.24
160,000.00	14,365.94	7,682.06	5,468.42	4,372.24	3,722.92
170,000.00	15,263.81	8,162.19	5,810.20	4,645.50	3,955.60
180,000.00	16,161.68	8,642.32	6,151.97	4,918.77	4,188.29
190,000.00	17,059.55	9,122.45	6,493.75	5,192.03	4,420.97
200,000.00	17,957.42	9,602.58	6,835.53	5,465.30	4,653.65
225,000.00	20,202.10	10,802.90	7,689.97	6,148.46	5,235.36
250,000.00	22,446.78	12,003.22	8,544.41	6,831.62	5,817.06
275,000.00	24,691.46	13,203.54	9,398.85	7,514.78	6,398.77
300,000.00	26,936.14	14,403.86	10,253.29	8,197.94	6,980.48
350,000.00	31,425.49	16,804.51	11,962.17	9,564.27	8,143.89
400,000.00	35,914.85	19,205.15	13,671.05	10,930.59	9,307.30
450,000.00	40,404.20	21,605.80	15,379.93	12,296.91	10,470.71
500,000.00	44,893.56	24,006.44	17,088.81	13,663.24	11,634.13

Monthly Mortgage Payment 14%

TABLE C

(Amount Necessary to Amortize a Loan)

10 Years	15 Years	TERM OF LOAN 20 Years	25 Years	30 Years	AMOUNT OF LOAN
$ .78	$ .67	$ .62	$ .60	$ .59	$ 50.00
1.55	1.33	1.24	1.20	1.18	100.00
3.11	2.66	2.49	2.41	2.37	200.00
4.66	4.00	3.73	3.61	3.55	300.00
6.21	5.33	4.97	4.82	4.74	400.00
7.76	6.66	6.22	6.02	5.92	500.00
15.53	13.32	12.44	12.04	11.85	1,000.00
31.05	26.63	24.87	24.08	23.70	2,000.00
46.58	39.95	37.31	36.11	35.55	3,000.00
62.11	53.27	49.74	48.15	47.39	4,000.00
77.63	66.59	62.18	60.19	59.24	5,000.00
155.27	133.17	124.35	120.38	118.49	10,000.00
232.90	199.76	186.53	180.56	177.73	15,000.00
310.53	266.35	248.70	240.75	236.97	20,000.00
388.17	332.94	310.88	300.94	296.22	25,000.00
465.80	399.52	373.06	361.13	355.46	30,000.00
543.43	466.11	435.23	421.32	414.71	35,000.00
621.07	532.70	497.41	481.50	473.95	40,000.00
698.70	599.28	559.58	541.69	533.19	45,000.00
776.33	665.87	621.76	601.88	592.44	50,000.00
853.97	732.46	683.94	662.07	651.68	55,000.00
931.60	799.04	746.11	722.26	710.92	60,000.00
1,009.23	865.63	808.29	782.44	770.17	65,000.00
1,086.87	932.22	870.46	842.63	829.41	70,000.00
1,164.50	998.81	932.64	902.82	888.65	75,000.00
1,242.13	1,065.39	994.82	963.01	947.90	80,000.00
1,319.76	1,131.98	1,056.99	1,023.20	1,007.14	85,000.00
1,397.40	1,198.57	1,119.17	1,083.38	1,066.38	90,000.00
1,475.03	1,265.15	1,181.34	1,143.57	1,125.63	95,000.00
1,552.66	1,331.74	1,243.52	1,203.76	1,184.87	100,000.00
1,707.93	1,464.92	1,367.87	1,324.14	1,303.36	110,000.00
1,863.20	1,598.09	1,492.22	1,444.51	1,421.85	120,000.00
2,018.46	1,731.26	1,616.58	1,564.89	1,540.33	130,000.00
2,173.73	1,864.44	1,740.93	1,685.27	1,658.82	140,000.00
2,329.00	1,997.61	1,865.28	1,805.64	1,777.31	150,000.00
2,484.26	2,130.79	1,989.63	1,926.02	1,895.79	160,000.00
2,639.53	2,263.96	2,113.99	2,046.39	2,014.28	170,000.00
2,794.80	2,397.13	2,238.34	2,166.77	2,132.77	180,000.00
2,950.06	2,530.31	2,362.69	2,287.15	2,251.26	190,000.00
3,105.33	2,663.48	2,487.04	2,407.52	2,369.74	200,000.00
3,493.49	2,996.42	2,797.92	2,708.46	2,665.96	225,000.00
3,881.66	3,329.35	3,108.80	3,009.40	2,962.18	250,000.00
4,269.83	3,662.29	3,419.68	3,310.34	3,258.40	275,000.00
4,657.99	3,995.22	3,730.56	3,611.28	3,554.62	300,000.00
5,434.33	4,661.09	4,352.32	4,213.16	4,147.05	350,000.00
6,210.66	5,326.97	4,974.08	4,815.04	4,739.49	400,000.00
6,986.99	5,992.84	5,595.84	5,416.92	5,331.92	450,000.00
7,763.32	6,658.71	6,217.60	6,018.81	5,924.36	500,000.00

TABLE C

(Amount Necessary to Amortize a Loan)

AMOUNT OF LOAN	TERM OF LOAN				
	1 Year	2 Years	3 Years	4 Years	5 Years
$ 50.00	$ 4.50	$ 2.41	$ 1.71	$ 1.37	$ 1.17
100.00	8.99	4.81	3.43	2.75	2.34
200.00	17.98	9.63	6.86	5.49	4.68
300.00	26.97	14.44	10.29	8.24	7.02
400.00	35.96	19.25	13.72	10.98	9.36
500.00	44.95	24.07	17.15	13.73	11.70
1,000.00	89.90	48.13	34.30	27.45	23.40
2,000.00	179.81	96.26	68.60	54.90	46.80
3,000.00	269.71	144.39	102.90	82.36	70.19
4,000.00	359.62	192.52	137.20	109.81	93.59
5,000.00	449.52	240.66	171.50	137.26	116.99
10,000.00	899.05	481.31	342.99	274.52	233.98
15,000.00	1,348.57	721.97	514.49	411.78	350.97
20,000.00	1,798.10	962.62	685.98	549.04	467.96
25,000.00	2,247.62	1,203.28	857.48	686.30	584.95
30,000.00	2,697.14	1,443.93	1,028.98	823.56	701.94
35,000.00	3,146.67	1,684.59	1,200.47	960.82	818.93
40,000.00	3,596.19	1,925.24	1,371.97	1,098.08	935.92
45,000.00	4,045.72	2,165.90	1,543.46	1,235.34	1,052.91
50,000.00	4,495.24	2,406.55	1,714.96	1,372.60	1,169.90
55,000.00	4,944.76	2,647.21	1,886.45	1,509.86	1,286.89
60,000.00	5,394.29	2,887.86	2,057.95	1,647.12	1,403.88
65,000.00	5,843.81	3,128.52	2,229.45	1,784.38	1,520.87
70,000.00	6,293.34	3,369.17	2,400.94	1,921.64	1,637.86
75,000.00	6,742.86	3,609.83	2,572.44	2,058.90	1,754.85
80,000.00	7,192.38	3,850.49	2,743.93	2,196.16	1,871.85
85,000.00	7,641.91	4,091.14	2,915.43	2,333.42	1,988.84
90,000.00	8,091.43	4,331.80	3,086.93	2,470.68	2,105.83
95,000.00	8,540.96	4,572.45	3,258.42	2,607.94	2,222.82
100,000.00	8,990.48	4,813.11	3,429.92	2,745.20	2,339.81
110,000.00	9,889.53	5,294.42	3,772.91	3,019.73	2,573.79
120,000.00	10,788.57	5,775.73	4,115.90	3,294.25	2,807.77
130,000.00	11,687.62	6,257.04	4,458.89	3,568.77	3,041.75
140,000.00	12,586.67	6,738.35	4,801.88	3,843.29	3,275.73
150,000.00	13,485.72	7,219.66	5,144.88	4,117.81	3,509.71
160,000.00	14,384.77	7,700.97	5,487.87	4,392.33	3,743.69
170,000.00	15,283.81	8,182.28	5,830.86	4,666.85	3,977.67
180,000.00	16,182.86	8,663.59	6,173.85	4,941.37	4,211.65
190,000.00	17,081.91	9,144.90	6,516.84	5,215.89	4,445.63
200,000.00	17,980.96	9,626.21	6,859.84	5,490.41	4,679.61
225,000.00	20,228.58	10,829.49	7,717.32	6,176.71	5,264.56
250,000.00	22,476.20	12,032.74	8,574.79	6,863.01	5,849.52
275,000.00	24,723.82	13,236.04	9,432.27	7,549.31	6,434.47
300,000.00	26,971.44	14,439.32	10,289.75	8,235.61	7,019.42
350,000.00	31,466.68	16,845.87	12,004.71	9,608.22	8,189.32
400,000.00	35,961.92	19,252.43	13,719.67	10,980.82	9,359.23
450,000.00	40,457.16	21,658.98	15,434.63	12,353.42	10,529.13
500,000.00	44,952.39	24,065.54	17,149.59	13,726.02	11,699.03

Monthly Mortgage Payment 14¼%

TABLE C

(Amount Necessary to Amortize a Loan)

10 Years	15 Years	TERM OF LOAN 20 Years	25 Years	30 Years	AMOUNT OF LOAN
$ .78	$ .67	$ .63	$ .61	$ .60	$ 50.00
1.57	1.35	1.26	1.22	1.20	100.00
3.14	2.70	2.52	2.45	2.41	200.00
4.70	4.05	3.79	3.67	3.61	300.00
6.27	5.39	5.05	4.89	4.82	400.00
7.84	6.74	6.31	6.11	6.02	500.00
15.68	13.49	12.62	12.23	12.05	1,000.00
31.35	26.97	25.23	24.46	24.09	2,000.00
47.03	40.46	37.85	36.69	36.14	3,000.00
62.71	53.94	50.47	48.92	48.19	4,000.00
78.39	67.43	63.09	61.15	60.23	5,000.00
156.77	134.86	126.17	122.29	120.47	10,000.00
235.16	202.29	189.26	183.44	180.70	15,000.00
313.55	269.72	252.34	244.59	240.94	20,000.00
391.93	337.14	315.43	305.73	301.17	25,000.00
470.32	404.57	378.52	366.88	361.41	30,000.00
548.71	472.00	441.60	428.02	421.64	35,000.00
627.09	539.43	504.69	489.17	481.87	40,000.00
705.48	606.86	567.77	550.32	542.11	45,000.00
783.87	674.29	630.86	611.46	602.34	50,000.00
862.25	741.72	693.95	672.61	662.58	55,000.00
940.64	809.15	757.03	733.76	722.81	60,000.00
1,019.03	876.58	820.12	794.90	783.05	65,000.00
1,097.41	944.01	883.20	856.05	843.28	70,000.00
1,175.80	1,011.43	946.29	917.20	903.52	75,000.00
1,254.18	1,078.86	1,009.38	978.34	963.75	80,000.00
1,332.57	1,146.29	1,072.46	1,039.49	1,023.98	85,000.00
1,410.96	1,213.72	1,135.55	1,100.63	1,084.22	90,000.00
1,489.34	1,281.15	1,198.63	1,161.78	1,144.45	95,000.00
1,567.73	1,348.58	1,261.72	1,222.93	1,204.69	100,000.00
1,724.50	1,483.44	1,387.89	1,345.22	1,325.16	110,000.00
1,881.28	1,618.30	1,514.06	1,467.51	1,445.62	120,000.00
2,038.05	1,753.15	1,640.23	1,589.81	1,566.09	130,000.00
2,194.82	1,888.01	1,766.41	1,712.10	1,686.56	140,000.00
2,351.60	2,022.87	1,892.58	1,834.39	1,807.03	150,000.00
2,508.37	2,157.73	2,018.75	1,956.68	1,927.50	160,000.00
2,665.14	2,292.59	2,144.92	2,078.98	2,047.97	170,000.00
2,821.92	2,427.44	2,271.09	2,201.27	2,168.44	180,000.00
2,978.69	2,562.30	2,397.27	2,323.56	2,288.91	190,000.00
3,135.46	2,697.16	2,523.44	2,445.86	2,409.37	200,000.00
3,527.39	3,034.30	2,838.87	2,751.59	2,710.55	225,000.00
3,919.33	3,371.45	3,154.30	3,057.32	3,011.72	250,000.00
4,311.26	3,708.59	3,469.73	3,363.05	3,312.89	275,000.00
4,703.19	4,045.74	3,785.16	3,668.78	3,614.06	300,000.00
5,487.06	4,720.03	4,416.02	4,280.25	4,216.40	350,000.00
6,270.92	5,394.32	5,046.88	4,891.71	4,818.75	400,000.00
7,054.79	6,068.61	5,677.74	5,503.17	5,421.09	450,000.00
7,838.66	6,742.90	6,308.59	6,114.64	6,023.44	500,000.00

14½%

TABLE C

(Amount Necessary to Amortize a Loan)

AMOUNT OF LOAN	TERM OF LOAN				
	1 Year	2 Years	3 Years	4 Years	5 Years
$ 50.00	$ 4.50	$ 2.41	$ 1.72	$ 1.38	$ 1.18
100.00	9.00	4.82	3.44	2.76	2.35
200.00	18.00	9.65	6.88	5.52	4.71
300.00	27.01	14.47	10.33	8.27	7.06
400.00	36.01	19.30	13.77	11.03	9.41
500.00	45.01	24.12	17.21	13.79	11.76
1,000.00	90.02	48.25	34.42	27.58	23.53
2,000.00	180.05	96.50	68.84	55.16	47.06
3,000.00	270.07	144.75	103.26	82.73	70.58
4,000.00	360.09	193.00	137.68	110.31	94.11
5,000.00	450.11	241.25	172.10	137.89	117.64
10,000.00	900.23	482.49	344.21	275.78	235.28
15,000.00	1,350.34	723.74	516.31	413.67	352.92
20,000.00	1,800.45	964.99	688.42	551.56	470.57
25,000.00	2,250.56	1,206.24	860.52	689.45	588.21
30,000.00	2,700.68	1,447.48	1,032.63	827.34	705.85
35,000.00	3,150.79	1,688.73	1,204.73	965.23	823.49
40,000.00	3,600.90	1,929.98	1,376.84	1,103.12	941.13
45,000.00	4,051.01	2,171.22	1,548.94	1,241.01	1,058.77
50,000.00	4,501.13	2,412.47	1,721.05	1,378.90	1,176.41
55,000.00	4,951.24	2,653.72	1,893.15	1,516.79	1,294.06
60,000.00	5,401.35	2,894.97	2,065.26	1,654.68	1,411.70
65,000.00	5,851.47	3,136.21	2,237.36	1,792.57	1,529.34
70,000.00	6,301.58	3,377.46	2,409.47	1,930.46	1,646.98
75,000.00	6,751.69	3,618.71	2,581.57	2,068.35	1,764.62
80,000.00	7,201.80	3,859.95	2,753.68	2,206.24	1,882.26
85,000.00	7,651.92	4,101.20	2,925.78	2,344.13	1,999.90
90,000.00	8,102.03	4,342.45	3,097.89	2,482.02	2,117.55
95,000.00	8,552.14	4,583.70	3,269.99	2,619.91	2,235.19
100,000.00	9,002.25	4,824.94	3,442.10	2,757.80	2,352.83
110,000.00	9,902.48	5,307.44	3,786.31	3,033.57	2,588.11
120,000.00	10,802.71	5,789.93	4,130.52	3,309.35	2,823.39
130,000.00	11,702.93	6,272.43	4,474.73	3,585.13	3,058.68
140,000.00	12,603.16	6,754.92	4,818.94	3,860.91	3,293.96
150,000.00	13,503.38	7,237.41	5,163.15	4,136.69	3,529.24
160,000.00	14,403.61	7,719.91	5,507.36	4,412.47	3,764.52
170,000.00	15,303.83	8,202.40	5,851.57	4,688.25	3,999.81
180,000.00	16,204.06	8,684.90	6,195.78	4,964.03	4,235.09
190,000.00	17,104.28	9,167.39	6,539.99	5,239.81	4,470.37
200,000.00	18,004.51	9,649.89	6,884.20	5,515.59	4,705.66
225,000.00	20,255.07	10,856.12	7,744.72	6,205.04	5,293.86
250,000.00	22,505.64	12,062.36	8,605.24	6,894.49	5,882.07
275,000.00	24,756.20	13,268.59	9,465.77	7,583.94	6,470.28
300,000.00	27,006.76	14,474.83	10,326.29	8,273.39	7,058.48
350,000.00	31,507.89	16,887.30	12,047.34	9,652.28	8,234.90
400,000.00	36,009.02	19,299.77	13,768.39	11,031.18	9,411.31
450,000.00	40,510.15	21,712.24	15,489.44	12,410.08	10,587.73
500,000.00	45,011.27	24,124.71	17,210.49	13,788.98	11,764.14

Monthly Mortgage Payment 14½%

TABLE C

(Amount Necessary to Amortize a Loan)

10 Years	15 Years	TERM OF LOAN 20 Years	25 Years	30 Years	AMOUNT OF LOAN
$ .79	$ .68	$ .64	$ .62	$ .61	$ 50.00
1.58	1.37	1.28	1.24	1.22	100.00
3.17	2.73	2.56	2.48	2.45	200.00
4.75	4.10	3.84	3.73	3.67	300.00
6.33	5.46	5.12	4.97	4.90	400.00
7.91	6.83	6.40	6.21	6.12	500.00
15.83	13.66	12.80	12.42	12.25	1,000.00
31.66	27.31	25.60	24.84	24.49	2,000.00
47.49	40.97	38.40	37.26	36.74	3,000.00
63.31	54.62	51.20	49.69	48.98	4,000.00
79.14	68.28	64.00	62.11	61.23	5,000.00
158.29	136.55	128.00	124.22	122.46	10,000.00
237.43	204.83	192.00	186.32	183.68	15,000.00
316.57	273.10	256.00	248.43	244.91	20,000.00
395.72	341.38	320.00	310.54	306.14	25,000.00
474.86	409.65	384.00	372.65	367.37	30,000.00
554.00	477.93	448.00	434.76	428.59	35,000.00
633.15	546.20	512.00	496.87	489.82	40,000.00
712.29	614.48	576.00	558.97	551.05	45,000.00
791.43	682.75	640.00	621.08	612.28	50,000.00
870.58	751.03	704.00	683.19	673.51	55,000.00
949.72	819.30	768.00	745.30	734.73	60,000.00
1,028.86	887.58	832.00	807.41	795.96	65,000.00
1,108.01	955.85	896.00	869.51	857.19	70,000.00
1,187.15	1,024.13	960.00	931.62	918.42	75,000.00
1,266.29	1,092.40	1,024.00	993.73	979.64	80,000.00
1,345.44	1,160.68	1,088.00	1,055.84	1,040.87	85,000.00
1,424.58	1,228.95	1,152.00	1,117.95	1,102.10	90,000.00
1,503.72	1,297.23	1,216.00	1,180.05	1,163.33	95,000.00
1,582.87	1,365.50	1,280.00	1,242.16	1,224.56	100,000.00
1,741.15	1,502.05	1,408.00	1,366.38	1,347.01	110,000.00
1,899.44	1,638.60	1,536.00	1,490.60	1,469.47	120,000.00
2,057.73	1,775.15	1,664.00	1,614.81	1,591.92	130,000.00
2,216.02	1,911.70	1,792.00	1,739.03	1,714.38	140,000.00
2,374.30	2,048.25	1,920.00	1,863.24	1,836.83	150,000.00
2,532.59	2,184.80	2,048.00	1,987.46	1,959.29	160,000.00
2,690.88	2,321.35	2,176.00	2,111.68	2,081.75	170,000.00
2,849.16	2,457.90	2,304.00	2,235.89	2,204.20	180,000.00
3,007.45	2,594.45	2,432.00	2,360.11	2,326.66	190,000.00
3,165.74	2,731.00	2,560.00	2,484.33	2,449.11	200,000.00
3,561.45	3,072.38	2,879.99	2,794.87	2,755.25	225,000.00
3,957.17	3,413.75	3,199.99	3,105.41	3,061.39	250,000.00
4,352.89	3,755.13	3,519.99	3,415.95	3,367.53	275,000.00
4,748.60	4,096.50	3,839.99	3,726.49	3,673.67	300,000.00
5,540.04	4,779.25	4,479.99	4,347.57	4,285.95	350,000.00
6,331.47	5,462.00	5,119.99	4,968.65	4,898.22	400,000.00
7,122.91	6,144.75	5,759.99	5,589.73	5,510.50	450,000.00
7,914.34	6,827.50	6,399.99	6,210.81	6,122.78	500,000.00

219

14¾% Figuring Out Your

TABLE C
(Amount Necessary to Amortize a Loan)

AMOUNT OF LOAN	TERM OF LOAN 1 Year	2 Years	3 Years	4 Years	5 Years
$ 50.00	$ 4.51	$ 2.42	$ 1.73	$ 1.39	$ 1.18
100.00	9.01	4.84	3.45	2.77	2.37
200.00	18.03	9.67	6.91	5.54	4.73
300.00	27.04	14.51	10.36	8.31	7.10
400.00	36.06	19.35	13.82	11.08	9.46
500.00	45.07	24.18	17.27	13.85	11.83
1,000.00	90.14	48.37	34.54	27.70	23.66
2,000.00	180.28	96.74	69.09	55.41	47.32
3,000.00	270.42	145.10	103.63	83.11	70.98
4,000.00	360.56	193.47	138.17	110.82	94.64
5,000.00	450.70	241.84	172.72	138.52	118.29
10,000.00	901.40	483.68	345.43	277.04	236.59
15,000.00	1,352.11	725.52	518.15	415.56	354.88
20,000.00	1,802.81	967.36	690.86	554.08	473.18
25,000.00	2,253.51	1,209.20	863.58	692.60	591.47
30,000.00	2,704.21	1,451.04	1,036.29	831.13	709.77
35,000.00	3,154.91	1,692.88	1,209.01	969.65	828.06
40,000.00	3,605.62	1,934.72	1,381.72	1,108.17	946.36
45,000.00	4,056.32	2,176.56	1,554.44	1,246.69	1,064.65
50,000.00	4,507.02	2,418.40	1,727.15	1,385.21	1,182.95
55,000.00	4,957.72	2,660.24	1,899.87	1,523.73	1,301.24
60,000.00	5,408.42	2,902.08	2,072.58	1,662.25	1,419.53
65,000.00	5,859.13	3,143.92	2,245.30	1,800.77	1,537.83
70,000.00	6,309.83	3,385.76	2,418.01	1,939.29	1,656.12
75,000.00	6,760.53	3,627.60	2,590.73	2,077.81	1,774.42
80,000.00	7,211.23	3,869.44	2,763.44	2,216.33	1,892.71
85,000.00	7,661.93	4,111.28	2,936.16	2,354.86	2,011.01
90,000.00	8,112.63	4,353.12	3,108.87	2,493.38	2,129.30
95,000.00	8,563.34	4,594.96	3,281.59	2,631.90	2,247.60
100,000.00	9,014.04	4,836.80	3,454.30	2,770.42	2,365.89
110,000.00	9,915.44	5,320.47	3,799.73	3,047.46	2,602.48
120,000.00	10,816.85	5,804.15	4,145.16	3,324.50	2,839.07
130,000.00	11,718.25	6,287.83	4,490.59	3,601.54	3,075.66
140,000.00	12,619.65	6,771.51	4,836.02	3,878.59	3,312.25
150,000.00	13,521.06	7,255.19	5,181.45	4,155.63	3,548.84
160,000.00	14,422.46	7,738.87	5,526.88	4,432.67	3,785.42
170,000.00	15,323.87	8,222.55	5,872.31	4,709.71	4,022.01
180,000.00	16,225.27	8,706.23	6,217.74	4,986.75	4,258.60
190,000.00	17,126.67	9,189.91	6,563.18	5,263.80	4,495.19
200,000.00	18,028.08	9,673.59	6,908.61	5,540.84	4,731.78
225,000.00	20,281.59	10,882.79	7,772.18	6,233.44	5,323.25
250,000.00	22,535.10	12,091.99	8,635.76	6,926.05	5,914.73
275,000.00	24,788.61	13,301.19	9,499.33	7,618.65	6,506.20
300,000.00	27,042.12	14,510.39	10,362.91	8,311.26	7,097.67
350,000.00	31,549.14	16,928.78	12,090.06	9,696.47	8,280.62
400,000.00	36,056.15	19,347.18	13,817.21	11,081.67	9,463.56
450,000.00	40,563.17	21,765.58	15,544.36	12,466.88	10,646.51
500,000.00	45,070.19	24,183.98	17,271.51	13,852.09	11,829.45

Monthly Mortgage Payment 14¾%

TABLE C
(Amount Necessary to Amortize a Loan)

| | TERM OF LOAN | | | | AMOUNT OF LOAN |
10 Years	15 Years	20 Years	25 Years	30 Years	
$ .80	$ .69	$ .65	$ .63	$ .62	$ 50.00
1.60	1.38	1.30	1.26	1.24	100.00
3.20	2.77	2.60	2.52	2.49	200.00
4.79	4.15	3.90	3.78	3.73	300.00
6.39	5.53	5.19	5.05	4.98	400.00
7.99	6.91	6.49	6.31	6.22	500.00
15.98	13.83	12.98	12.61	12.44	1,000.00
31.96	27.65	25.97	25.23	24.89	2,000.00
47.94	41.48	38.95	37.84	37.33	3,000.00
63.92	55.30	51.93	50.46	49.78	4,000.00
79.90	69.13	64.92	63.07	62.22	5,000.00
159.81	138.25	129.84	126.15	124.45	10,000.00
239.71	207.38	194.75	189.22	186.67	15,000.00
319.61	276.50	259.67	252.29	248.90	20,000.00
399.52	345.63	324.59	315.37	311.12	25,000.00
479.42	414.75	389.51	378.44	373.34	30,000.00
559.33	483.88	454.42	441.51	435.57	35,000.00
639.23	553.00	519.34	504.59	497.79	40,000.00
719.13	622.13	584.26	567.66	560.01	45,000.00
799.04	691.25	649.18	630.73	622.24	50,000.00
878.94	760.38	714.10	693.81	684.46	55,000.00
958.84	829.50	779.01	756.88	746.69	60,000.00
1,038.75	898.63	843.93	819.95	808.91	65,000.00
1,118.65	967.75	908.85	883.03	871.13	70,000.00
1,198.56	1,036.88	973.77	946.10	933.36	75,000.00
1,278.46	1,106.00	1,038.68	1,009.17	995.58	80,000.00
1,358.36	1,175.13	1,103.60	1,072.25	1,057.80	85,000.00
1,438.27	1,244.25	1,168.52	1,135.32	1,120.03	90,000.00
1,518.17	1,313.38	1,233.44	1,198.39	1,182.25	95,000.00
1,598.07	1,382.50	1,298.36	1,261.46	1,244.48	100,000.00
1,757.88	1,520.75	1,428.19	1,387.61	1,368.92	110,000.00
1,917.69	1,659.00	1,558.03	1,513.76	1,493.37	120,000.00
2,077.50	1,797.25	1,687.86	1,639.90	1,617.82	130,000.00
2,237.30	1,935.51	1,817.70	1,766.05	1,742.27	140,000.00
2,397.11	2,073.76	1,947.53	1,892.20	1,866.71	150,000.00
2,556.92	2,212.01	2,077.37	2,018.34	1,991.16	160,000.00
2,716.73	2,350.26	2,207.20	2,144.49	2,115.61	170,000.00
2,876.53	2,488.51	2,337.04	2,270.64	2,240.06	180,000.00
3,036.34	2,626.76	2,466.88	2,396.78	2,364.50	190,000.00
3,196.15	2,765.01	2,596.71	2,522.93	2,488.95	200,000.00
3,595.67	3,110.63	2,921.30	2,838.30	2,800.07	225,000.00
3,995.19	3,456.26	3,245.89	3,153.66	3,111.19	250,000.00
4,394.70	3,801.89	3,570.48	3,469.03	3,422.31	275,000.00
4,794.22	4,147.51	3,895.07	3,784.39	3,733.43	300,000.00
5,593.26	4,838.76	4,544.24	4,415.13	4,355.67	350,000.00
6,392.30	5,530.02	5,193.42	5,045.86	4,977.90	400,000.00
7,191.33	6,221.27	5,842.60	5,676.59	5,600.14	450,000.00
7,990.37	6,912.52	6,491.78	6,307.32	6,222.38	500,000.00

15[%] Figuring Out Your

TABLE C
(Amount Necessary to Amortize a Loan)

AMOUNT OF LOAN	TERM OF LOAN				
	1 Year	2 Years	3 Years	4 Years	5 Years
$ 50.00	$ 4.51	$ 2.42	$ 1.73	$ 1.39	$ 1.19
100.00	9.03	4.85	3.47	2.78	2.38
200.00	18.05	9.70	6.93	5.57	4.76
300.00	27.08	14.55	10.40	8.35	7.14
400.00	36.10	19.39	13.87	11.13	9.52
500.00	45.13	24.24	17.33	13.92	11.89
1,000.00	90.26	48.49	34.67	27.83	23.79
2,000.00	180.52	96.97	69.33	55.66	47.58
3,000.00	270.77	145.46	104.00	83.49	71.37
4,000.00	361.03	193.95	138.66	111.32	95.16
5,000.00	451.29	242.43	173.33	139.15	118.95
10,000.00	902.58	484.87	346.65	278.31	237.90
15,000.00	1,353.87	727.30	519.98	417.46	356.85
20,000.00	1,805.17	969.73	693.31	556.61	475.80
25,000.00	2,256.46	1,212.17	866.63	695.77	594.75
30,000.00	2,707.75	1,454.60	1,039.96	834.92	713.70
35,000.00	3,159.04	1,697.03	1,213.29	974.08	832.65
40,000.00	3,610.33	1,939.47	1,386.61	1,113.23	951.60
45,000.00	4,061.62	2,181.90	1,559.94	1,252.38	1,070.55
50,000.00	4,512.92	2,424.33	1,733.27	1,391.54	1,189.50
55,000.00	4,964.21	2,666.77	1,906.59	1,530.69	1,308.45
60,000.00	5,415.50	2,909.20	2,079.92	1,669.84	1,427.40
65,000.00	5,866.79	3,151.63	2,253.25	1,809.00	1,546.35
70,000.00	6,318.08	3,394.07	2,426.57	1,948.15	1,665.30
75,000.00	6,769.37	3,636.50	2,599.90	2,087.31	1,784.24
80,000.00	7,220.66	3,878.93	2,773.23	2,226.46	1,903.19
85,000.00	7,671.96	4,121.37	2,946.55	2,365.61	2,022.14
90,000.00	8,123.25	4,363.80	3,119.88	2,504.77	2,141.09
95,000.00	8,574.54	4,606.23	3,293.21	2,643.92	2,260.04
100,000.00	9,025.83	4,848.66	3,466.53	2,783.07	2,378.99
110,000.00	9,928.41	5,333.53	3,813.19	3,061.38	2,616.89
120,000.00	10,831.00	5,818.40	4,159.84	3,339.69	2,854.79
130,000.00	11,733.58	6,303.26	4,506.49	3,618.00	3,092.69
140,000.00	12,636.16	6,788.13	4,853.15	3,896.30	3,330.59
150,000.00	13,538.75	7,273.00	5,199.80	4,174.61	3,568.49
160,000.00	14,441.33	7,757.86	5,546.45	4,452.92	3,806.39
170,000.00	15,343.91	8,242.73	5,893.11	4,731.23	4,044.29
180,000.00	16,246.50	8,727.60	6,239.76	5,009.53	4,282.19
190,000.00	17,149.08	9,212.46	6,586.41	5,287.84	4,520.09
200,000.00	18,051.66	9,697.33	6,933.07	5,566.15	4,757.99
225,000.00	20,308.12	10,909.50	7,799.70	6,261.92	5,352.73
250,000.00	22,564.58	12,121.66	8,666.33	6,957.69	5,947.48
275,000.00	24,821.04	13,333.83	9,532.97	7,653.46	6,542.23
300,000.00	27,077.49	14,545.99	10,399.60	8,349.22	7,136.98
350,000.00	31,590.41	16,970.33	12,132.86	9,740.76	8,326.48
400,000.00	36,103.32	19,394.66	13,866.13	11,132.30	9,515.97
450,000.00	40,616.24	21,818.99	15,599.40	12,523.84	10,705.47
500,000.00	45,129.16	24,243.32	17,332.66	13,915.37	11,894.97

Monthly Mortgage Payment

15%

TABLE C

(Amount Necessary to Amortize a Loan)

10 Years	15 Years	TERM OF LOAN 20 Years	25 Years	30 Years	AMOUNT OF LOAN
$ .81	$ .70	$ .66	$ .64	$ .63	$ 50.00
1.61	1.40	1.32	1.28	1.26	100.00
3.23	2.80	2.63	2.56	2.53	200.00
4.84	4.20	3.95	3.84	3.79	300.00
6.45	5.60	5.27	5.12	5.06	400.00
8.07	7.00	6.58	6.40	6.32	500.00
16.13	14.00	13.17	12.81	12.64	1,000.00
32.27	27.99	26.34	25.62	25.29	2,000.00
48.40	41.99	39.50	38.42	37.93	3,000.00
64.53	55.98	52.67	51.23	50.58	4,000.00
80.67	69.98	65.84	64.04	63.22	5,000.00
161.33	139.96	131.68	128.08	126.44	10,000.00
242.00	209.94	197.52	192.12	189.67	15,000.00
322.67	279.92	263.36	256.17	252.89	20,000.00
403.34	349.90	329.20	320.21	316.11	25,000.00
484.00	419.88	395.04	384.25	379.33	30,000.00
564.67	489.86	460.88	448.29	442.56	35,000.00
645.34	559.83	526.72	512.33	505.78	40,000.00
726.01	629.81	592.56	576.37	569.00	45,000.00
806.67	699.79	658.39	640.42	632.22	50,000.00
887.34	769.77	724.23	704.46	695.44	55,000.00
968.01	839.75	790.07	768.50	758.67	60,000.00
1,048.68	909.73	855.91	832.54	821.89	65,000.00
1,129.34	979.71	921.75	896.58	885.11	70,000.00
1,210.01	1,049.69	987.59	960.62	948.33	75,000.00
1,290.68	1,119.67	1,053.43	1,024.66	1,011.56	80,000.00
1,371.35	1,189.65	1,119.27	1,088.71	1,074.78	85,000.00
1,452.01	1,259.63	1,185.11	1,152.75	1,138.00	90,000.00
1,532.68	1,329.61	1,250.95	1,216.79	1,201.22	95,000.00
1,613.35	1,399.59	1,316.79	1,280.83	1,264.44	100,000.00
1,774.68	1,539.55	1,448.47	1,408.91	1,390.89	110,000.00
1,936.02	1,679.50	1,580.15	1,537.00	1,517.33	120,000.00
2,097.35	1,819.46	1,711.83	1,665.08	1,643.78	130,000.00
2,258.69	1,959.42	1,843.51	1,793.16	1,770.22	140,000.00
2,420.02	2,099.38	1,975.18	1,921.25	1,896.67	150,000.00
2,581.36	2,239.34	2,106.86	2,049.33	2,023.11	160,000.00
2,742.69	2,379.30	2,238.54	2,177.41	2,149.55	170,000.00
2,904.03	2,519.26	2,370.22	2,305.50	2,276.00	180,000.00
3,065.36	2,659.22	2,501.90	2,433.58	2,402.44	190,000.00
3,226.70	2,799.17	2,633.58	2,561.66	2,528.89	200,000.00
3,630.04	3,149.07	2,962.78	2,881.87	2,845.00	225,000.00
4,033.37	3,498.97	3,291.97	3,202.08	3,161.11	250,000.00
4,436.71	3,848.86	3,621.17	3,522.28	3,477.22	275,000.00
4,840.05	4,198.76	3,950.37	3,842.49	3,793.33	300,000.00
5,646.72	4,898.55	4,608.76	4,482.91	4,425.55	350,000.00
6,453.40	5,598.35	5,267.16	5,123.32	5,057.78	400,000.00
7,260.07	6,298.14	5,925.55	5,763.74	5,690.00	450,000.00
8,066.75	6,997.94	6,583.95	6,404.15	6,322.22	500,000.00

TABLE C
(Amount Necessary to Amortize a Loan)

AMOUNT OF LOAN	TERM OF LOAN				
	1 Year	2 Years	3 Years	4 Years	5 Years
$ 50.00	$ 4.52	$ 2.43	$ 1.74	$ 1.40	$ 1.20
100.00	9.04	4.86	3.48	2.80	2.39
200.00	18.08	9.72	6.96	5.59	4.78
300.00	27.11	14.58	10.44	8.39	7.18
400.00	36.15	19.44	13.92	11.18	9.57
500.00	45.19	24.30	17.39	13.98	11.96
1,000.00	90.38	48.61	34.79	27.96	23.92
2,000.00	180.75	97.21	69.58	55.92	47.84
3,000.00	271.13	145.82	104.36	83.87	71.76
4,000.00	361.51	194.42	139.15	111.83	95.69
5,000.00	451.88	243.03	173.94	139.79	119.61
10,000.00	903.76	486.06	347.88	279.58	239.21
15,000.00	1,355.64	729.08	521.82	419.36	358.82
20,000.00	1,807.53	972.11	695.76	559.15	478.43
25,000.00	2,259.41	1,215.14	869.70	698.94	598.03
30,000.00	2,711.29	1,458.17	1,043.64	838.73	717.64
35,000.00	3,163.17	1,701.19	1,217.58	978.52	837.25
40,000.00	3,615.05	1,944.22	1,391.52	1,118.31	956.85
45,000.00	4,066.93	2,187.25	1,565.45	1,258.09	1,076.46
50,000.00	4,518.82	2,430.28	1,739.39	1,397.88	1,196.07
55,000.00	4,970.70	2,673.30	1,913.33	1,537.67	1,315.67
60,000.00	5,422.58	2,916.33	2,087.27	1,677.46	1,435.28
65,000.00	5,874.46	3,159.36	2,261.21	1,817.25	1,554.89
70,000.00	6,326.34	3,402.39	2,435.15	1,957.03	1,674.50
75,000.00	6,778.22	3,645.41	2,609.09	2,096.82	1,794.10
80,000.00	7,230.11	3,888.44	2,783.03	2,236.61	1,913.71
85,000.00	7,681.99	4,131.47	2,956.97	2,376.40	2,033.32
90,000.00	8,133.87	4,374.50	3,130.91	2,516.19	2,152.92
95,000.00	8,585.75	4,617.52	3,304.85	2,655.98	2,272.53
100,000.00	9,037.63	4,860.55	3,478.79	2,795.76	2,392.14
110,000.00	9,941.40	5,346.61	3,826.67	3,075.34	2,631.35
120,000.00	10,845.16	5,832.66	4,174.55	3,354.92	2,870.56
130,000.00	11,748.92	6,318.72	4,522.42	3,634.49	3,109.78
140,000.00	12,652.69	6,804.77	4,870.30	3,914.07	3,348.99
150,000.00	13,556.45	7,290.83	5,218.18	4,193.65	3,588.20
160,000.00	14,460.21	7,776.88	5,566.06	4,473.22	3,827.42
170,000.00	15,363.97	8,262.94	5,913.94	4,752.80	4,066.63
180,000.00	16,267.74	8,748.99	6,261.82	5,032.38	4,305.84
190,000.00	17,171.50	9,235.05	6,609.70	5,311.95	4,545.06
200,000.00	18,075.26	9,721.10	6,957.58	5,591.53	4,784.27
225,000.00	20,334.67	10,936.24	7,827.27	6,290.47	5,382.31
250,000.00	22,594.08	12,151.38	8,696.97	6,989.41	5,980.34
275,000.00	24,853.49	13,366.52	9,566.67	7,688.35	6,578.37
300,000.00	27,112.90	14,581.65	10,436.36	8,387.29	7,176.41
350,000.00	31,631.71	17,011.93	12,175.76	9,785.17	8,372.48
400,000.00	36,150.53	19,442.20	13,915.15	11,183.06	9,568.54
450,000.00	40,669.34	21,872.48	15,654.55	12,580.94	10,764.61
500,000.00	45,188.16	24,302.76	17,393.94	13,978.82	11,960.68

Monthly Mortgage Payment   15¼%

TABLE C

(Amount Necessary to Amortize a Loan)

10 Years	15 Years	TERM OF LOAN 20 Years	25 Years	30 Years	AMOUNT OF LOAN
$ .81	$ .71	$ .67	$ .65	$ .64	$ 50.00
1.63	1.42	1.34	1.30	1.28	100.00
3.26	2.83	2.67	2.60	2.57	200.00
4.89	4.25	4.01	3.90	3.85	300.00
6.51	5.67	5.34	5.20	5.14	400.00
8.14	7.08	6.68	6.50	6.42	500.00
16.29	14.17	13.35	13.00	12.84	1,000.00
32.57	28.33	26.71	26.01	25.69	2,000.00
48.86	42.50	40.06	39.01	38.53	3,000.00
65.15	56.67	53.41	52.01	51.38	4,000.00
81.43	70.84	66.76	65.01	64.22	5,000.00
162.87	141.67	133.53	130.03	128.45	10,000.00
244.30	212.51	200.29	195.04	192.67	15,000.00
325.74	283.35	267.06	260.05	256.89	20,000.00
407.17	354.19	333.82	325.06	321.11	25,000.00
488.61	425.02	400.59	390.08	385.34	30,000.00
570.04	495.86	467.35	455.09	449.56	35,000.00
651.48	566.70	534.12	520.10	513.78	40,000.00
732.91	637.54	600.88	585.12	578.01	45,000.00
814.35	708.37	667.65	650.13	642.23	50,000.00
895.78	779.21	734.41	715.14	706.45	55,000.00
977.22	850.05	801.18	780.15	770.68	60,000.00
1,058.65	920.89	867.94	845.17	834.90	65,000.00
1,140.09	991.72	934.71	910.18	899.12	70,000.00
1,221.52	1,062.56	1,001.47	975.19	963.34	75,000.00
1,302.95	1,133.40	1,068.24	1,040.21	1,027.57	80,000.00
1,384.39	1,204.24	1,135.00	1,105.22	1,091.79	85,000.00
1,465.82	1,275.07	1,201.77	1,170.23	1,156.01	90,000.00
1,547.26	1,345.91	1,268.53	1,235.25	1,220.24	95,000.00
1,628.69	1,416.75	1,335.30	1,300.26	1,284.46	100,000.00
1,791.56	1,558.42	1,468.83	1,430.28	1,412.90	110,000.00
1,954.43	1,700.10	1,602.36	1,560.31	1,541.35	120,000.00
2,117.30	1,841.77	1,735.89	1,690.34	1,669.80	130,000.00
2,280.17	1,983.45	1,869.42	1,820.36	1,798.24	140,000.00
2,443.04	2,125.12	2,002.95	1,950.39	1,926.69	150,000.00
2,605.91	2,266.80	2,136.48	2,080.41	2,055.13	160,000.00
2,768.78	2,408.47	2,270.01	2,210.44	2,183.58	170,000.00
2,931.65	2,550.15	2,403.54	2,340.46	2,312.03	180,000.00
3,094.52	2,691.82	2,537.07	2,470.49	2,440.47	190,000.00
3,257.39	2,833.50	2,670.60	2,600.52	2,568.92	200,000.00
3,664.56	3,187.69	3,004.42	2,925.58	2,890.03	225,000.00
4,071.73	3,541.87	3,338.25	3,250.65	3,211.15	250,000.00
4,478.91	3,896.06	3,672.07	3,575.71	3,532.26	275,000.00
4,886.08	4,250.25	4,005.90	3,900.77	3,853.38	300,000.00
5,700.43	4,958.62	4,673.55	4,550.90	4,495.60	350,000.00
6,514.77	5,667.00	5,341.19	5,201.03	5,137.83	400,000.00
7,329.12	6,375.37	6,008.84	5,851.16	5,780.06	450,000.00
8,143.47	7,083.75	6,676.49	6,501.29	6,422.29	500,000.00

15½%   Figuring Out Your

TABLE C

(Amount Necessary to Amortize a Loan)

AMOUNT OF LOAN	1 Year	2 Years	3 Years	4 Years	5 Years
$ 50.00	$ 4.52	$ 2.44	$ 1.75	$ 1.40	$ 1.20
100.00	9.05	4.87	3.49	2.81	2.41
200.00	18.10	9.74	6.98	5.62	4.81
300.00	27.15	14.62	10.47	8.43	7.22
400.00	36.20	19.49	13.96	11.23	9.62
500.00	45.25	24.36	17.46	14.04	12.03
1,000.00	90.49	48.72	34.91	28.08	24.05
2,000.00	180.99	97.45	69.82	56.17	48.11
3,000.00	271.48	146.17	104.73	84.25	72.16
4,000.00	361.98	194.90	139.64	112.34	96.21
5,000.00	452.47	243.62	174.55	140.42	120.27
10,000.00	904.94	487.25	349.11	280.85	240.53
15,000.00	1,357.42	730.87	523.66	421.27	360.80
20,000.00	1,809.89	974.49	698.21	561.70	481.06
25,000.00	2,262.36	1,218.11	872.77	702.12	601.33
30,000.00	2,714.83	1,461.74	1,047.32	842.55	721.60
35,000.00	3,167.30	1,705.36	1,221.87	982.97	841.86
40,000.00	3,619.78	1,948.98	1,396.43	1,123.39	962.13
45,000.00	4,072.25	2,192.60	1,570.98	1,263.82	1,082.39
50,000.00	4,524.72	2,436.23	1,745.53	1,404.24	1,202.66
55,000.00	4,977.19	2,679.85	1,920.09	1,544.67	1,322.93
60,000.00	5,429.66	2,923.47	2,094.64	1,685.09	1,443.19
65,000.00	5,882.14	3,167.10	2,269.19	1,825.52	1,563.46
70,000.00	6,334.61	3,410.72	2,443.75	1,965.94	1,683.72
75,000.00	6,787.08	3,654.34	2,618.30	2,106.36	1,803.99
80,000.00	7,239.55	3,897.96	2,792.85	2,246.79	1,924.26
85,000.00	7,692.03	4,141.59	2,967.41	2,387.21	2,044.52
90,000.00	8,144.50	4,385.21	3,141.96	2,527.64	2,164.79
95,000.00	8,596.97	4,628.83	3,316.51	2,668.06	2,285.05
100,000.00	9,049.44	4,872.45	3,491.07	2,808.49	2,405.32
110,000.00	9,954.39	5,359.70	3,840.17	3,089.33	2,645.85
120,000.00	10,859.33	5,846.95	4,189.28	3,370.18	2,886.38
130,000.00	11,764.27	6,334.19	4,538.39	3,651.03	3,126.91
140,000.00	12,669.22	6,821.44	4,887.50	3,931.88	3,367.45
150,000.00	13,574.16	7,308.68	5,236.60	4,212.73	3,607.98
160,000.00	14,479.11	7,795.93	5,585.71	4,493.58	3,848.51
170,000.00	15,384.05	8,283.17	5,934.82	4,774.43	4,089.04
180,000.00	16,288.99	8,770.42	6,283.92	5,055.27	4,329.57
190,000.00	17,193.94	9,257.66	6,633.03	5,336.12	4,570.11
200,000.00	18,098.88	9,744.91	6,982.14	5,616.97	4,810.64
225,000.00	20,361.24	10,963.02	7,854.90	6,319.09	5,411.97
250,000.00	22,623.60	12,181.14	8,727.67	7,021.21	6,013.30
275,000.00	24,885.96	13,399.25	9,600.44	7,723.34	6,614.63
300,000.00	27,148.32	14,617.36	10,473.20	8,425.46	7,215.96
350,000.00	31,673.05	17,053.59	12,218.74	9,829.70	8,418.62
400,000.00	36,197.77	19,489.82	13,964.27	11,233.94	9,621.28
450,000.00	40,722.49	21,926.04	15,709.81	12,638.19	10,823.94
500,000.00	45,247.21	24,362.27	17,455.34	14,042.43	12,026.60

Monthly Mortgage Payment   15½%

TABLE C
(Amount Necessary to Amortize a Loan)

		TERM OF LOAN			AMOUNT
10 Years	15 Years	20 Years	25 Years	30 Years	OF LOAN
$ .82	$ .72	$ .68	$ .66	$ .65	$ 50.00
1.64	1.43	1.35	1.32	1.30	100.00
3.29	2.87	2.71	2.64	2.61	200.00
4.93	4.30	4.06	3.96	3.91	300.00
6.58	5.74	5.42	5.28	5.22	400.00
8.22	7.17	6.77	6.60	6.52	500.00
16.44	14.34	13.54	13.20	13.05	1,000.00
32.88	28.68	27.08	26.39	26.09	2,000.00
49.32	43.02	40.62	39.59	39.14	3,000.00
65.76	57.36	54.16	52.79	52.18	4,000.00
82.21	71.70	67.69	65.99	65.23	5,000.00
164.41	143.40	135.39	131.97	130.45	10,000.00
246.62	215.10	203.08	197.96	195.68	15,000.00
328.82	286.80	270.78	263.95	260.90	20,000.00
411.03	358.50	338.47	329.94	326.13	25,000.00
493.23	430.20	406.16	395.92	391.36	30,000.00
575.44	501.90	473.86	461.91	456.58	35,000.00
657.64	573.60	541.55	527.90	521.81	40,000.00
739.85	645.30	609.25	593.89	587.03	45,000.00
822.05	717.00	676.94	659.87	652.26	50,000.00
904.26	788.69	744.63	725.86	717.48	55,000.00
986.46	860.39	812.33	791.85	782.71	60,000.00
1,068.67	932.09	880.02	857.83	847.94	65,000.00
1,150.87	1,003.79	947.72	923.82	913.16	70,000.00
1,233.08	1,075.49	1,015.41	989.81	978.39	75,000.00
1,315.28	1,147.19	1,083.10	1,055.80	1,043.61	80,000.00
1,397.49	1,218.89	1,150.80	1,121.78	1,108.84	85,000.00
1,479.69	1,290.59	1,218.49	1,187.77	1,174.07	90,000.00
1,561.90	1,362.29	1,286.19	1,253.76	1,239.29	95,000.00
1,644.11	1,433.99	1,353.88	1,319.75	1,304.52	100,000.00
1,808.52	1,577.39	1,489.27	1,451.72	1,434.97	110,000.00
1,972.93	1,720.79	1,624.66	1,583.69	1,565.42	120,000.00
2,137.34	1,864.19	1,760.04	1,715.67	1,695.87	130,000.00
2,301.75	2,007.59	1,895.43	1,847.64	1,826.32	140,000.00
2,466.16	2,150.99	2,030.82	1,979.62	1,956.78	150,000.00
2,630.57	2,294.38	2,166.21	2,111.59	2,087.23	160,000.00
2,794.98	2,437.78	2,301.60	2,243.57	2,217.68	170,000.00
2,959.39	2,581.18	2,436.99	2,375.54	2,348.13	180,000.00
3,123.80	2,724.58	2,572.37	2,507.52	2,478.58	190,000.00
3,288.21	2,867.98	2,707.76	2,639.49	2,609.03	200,000.00
3,699.24	3,226.48	3,046.23	2,969.43	2,935.16	225,000.00
4,110.26	3,584.98	3,384.70	3,299.36	3,261.29	250,000.00
4,521.29	3,943.47	3,723.17	3,629.30	3,587.42	275,000.00
4,932.32	4,301.97	4,061.64	3,959.24	3,913.55	300,000.00
5,754.37	5,018.97	4,738.58	4,619.11	4,565.81	350,000.00
6,576.42	5,735.96	5,415.52	5,278.98	5,218.07	400,000.00
7,398.47	6,452.96	6,092.46	5,938.85	5,870.33	450,000.00
8,220.53	7,169.95	6,769.40	6,598.73	6,522.58	500,000.00

TABLE C

(Amount Necessary to Amortize a Loan)

AMOUNT OF LOAN	TERM OF LOAN				
	1 Year	2 Years	3 Years	4 Years	5 Years
$ 50.00	$ 4.53	$ 2.44	$ 1.75	$ 1.41	$ 1.21
100.00	9.06	4.88	3.50	2.82	2.42
200.00	18.12	9.77	7.01	5.64	4.84
300.00	27.18	14.65	10.51	8.46	7.26
400.00	36.25	19.54	14.01	11.28	9.67
500.00	45.31	24.42	17.52	14.11	12.09
1,000.00	90.61	48.84	35.03	28.21	24.19
2,000.00	181.23	97.69	70.07	56.42	48.37
3,000.00	271.84	146.53	105.10	84.64	72.56
4,000.00	362.45	195.37	140.13	112.85	96.74
5,000.00	453.06	244.22	175.17	141.06	120.93
10,000.00	906.13	488.44	350.34	282.12	241.85
15,000.00	1,359.19	732.66	525.51	423.19	362.78
20,000.00	1,812.25	976.87	700.67	564.25	483.71
25,000.00	2,265.31	1,221.09	875.84	705.31	604.64
30,000.00	2,718.38	1,465.31	1,051.01	846.37	725.56
35,000.00	3,171.44	1,709.53	1,226.18	987.43	846.49
40,000.00	3,624.50	1,953.75	1,401.35	1,128.50	967.42
45,000.00	4,077.57	2,197.97	1,576.52	1,269.56	1,088.34
50,000.00	4,530.63	2,442.19	1,751.69	1,410.62	1,209.27
55,000.00	4,983.69	2,686.41	1,926.86	1,551.68	1,330.20
60,000.00	5,436.76	2,930.62	2,102.02	1,692.74	1,451.13
65,000.00	5,889.82	3,174.84	2,277.19	1,833.81	1,572.05
70,000.00	6,342.88	3,419.06	2,452.36	1,974.87	1,692.98
75,000.00	6,795.94	3,663.28	2,627.53	2,115.93	1,813.91
80,000.00	7,249.01	3,907.50	2,802.70	2,256.99	1,934.83
85,000.00	7,702.07	4,151.72	2,977.87	2,398.05	2,055.76
90,000.00	8,155.13	4,395.94	3,153.04	2,539.12	2,176.69
95,000.00	8,608.20	4,640.16	3,328.20	2,680.18	2,297.62
100,000.00	9,061.26	4,884.37	3,503.37	2,821.24	2,418.54
110,000.00	9,967.39	5,372.81	3,853.71	3,103.36	2,660.40
120,000.00	10,873.51	5,861.25	4,204.05	3,385.49	2,902.25
130,000.00	11,779.64	6,349.69	4,554.39	3,667.61	3,144.11
140,000.00	12,685.76	6,838.12	4,904.72	3,949.74	3,385.96
150,000.00	13,591.89	7,326.56	5,255.06	4,231.86	3,627.81
160,000.00	14,498.02	7,815.00	5,605.40	4,513.98	3,869.67
170,000.00	15,404.14	8,303.44	5,955.73	4,796.11	4,111.52
180,000.00	16,310.27	8,791.87	6,306.07	5,078.23	4,353.38
190,000.00	17,216.39	9,280.31	6,656.41	5,360.36	4,595.23
200,000.00	18,122.52	9,768.75	7,006.75	5,642.48	4,837.08
225,000.00	20,387.83	10,989.84	7,882.59	6,347.79	5,441.72
250,000.00	22,653.15	12,210.94	8,758.43	7,053.10	6,046.36
275,000.00	24,918.46	13,432.03	9,634.28	7,758.41	6,650.99
300,000.00	27,183.78	14,653.12	10,510.12	8,463.72	7,255.63
350,000.00	31,714.41	17,095.31	12,261.81	9,874.34	8,464.90
400,000.00	36,245.04	19,537.50	14,013.49	11,284.96	9,674.17
450,000.00	40,775.67	21,979.68	15,765.18	12,695.58	10,883.44
500,000.00	45,306.30	24,421.87	17,516.87	14,106.20	12,092.71

Monthly Mortgage Payment 15¾%

TABLE C
(Amount Necessary to Amortize a Loan)

10 Years	15 Years	TERM OF LOAN 20 Years	25 Years	30 Years	AMOUNT OF LOAN
$ .83	$ .73	$ .69	$ .67	$ .66	$ 50.00
1.66	1.45	1.37	1.34	1.32	100.00
3.32	2.90	2.75	2.68	2.65	200.00
4.98	4.35	4.12	4.02	3.97	300.00
6.64	5.81	5.49	5.36	5.30	400.00
8.30	7.26	6.86	6.70	6.62	500.00
16.60	14.51	13.73	13.39	13.25	1,000.00
33.19	29.03	27.45	26.79	26.49	2,000.00
49.79	43.54	41.18	40.18	39.74	3,000.00
66.38	58.05	54.90	53.57	52.98	4,000.00
82.98	72.57	68.63	66.96	66.23	5,000.00
165.96	145.13	137.25	133.93	132.46	10,000.00
248.94	217.70	205.88	200.89	198.69	15,000.00
331.92	290.26	274.51	267.86	264.92	20,000.00
414.90	362.83	343.13	334.82	331.15	25,000.00
497.88	435.39	411.76	401.79	397.39	30,000.00
580.85	507.96	480.39	468.75	463.62	35,000.00
663.83	580.52	549.01	535.72	529.85	40,000.00
746.81	653.09	617.64	602.68	596.08	45,000.00
829.79	725.65	686.27	669.64	662.31	50,000.00
912.77	798.22	754.89	736.61	728.54	55,000.00
995.75	870.78	823.52	803.57	794.77	60,000.00
1,078.73	943.35	892.15	870.54	861.00	65,000.00
1,161.71	1,015.92	960.77	937.50	927.23	70,000.00
1,244.69	1,088.48	1,029.40	1,004.47	993.46	75,000.00
1,327.67	1,161.05	1,098.03	1,071.43	1,059.69	80,000.00
1,410.65	1,233.61	1,166.65	1,138.40	1,125.92	85,000.00
1,493.63	1,306.18	1,235.28	1,205.36	1,192.16	90,000.00
1,576.61	1,378.74	1,303.91	1,272.33	1,258.39	95,000.00
1,659.58	1,451.31	1,372.53	1,339.29	1,324.62	100,000.00
1,825.54	1,596.44	1,509.79	1,473.22	1,457.08	110,000.00
1,991.50	1,741.57	1,647.04	1,607.15	1,589.54	120,000.00
2,157.46	1,886.70	1,784.29	1,741.08	1,722.00	130,000.00
2,323.42	2,031.83	1,921.55	1,875.01	1,854.46	140,000.00
2,489.38	2,176.96	2,058.80	2,008.93	1,986.93	150,000.00
2,655.34	2,322.09	2,196.05	2,142.86	2,119.39	160,000.00
2,821.29	2,467.22	2,333.31	2,276.79	2,251.85	170,000.00
2,987.25	2,612.35	2,470.56	2,410.72	2,384.31	180,000.00
3,153.21	2,757.48	2,607.81	2,544.65	2,516.77	190,000.00
3,319.17	2,902.62	2,745.07	2,678.58	2,649.23	200,000.00
3,734.07	3,265.44	3,088.20	3,013.40	2,980.39	225,000.00
4,148.96	3,628.27	3,431.33	3,348.22	3,311.54	250,000.00
4,563.86	3,991.10	3,774.47	3,683.05	3,642.70	275,000.00
4,978.75	4,353.92	4,117.60	4,017.87	3,973.85	300,000.00
5,808.55	5,079.58	4,803.87	4,687.51	4,636.16	350,000.00
6,638.34	5,805.23	5,490.13	5,357.16	5,298.47	400,000.00
7,468.13	6,530.88	6,176.40	6,026.80	5,960.78	450,000.00
8,297.92	7,256.54	6,862.67	6,696.45	6,623.09	500,000.00

TABLE C

(Amount Necessary to Amortize a Loan)

AMOUNT OF LOAN	TERM OF LOAN				
	1 Year	2 Years	3 Years	4 Years	5 Years
$ 50.00	$ 4.54	$ 2.45	$ 1.76	$ 1.42	$ 1.22
100.00	9.07	4.90	3.52	2.83	2.43
200.00	18.15	9.79	7.03	5.67	4.86
300.00	27.22	14.69	10.55	8.50	7.30
400.00	36.29	19.59	14.06	11.34	9.73
500.00	45.37	24.48	17.58	14.17	12.16
1,000.00	90.73	48.96	35.16	28.34	24.32
2,000.00	181.46	97.93	70.31	56.68	48.64
3,000.00	272.19	146.89	105.47	85.02	72.95
4,000.00	362.92	195.85	140.63	113.36	97.27
5,000.00	453.65	244.82	175.79	141.70	121.59
10,000.00	907.31	489.63	351.57	283.40	243.18
15,000.00	1,360.96	734.45	527.36	425.10	364.77
20,000.00	1,814.62	979.26	703.14	566.81	486.36
25,000.00	2,268.27	1,224.08	878.93	708.51	607.95
30,000.00	2,721.93	1,468.89	1,054.71	850.21	729.54
35,000.00	3,175.58	1,713.71	1,230.50	991.91	851.13
40,000.00	3,629.23	1,958.52	1,406.28	1,133.61	972.72
45,000.00	4,082.89	2,203.34	1,582.07	1,275.31	1,094.31
50,000.00	4,536.54	2,448.16	1,757.85	1,417.01	1,215.90
55,000.00	4,990.20	2,692.97	1,933.64	1,558.72	1,337.49
60,000.00	5,443.85	2,937.79	2,109.42	1,700.42	1,459.08
65,000.00	5,897.51	3,182.60	2,285.21	1,842.12	1,580.67
70,000.00	6,351.16	3,427.42	2,460.99	1,983.82	1,702.26
75,000.00	6,804.81	3,672.23	2,636.78	2,125.52	1,823.85
80,000.00	7,258.47	3,917.05	2,812.56	2,267.22	1,945.44
85,000.00	7,712.12	4,161.86	2,988.35	2,408.92	2,067.03
90,000.00	8,165.78	4,406.68	3,164.13	2,550.63	2,188.63
95,000.00	8,619.43	4,651.50	3,339.92	2,692.33	2,310.22
100,000.00	9,073.09	4,896.31	3,515.70	2,834.03	2,431.81
110,000.00	9,980.39	5,385.94	3,867.27	3,117.43	2,674.99
120,000.00	10,887.70	5,875.57	4,218.84	3,400.83	2,918.17
130,000.00	11,795.01	6,365.20	4,570.41	3,684.24	3,161.35
140,000.00	12,702.32	6,854.84	4,921.98	3,967.64	3,404.53
150,000.00	13,609.63	7,344.47	5,273.55	4,251.04	3,647.71
160,000.00	14,516.94	7,834.10	5,625.13	4,534.44	3,890.89
170,000.00	15,424.25	8,323.73	5,976.70	4,817.85	4,134.07
180,000.00	16,331.55	8,813.36	6,328.27	5,101.25	4,377.25
190,000.00	17,238.86	9,302.99	6,679.84	5,384.65	4,620.43
200,000.00	18,146.17	9,792.62	7,031.41	5,668.06	4,863.61
225,000.00	20,414.44	11,016.70	7,910.33	6,376.56	5,471.56
250,000.00	22,682.71	12,240.78	8,789.26	7,085.07	6,079.51
275,000.00	24,950.99	13,464.86	9,668.18	7,793.58	6,687.47
300,000.00	27,219.26	14,688.93	10,547.11	8,502.08	7,295.42
350,000.00	31,755.80	17,137.09	12,304.96	9,919.10	8,511.32
400,000.00	36,292.34	19,585.24	14,062.81	11,336.11	9,727.22
450,000.00	40,828.89	22,033.40	15,820.66	12,753.13	10,943.13
500,000.00	45,365.43	24,481.56	17,578.52	14,170.14	12,159.03

Monthly Mortgage Payment 16%

TABLE C
(Amount Necessary to Amortize a Loan)

10 Years	15 Years	TERM OF LOAN 20 Years	25 Years	30 Years	AMOUNT OF LOAN
$ .84	$ .73	$ .70	$ .68	$ .67	$ 50.00
1.68	1.47	1.39	1.36	1.34	100.00
3.35	2.94	2.78	2.72	2.69	200.00
5.03	4.41	4.17	4.08	4.03	300.00
6.70	5.87	5.57	5.44	5.38	400.00
8.38	7.34	6.96	6.79	6.72	500.00
16.75	14.69	13.91	13.59	13.45	1,000.00
33.50	29.37	27.83	27.18	26.90	2,000.00
50.25	44.06	41.74	40.77	40.34	3,000.00
67.01	58.75	55.65	54.36	53.79	4,000.00
83.76	73.44	69.56	67.94	67.24	5,000.00
167.51	146.87	139.13	135.89	134.48	10,000.00
251.27	220.31	208.69	203.83	201.71	15,000.00
335.03	293.74	278.25	271.78	268.95	20,000.00
418.78	367.18	347.81	339.72	336.19	25,000.00
502.54	440.61	417.38	407.67	403.43	30,000.00
586.30	514.05	486.94	475.61	470.66	35,000.00
670.05	587.48	556.50	543.56	537.90	40,000.00
753.81	660.92	626.07	611.50	605.14	45,000.00
837.57	734.35	695.63	679.44	672.38	50,000.00
921.32	807.79	765.19	747.39	739.62	55,000.00
1,005.08	881.22	834.75	815.33	806.85	60,000.00
1,088.84	954.66	904.32	883.28	874.09	65,000.00
1,172.59	1,028.09	973.88	951.22	941.33	70,000.00
1,256.35	1,101.53	1,043.44	1,019.17	1,008.57	75,000.00
1,340.10	1,174.96	1,113.00	1,087.11	1,075.81	80,000.00
1,423.86	1,248.40	1,182.57	1,155.06	1,143.04	85,000.00
1,507.62	1,321.83	1,252.13	1,223.00	1,210.28	90,000.00
1,591.37	1,395.27	1,321.69	1,290.94	1,277.52	95,000.00
1,675.13	1,468.70	1,391.26	1,358.89	1,344.76	100,000.00
1,842.64	1,615.57	1,530.38	1,494.78	1,479.23	110,000.00
2,010.16	1,762.44	1,669.51	1,630.67	1,613.71	120,000.00
2,177.67	1,909.31	1,808.63	1,766.56	1,748.18	130,000.00
2,345.18	2,056.18	1,947.76	1,902.44	1,882.66	140,000.00
2,512.70	2,203.05	2,086.88	2,038.33	2,017.14	150,000.00
2,680.21	2,349.92	2,226.01	2,174.22	2,151.61	160,000.00
2,847.72	2,496.79	2,365.14	2,310.11	2,286.09	170,000.00
3,015.24	2,643.66	2,504.26	2,446.00	2,420.56	180,000.00
3,182.75	2,790.53	2,643.39	2,581.89	2,555.04	190,000.00
3,350.26	2,937.40	2,782.51	2,717.78	2,689.51	200,000.00
3,769.05	3,304.58	3,130.33	3,057.50	3,025.70	225,000.00
4,187.83	3,671.75	3,478.14	3,397.22	3,361.89	250,000.00
4,606.61	4,038.93	3,825.95	3,736.94	3,698.08	275,000.00
5,025.39	4,406.10	4,173.77	4,076.67	4,034.27	300,000.00
5,862.96	5,140.45	4,869.40	4,756.11	4,706.65	350,000.00
6,700.52	5,874.80	5,565.02	5,435.56	5,379.03	400,000.00
7,538.09	6,609.15	6,260.65	6,115.00	6,051.41	450,000.00
8,375.66	7,343.50	6,956.28	6,794.44	6,723.78	500,000.00

231

TABLE C

(Amount Necessary to Amortize a Loan)

AMOUNT OF LOAN	TERM OF LOAN				
	1 Year	2 Years	3 Years	4 Years	5 Years
$ 50.00	$ 4.54	$ 2.45	$ 1.76	$ 1.42	$ 1.22
100.00	9.08	4.91	3.53	2.85	2.45
200.00	18.17	9.82	7.06	5.69	4.89
300.00	27.25	14.72	10.58	8.54	7.34
400.00	36.34	19.63	14.11	11.39	9.78
500.00	45.42	24.54	17.64	14.23	12.23
1,000.00	90.85	49.08	35.28	28.47	24.45
2,000.00	181.70	98.17	70.56	56.94	48.90
3,000.00	272.55	147.25	105.84	85.41	73.35
4,000.00	363.40	196.33	141.12	113.87	97.80
5,000.00	454.25	245.41	176.40	142.34	122.26
10,000.00	908.49	490.83	352.81	284.68	244.51
15,000.00	1,362.74	736.24	529.21	427.03	366.77
20,000.00	1,816.98	981.65	705.61	569.37	489.02
25,000.00	2,271.23	1,227.07	882.01	711.71	611.28
30,000.00	2,725.48	1,472.48	1,058.42	854.05	733.53
35,000.00	3,179.72	1,717.89	1,234.82	996.40	855.79
40,000.00	3,633.97	1,963.31	1,411.22	1,138.74	978.04
45,000.00	4,088.21	2,208.72	1,587.63	1,281.08	1,100.30
50,000.00	4,542.46	2,454.13	1,764.03	1,423.42	1,222.55
55,000.00	4,996.71	2,699.55	1,940.43	1,565.77	1,344.81
60,000.00	5,450.95	2,944.96	2,116.83	1,708.11	1,467.07
65,000.00	5,905.20	3,190.37	2,293.24	1,850.45	1,589.32
70,000.00	6,359.44	3,435.79	2,469.64	1,992.79	1,711.58
75,000.00	6,813.69	3,681.20	2,646.04	2,135.14	1,833.83
80,000.00	7,267.94	3,926.61	2,822.45	2,277.48	1,956.09
85,000.00	7,722.18	4,172.02	2,998.85	2,419.82	2,078.34
90,000.00	8,176.43	4,417.44	3,175.25	2,562.16	2,200.60
95,000.00	8,630.67	4,662.85	3,351.66	2,704.51	2,322.85
100,000.00	9,084.92	4,908.26	3,528.06	2,846.85	2,445.11
110,000.00	9,993.41	5,399.09	3,880.86	3,131.53	2,689.62
120,000.00	10,901.90	5,889.92	4,233.67	3,416.22	2,934.13
130,000.00	11,810.40	6,380.74	4,586.48	3,700.90	3,178.64
140,000.00	12,718.89	6,871.57	4,939.28	3,985.59	3,423.15
150,000.00	13,627.38	7,362.40	5,292.09	4,270.27	3,667.66
160,000.00	14,535.87	7,853.22	5,644.89	4,554.96	3,912.17
170,000.00	15,444.36	8,344.05	5,997.70	4,839.64	4,156.69
180,000.00	16,352.86	8,834.88	6,350.50	5,124.33	4,401.20
190,000.00	17,261.35	9,325.70	6,703.31	5,409.01	4,645.71
200,000.00	18,169.84	9,816.53	7,056.12	5,693.70	4,890.22
225,000.00	20,441.07	11,043.60	7,938.13	6,405.41	5,501.50
250,000.00	22,712.30	12,270.66	8,820.15	7,117.12	6,112.77
275,000.00	24,983.53	13,497.73	9,702.16	7,828.83	6,724.05
300,000.00	27,254.76	14,724.79	10,584.17	8,540.54	7,335.33
350,000.00	31,797.22	17,178.93	12,348.20	9,963.97	8,557.88
400,000.00	36,339.68	19,633.06	14,112.23	11,387.39	9,780.44
450,000.00	40,882.14	22,087.19	15,876.26	12,810.82	11,002.99
500,000.00	45,424.60	24,541.32	17,640.29	14,234.24	12,225.54

Monthly Mortgage Payment 16¼%

TABLE C

(Amount Necessary to Amortize a Loan)

\$ .85	\$ .74	\$ .71	\$ .69	\$ .68	\$ 50.00
		TERM OF LOAN			AMOUNT
10 Years	15 Years	20 Years	25 Years	30 Years	OF LOAN
\$ .85	\$ .74	\$ .71	\$ .69	\$ .68	\$ 50.00
1.69	1.49	1.41	1.38	1.36	100.00
3.38	2.97	2.82	2.76	2.73	200.00
5.07	4.46	4.23	4.14	4.09	300.00
6.76	5.94	5.64	5.51	5.46	400.00
8.45	7.43	7.05	6.89	6.82	500.00
16.91	14.86	14.10	13.79	13.65	1,000.00
33.81	29.72	28.20	27.57	27.30	2,000.00
50.72	44.59	42.30	41.36	40.95	3,000.00
67.63	59.45	56.40	55.14	54.60	4,000.00
84.54	74.31	70.50	68.93	68.25	5,000.00
169.07	148.62	141.00	137.85	136.49	10,000.00
253.61	222.93	211.51	206.78	204.74	15,000.00
338.15	297.23	282.01	275.71	272.99	20,000.00
422.69	371.54	352.51	344.64	341.23	25,000.00
507.22	445.85	423.01	413.56	409.48	30,000.00
591.76	520.16	493.52	482.49	477.73	35,000.00
676.30	594.47	564.02	551.42	545.97	40,000.00
760.83	668.78	634.52	620.34	614.22	45,000.00
845.37	743.08	705.02	689.27	682.47	50,000.00
929.91	817.39	775.53	758.20	750.71	55,000.00
1,014.45	891.70	846.03	827.12	818.96	60,000.00
1,098.98	966.01	916.53	896.05	887.21	65,000.00
1,183.52	1,040.32	987.03	964.98	955.45	70,000.00
1,268.06	1,114.63	1,057.53	1,033.91	1,023.70	75,000.00
1,352.60	1,188.93	1,128.04	1,102.83	1,091.95	80,000.00
1,437.13	1,263.24	1,198.54	1,171.76	1,160.19	85,000.00
1,521.67	1,337.55	1,269.04	1,240.69	1,228.44	90,000.00
1,606.21	1,411.86	1,339.54	1,309.61	1,296.69	95,000.00
1,690.74	1,486.17	1,410.05	1,378.54	1,364.93	100,000.00
1,859.82	1,634.78	1,551.05	1,516.40	1,501.43	110,000.00
2,028.89	1,783.40	1,692.05	1,654.25	1,637.92	120,000.00
2,197.97	1,932.02	1,833.06	1,792.10	1,774.42	130,000.00
2,367.04	2,080.64	1,974.06	1,929.96	1,910.91	140,000.00
2,536.12	2,229.25	2,115.07	2,067.81	2,047.40	150,000.00
2,705.19	2,377.87	2,256.07	2,205.67	2,183.90	160,000.00
2,874.27	2,526.49	2,397.08	2,343.52	2,320.39	170,000.00
3,043.34	2,675.10	2,538.08	2,481.37	2,456.88	180,000.00
3,212.41	2,823.72	2,679.09	2,619.23	2,593.38	190,000.00
3,381.49	2,972.34	2,820.09	2,757.08	2,729.87	200,000.00
3,804.17	3,343.88	3,172.60	3,101.72	3,071.10	225,000.00
4,226.86	3,715.42	3,525.11	3,446.35	3,412.34	250,000.00
4,649.55	4,086.96	3,877.63	3,790.99	3,753.57	275,000.00
5,072.23	4,458.50	4,230.14	4,135.62	4,094.80	300,000.00
5,917.60	5,201.59	4,935.16	4,824.89	4,777.27	350,000.00
6,762.98	5,944.67	5,640.18	5,514.17	5,459.74	400,000.00
7,608.35	6,687.76	6,345.20	6,203.44	6,142.21	450,000.00
8,453.72	7,430.84	7,050.23	6,892.71	6,824.67	500,000.00

16½%

Figuring Out Your

TABLE C
(Amount Necessary to Amortize a Loan)

AMOUNT OF LOAN	1 Year	2 Years	3 Years	4 Years	5 Years
$ 50.00	$ 4.55	$ 2.46	$ 1.77	$ 1.43	$ 1.23
100.00	9.10	4.92	3.54	2.86	2.46
200.00	18.19	9.84	7.08	5.72	4.92
300.00	27.29	14.76	10.62	8.58	7.38
400.00	36.39	19.68	14.16	11.44	9.83
500.00	45.48	24.60	17.70	14.30	12.29
1,000.00	90.97	49.20	35.40	28.60	24.58
2,000.00	181.94	98.40	70.81	57.19	49.17
3,000.00	272.90	147.61	106.21	85.79	73.75
4,000.00	363.87	196.81	141.62	114.39	98.34
5,000.00	454.84	246.01	177.02	142.99	122.92
10,000.00	909.68	492.02	354.04	285.97	245.85
15,000.00	1,364.51	738.04	531.07	428.96	368.77
20,000.00	1,819.35	984.05	708.09	571.94	491.69
25,000.00	2,274.19	1,230.06	885.11	714.93	614.61
30,000.00	2,729.03	1,476.07	1,062.13	857.91	737.54
35,000.00	3,183.87	1,722.08	1,239.15	1,000.90	860.46
40,000.00	3,638.71	1,968.09	1,416.18	1,143.88	983.38
45,000.00	4,093.54	2,214.11	1,593.20	1,286.87	1,106.30
50,000.00	4,548.38	2,460.12	1,770.22	1,429.85	1,229.23
55,000.00	5,003.22	2,706.13	1,947.24	1,572.84	1,352.15
60,000.00	5,458.06	2,952.14	2,124.26	1,715.82	1,475.07
65,000.00	5,912.90	3,198.15	2,301.28	1,858.81	1,597.99
70,000.00	6,367.73	3,444.16	2,478.31	2,001.79	1,720.92
75,000.00	6,822.57	3,690.18	2,655.33	2,144.78	1,843.84
80,000.00	7,277.41	3,936.19	2,832.35	2,287.76	1,966.76
85,000.00	7,732.25	4,182.20	3,009.37	2,430.75	2,089.68
90,000.00	8,187.09	4,428.21	3,186.39	2,573.73	2,212.61
95,000.00	8,641.93	4,674.22	3,363.42	2,716.72	2,335.53
100,000.00	9,096.76	4,920.24	3,540.44	2,859.70	2,458.45
110,000.00	10,006.44	5,412.26	3,894.48	3,145.67	2,704.30
120,000.00	10,916.12	5,904.28	4,248.53	3,431.64	2,950.14
130,000.00	11,825.79	6,396.31	4,602.57	3,717.61	3,195.99
140,000.00	12,735.47	6,888.33	4,956.61	4,003.58	3,441.83
150,000.00	13,645.15	7,380.35	5,310.66	4,289.55	3,687.68
160,000.00	14,554.82	7,872.38	5,664.70	4,575.52	3,933.52
170,000.00	15,464.50	8,364.40	6,018.75	4,861.49	4,179.37
180,000.00	16,374.17	8,856.42	6,372.79	5,147.46	4,425.21
190,000.00	17,283.85	9,348.45	6,726.83	5,433.43	4,671.06
200,000.00	18,193.53	9,840.47	7,080.88	5,719.40	4,916.90
225,000.00	20,467.72	11,070.53	7,965.99	6,434.33	5,531.52
250,000.00	22,741.91	12,300.59	8,851.10	7,149.25	6,146.13
275,000.00	25,016.10	13,530.65	9,736.21	7,864.18	6,760.74
300,000.00	27,290.29	14,760.71	10,621.31	8,579.10	7,375.36
350,000.00	31,838.67	17,220.82	12,391.53	10,008.95	8,604.58
400,000.00	36,387.05	19,680.94	14,161.75	11,438.80	9,833.81
450,000.00	40,935.44	22,141.06	15,931.97	12,868.65	11,063.03
500,000.00	45,483.82	24,601.18	17,702.19	14,298.50	12,292.26

234

Monthly Mortgage Payment 16½%

TABLE C

(Amount Necessary to Amortize a Loan)

| TERM OF LOAN | | | | | AMOUNT OF LOAN |
10 Years	15 Years	20 Years	25 Years	30 Years	
$ .85	$ .75	$ .71	$ .70	$ .69	$ 50.00
1.71	1.50	1.43	1.40	1.39	100.00
3.41	3.01	2.86	2.80	2.77	200.00
5.12	4.51	4.29	4.19	4.16	300.00
6.83	6.01	5.72	5.59	5.54	400.00
8.53	7.52	7.14	6.99	6.93	500.00
17.06	15.04	14.29	13.98	13.85	1,000.00
34.13	30.07	28.58	27.96	27.70	2,000.00
51.19	45.11	42.87	41.95	41.55	3,000.00
68.26	60.15	57.16	55.93	55.41	4,000.00
85.32	75.19	71.45	69.91	69.26	5,000.00
170.64	150.37	142.89	139.82	138.51	10,000.00
255.96	225.56	214.34	209.74	207.77	15,000.00
341.28	300.74	285.78	279.65	277.03	20,000.00
426.61	375.93	357.23	349.56	346.29	25,000.00
511.93	451.11	428.67	419.47	415.54	30,000.00
597.25	526.30	500.12	489.39	484.80	35,000.00
682.57	601.48	571.56	559.30	554.06	40,000.00
767.89	676.67	643.01	629.21	623.32	45,000.00
853.21	751.85	714.45	699.12	692.57	50,000.00
938.53	827.04	785.90	769.03	761.83	55,000.00
1,023.85	902.23	857.34	838.95	831.09	60,000.00
1,109.17	977.41	928.79	908.86	900.35	65,000.00
1,194.50	1,052.60	1,000.23	978.77	969.60	70,000.00
1,279.82	1,127.78	1,071.68	1,048.68	1,038.86	75,000.00
1,365.14	1,202.97	1,143.12	1,118.60	1,108.12	80,000.00
1,450.46	1,278.15	1,214.57	1,188.51	1,177.38	85,000.00
1,535.78	1,353.34	1,286.01	1,258.42	1,246.63	90,000.00
1,621.10	1,428.52	1,357.46	1,328.33	1,315.89	95,000.00
1,706.42	1,503.71	1,428.90	1,398.24	1,385.15	100,000.00
1,877.07	1,654.08	1,571.79	1,538.07	1,523.66	110,000.00
2,047.71	1,804.45	1,714.68	1,677.89	1,662.18	120,000.00
2,218.35	1,954.82	1,857.57	1,817.72	1,800.69	130,000.00
2,388.99	2,105.19	2,000.46	1,957.54	1,939.21	140,000.00
2,559.63	2,255.56	2,143.35	2,097.37	2,077.72	150,000.00
2,730.28	2,405.93	2,286.24	2,237.19	2,216.24	160,000.00
2,900.92	2,556.30	2,429.13	2,377.02	2,354.75	170,000.00
3,071.56	2,706.68	2,572.02	2,516.84	2,493.27	180,000.00
3,242.20	2,857.05	2,714.91	2,656.66	2,631.78	190,000.00
3,412.85	3,007.42	2,857.80	2,796.49	2,770.30	200,000.00
3,839.45	3,383.34	3,215.03	3,146.05	3,116.58	225,000.00
4,266.06	3,759.27	3,572.25	3,495.61	3,462.87	250,000.00
4,692.66	4,135.20	3,929.48	3,845.17	3,809.16	275,000.00
5,119.27	4,511.13	4,286.70	4,194.73	4,155.44	300,000.00
5,972.48	5,262.98	5,001.15	4,893.86	4,848.02	350,000.00
6,825.69	6,014.83	5,715.60	5,592.98	5,540.59	400,000.00
7,678.90	6,766.69	6,430.05	6,292.10	6,233.17	450,000.00
8,532.11	7,518.54	7,144.50	6,991.22	6,925.74	500,000.00

Figuring Out Your

TABLE C

(Amount Necessary to Amortize a Loan)

AMOUNT OF LOAN	TERM OF LOAN				
	1 Year	2 Years	3 Years	4 Years	5 Years
$ 50.00	$ 4.55	$ 2.47	$ 1.78	$ 1.44	$ 1.24
100.00	9.11	4.93	3.55	2.87	2.47
200.00	18.22	9.86	7.11	5.75	4.94
300.00	27.33	14.80	10.66	8.62	7.42
400.00	36.43	19.73	14.21	11.49	9.89
500.00	45.54	24.66	17.76	14.36	12.36
1,000.00	91.09	49.32	35.53	28.73	24.72
2,000.00	182.17	98.64	71.06	57.45	49.44
3,000.00	273.26	147.97	106.59	86.18	74.16
4,000.00	364.34	197.29	142.11	114.90	98.87
5,000.00	455.43	246.61	177.64	143.63	123.59
10,000.00	910.86	493.22	355.28	287.26	247.18
15,000.00	1,366.29	739.83	532.93	430.89	370.78
20,000.00	1,821.72	986.44	710.57	574.52	494.37
25,000.00	2,277.15	1,233.06	888.21	718.15	617.96
30,000.00	2,732.58	1,479.67	1,065.85	861.78	741.55
35,000.00	3,188.02	1,726.28	1,243.50	1,005.41	865.14
40,000.00	3,643.45	1,972.89	1,421.14	1,149.03	988.73
45,000.00	4,098.88	2,219.50	1,598.78	1,292.66	1,112.33
50,000.00	4,554.31	2,466.11	1,776.42	1,436.29	1,235.92
55,000.00	5,009.74	2,712.72	1,954.06	1,579.92	1,359.51
60,000.00	5,465.17	2,959.33	2,131.71	1,723.55	1,483.10
65,000.00	5,920.60	3,205.94	2,309.35	1,867.18	1,606.69
70,000.00	6,376.03	3,452.56	2,486.99	2,010.81	1,730.28
75,000.00	6,831.46	3,699.17	2,664.63	2,154.44	1,853.88
80,000.00	7,286.89	3,945.78	2,842.27	2,298.07	1,977.47
85,000.00	7,742.32	4,192.39	3,019.92	2,441.70	2,101.06
90,000.00	8,197.75	4,439.00	3,197.56	2,585.33	2,224.65
95,000.00	8,653.18	4,685.61	3,375.20	2,728.96	2,348.24
100,000.00	9,108.62	4,932.22	3,552.84	2,872.59	2,471.84
110,000.00	10,019.48	5,425.44	3,908.13	3,159.84	2,719.02
120,000.00	10,930.34	5,918.67	4,263.41	3,447.10	2,966.20
130,000.00	11,841.20	6,411.89	4,618.70	3,734.36	3,213.39
140,000.00	12,752.06	6,905.11	4,973.98	4,021.62	3,460.57
150,000.00	13,662.92	7,398.33	5,329.26	4,308.88	3,707.75
160,000.00	14,573.78	7,891.56	5,684.55	4,596.14	3,954.94
170,000.00	15,484.65	8,384.78	6,039.83	4,883.40	4,202.12
180,000.00	16,395.51	8,878.00	6,395.12	5,170.66	4,449.30
190,000.00	17,306.37	9,371.22	6,750.40	5,457.91	4,696.49
200,000.00	18,217.23	9,864.44	7,105.69	5,745.17	4,943.67
225,000.00	20,494.38	11,097.50	7,993.90	6,463.32	5,561.63
250,000.00	22,771.54	12,330.56	8,882.11	7,181.47	6,179.59
275,000.00	25,048.69	13,563.61	9,770.32	7,899.61	6,797.55
300,000.00	27,325.85	14,796.67	10,658.53	8,617.76	7,415.51
350,000.00	31,880.15	17,262.78	12,434.95	10,054.05	8,651.42
400,000.00	36,434.46	19,728.89	14,211.37	11,490.35	9,887.34
450,000.00	40,988.77	22,195.00	15,987.79	12,926.64	11,123.26
500,000.00	45,543.08	24,661.11	17,764.22	14,362.93	12,359.18

Monthly Mortgage Payment 16¾%

TABLE C

(Amount Necessary to Amortize a Loan)

10 Years	15 Years	TERM OF LOAN 20 Years	25 Years	30 Years	AMOUNT OF LOAN
$ .86	$ .76	$ .72	$ .71	$ .70	$ 50.00
1.72	1.52	1.45	1.42	1.41	100.00
3.44	3.04	2.90	2.84	2.81	200.00
5.17	4.56	4.34	4.25	4.22	300.00
6.89	6.09	5.79	5.67	5.62	400.00
8.61	7.61	7.24	7.09	7.03	500.00
17.22	15.21	14.48	14.18	14.05	1,000.00
34.44	30.43	28.96	28.36	28.11	2,000.00
51.67	45.64	43.43	42.54	42.16	3,000.00
68.89	60.85	57.91	56.72	56.22	4,000.00
86.11	76.07	72.39	70.90	70.27	5,000.00
172.22	152.13	144.78	141.80	140.54	10,000.00
258.33	228.20	217.17	212.70	210.81	15,000.00
344.43	304.26	289.56	283.60	281.08	20,000.00
430.54	380.33	361.95	354.50	351.35	25,000.00
516.65	456.40	434.35	425.40	421.62	30,000.00
602.76	532.46	506.74	496.30	491.89	35,000.00
688.87	608.53	579.13	567.20	562.16	40,000.00
774.98	684.59	651.52	638.10	632.43	45,000.00
861.08	760.66	723.91	709.00	702.70	50,000.00
947.19	836.73	796.30	779.90	772.97	55,000.00
1,033.30	912.79	868.69	850.80	843.24	60,000.00
1,119.41	988.86	941.08	921.70	913.51	65,000.00
1,205.52	1,064.92	1,013.47	992.60	983.78	70,000.00
1,291.63	1,140.99	1,085.86	1,063.50	1,054.05	75,000.00
1,377.73	1,217.06	1,158.26	1,134.40	1,124.32	80,000.00
1,463.84	1,293.12	1,230.65	1,205.30	1,194.59	85,000.00
1,549.95	1,369.19	1,303.04	1,276.20	1,264.86	90,000.00
1,636.06	1,445.26	1,375.43	1,347.10	1,335.13	95,000.00
1,722.17	1,521.32	1,447.82	1,418.00	1,405.40	100,000.00
1,894.38	1,673.45	1,592.60	1,559.80	1,545.94	110,000.00
2,066.60	1,825.59	1,737.38	1,701.60	1,686.47	120,000.00
2,238.82	1,977.72	1,882.17	1,843.40	1,827.01	130,000.00
2,411.03	2,129.85	2,026.95	1,985.20	1,967.55	140,000.00
2,583.25	2,281.98	2,171.73	2,127.00	2,108.09	150,000.00
2,755.47	2,434.11	2,316.51	2,268.80	2,248.63	160,000.00
2,927.68	2,586.25	2,461.29	2,410.59	2,389.17	170,000.00
3,099.90	2,738.38	2,606.08	2,552.39	2,529.71	180,000.00
3,272.12	2,890.51	2,750.86	2,694.19	2,670.25	190,000.00
3,444.33	3,042.64	2,895.64	2,835.99	2,810.79	200,000.00
3,874.88	3,422.97	3,257.59	3,190.49	3,162.14	225,000.00
4,305.42	3,803.30	3,619.55	3,544.99	3,513.49	250,000.00
4,735.96	4,183.63	3,981.50	3,899.49	3,864.84	275,000.00
5,166.50	4,563.96	4,343.46	4,253.99	4,216.19	300,000.00
6,027.59	5,324.62	5,067.37	4,962.99	4,918.88	350,000.00
6,888.67	6,085.28	5,791.28	5,671.99	5,621.58	400,000.00
7,749.75	6,845.94	6,515.19	6,380.99	6,324.28	450,000.00
8,610.84	7,606.61	7,239.10	7,089.99	7,026.98	500,000.00

17%   **Figuring Out Your**

TABLE C

(Amount Necessary to Amortize a Loan)

AMOUNT OF LOAN	TERM OF LOAN 1 Year	2 Years	3 Years	4 Years	5 Years
$ 50.00	$ 4.56	$ 2.47	$ 1.78	$ 1.44	$ 1.24
100.00	9.12	4.94	3.57	2.89	2.49
200.00	18.24	9.89	7.13	5.77	4.97
300.00	27.36	14.83	10.70	8.66	7.46
400.00	36.48	19.78	14.26	11.54	9.94
500.00	45.60	24.72	17.83	14.43	12.43
1,000.00	91.20	49.44	35.65	28.86	24.85
2,000.00	182.41	98.88	71.31	57.71	49.71
3,000.00	273.61	148.33	106.96	86.57	74.56
4,000.00	364.82	197.77	142.61	115.42	99.41
5,000.00	456.02	247.21	178.26	144.28	124.26
10,000.00	912.05	494.42	356.53	288.55	248.53
15,000.00	1,368.07	741.63	534.79	432.83	372.79
20,000.00	1,824.10	988.85	713.05	577.10	497.05
25,000.00	2,280.12	1,236.06	891.32	721.38	621.31
30,000.00	2,736.14	1,483.27	1,069.58	865.65	745.58
35,000.00	3,192.17	1,730.48	1,247.85	1,009.93	869.84
40,000.00	3,648.19	1,977.69	1,426.11	1,154.20	994.10
45,000.00	4,104.21	2,224.90	1,604.37	1,298.48	1,118.37
50,000.00	4,560.24	2,472.11	1,782.64	1,442.75	1,242.63
55,000.00	5,016.26	2,719.32	1,960.90	1,587.03	1,366.89
60,000.00	5,472.29	2,966.54	2,139.16	1,731.30	1,491.15
65,000.00	5,928.31	3,213.75	2,317.43	1,875.58	1,615.42
70,000.00	6,384.33	3,460.96	2,495.69	2,019.85	1,739.68
75,000.00	6,840.36	3,708.17	2,673.95	2,164.13	1,863.94
80,000.00	7,296.38	3,955.38	2,852.22	2,308.40	1,988.21
85,000.00	7,752.40	4,202.59	3,030.48	2,452.68	2,112.47
90,000.00	8,208.43	4,449.80	3,208.75	2,596.95	2,236.73
95,000.00	8,664.45	4,697.02	3,387.01	2,741.23	2,360.99
100,000.00	9,120.48	4,944.23	3,565.27	2,885.50	2,485.26
110,000.00	10,032.52	5,438.65	3,921.80	3,174.05	2,733.78
120,000.00	10,944.57	5,933.07	4,278.33	3,462.61	2,982.31
130,000.00	11,856.62	6,427.49	4,634.85	3,751.16	3,230.83
140,000.00	12,768.67	6,921.92	4,991.38	4,039.71	3,479.36
150,000.00	13,680.71	7,416.34	5,347.91	4,328.26	3,727.89
160,000.00	14,592.76	7,910.76	5,704.44	4,616.81	3,976.41
170,000.00	15,504.81	8,405.18	6,060.96	4,905.36	4,224.94
180,000.00	16,416.86	8,899.61	6,417.49	5,193.91	4,473.46
190,000.00	17,328.90	9,394.03	6,774.02	5,482.46	4,721.99
200,000.00	18,240.95	9,888.45	7,130.55	5,771.01	4,970.52
225,000.00	20,521.07	11,124.51	8,021.86	6,492.38	5,591.83
250,000.00	22,801.19	12,360.57	8,913.18	7,213.76	6,213.14
275,000.00	25,081.31	13,596.62	9,804.50	7,935.14	6,834.46
300,000.00	27,361.43	14,832.68	10,695.82	8,656.51	7,455.77
350,000.00	31,921.66	17,304.79	12,478.45	10,099.26	8,698.40
400,000.00	36,481.90	19,776.91	14,261.09	11,542.02	9,941.03
450,000.00	41,042.14	22,249.02	16,043.73	12,984.77	11,183.66
500,000.00	45,602.38	24,721.13	17,826.36	14,427.52	12,426.29

Monthly Mortgage Payment

TABLE C

(Amount Necessary to Amortize a Loan)

10 Years	15 Years	TERM OF LOAN 20 Years	25 Years	30 Years	AMOUNT OF LOAN
$ .87	$ .77	$ .73	$ .72	$ .71	$ 50.00
1.74	1.54	1.47	1.44	1.43	100.00
3.48	3.08	2.93	2.88	2.85	200.00
5.21	4.62	4.40	4.31	4.28	300.00
6.95	6.16	5.87	5.75	5.70	400.00
8.69	7.70	7.33	7.19	7.13	500.00
17.38	15.39	14.67	14.38	14.26	1,000.00
34.76	30.78	29.34	28.76	28.51	2,000.00
52.14	46.17	44.00	43.13	42.77	3,000.00
69.52	61.56	58.67	57.51	57.03	4,000.00
86.90	76.95	73.34	71.89	71.28	5,000.00
173.80	153.90	146.68	143.78	142.57	10,000.00
260.70	230.85	220.02	215.67	213.85	15,000.00
347.60	307.80	293.36	287.56	285.14	20,000.00
434.49	384.75	366.70	359.45	356.42	25,000.00
521.39	461.70	440.04	431.34	427.70	30,000.00
608.29	538.65	513.38	503.23	498.99	35,000.00
695.19	615.60	586.72	575.12	570.27	40,000.00
782.09	692.55	660.06	647.01	641.55	45,000.00
868.99	769.50	733.40	718.90	712.84	50,000.00
955.89	846.45	806.74	790.79	784.12	55,000.00
1,042.79	923.40	880.08	862.68	855.41	60,000.00
1,129.68	1,000.35	953.42	934.57	926.69	65,000.00
1,216.58	1,077.30	1,026.76	1,006.46	997.97	70,000.00
1,303.48	1,154.25	1,100.10	1,078.35	1,069.26	75,000.00
1,390.38	1,231.20	1,173.44	1,150.24	1,140.54	80,000.00
1,477.28	1,308.15	1,246.78	1,222.13	1,211.82	85,000.00
1,564.18	1,385.10	1,320.12	1,294.02	1,283.11	90,000.00
1,651.08	1,462.05	1,393.46	1,365.91	1,354.39	95,000.00
1,737.98	1,539.00	1,466.80	1,437.80	1,425.68	100,000.00
1,911.77	1,692.90	1,613.48	1,581.58	1,568.24	110,000.00
2,085.57	1,846.81	1,760.16	1,725.36	1,710.81	120,000.00
2,259.37	2,000.71	1,906.84	1,869.14	1,853.38	130,000.00
2,433.17	2,154.61	2,053.52	2,012.92	1,995.95	140,000.00
2,606.96	2,308.51	2,200.20	2,156.69	2,138.51	150,000.00
2,780.76	2,462.41	2,346.88	2,300.47	2,281.08	160,000.00
2,954.56	2,616.31	2,493.56	2,444.25	2,423.65	170,000.00
3,128.36	2,770.21	2,640.24	2,588.03	2,566.22	180,000.00
3,302.16	2,924.11	2,786.92	2,731.81	2,708.78	190,000.00
3,475.95	3,078.01	2,933.60	2,875.59	2,851.35	200,000.00
3,910.45	3,462.76	3,300.30	3,235.04	3,207.77	225,000.00
4,344.94	3,847.51	3,667.00	3,594.49	3,564.19	250,000.00
4,779.44	4,232.26	4,033.70	3,953.94	3,920.61	275,000.00
5,213.93	4,617.01	4,400.40	4,313.39	4,277.03	300,000.00
6,082.92	5,386.52	5,133.80	5,032.29	4,989.86	350,000.00
6,951.91	6,156.02	5,867.20	5,751.19	5,702.70	400,000.00
7,820.89	6,925.52	6,600.60	6,470.08	6,415.54	450,000.00
8,689.88	7,695.02	7,334.00	7,188.98	7,128.38	500,000.00

TABLE C

(Amount Necessary to Amortize a Loan)

AMOUNT OF LOAN	TERM OF LOAN				
	1 Year	2 Years	3 Years	4 Years	5 Years
$ 50.00	$ 4.57	$ 2.48	$ 1.79	$ 1.45	$ 1.25
100.00	9.13	4.96	3.58	2.90	2.50
200.00	18.26	9.91	7.16	5.80	5.00
300.00	27.40	14.87	10.73	8.70	7.50
400.00	36.53	19.82	14.31	11.59	9.99
500.00	45.66	24.78	17.89	14.49	12.49
1,000.00	91.32	49.56	35.78	28.98	24.99
2,000.00	182.65	99.12	71.55	57.97	49.97
3,000.00	273.97	148.69	107.33	86.95	74.96
4,000.00	365.29	198.25	143.11	115.94	99.95
5,000.00	456.62	247.81	178.89	144.92	124.94
10,000.00	913.23	495.62	357.77	289.85	249.87
15,000.00	1,369.85	743.44	536.66	434.77	374.81
20,000.00	1,826.47	991.25	715.55	579.69	499.74
25,000.00	2,283.09	1,239.06	894.43	724.61	624.68
30,000.00	2,739.70	1,486.87	1,073.32	869.54	749.62
35,000.00	3,196.32	1,734.69	1,252.20	1,014.46	874.55
40,000.00	3,652.94	1,982.50	1,431.09	1,159.38	999.49
45,000.00	4,109.55	2,230.31	1,609.98	1,304.30	1,124.42
50,000.00	4,566.17	2,478.12	1,788.86	1,449.23	1,249.36
55,000.00	5,022.79	2,725.94	1,967.75	1,594.15	1,374.30
60,000.00	5,479.41	2,973.75	2,146.64	1,739.07	1,499.23
65,000.00	5,936.02	3,221.56	2,325.52	1,884.00	1,624.17
70,000.00	6,392.64	3,469.37	2,504.41	2,028.92	1,749.10
75,000.00	6,849.26	3,717.19	2,683.30	2,173.84	1,874.04
80,000.00	7,305.87	3,965.00	2,862.18	2,318.76	1,998.98
85,000.00	7,762.49	4,212.81	3,041.07	2,463.69	2,123.91
90,000.00	8,219.11	4,460.62	3,219.95	2,608.61	2,248.85
95,000.00	8,675.73	4,708.43	3,398.84	2,753.53	2,373.78
100,000.00	9,132.34	4,956.25	3,577.73	2,898.45	2,498.72
110,000.00	10,045.58	5,451.87	3,935.50	3,188.30	2,748.59
120,000.00	10,958.81	5,947.50	4,293.27	3,478.15	2,998.46
130,000.00	11,872.05	6,443.12	4,651.05	3,767.99	3,248.34
140,000.00	12,785.28	6,938.75	5,008.82	4,057.84	3,498.21
150,000.00	13,698.52	7,434.37	5,366.59	4,347.68	3,748.08
160,000.00	14,611.75	7,930.00	5,724.36	4,637.53	3,997.95
170,000.00	15,524.98	8,425.62	6,082.14	4,927.37	4,247.82
180,000.00	16,438.22	8,921.24	6,439.91	5,217.22	4,497.70
190,000.00	17,351.45	9,416.87	6,797.68	5,507.06	4,747.57
200,000.00	18,264.69	9,912.49	7,155.45	5,796.91	4,997.44
225,000.00	20,547.77	11,151.56	8,049.89	6,521.52	5,622.12
250,000.00	22,830.86	12,390.62	8,944.32	7,246.14	6,246.80
275,000.00	25,113.94	13,629.68	9,838.75	7,970.75	6,871.48
300,000.00	27,397.03	14,868.74	10,733.18	8,695.36	7,496.16
350,000.00	31,963.20	17,346.87	12,522.05	10,144.59	8,745.52
400,000.00	36,529.37	19,824.99	14,310.91	11,593.82	9,994.88
450,000.00	41,095.55	22,303.11	16,099.77	13,043.05	11,244.24
500,000.00	45,661.72	24,781.24	17,888.64	14,492.27	12,493.60

Monthly Mortgage Payment 17¼%

TABLE C
(Amount Necessary to Amortize a Loan)

10 Years	15 Years	TERM OF LOAN 20 Years	25 Years	30 Years	AMOUNT OF LOAN
$ .88	$ .78	$ .74	$ .73	$ .72	$ 50.00
1.75	1.56	1.49	1.46	1.45	100.00
3.51	3.11	2.97	2.92	2.89	200.00
5.26	4.67	4.46	4.37	4.34	300.00
7.02	6.23	5.94	5.83	5.78	400.00
8.77	7.78	7.43	7.29	7.23	500.00
17.54	15.57	14.86	14.58	14.46	1,000.00
35.08	31.14	29.72	29.15	28.92	2,000.00
52.62	46.70	44.58	43.73	43.38	3,000.00
70.15	62.27	59.43	58.31	57.84	4,000.00
87.69	77.84	74.29	72.88	72.30	5,000.00
175.39	155.68	148.58	145.76	144.60	10,000.00
263.08	233.51	222.88	218.65	216.90	15,000.00
350.77	311.35	297.17	291.53	289.20	20,000.00
438.46	389.19	371.46	364.41	361.50	25,000.00
526.16	467.03	445.75	437.29	433.80	30,000.00
613.85	544.86	520.04	510.17	506.10	35,000.00
701.54	622.70	594.34	583.06	578.39	40,000.00
789.23	700.54	668.63	655.94	650.69	45,000.00
876.93	778.38	742.92	728.82	722.99	50,000.00
964.62	856.22	817.21	801.70	795.29	55,000.00
1,052.31	934.05	891.51	874.58	867.59	60,000.00
1,140.00	1,011.89	965.80	947.47	939.89	65,000.00
1,227.70	1,089.73	1,040.09	1,020.35	1,012.19	70,000.00
1,315.39	1,167.57	1,114.38	1,093.23	1,084.49	75,000.00
1,403.08	1,245.41	1,188.67	1,166.11	1,156.79	80,000.00
1,490.77	1,323.24	1,262.97	1,239.00	1,229.09	85,000.00
1,578.47	1,401.08	1,337.26	1,311.88	1,301.39	90,000.00
1,666.16	1,478.92	1,411.55	1,384.76	1,373.69	95,000.00
1,753.85	1,556.76	1,485.84	1,457.64	1,445.99	100,000.00
1,929.24	1,712.43	1,634.43	1,603.41	1,590.58	110,000.00
2,104.62	1,868.11	1,783.01	1,749.17	1,735.18	120,000.00
2,280.01	2,023.78	1,931.59	1,894.93	1,879.78	130,000.00
2,455.39	2,179.46	2,080.18	2,040.70	2,024.38	140,000.00
2,630.78	2,335.14	2,228.76	2,186.46	2,168.98	150,000.00
2,806.16	2,490.81	2,377.35	2,332.23	2,313.58	160,000.00
2,981.55	2,646.49	2,525.93	2,477.99	2,458.18	170,000.00
3,156.93	2,802.16	2,674.52	2,623.75	2,602.77	180,000.00
3,332.32	2,957.84	2,823.10	2,769.52	2,747.37	190,000.00
3,507.70	3,113.51	2,971.68	2,915.28	2,891.97	200,000.00
3,946.16	3,502.70	3,343.14	3,279.69	3,253.47	225,000.00
4,384.63	3,891.89	3,714.60	3,644.10	3,614.96	250,000.00
4,823.09	4,281.08	4,086.07	4,008.51	3,976.46	275,000.00
5,261.55	4,670.27	4,457.53	4,372.92	4,337.96	300,000.00
6,138.48	5,448.65	5,200.45	5,101.74	5,060.95	350,000.00
7,015.40	6,227.03	5,943.37	5,830.57	5,783.94	400,000.00
7,892.33	7,005.41	6,686.29	6,559.39	6,506.94	450,000.00
8,769.25	7,783.79	7,429.21	7,288.21	7,229.93	500,000.00

TABLE C

(Amount Necessary to Amortize a Loan)

AMOUNT OF LOAN	TERM OF LOAN				
	1 Year	2 Years	3 Years	4 Years	5 Years
$ 50.00	$ 4.57	$ 2.48	$ 1.80	$ 1.46	$ 1.26
100.00	9.14	4.97	3.59	2.91	2.51
200.00	18.29	9.94	7.18	5.82	5.02
300.00	27.43	14.90	10.77	8.73	7.54
400.00	36.58	19.87	14.36	11.65	10.05
500.00	45.72	24.84	17.95	14.56	12.56
1,000.00	91.44	49.68	35.90	29.11	25.12
2,000.00	182.88	99.37	71.80	58.23	50.24
3,000.00	274.33	149.05	107.71	87.34	75.37
4,000.00	365.77	198.73	143.61	116.46	100.49
5,000.00	457.21	248.41	179.51	145.57	125.61
10,000.00	914.42	496.83	359.02	291.14	251.22
15,000.00	1,371.63	745.24	538.53	436.72	376.83
20,000.00	1,828.84	993.66	718.04	582.29	502.44
25,000.00	2,286.06	1,242.07	897.55	727.86	628.06
30,000.00	2,743.27	1,490.49	1,077.06	873.43	753.67
35,000.00	3,200.48	1,738.90	1,256.57	1,019.00	879.28
40,000.00	3,657.69	1,987.31	1,436.08	1,164.57	1,004.89
45,000.00	4,114.90	2,235.73	1,615.59	1,310.15	1,130.50
50,000.00	4,572.11	2,484.14	1,795.10	1,455.72	1,256.11
55,000.00	5,029.32	2,732.56	1,974.61	1,601.29	1,381.72
60,000.00	5,486.53	2,980.97	2,154.12	1,746.86	1,507.33
65,000.00	5,943.74	3,229.39	2,333.63	1,892.43	1,632.94
70,000.00	6,400.95	3,477.80	2,513.14	2,038.01	1,758.55
75,000.00	6,858.17	3,726.21	2,692.65	2,183.58	1,884.17
80,000.00	7,315.38	3,974.63	2,872.17	2,329.15	2,009.78
85,000.00	7,772.59	4,223.04	3,051.68	2,474.72	2,135.39
90,000.00	8,229.80	4,471.46	3,231.19	2,620.29	2,261.00
95,000.00	8,687.01	4,719.87	3,410.70	2,765.87	2,386.61
100,000.00	9,144.22	4,968.28	3,590.21	2,911.44	2,512.22
110,000.00	10,058.64	5,465.11	3,949.23	3,202.58	2,763.44
120,000.00	10,973.06	5,961.94	4,308.25	3,493.72	3,014.67
130,000.00	11,887.49	6,458.77	4,667.27	3,784.87	3,265.89
140,000.00	12,801.91	6,955.60	5,026.29	4,076.01	3,517.11
150,000.00	13,716.33	7,452.43	5,385.31	4,367.16	3,768.33
160,000.00	14,630.75	7,949.26	5,744.33	4,658.30	4,019.55
170,000.00	15,545.17	8,446.08	6,103.35	4,949.44	4,270.78
180,000.00	16,459.60	8,942.91	6,462.37	5,240.59	4,522.00
190,000.00	17,374.02	9,439.74	6,821.39	5,531.73	4,773.22
200,000.00	18,288.44	9,936.57	7,180.41	5,822.87	5,024.44
225,000.00	20,574.50	11,178.64	8,077.96	6,550.73	5,652.50
250,000.00	22,860.55	12,420.71	8,975.52	7,278.59	6,280.55
275,000.00	25,146.61	13,662.78	9,873.07	8,006.45	6,908.61
300,000.00	27,432.66	14,904.85	10,770.62	8,734.31	7,536.66
350,000.00	32,004.77	17,389.00	12,565.72	10,190.03	8,792.77
400,000.00	36,576.88	19,873.14	14,360.83	11,645.75	10,048.89
450,000.00	41,148.99	22,357.28	16,155.93	13,101.47	11,305.00
500,000.00	45,721.10	24,841.42	17,951.03	14,557.19	12,561.11

Monthly Mortgage Payment 17½%

TABLE C
(Amount Necessary to Amortize a Loan)

10 Years	15 Years	TERM OF LOAN 20 Years	25 Years	30 Years	AMOUNT OF LOAN
$ .88	$ .79	$ .75	$ .74	$ .73	$ 50.00
1.77	1.57	1.50	1.48	1.47	100.00
3.54	3.15	3.01	2.96	2.93	200.00
5.31	4.72	4.51	4.43	4.40	300.00
7.08	6.30	6.02	5.91	5.87	400.00
8.85	7.87	7.52	7.39	7.33	500.00
17.70	15.75	15.05	14.78	14.66	1,000.00
35.40	31.49	30.10	29.55	29.33	2,000.00
53.09	47.24	45.15	44.33	43.99	3,000.00
70.79	62.98	60.20	59.10	58.65	4,000.00
88.49	78.73	75.25	73.88	73.32	5,000.00
176.98	157.46	150.49	147.75	146.63	10,000.00
265.47	236.19	225.74	221.63	219.95	15,000.00
353.96	314.92	300.99	295.51	293.27	20,000.00
442.45	393.64	376.24	369.38	366.58	25,000.00
530.94	472.37	451.48	443.26	439.90	30,000.00
619.43	551.10	526.73	517.14	513.21	35,000.00
707.92	629.83	601.98	591.01	586.53	40,000.00
796.40	708.56	677.22	664.89	659.85	45,000.00
884.89	787.29	752.47	738.76	733.16	50,000.00
973.38	866.02	827.72	812.64	806.48	55,000.00
1,061.87	944.75	902.97	886.52	879.80	60,000.00
1,150.36	1,023.48	978.21	960.39	953.11	65,000.00
1,238.85	1,102.20	1,053.46	1,034.27	1,026.43	70,000.00
1,327.34	1,180.93	1,128.71	1,108.15	1,099.74	75,000.00
1,415.83	1,259.66	1,203.95	1,182.02	1,173.06	80,000.00
1,504.32	1,338.39	1,279.20	1,255.90	1,246.38	85,000.00
1,592.81	1,417.12	1,354.45	1,329.78	1,319.69	90,000.00
1,681.30	1,495.85	1,429.69	1,403.65	1,393.01	95,000.00
1,769.79	1,574.58	1,504.94	1,477.53	1,466.33	100,000.00
1,946.77	1,732.04	1,655.44	1,625.28	1,612.96	110,000.00
2,123.75	1,889.49	1,805.93	1,773.04	1,759.59	120,000.00
2,300.72	2,046.95	1,956.42	1,920.79	1,906.22	130,000.00
2,477.70	2,204.41	2,106.92	2,068.54	2,052.86	140,000.00
2,654.68	2,361.87	2,257.41	2,216.29	2,199.49	150,000.00
2,831.66	2,519.33	2,407.91	2,364.05	2,346.12	160,000.00
3,008.64	2,676.78	2,558.40	2,511.80	2,492.75	170,000.00
3,185.62	2,834.24	2,708.90	2,659.55	2,639.39	180,000.00
3,362.60	2,991.70	2,859.39	2,807.31	2,786.02	190,000.00
3,539.58	3,149.16	3,009.88	2,955.06	2,932.65	200,000.00
3,982.02	3,542.80	3,386.12	3,324.44	3,299.23	225,000.00
4,424.47	3,936.45	3,762.35	3,693.82	3,665.81	250,000.00
4,866.92	4,330.09	4,138.59	4,063.21	4,032.39	275,000.00
5,309.36	4,723.73	4,514.83	4,432.59	4,398.98	300,000.00
6,194.26	5,511.02	5,267.30	5,171.35	5,132.14	350,000.00
7,079.15	6,298.31	6,019.77	5,910.12	5,865.30	400,000.00
7,964.04	7,085.60	6,772.24	6,648.88	6,598.46	450,000.00
8,848.94	7,872.89	7,524.71	7,387.65	7,331.63	500,000.00

TABLE C
(Amount Necessary to Amortize a Loan)

AMOUNT OF LOAN	TERM OF LOAN				
	1 Year	2 Years	3 Years	4 Years	5 Years
$ 50.00	$ 4.58	$ 2.49	$ 1.80	$ 1.46	$ 1.26
100.00	9.16	4.98	3.60	2.92	2.53
200.00	18.31	9.96	7.21	5.85	5.05
300.00	27.47	14.94	10.81	8.77	7.58
400.00	36.62	19.92	14.41	11.70	10.10
500.00	45.78	24.90	18.01	14.62	12.63
1,000.00	91.56	49.80	36.03	29.24	25.26
2,000.00	183.12	99.61	72.05	58.49	50.52
3,000.00	274.68	149.41	108.08	87.73	75.77
4,000.00	366.24	199.21	144.11	116.98	101.03
5,000.00	457.81	249.02	180.14	146.22	126.29
10,000.00	915.61	498.03	360.27	292.45	252.58
15,000.00	1,373.42	747.05	540.41	438.67	378.86
20,000.00	1,831.22	996.07	720.54	584.89	505.15
25,000.00	2,289.03	1,245.08	900.68	731.11	631.44
30,000.00	2,746.83	1,494.10	1,080.81	877.34	757.73
35,000.00	3,204.64	1,743.12	1,260.95	1,023.56	884.02
40,000.00	3,662.44	1,992.14	1,441.08	1,169.78	1,010.30
45,000.00	4,120.25	2,241.15	1,621.22	1,316.00	1,136.59
50,000.00	4,578.05	2,490.17	1,801.36	1,462.23	1,262.88
55,000.00	5,035.86	2,739.19	1,981.49	1,608.45	1,389.17
60,000.00	5,493.66	2,988.20	2,161.63	1,754.67	1,515.46
65,000.00	5,951.47	3,237.22	2,341.76	1,900.89	1,641.75
70,000.00	6,409.27	3,486.24	2,521.90	2,047.12	1,768.03
75,000.00	6,867.08	3,735.25	2,702.03	2,193.34	1,894.32
80,000.00	7,324.88	3,984.27	2,882.17	2,339.56	2,020.61
85,000.00	7,782.69	4,233.29	3,062.30	2,485.78	2,146.90
90,000.00	8,240.50	4,482.31	3,242.44	2,632.01	2,273.19
95,000.00	8,698.30	4,731.32	3,422.58	2,778.23	2,399.47
100,000.00	9,156.11	4,980.34	3,602.71	2,924.45	2,525.76
110,000.00	10,071.72	5,478.37	3,962.98	3,216.90	2,778.34
120,000.00	10,987.33	5,976.41	4,323.25	3,509.34	3,030.91
130,000.00	11,902.94	6,474.44	4,683.52	3,801.79	3,283.49
140,000.00	12,818.55	6,972.47	5,043.79	4,094.23	3,536.07
150,000.00	13,734.16	7,470.51	5,404.07	4,386.68	3,788.64
160,000.00	14,649.77	7,968.54	5,764.34	4,679.12	4,041.22
170,000.00	15,565.38	8,466.58	6,124.61	4,971.57	4,293.80
180,000.00	16,480.99	8,964.61	6,484.88	5,264.01	4,546.37
190,000.00	17,396.60	9,462.64	6,845.15	5,556.46	4,798.95
200,000.00	18,312.21	9,960.68	7,205.42	5,848.91	5,051.52
225,000.00	20,601.24	11,205.76	8,106.10	6,580.02	5,682.97
250,000.00	22,890.26	12,450.85	9,006.78	7,311.13	6,314.41
275,000.00	25,179.29	13,695.93	9,907.45	8,042.24	6,945.85
300,000.00	27,468.32	14,941.02	10,808.13	8,773.36	7,577.29
350,000.00	32,046.37	17,431.19	12,609.49	10,235.58	8,840.17
400,000.00	36,624.42	19,921.36	14,410.84	11,697.81	10,103.05
450,000.00	41,202.48	22,411.53	16,212.20	13,160.04	11,365.93
500,000.00	45,780.53	24,901.70	18,013.55	14,622.26	12,628.81

Monthly Mortgage Payment 17¾%

TABLE C
(Amount Necessary to Amortize a Loan)

10 Years	15 Years	TERM OF LOAN 20 Years	25 Years	30 Years	AMOUNT OF LOAN
$ .89	$ .80	$ .76	$ .75	$ .74	$ 50.00
1.79	1.59	1.52	1.50	1.49	100.00
3.57	3.18	3.05	2.99	2.97	200.00
5.36	4.78	4.57	4.49	4.46	300.00
7.14	6.37	6.10	5.99	5.95	400.00
8.93	7.96	7.62	7.49	7.43	500.00
17.86	15.92	15.24	14.97	14.87	1,000.00
35.72	31.85	30.48	29.95	29.73	2,000.00
53.57	47.77	45.72	44.92	44.60	3,000.00
71.43	63.70	60.96	59.90	59.47	4,000.00
89.29	79.62	76.20	74.87	74.33	5,000.00
178.58	159.25	152.41	149.75	148.67	10,000.00
267.87	238.87	228.61	224.62	223.00	15,000.00
357.16	318.49	304.82	299.49	297.34	20,000.00
446.45	398.12	381.02	374.36	371.67	25,000.00
535.74	477.74	457.23	449.24	446.01	30,000.00
625.03	557.36	533.43	524.11	520.34	35,000.00
714.32	636.99	609.64	598.98	594.68	40,000.00
803.60	716.61	685.84	673.86	669.01	45,000.00
892.89	796.23	762.05	748.73	743.35	50,000.00
982.18	875.86	838.25	823.60	817.68	55,000.00
1,071.47	955.48	914.46	898.48	892.02	60,000.00
1,160.76	1,035.10	990.66	973.35	966.35	65,000.00
1,250.05	1,114.73	1,066.87	1,048.22	1,040.68	70,000.00
1,339.34	1,194.35	1,143.07	1,123.09	1,115.02	75,000.00
1,428.63	1,273.97	1,219.28	1,197.97	1,189.35	80,000.00
1,517.92	1,353.60	1,295.48	1,272.84	1,263.69	85,000.00
1,607.21	1,433.22	1,371.69	1,347.71	1,338.02	90,000.00
1,696.50	1,512.84	1,447.89	1,422.59	1,412.36	95,000.00
1,785.79	1,592.47	1,524.10	1,497.46	1,486.69	100,000.00
1,964.37	1,751.71	1,676.51	1,647.21	1,635.36	110,000.00
2,142.95	1,910.96	1,828.92	1,796.95	1,784.03	120,000.00
2,321.52	2,070.21	1,981.33	1,946.70	1,932.70	130,000.00
2,500.10	2,229.45	2,133.74	2,096.44	2,081.37	140,000.00
2,678.68	2,388.70	2,286.15	2,246.19	2,230.04	150,000.00
2,857.26	2,547.95	2,438.56	2,395.94	2,378.71	160,000.00
3,035.84	2,707.19	2,590.97	2,545.68	2,527.38	170,000.00
3,214.42	2,866.44	2,743.38	2,695.43	2,676.05	180,000.00
3,393.00	3,025.69	2,895.79	2,845.17	2,824.72	190,000.00
3,571.58	3,184.93	3,048.20	2,994.92	2,973.38	200,000.00
4,018.02	3,583.05	3,429.22	3,369.28	3,345.06	225,000.00
4,464.47	3,981.17	3,810.25	3,743.65	3,716.73	250,000.00
4,910.92	4,379.28	4,191.27	4,118.01	4,088.40	275,000.00
5,357.37	4,777.40	4,572.30	4,492.38	4,460.08	300,000.00
6,250.26	5,573.63	5,334.35	5,241.11	5,203.42	350,000.00
7,143.15	6,369.87	6,096.40	5,989.84	5,946.77	400,000.00
8,036.05	7,166.10	6,858.45	6,738.57	6,690.12	450,000.00
8,928.94	7,962.33	7,620.50	7,487.30	7,433.46	500,000.00